AF740763

INTERNATIONAL LAW AND THE MOVEMENT OF PERSONS BETWEEN STATES

INTERNATIONAL LAW AND THE MOVEMENT OF PERSONS BETWEEN STATES

BY

GUY S. GOODWIN-GILL

Legal Adviser in the Office of the United Nations High Commissioner for Refugees

1478

1978

CLARENDON PRESS · OXFORD

UNIV DUNELM

16. JAN. 1979

342.082
GOO

Oxford University Press, Walton Street, Oxford OX2 6DP

OXFORD LONDON GLASGOW
NEW YORK TORONTO MELBOURNE WELLINGTON
IBADAN NAIROBI DAR ES SALAAM LUSAKA CAPE TOWN
KUALA LUMPUR SINGAPORE JAKARTA HONG KONG TOKYO
DELHI BOMBAY CALCUTTA MADRAS KARACHI

© *Oxford University Press 1978*

All rights reserved. No part of this publication may be reproduced, stored in a retrieval system, or transmitted, in any form or by any means, electronic, mechanical, photocopying, recording, or otherwise, without the prior permission of Oxford University Press

British Library Cataloguing in Publication Data
Goodwin-Gill, Guy S
International law and the movement of persons between states.
1. Aliens
I. Title
341.48.4 JX4255 77-30244

ISBN 0 19 825333 8

341.515
GOO
AGJ 612

Printed in Great Britain by William Clowes & Sons, Limited
London, Beccles and Colchester

PREFACE

FEW SUBJECTS arouse quite the same degree of passionate and partisan argument as the presence of aliens upon State territory. The conditions of their entry, if it be allowed at all, the treatment due to those admitted and the permitted circumstances of their expulsion are matters commonly consigned, without further inquiry, to the realm of sovereign State powers. While there can be no doubt that States do possess a broad competence in regard to foreign nationals generally, the central thesis of this work is that such competence is clearly limited and confined by established and emergent rules and standards of international law. On occasion it may be that such limitations operate only at the outermost edges of an apparently illimitable power, as is often the case where expulsion is ordered of an alien deemed to be a risk to national security. But such cases are exceptional, and it is more usual to find the existence of rules which operate to limit the ambit of the power in question and to direct the manner of its exercise. Such rules have their origins in treaty, in the practice of States, and in general principles of law.

In seeing what States claim for themselves and what they object to in others I have relied not only on a large number of individual examples of State practice, but I have also taken the opportunity to examine in some detail the elaborated legal regimes operating in the United Kingdom, the United States of America, France, the Federal Republic of Germany, and the European Communities. Attention to these systems may suggest an unrepresentative bias, but I hope to have compensated for this by reference to practice across a broader field and to more general developments in international law, in particular, in the matter of human rights. I have thought it important, therefore, to pay special attention to recent covenants and conventions. But it is evident, as post-Helsinki experience would indicate, that not inconsiderable problems remain in regard to the permissible or claimable extent of the reserved domain of domestic jurisdiction. The application of the principle of non-discrimination in matters affecting aliens and nationals presents the issue in particularly pertinent fashion, while it will be seen that further development, in theory and in practice, is called for in respect of related concepts of international obligation.

Part of this book, which has its origins in my work for the degree of Doctor of Philosophy in the University of Oxford, has already been published in volume 47 of the *British Yearbook of International Law*. I would like to thank the many who have assisted me over the years; in particular, I am grateful to Mary Melling for typing but more for patience; to the staff of the Oxford University Press for their courtesy and attention; and to Professor R. Y. Jennings of Jesus College, Cambridge, who read a substantial part of the manuscript and whose knowledge and critical insight proved a formative source of inspiration. My greatest debt I owe to Professor Ian Brownlie, now of the London School of Economics, who was first my tutor and then my supervisor during my time at Wadham College, Oxford. Without the benefit of his original thinking, his sound instruction in the making and the substance of public international law, and his constant and continuing advice and encouragement, I would not have written this book. For such errors and omissions as none the less occur, I alone remain responsible; moreover, the views expressed are my own and are not necessarily shared by the Office of the United Nations High Commissioner for Refugees.

GUY S. GOODWIN-GILL

London
November 1977

CONTENTS

PART II: THE ENTRY AND EXCLUSION OF FOREIGN NATIONALS

SELECTED ABBREVIATIONS

AuslG.	Ausländergesetz 1965 (Aliens Law of the Federal Republic of Germany)
BGBl.	Bundesgesetzblatt (published laws of the Federal Republic of Germany)
BGHSt.	Bundesgerichtshof Strafsachen (Federal Court, Criminal Matters)
BVerfGE.	Entscheidungen des Bundesverfassungsgerichts (BVerfGe) (Decisions of the Federal Constitutional Court of the Federal Republic of Germany)
BVerwGE.	Entscheidungen des Bundesverwaltungsgerichts (BVerwGe) (Decisions of the Federal Administrative Court of the Federal Republic of Germany)
DAG	Deutsches Auslieferungsgesetz 1925 (German Extradition Law)
GBl.	Gesetzblatt (published laws of the German Democratic Republic)
GG	Grundgesetz 1949 (Basic Law of the Federal Republic of Germany)
OVG	Oberverwaltungsgericht (Higher Administrative Court)
VerwRspr.	Verwaltungsrechtsprechung in Deutschland (collection of administrative law decisions)
1973 H.C. No. 79	Statement of Immigration Rules for Control on Entry (Commonwealth Citizens), January 1973
1973 H.C. No. 80	Statement of Immigration Rules for Control after Entry (Commonwealth Citizens), January 1973
1973 H.C. No. 81	Statement of Immigration Rules for Control on Entry (EEC and other Non-Commonwealth Nationals), January 1973
1973 H.C. No. 82	Statement of Immigration Rules for Control after Entry (EEC and other Non-Commonwealth Nationals), January 1973

TABLE OF CASES

Cases brought under the European Convention on Human Rights

Decisions of the European Court of Justice and of National Courts relating to the Treaty of Rome

United States of America

France

Federal Republic of Germany

Miscellaneous

TABLE OF STATUTES

United States of America

PART I

PRELIMINARY MATTERS

I

INTRODUCTION

THE MOVEMENT of persons across frontiers represents an area of particular problems for international law. Both emigration and immigration touch the self-interest of States, and it is common to find expressed the view that these are matters pre-eminently within the reserved domain of domestic jurisdiction. By this characterization it is understood that the State enjoys an absolute and uncontrolled discretion, or sovereign power, to determine whether it will permit its subjects to travel abroad and whether, and on what conditions, it will permit the entry and establishment of aliens.

This first reference to 'discretion' demands qualification. In the course of examining the *South West Africa Cases* (*Second Phase*), Dr. Brownlie makes the point that no power is in the ultimate sense discretionary, since the very notion of power involves an idea of design, of a *defined* objective, purpose, or competence.[1] A related, but somewhat different approach has been suggested recently by K. C. Davis in his work, *Discretionary Justice*.[2] He is concerned with discretion within a system of municipal law, but his views would seem to be of more general application. Thus, he proposes the objective of 'confining and structuring' discretion.[3] The governing premiss is that of control according to laws, rules, and regulations. Such control is of two kinds: first, it sets the limits to the power in question, that is, it says what can and what cannot be done; secondly, it prescribes the manner of exercise of the power. A characterization of this nature is particularly well suited for application to a variety of the powers of States in general, and especially to the powers of exclusion and expulsion.

There is nothing novel in this basic approach, which already has ample support in the jurisprudence of the World Court. For ex-

[1] Brownlie, *Principles of Public International Law* (2nd ed., 1973), pp. 462–3.

[2] *Discretionary Justice—A Preliminary Inquiry* (1971).

[3] Davis, op. cit., pp. 55, 97. As they are used below, the words 'confining' and 'structuring' indicate the distinction between the two functions of legal rules which are (i) to set the limits and (ii) to prescribe the manner of exercise of a given power.

UNIV DUNELM

ample, in the *Nationality Decrees Case*, the Court noted that, wherever its international implications were concerned, 'jurisdiction which, in principle, belongs solely to the State is limited by rules of international law'.[1] Similarly, in the *Lotus Case*, the Court qualified its reference to the 'wide measure of discretion' which a State enjoys regarding the extent of its jurisdiction by express mention of the limits which international law imposes.[2]

The word 'discretion' and the phrase 'discretionary power' are commonly used to signify the presence of uncontrolled freedom of action; the implication is of an arbitrary power, which is in turn opposed to the ideal of the rule of law. While such a meaning in relation to certain powers may be justified by first impressions, it is the object of the present work to advance a more detailed description of discretionary powers, and to show how they exist within legal limits. Such limits may specify the courses of action which are available and may also indicate matters which require to be taken into account before a decision is made. There is, correspondingly, an absence of complete freedom in regard both to the decision, what is to be done, and to the manner in which that decision is to be reached. Certainly, a wide margin of appreciation may be conceded to the holder of the power, and this is frequently the case in regard to the power of the State to exclude or to expel an alien. To that extent, the controls may be operative only at the outermost edges of an apparently absolute competence. The present aim remains, to determine with greater precision where the limits to such powers may be found, and what rules and standards govern their exercise.

(1) GENERAL PRINCIPLES LIMITING THE COMPETENCE OF STATES IN MATTERS OF NATIONALITY

The issue of nationality is inextricably bound up with the crossing of frontiers. Whether an individual is a citizen, an alien, or a treaty national may determine the extent of his rights, if any, to enter a State, to remain and work there, to leave that State and not to be

[1] P.C.I.J. (1923), Ser. B, No. 4, pp. 23–4.

[2] P.C.I.J. (1927), Ser. A, No. 10, p. 18. See also *Anglo-Norwegian Fisheries Case*, I.C.J. Rep., 1951, p. 3, and, more recently, the recognition of a 'qualified right' to extend exclusive fishing zones, as expressed in the Judgment of the Court in the *Fisheries Jurisdiction Cases*, I.C.J. Rep., 1974, p. 3. Cf. the conception of *jus aequum* in the terminology of Professor Schwarzenberger: *International Law and Order* (1971), pp. 5, 6.

expelled. The precise status of the individual may similarly determine the rights of other States, and whether any of them has a sufficient interest to exercise diplomatic protection in regard to the treatment afforded to that individual.[1]

The allocation of people to one rather than another subject of international law is manifestly an issue upon which both municipal law and international law may pronounce.[2] States are generally free to decide for themselves whether to have different categories of nationals, and whether such categories are to be subject to varying rights and obligations. It will be seen that a class of persons which occupies an intermediate status between that of the citizen and that of the alien is frequently of major significance in matters of immigration, but the consequences of such a status are generally a matter for internal law alone or, occasionally, for internal law in conjunction with specific treaty obligations.

The decisions of international tribunals have often emphasized the necessity of a continuing distinction between the internal and the international aspects of nationality. Oppenheim observes:

Nationality of an individual in his quality of being a subject of a certain State, and therefore its citizen. It is not for international law but for municipal law to determine who is, and who is not, to be considered a subject.[3]

This general statement is then qualified by reference to the principle of customary international law that such nationality is required to be recognized by other States only in so far as it conforms with international law. Schwarzenberger is more precise:

If the individual is an object of international law, international law must ultimately determine the criteria for allocating any such object to one rather than another subject of international law. The primary test is that of nationality.[4]

Weis chooses to underline the twin aspects of the institution:

As a concept of municipal law [nationality] is defined by municipal law; as a concept of international law, it is defined by international law. From

[1] In some cases an international body may also be involved, as where that body has a recognized interest in the protection of the individual's human rights.

[2] Schwarzenberger, *International Law* (3rd ed., 1957), vol. I, p. 354.

[3] Oppenheim, *International Law* (8th ed., 1955), vol. I, pp. 642–3. See also O'Connell, *International Law* (2nd ed., 1970), p. 670.

[4] *International Law* (3rd ed., 1957), vol. I, p. 354.

the aspect of municipal law there is, therefore, no one concept of nationality but as many concepts as there are municipal laws.[1]

The freedom which States possess in this field leads inevitably to the anomalies of dual and multiple nationality and statelessness. Municipal law does show some conformity, however, particularly in regard to accepted methods for the acquisition of nationality,[2] and the final result may not be so chaotic.[3]

The essential quality of a State's power or competence in the matter of nationality is its discretionary nature. It will be argued subsequently that this same characteristic pertains to the powers which a State enjoys generally in regard to the entry and expulsion of aliens. Moreover, it is by way of the concept of discretion, confined and structured by law,[4] that one may progress towards a theory of 'sovereign rights' which is more fully compatible with the existence of international obligations. The limitations which international law imposes upon States in the present context are revealed by three situations in particular: (*a*) the imposition of nationality upon immigrants or residents; (*b*) denationalization; and (*c*) the issue of nationality in relation to the exercise of diplomatic protection.

(*a*) *The Imposition of Nationality upon Immigrants or Residents*

As Brownlie observes, the automatic imposition of nationality upon all those persons entering a State's territory would, if accepted, enable that State to avoid its duties to aliens resident or passing through.[5] Today the general view is that recognition need not be accorded to such measures if imposed without request or

[1] Weis, *Nationality and Statelessness in International Law* (1956), p. 239.

[2] Cf. Oppenheim, *International Law* (1st ed., 1905), vol. I, pp. 352–6; id., 8th ed., 1955, vol. I, pp. 649–60.

[3] See 5 *B.D.I.L.* 7. The development of the concepts of nationality, citizenship, and alienage have been thoroughly explored elsewhere. See Hoebel, *The Law of Primitive Man* (1954), p. 7; Radcliffe-Brown, Preface to Fortes and Evans-Pritchard, *African Legal Systems* (1940), p. xiv; Hartland, *Primitive Law* (1924), p. 118; Manson, 'The Admission of Aliens', 4 Jour. Soc. Comp. Leg. (1902), 114; Del Vecchio, 'The Evolution of Hospitality', 4 Sydney L.R. 205; Wolff, *Jus Gentium*, s. 156; Hebrews 13: 2. On the evolution of British nationality and the concept of allegiance, see Jones, *British Nationality Law and Practice* (1947); Pollock and Maitland, *History of English Law* (2nd ed., 1968), vol. I, pp. 458–67; Holdsworth, 9 *H.E.L.* 72–104; 5 *B.D.I.L.* 43 ff.; Plender, *International Migration Law* (1972), pp. 1–37; Salmond, 'Citizenship and Allegiance', Pt. I, 17 L.Q.R. (1901), 270; Pt. II, 18 L.Q.R. (1902), 49.

[4] Admittedly with varying degrees of certainty.

[5] Brownlie, op. cit., pp. 383–4.

consent, unless the individual has a genuine connection with the State by both parentage and permanent domicile.[1]

Consent, or acquiescence, of the individuals affected is of continuing importance in cases involving a change of territorial sovereignty. Formerly, it may have been that the nationality of resident or domiciled inhabitants automatically followed the change of sovereign, although they would not always lose their former status.[2] It was commonly accepted, however, that there must be a 'sufficient link', whether described in terms of domicile or of habitual residence, between the successor State and those whom it claimed as nationals.[3] Modern treaties of cession and for the regulation of nationality tend to apply the criteria of permanent or habitual residence, in conjunction with recognition of the right of option.[4] However, it is doubtful whether there is any rule of customary international law which insists upon such a right.[5] Indeed, its recognition by treaty may only be evidence of a limited exception to the general rule which relates nationality to the criterion of genuine or substantial connection with the territory in question.

(*b*) '*Denationalization*'

National legal systems commonly provide for deprivation of nationality in certain circumstances,[6] and current State practice does not support any general rule prohibiting such measures.[7] Once again this is an area of discretion in which States' powers are only indistinctly confined by rules of international law. Statelessness

[1] 5 *B.D.I.L.* 25–30; Weis, op. cit., pp. 110–13; Brownlie, op. cit., p. 392; Schwarzenberger, op. cit., p. 360.

[2] See 5 *B.D.I.L.* 32–8.

[3] *Peinitsch* v. *German State*, Ann. Dig., 1923–4, Case No. 121; O'Connell, *International Law*, pp. 391–3, and *State Succession in Municipal Law and International Law*, vol. I, pp. 499 ff.

[4] See the 1956 Treaty between the Federal Republic of Germany and Belgium: BGBl. 1958, II, S. 263; 1960 Treaty between the Federal Republic of Germany and the Netherlands: BGBl. 1963, II, S. 463; 1956 Treaty between Federal Republic of Germany and France over the Saar: BGBl. 1956, II, S. 1589; 1969 Treaty between the German Democratic Republic and the U.S.S.R. on dual nationality: GBl., D.D.R., 1969, Teil I, S. 108. The treaties are printed in Makarov, *Deutsches Staatsangehörigkeitsrecht, Kommentar* (2nd ed., 1971), at pp. 577, 582, 588, and 622.

[5] O'Connell, *International Law*, p. 393.

[6] See Oppenheim, *International Law* (8th ed.), vol. I, pp. 657–60.

[7] Brownlie, op. cit., p. 391. Cf. Weis, 'The United Nations Convention on the Reduction of Statelessness', 11 I.C.L.Q. (1962), 1073; Lauterpacht, *International Law and Human Rights* (1950), pp. 433 f.

is a continuing phenomenon, and yet an indication of the circumstances in which denationalization would be unlawful can be gathered from a consideration of some of the established incidents of nationality. From among them, Oppenheim selects one particular right and one particular duty:

> The right is that of protection over its citizens abroad which every State holds . . . The duty is that of receiving on its territory such of its citizens as are not allowed to remain on the territory of other States.[1]

Just as a State cannot avoid its international obligations towards aliens by the imposition of nationality on them, so too it is barred from avoidance of the duty to admit nationals by a measure of '*ad hoc* denationalization'. Every case would need to be considered in the light of its facts and of the reasons behind such a decision, but as Brownlie notes:

> In appropriate circumstances responsibility would be created for the breach of duty if it were shown that the withdrawal of nationality was itself a part of the delictual conduct facilitating the result.[2]

At the present time the competence of States to introduce denationalization measures cannot be doubted. On occasion they may have effect only internally, as in the case of a suspension of political rights, but the issues are less straightforward in regard to other States. Whereas every State is generally free to refuse admission to any individuals who have been rendered stateless, in practice this freedom is often restricted by treaty and other obligations towards refugees and persons similarly placed.[3]

(*c*) *Nationality and Diplomatic Protection*

In many cases it is impossible to separate the right to exercise diplomatic protection from the fact of nationality.[4] In its opinion in the *Panevezys-Saldutiskis Railways Case*, the Permanent Court of International Justice observed: 'in the absence of a special agreement, it is the bond of nationality between the State and the individual

[1] Op. cit., pp. 645–6.
[2] Op. cit., p. 383.
[3] See further below, pp. 137–46. Cf. British Nationality Act 1948, section 20; 5 *B.D.I.L.* 295–6, 335–7.
[4] See 5 *B.D.I.L.* 3 and *passim*.

which alone confers upon the State the right of diplomatic protection.'[1] Taken out of context, this statement is not very helpful. It is of even less assistance when accompanied by references to the well-known dictum of the same Court in the *Nationality Decrees Case*, to the effect that questions of nationality are in principle within the reserved domain of domestic jurisdiction.[2] Be that as it may, Schwarzenberger remarks that the reason why any State is not entitled to intervene on behalf of any individual lies in the fact that,

> in so far as the relations between any subject of international law and its own nationals are concerned, at least under customary international law, these are matters within the exclusive jurisdiction of that particular subject of international law.[3]

It may be that today this conclusion is open to re-examination in the light of the distinction drawn by the International Court of Justice between international obligations *erga omnes* and international obligations the performance of which is the subject of diplomatic protection. It is in the latter case, said the Court, that a State must first establish its right or interest in order to bring a claim.[4]

In the typical case, the claimant State will prove its interest by showing that the individual concerned is its national. There may be problems, however, if the local law has little or nothing to say about the nationality of the *de cuius*. In the *Cayuga Indians Case*[5] the decision of the Tribunal that those Indians resident in Canada were British nationals under the protection of the Crown rested principally on the fact of residence and attachment, as also upon the fact that the Crown was in lawful administration of the territory wherein they resided.[6] As O'Connell observes with considerable justification,

[1] P.C.I.J. (1939), Ser. A/B, No. 70, p. 16.

[2] P.C.I.J. (1923), Ser. B, No. 4, p. 23.

[3] Op. cit., p. 355

[4] *Barcelona Traction Case*, I.C.J. Rep., 1970, p. 3 at p. 32.

[5] U.N. Rep., vol. VI, p. 173 (1926).

[6] Ibid., p. 177. Cf. Brownlie, op. cit., at pp. 388–9: 'if a right of protection arises by virtue of lawful administration of territory, then it would seem that nationality may be said to arise from the fact of the right of protection.' Note also the category of 'British protected persons'; in 1897 the Legal Adviser to the Foreign Office declared, 'There is no law to prevent Her Majesty from extending her protection to any body she pleases, and therefore, technically, I can hardly say that there is any "legal objection".' *Illegitimate Anglo-Chinese*: 5 *B.D.I.L.* 465–7. This statement must, of course, be read in relation to the competing rights of other States; in the case in point the Chinese authorities did not wish to claim the individuals in question as Chinese subjects. See also 5 *B.D.I.L.* 439–48; O'Connell, *International Law*, pp. 677–8; Parry, *Nationality and Citizenship Laws of the Commonwealth and the Republic of Ireland*, vol. I (1957), pp. 11–15; Jones, *British Nationality Law* (1956), pp. 84, 185 ff.

it is impossible to disengage nationality in its international sense from the social fact of attachment to a given legal society.[1] It is this practical point which is the most striking in the judgment of the International Court of Justice in the *Nottebohm Case*:

the diversity of demographic conditions has thus far made it impossible for any general agreement to be reached on the rules relating to nationality, although the latter by its very nature affects international relations. It has been considered that the best way of making such rules accord with the varying demographic conditions in different countries is to leave the fixing of such rules to the competence of each State. On the other hand, a State cannot claim that the rules it has thus laid down are entitled to recognition by another State unless it has acted in conformity with this general aim of making the legal bond of nationality accord with the individual's genuine connection with the State which assumes the defence of its citizens by means of protection as against other States . . . [Nationality] is a legal bond having as its basis a social fact of attachment, a genuine connection of existence, interests and sentiments, together with the existence of reciprocal rights and duties. It may be said to constitute the juridical expression of the fact that the individual upon whom it is conferred, either directly by the law or as the result of an act of the authorities, is in fact more closely connected with the population of the State conferring nationality than with that of any other State. Conferred by a State, it only entitles that State to exercise protection vis-à-vis another State, if it constitutes a translation into juridical terms of the individual's connection with the State which has made him its national.[2]

Earlier the Court affirmed that it is international law which determines whether a State is entitled to exercise protection and to seise the court.[3] This it may generally do by showing the 'internationally required prerequisite of genuine connection between itself and the individual'.[4] A simple assertion, or the formal appearance of nationality, may not be enough. So it is that the competence of

[1] O'Connell, *International Law*, p. 671; see also the Israeli case, *A.B.* v. *M.B.* 17 I.L.R. (1950), 111.

[2] I.C.J. Rep., 1955, p. 4 at p. 23.

[3] Ibid., p. 21. Cf. Articles 1 and 2, 1930 Hague Convention on Certain Questions relating to the Conflict of Nationality Laws: 179 L.N.T.S. 89.

[4] Schwarzenberger, op. cit., p. 359. See also ibid., pp. 361–2, where the writer goes on to argue that 'if the necessary distinction between nationality for the purposes of international and municipal law is made . . . for the purposes of international law, nationality is regulated by rules of international law and, thus, neither exclusively nor essentially within the domestic jurisdiction of States.'

States to regulate nationality has been compared with their competence in matters of territory and jurisdiction.[1] In each case the issue is on the international plane, and an international tribunal is competent to examine the validity of a State's actions in that respect.[2] It may be that there is a presumption in favour of the local law, but this is clearly limited by the controlling precepts of international law. Nevertheless, the effect of international law upon such normal incidents of nationality as the 'right' to enter one's own State is far from clear. In the words of Schwarzenberger, the question is, 'Whether a genuine connection, which establishes the right of diplomatic protection, creates also an international duty on the part of a State to accept international obligations which result from this relationship.'[3]

(2) NATIONALITY AND RIGHTS OF ENTRY IN MUNICIPAL LAW

By reason of the relation existing between nationality and the 'right' to enter a State, it becomes necessary to consider the extent to which the two may coincide in practice.

(*a*) *British Nationality and Citizenship of the United Kingdom and Colonies*

The characteristics of British nationality and of alienage were summarized in the British Nationality and Status of Aliens Act 1914, section 1 of which declared that natural-born British subjects comprised (*a*) any person born within His Majesty's dominions and allegiance; and (*b*) any person born out of His Majesty's dominions if, *inter alia*, his father was born within His Majesty's allegiance. This was an Imperial enactment, intended to provide the basis for a common status, but it was never applied uniformly and did not preclude discrimination in the policies followed by Commonwealth countries *vis-à-vis* one another, even during the period prior to the Statute of Westminster 1931. Thus, in Canada, South Africa, Australia, and New Zealand, the immigration of Orientals in particular was at the least severely restricted, notwithstanding their

[1] O'Connell, *International Law*, p. 760; Brownlie, op. cit., p. 369; Parry, op. cit., vol. I, p. 27.

[2] See the *Flegenheimer Claim*, 25 I.L.R. 91.

[3] Op. cit., p. 360.

common status as British subjects.[1] The Canadian case *Re Munshi Singh* illustrates attitudes prevailing in 1914, and on the subject of immigration to Canada the Chief Justice declared: 'in my opinion the British subject has no higher right than an alien in coming to the shores of Canada.'[2] The common status continued to be respected in the law of the United Kingdom, however, and restrictions on entry imposed during the First World War were directed solely at the alien, that is, 'any person who is not a British subject'.[3]

The movement towards greater autonomy among Commonwealth nations after the Second World War was reflected in the radical changes introduced by the British Nationality Act 1948. In one commentator's words, it was 'of the essence of the new scheme that each [Commonwealth] country decides who are its citizens', and a feature 'that each country acknowledges the citizens of the others not to be aliens'.[4] In pursuit of this aim the Act makes a distinction between citizens of the United Kingdom and Colonies (treated with the Channel Islands and the Isle of Man as one unit) and those of Commonwealth countries specified in section 1 (3), as amended.[5] The Act speaks of having the status of a British subject and 'being known' as a British subject, but it does not define that status. Indeed, from the point of United Kingdom law, no satisfactory definition is possible without taking account of the combined effect of all Commonwealth legislation in the matter. The terms 'British subject' and 'Commonwealth citizen' are also declared to have the same meaning,[6] but again their meaning is only comprehensible in the light of internal law provisions governing citizenship of the United King-

[1] See the following examples of Commonwealth legislation discriminating against classes of Commonwealth immigrants: Canada R.S.C., pp. 2121, 3134, 3162 (1952); New Zealand, Act No. 44 of 1919, New Zealand Statutes 1955, p. 1677; Act No. 23 of 1920, ibid., p. 1681; Australia, Commonwealth Acts 1901–50, pp. 2003–5; see also Pakistan, Control of Entry Act 1952, The Central Acts and Ordinances of Pakistan 1952, Act No. 15; India, Influx from Pakistan Control Act 1949 (1949) All. Ind. Rep., Act No. 102, and (1952) All Ind. Rep., Act No. 108.

[2] 6 Western Weekly Rep. 1347 (1914). See also *Re 39 Hindus* 15 D.L.R. 189 (1913).

[3] British Nationality and Status of Aliens Act 1914, section 27; this definition is expressly preserved by British Nationality Act 1948, section 32. A British subject might nevertheless be treated as an alien by virtue of the Aliens Restrictions Acts 1914 and 1919 and Article 15, Aliens Order 1920, unless he could prove his status by producing a passport or other document establishing his identity. See now Immigration Act 1971, section 3 (8); Sch. 2, paras. 2, 4, and below, pp. 103–4, 108.

[4] Parry, op. cit., vol. I, p. 112.

[5] British Nationality Acts 1948–1965; see also Bangladesh Act 1973; Pakistan Act 1973.

[6] British Nationality Act 1948, section 1 (2).

dom and Colonies and of independent Commonwealth countries respectively. Additional difficulties are created by the anomalous position of the Republic of Ireland, which is neither a Commonwealth country nor a part of Her Majesty's dominions. Under the law of the United Kingdom it is not a foreign country either, and its citizens, although not Commonwealth citizens, are not treated as aliens.[1]

A leading feature of the British Nationality Act, although one which is of less and less practical importance, is the common or multiple status which it creates within the term British subject/ Commonwealth citizen.[2] Even at the time of its affirmation, however, it was admitted that such status would not prevent discrimination in the policies followed by Commonwealth countries in their *inter se* relations.[3] Indeed, one of the principal objects of the Act was to recognize and give effect to the wish of independent Commonwealth States to enact their own citizenship laws.

None the less, as regards the United Kingdom itself, from 1949 to 1962 an unconditional right of entry and residence extended both to citizens of the United Kingdom and Colonies[4] and to the citizens of independent Commonwealth countries. This right of entry has been progressively cut back,[5] and admission to the United Kingdom depends now not upon citizenship or subjecthood, but on the concept of *patriality*, the quality of 'belonging' to the United Kingdom. The class of *patrials* is in many ways anomalous, for not only does it include certain citizens of independent Commonwealth countries, it also excludes certain classes of United Kingdom citizens.

Under the Immigration Act 1971, those who enjoy the right of abode are comprised within the following categories: (*a*) citizens of the United Kingdom and Colonies who acquired that status by birth, adoption, naturalization or registration in the United Kingdom;[6]

[1] Ibid., section 32 (1); Ireland Act 1949, sections 2 (1), 3 (1).

[2] See generally, Clute, 'Nationality and Citizenship', in Wilson, ed., *The International Law Standard and Commonwealth Developments* (1966), p. 105.

[3] 155 H.L. Deb., col. 1. See also *De Marigny* v. *Langlais* Criminal Reports, Canada, vol. 5 (1948), 256; *Thornton* v. *The Police* [1962] A.C. 339 (P.C.).

[4] See Macdonald, *The New Immigration Law* (1972), pp. 24–30, for a summary of the methods of acquisition and loss of citizenship of the United Kingdom and Colonies. On proposals for reform see Dummett, *Citizenship and Nationality* (1976); *British Nationality Law: Discussion of Possible Changes*, Cmnd. 6795 (1977).

[5] See below, pp. 97–103.

[6] Immigration Act 1971, section 2 (1) (a). The reference to registration applies also to registration in an independent Commonwealth country by the United Kingdom High Commissioner (under section 8 (2), British Nationality Act 1948), except that in the case of registration of a minor under section 7 of that Act, such registration must have been effected prior to the passing of the Immigration Act 1971 (28 Oct. 1971): section 2 (4).

(*b*) citizens of the United Kingdom and Colonies born to or adopted by such citizens as are within (*a*) above, or whose parent had obtained citizenship in the manner prescribed by (*a*) above;[1] (*c*) citizens of the United Kingdom and Colonies at any time settled in the United Kingdom and ordinarily resident there for five years or more;[2] (*d*) Commonwealth citizens born to or adopted by a citizen of the United Kingdom and Colonies who acquired such citizenship by birth in the United Kingdom;[3] and (*e*) women who are Commonwealth citizens and married to patrials within any of the above categories (*a*)–(*d*), that is, whether those patrials are themselves United Kingdom citizens or Commonwealth citizens.[4]

The concept of patriality is but one example of the way in which States may, for the purposes of controlling immigration, distinguish between various classes of 'nationals'. Under present United Kingdom law, the class of those who have the right of abode by no means corresponds with that class of nationals on whose behalf the United Kingdom may exercise diplomatic protection. The class of non-patrial citizens, although they may not satisfy the requirement of substantial connection, nevertheless continue to enjoy the benefit of diplomatic protection. In their case, the principle of effective nationality has to be applied in relation to other principles also, such as estoppel.[5]

(*b*) *French Nationality*

In an earlier period French law drew a distinction between 'citoyens français' and 'sujets français', the latter deriving their status from connection with the overseas colonies. The essence of this distinction was abolished by virtue of the 1946 Constitution which

[1] Ibid., section 2 (1) (b) (i) and (ii). As there was no United Kingdom citizenship before 1949, references to citizenship before that date are to be construed as references to British nationality: ibid., section 2 (3) (c).

[2] Ibid., section 2 (1) (c). The Act provides that a person is not to be treated as ordinarily resident in the United Kingdom at a time when he is there in breach of the immigration laws: section 33 (2). The Act in effect follows the Court of Appeal ruling in *Re Abdul Manan* [1971] 1 W.L.R. 859; see also sections 2 (3) (d), 33 (1).

[3] Immigration Act 1971, section 2 (1) (d).

[4] Ibid., section 2 (2) (a); this provision applies also in respect of women who are non-patrial United Kingdom citizens. Section 2 (2) (b) extends the right of abode to the former wives of United Kingdom or Commonwealth citizens within the same categories.

[5] In respect of United Kingdom citizens resident in East Africa, for example, the principle of effective nationality has to be considered in the light of the citizenship laws and other agreements entered into at the time of independence of the various States. It would appear that these had the effect of keeping alive the United Kingdom's responsibility for, and right of diplomatic protection over, its non-patrial citizens.

introduced the single status of 'citoyen de l'union française'. This status was enjoyed by all those who had the necessary associations either with France and the non-metropolitan territories, or with colonies, protectorates, and mandated territories.[1] The 1945 Code de la Nationalité prescribed the relevant connections in a comprehensive piece of legislation notable, in one commentator's view, 'pour sa préoccupation . . . de faire le plus de français possible'.[2]

The idea of a single citizenship was affirmed by Article 77 of the 1958 Constitution,[3] but in practice special provisions continued to apply to the category of persons known solely as 'ressortissants'. However, the 1945 law has been reenacted with substantial amendments by the law of 9 January 1973,[4] which contains no reference to the colonies as such. The area of application of the new law, 's'étend du territoire métropolitain, des départements et des territoires d'outre-mer'.[5] Where such *départements* and overseas territories achieve independence, the general rule is that the local population acquires the nationality of the new State.[6] Although provision is made for the retention of nationality by those domiciled in such territories who derive their status through a connection with metropolitan France,[7] there is no provision for a further status comparable to that of British subject or Commonwealth citizen.

The class of 'ressortissants', referred to above, has been characterized as follows:

Les ressortissants d'un État sont toutes les personnes qui relèvent à un titre quelconque de son autorité. En particulier, ont été considérés comme ressortissants de l'État: ses nationaux, les sujets de ses colonies, ceux des mandats qu'il administrait, ceux de ses protectorats; . . . il a été affirmé que le terme 'Français' figurant dans les traités conclus par la France au

[1] Articles 6 and 7 of the ordonnance du 19 octobre 1945 previously described the areas covered by the terms 'en France' and 'aux Colonies'; Boulbès observed, in relation to these articles that they have 'un caractère exclusif. Tout territoire qui ne se situe ni 'en France' ni 'aux Colonies' est nécessairement l'étranger pour l'application du Code de la Nationalité et, en général, des lois sur la nationalité. . . . L'extranéité pure et simple est la situation de l'individu qui n'est pas un Français.' *Droit français de la nationalité* (1956), pp. 27, 469.

[2] Savatier, Dalloz, *Jurisprudence Générale*, 1946, L. 10, 17.

[3] Boulbès, op. cit., p. 45.

[4] Loi no. 73-42 du 9 janvier 1973: *Recueil* Dalloz Sirey, 1973, L. 85; Plender, 'The New French Nationality Law', 23 I.C.L.Q. (1974), 709.

[5] Loi du 9 janvier, article 1, amending article 6 of the 1945 law.

[6] Articles 12 and 13 of the law of 1945, as amended by article 1 of the law of 1973; articles 152–7, as amended by article 20.

[7] Articles 152–7, as amended.

19ème siècle était l'équivalent du terme 'ressortissant français' en comprenant l'ensemble des individus ressortissants à un titre quelconque du Gouvernement de la République française.[1]

Essentially this description reproduces that class of persons on whose behalf France might justifiably exercise the right of diplomatic protection.[2] Within metropolitan France, however, many *ressortissants* were treated as aliens. The decision of the Conseil d'État in the case of *Hamar ben Brahim ben Mohamed, dit Paci* illustrates this point.[3] The question to be decided was whether a Moroccan subject could legally be made the subject of a deportation order. The court took the view that a Moroccan subject was clearly not a French national within the meaning of the Code de la Nationalité and that, moreover, he was not entitled to the privileges granted to the 'ressortissants de l'Union française' by Article 81 of the 1946 Constitution. The court concluded that his quality as a subject of a French protected State was no defence to the order expelling him from French territory.[4] Here again the class of nationals described by international law for the purposes of protection is divided up for the purpose of an application of the immigration laws by the protecting power.

(*c*) *Nationality of the Federal Republic of Germany*

Article 1 (2) of the 1965 Ausländergesetz (*AuslG.*) declares simply: 'Ausländer ist jeder, der nicht Deutscher im Sinne des Artikels 116 Absatz 1 des Grundgesetzes ist.'[5] The article of the Constitution to which this provision refers in turn declares:

Deutscher im Sinne dieses Grundgesetzes ist, vorbehaltlich anderweitiger gesetzlicher Regelung, wer die deutsche Staatsangehörigkeit besitzt oder als Flüchtling oder Vertriebener deutscher Volkszugehörigkeit oder als

[1] Kiss, *Répertoire de la pratique française en matière de droit international public*, vol. II (1966), pp. 233–8. Cf. Schwarzenberger, *International Law* (3rd ed.), vol. I, pp. 377–8.

[2] '*Au point de vue international*, les sujets ou les protégés français doivent être considérés comme des ressortissants français': Rapport au Président de la République Française, 1913: *Clunet*, 1914, p. 311; Kiss, op. cit., p. 236, s. 437.

[3] Arrêt au 18 mars 1955: Kiss, op. cit., pp. 541–2, s. 949.

[4] See also the *Samné* case, Conseil d'État, arrêt du 5 février 1931: *Recueil* Dalloz Sirey, 1931, p. 136, in which a Libyan subject, also a 'protégé français', was found to be an alien—'tout individu qui n'a pas la qualité de Français'.

[5] 'An alien is anyone who is not a German within the meaning of Article 116 (1) of the Basic Law.' BGBl. 1965, I, 353.

dessen Ehegatte oder Abkömmling in dem Gebiete des Deutschen Reiches nach dem Stande vom 31. Dezember 1937 Aufnahme gefunden hat.[1]

This means that, unless otherwise ordered by law, a 'German' is either one who possesses German nationality or one who, as a refugee or exile of the German race, has been accepted within the territory of the German Reich as it stood on 31 December 1937.[2] It is apparent that the concept of 'Deutscher' is not so easy of comprehension as the affirmative declaration of Article 1 of the *AuslG.* might lead one to believe. The inclusion of non-national, ethnic Germans can give rise to problems, particularly where they retain the nationality of another State. Nevertheless, the basic premiss of the aliens law is that 'Germans', however described, are to be set over and against all others.[3]

The class of persons comprised within the category, 'deutscher Vokszugehöriger' is itself divided. Only those ethnic Germans who qualify as 'Flüchtlinge' or 'Vertriebenen' come within the constitutional definition of 'Deutscher'. Makarov observes that nevertheless both categories of 'Deutscher' can, in addition to their constitutional status, possess a foreign nationality; they may even be stateless.[4] Leaving aside the problems of dual nationality, it is clear that, from the point of view of international law, the category of Germans without German nationality is less likely to satisfy the requirement of substantial connection in such a way as to permit the exercise of diplomatic protection in their favour. The law, however, gives them a qualified right to be naturalized on demand, provided that they do not endanger the internal or external security of the Federal Republic or of the individual *Länder*.[5] This right is further limited by the constitutional requirement that the individuals concerned should have been received within the territory of the former German Reich. On the assumption that this anticipates the establishment of permanent residence, and that this in turn takes place

[1] Article 116 (1), Bonner Grundgesetz 1949. See also the Bundesvertriebenengesetz, BGBl. 1953, I, 201, Article I; BGBl. 1957, I, 1215, 1330; BGBl. 1961, I, 813, 1882.

[2] The latter category extends also to the spouse or descendant of such refugee or exile. In some cases this description has only notional application, for example, in regard to those portions of the German Reich now under Polish sovereignty.

[3] Schiedermair, *Handbuch des Ausländerrechts der Bundesrepublik Deutschland*, p. 15.

[4] Makarov, *Deutsches Staatsangehörigkeitsrecht*, *Kommentar* (2nd ed., 1971), p. 243.

[5] Staatsangehörigkeitsregelungsgesetz 1955, Article 6 (1). Paragraph (2) provides that on it becoming clear that the individual has declined to exercise his right, he loses his legal status as a German ('verliert . . . die Rechtsstellung eines Deutschen').

within the area presently subject to the jurisdiction of the Federal Republic, then the criterion of genuine link would appear to be satisfied.[1]

The application of Article 116 (1) of the Constitution was considered in 1971 by the Bundesverwaltungsgericht.[2] The applicant had been born in 1909 as a German national and had lived in X all her life until 1963. She was first married to a German who was killed in 1944, and in 1946 she married a Polish national, the second applicant. At the end of the war X came under Polish sovereignty and, in 1959, after an exchange of territories, under Czechoslovak sovereignty. In 1963 the applicant and her family emigrated to the Federal Republic. The Court found that although on her second marriage she had lost her German nationality, she qualified as a German without German nationality.[3] The applicant thus came within the constitutional provision, and her husband and children also partook of this status.[4]

The category of 'Personen deutscher Volkszugehörigkeit' has been further elaborated in the Bundesvertriebenengesetz 1953, as amended, article 6 of which provides:

> Deutscher Volkszugehöriger im Sinne dieses Gesetzes ist, wer sich in seiner Heimat zum deutschen Volkstum bekannt hat, sofern dieses Bekenntnis durch bestimmte Merkmale wie Abstammung, Sprache, Erziehung, Kultur bestätigt wird.[5]

This concentration upon objective signs of belonging to the German race illustrates the point that this intermediate class of non-citizens is of relevance principally for the purpose of privileged treatment in naturalization. These provisions of German law are in many ways comparable to the different criteria applicable, under United King-

[1] See *Oppenheimer* v. *Cattermole* [1975] 2 W.L.R. 347. Note that Article 8 (1) of the law of 1955, which grants a similar right to be naturalized to other ethnic Germans, requires both permanent residence and the impossibility of returning home.

[2] *VerwRspr*. Bd. 23, S. 284 (BVerwGe., 1971).

[3] *VerwRspr*. Bd. 23, S. 284, at 287.

[4] Ibid., p. 288. See also *BVerwGE*. Bd. 23, S. 272 (1966), in which a refugee from Czechoslovakia was recognized as a German without German nationality, although born of an Italian father and an Austrian mother, thereby being an Italian national. He had been expelled as a 'Volksdeutscher' and had then taken up residence in the Federal Republic.

[5] 'An ethnic German within the meaning of this law comprises anyone who, in his homeland, acknowledged the German nation, in as much as this acknowledgement is corroborated by positive features, such as birth, language, upbringing and culture.' BGBl. 1957, I, 1215, 1330; BGBl. 1961, I, 813, 1882; Makarov, op. cit., p. 246.

dom law, to the registration of Commonwealth citizens as citizens of the United Kingdom and Colonies, and to the naturalization of aliens. Strictly speaking, the application and effect of such laws is of little concern to international law.

An issue which has been a steady source of controversy is that concerning the status of citizens of the German Democratic Republic, and at present there is some division of academic opinion on the point. In 1968 Schiedermair put forward the following view:

Nach hM gibt es trotz der Teilung Deutschlands nur eine einheitliche deutsche Staatsangehörigkeit. . . . Die Angehörigen der DDR sind somit für die BRD deutsche Staatsangehörige und unterliegen daher nicht den für Ausländer geltenden Bestimmungen. An dieser Auffassung ist festzuhalten, obwohl die DDR in jüngster Zeit eine eigene Staatsangehörigkeit eingeführt hat.[1]

This expresses the traditional view, but fails to reflect present realities. In 1967 the German Democratic Republic (DDR) enacted its own citizenship law, which is the only one recognized throughout East Germany.[2] This provides that citizens of the DDR shall comprise all those who, at the time of its founding,[3] were German nationals domiciled or ordinarily resident in the State, and who have not since lost their citizenship.[4] It also includes all those domiciled or resident outside the State, with no other nationality, who registered their status, and those who have been naturalized.[5] In 1968 the DDR adopted a new constitution and, in effect, completed a process of severance from legal sources previously shared in common with the Federal Republic.[6] In the latest edition of his work, Makarov notes that earlier the Federal Republic had not recognized the DDR as a State; it could not, therefore, logically recognize a nationality deriving from a non-entity.[7] Refugees from the East have never been treated as aliens, but Makarov suggests

[1] 'According to modern opinion there exists, despite the partition of Germany, only one German nationality . . . Consequently, those who "belong" to the German Democratic Republic are, from the point of view of the Federal Republic of Germany, German nationals and do not fall under the rules applicable to aliens. This view is to be supported, even though in recent times the German Democratic Republic has introduced its own nationality.' Schiedermair, op. cit., p. 16; see also Makarov, op. cit., 1st ed., 1966, pp. 21, 24.

[2] Gesetz über die Staatsbürgerschaft, DDR, 20 June 1967: GBl. 1967, I, 3.

[3] 7 October 1949.

[4] Article I (a).

[5] Article I (b), (c).

[6] e.g. Reichs- und Staatsangehörigkeitsrecht 1913.

[7] Makarov, op. cit., 2nd ed., 1971, pp. 21–8.

that some re-examination of previous theories is necessary in the light of recent developments.[1]

(*d*) *Conclusions*

This examination of the provisions of a number of municipal systems has illustrated the variety of local concepts of nationality. It has been seen, in particular, how States will quite frequently establish intermediate classes of 'non-citizen nationals'. The reasons which underlie such provisions are legion and are perhaps best exemplified by the development and demise of the so-called 'common status' of Commonwealth citizens. While such categories will often bear little or no relation to the class of persons who are allocated to a State under general international law, they nevertheless remain important for the purposes of immigration and the right of entry into a State. In such cases the continuing concept of the reserved domain of domestic jurisdiction is of singular significance. While international law is concerned with nationality for the purposes of diplomatic protection, and also in the matter of the reception of those expelled from the territory of other States, it leaves to States a much wider discretion in the regulation of the incidents of nationality, and in the creation of privileged classes, whether of aliens or citizens.

Since its inclusion in the Universal Declaration in 1948, the right to freedom of movement, both within State territory and for the purpose of entering and leaving it, has often come to figure prominently among the human rights declared fundamental to all men.[2] It may be that this right is inextricably bound up with other human rights, but, if so, its development has been hampered by a corresponding reluctance on the part of States to accord full recognition within the general field. Wherever such a right of entry can

[1] But cf. Mann, 45 *B.Y.I.L.* (1971), 470–1. A useful introduction to the problems of German nationality is provided by the litigation in *Oppenheimer* v. *Cattermole* [1973] Ch. 264 (C.A.); [1975] 2 W.L.R. 347 (H.L.); see also Mann, 89 L.Q.R. (1973), 194; Merrills, 23 I.C.L.Q. (1974), 143; 24 I.C.L.Q. (1975), 617.

[2] See Article 13, Universal Declaration of Human Rights; Article 5, International Convention on the Elimination of All Forms of Racial Discrimination; Article 12, International Covenant on Civil and Political Rights. See also Inglés, *Study of Discrimination in respect of the Right of Everyone to leave any Country, including his own, and to return to his Country*: U.N. Doc. E/CN.4/Sub.2/229/Rev.1 (1964). This report has been consistently ignored by the U.N. Human Rights Commission, and at its 19th Session in 1973 it was disposed of by a general recommendation to the General Assembly: *Review of the International Commission of Jurists*, June 1973, p. 1.

be said to exist today, it may usually be traced to one of three sources: (*a*) to municipal law, as an incident of citizenship; or (*b*) to treaties, which may create specific rights in favour of certain classes of aliens, including refugees and stateless persons; or (*c*) to general international law, in so far as this affirms the duty of a State to receive back its nationals expelled from other States or, possibly, in so far as it recognizes the human rights aspect and the right of entry as belonging to the individual citizen.

(3) STATE POWERS IN RELATION TO THE ENTRY AND EXPULSION OF FOREIGN NATIONALS

Just as the rules of international law regulate the power of States to determine the class of persons who shall be nationals, so too are limitations placed upon the discretionary competence of States in regard to the entry and expulsion of aliens. States retain a varying amount of freedom of action, but their powers are limited in extent and in the manner of exercise by the legal relations existing between States. Traditional modes of description, to the effect that the State enjoys 'sovereign rights' of exclusion and expulsion, tend to overplay the competence and to leave unresolved the conflict between claims to exclusive jurisdiction, on the one hand, and competing principles of accommodation and good faith, on the other. It must be emphasized that these general principles are backed up by particular rules regulating the exercise of the powers in question, in given circumstances.

The validity of an exclusion or an expulsion must be determined in the light of the State's obligations, whether they derive from custom, treaty, or general principles of law. In this instance, the obligations which limit State competence fall into three broad classes.

(*a*) *Bilateral Obligations*

Two categories of bilateral obligations may be identified in this field. First, there are those obligations which derive from treaties of limited application, such as treaties of commerce and establishment. Where such are operative, any claim to exclusive jurisdiction by the territorial sovereign over the nationals of the other party requires to be balanced against the terms of the treaty and its object and purpose.[1] Secondly, there are obligations which have their source in

[1] See below, pp. 160–97, 292–9.

that legal relationship created by the admission of a foreign national. By its consent to such admission, the receiving State becomes entitled to the local allegiance of the alien and binds itself to accord a certain standard of treatment to him. The receiving State also acquires the right to terminate the relationship by deportation, the State of nationality being under a duty to admit its national.[1]

It may be that other considerations, appertaining more particularly to the issue of State succession, apply in the case of a new State emerging with an alien minority already present on its territory. That State, it can be argued, had no choice regarding the presence of the class of foreign nationals and is therefore free to deal with them at will. But it may still be the case that, regardless of express consent, the State remains bound to a certain course of conduct. As has been noted in another context, there is no general support for the doctrine that any derogation from the freedom of action of States *must* be deduced from an express manifestation of their will.[2] In the present example, limitations on freedom of action may be traced to principles of general international law prohibiting discrimination and requiring respect for acquired rights.[3]

(*b*) *Obligations having a Regional or Multilateral Basis*

Obligations on a regional level will derive principally from treaty. The leading example here is the European Convention on Human Rights, which expressly confers on each Contracting State the right to refer any alleged breach of the Convention to the European Commission. The impact of this Convention on the State's powers of exclusion and expulsion is the subject of detailed study below.[4]

Still broader-based multilateral treaties also require to be considered, and attention will be drawn to the impression made by recent human rights conventions in particular, and to the extent to which these may impose, directly or indirectly, certain standards of treatment.

(*c*) *Universal Obligations, or Obligations owed* erga omnes

In one well-known dictum in its Judgment in the *Barcelona*

[1] See below, pp. 136–7; 201–3.

[2] Lauterpacht, *The Development of International Law by the International Court* (1958), p. 359.

[3] See in particular *German Settlers in Poland*, P.C.I.J. Ser. B, No. 6, (1923), pp. 33, 36, 39.

[4] See below, pp. 160–97; 282–306.

Traction Case the International Court of Justice expressed its recognition of a concept of obligations owed to the community of States as a whole:

> an essential distinction should be drawn between the obligations of a State towards the international community as a whole and those arising vis-à-vis another State in the field of diplomatic protection. By their very nature the former are the concern of all States. In view of the importance of the rights involved, all States can be held to have a legal interest in their protection; they are obligations *erga omnes*. Such obligations derive, for example, in contemporary international law, from the outlawing of acts of aggression, and of genocide, as also from the principles and rules concerning the basic rights of the human person, including protection from slavery and racial discrimination . . .[1]

The Court went on to observe that corresponding 'rights of protection' are to be found in the body of general international law and conferred by international instruments of a universal or quasi-universal character.

No cogent theory of obligation has yet been erected on these dicta. In particular, it remains unclear as to where the sources of the various obligations may be found, and as to what are the consequences of a breach of any such obligation. It may be that at present the traffic is all one way; obligations are owed at large, and the existence of such obligations provides the justification for expressions of international concern in the event of breach. The obligation gives a basis for criticism or condemnation, but not a sufficient *locus standi* for the initiation of a legal claim, strictly so called, in the sense of a claim for reparation. None the less, those obligations which are proposed for inclusion within the class of obligations *erga omnes* are not generally of the type which is susceptible to direct enforcement in this manner. An indication will be given below of the way in which such obligations may yet oblige States to a certain course of conduct, and of the direction in which the general class may be expected to develop.

[1] I.C.J. Rep., 1970, p. 3 at p. 32.

II

INTERNATIONAL LAW AND THE PASSPORT REGIME

IN THE context of contemporary international migration, nationality is closely bound up with one other institution of municipal law: namely, the passport. Passports and other travel documents are well established in the practice which governs the movement of persons across frontiers. There is more or less universal compliance with the recommendations of the 1920 League of Nations Conference as to the format of the international-style passport, but as yet very little consensus as to the role which passports are intended to play, whether in the international or the municipal sphere.[1]

Because so much of passport practice is dependent upon the provisions of municipal law, at times this aspect appears to dominate. But the passport also touches upon the relations between States, which include, particularly, the issues of nationality and its proof, diplomatic protection, and the 'returnability' of the holder to the State of issue. On the controversial question of the right to travel as a human right, municipal systems vary considerably. Thus, it is not always clear whether possession of a passport is a legal prerequisite to travel abroad, whether the individual has an enforceable right to be issued with a passport, and whether due process or alternative guarantees are applicable in such matters. These problems in turn raise the question of the precise nature of the passport and the place which it occupies in the local administration of States, whether or not the issue of a passport is a matter of foreign policy, as has often been argued in the United States, and therefore open to executive and arbitrary control.

Passport practice, although in many details purely dependent on local jurisdiction, does involve principles which affect the international relationships which lie behind (*a*) the passport's role as an identity document, (*b*) nationality; and (*c*) the diplomatic protection of citizens abroad. Nevertheless, while passports continue to be of paramount importance to the individual who seeks to travel abroad,

[1] Turack, *The Passport in International Law* (1972), ch. 22 and *passim*.

the 'rights' of that individual in respect to this particular freedom are still largely unrecognized. The practical value of a passport is still sufficiently reflected by the following comment, made in 1934:

le passeport n'est pas seulement un titre de voyage et une pièce d'identité. Il n'est pas seulement nécessaire pour se déplacer d'un pays à un autre. Il l'est pour obtenir du travail, pour participer au bénéfice de lois sociales, pour obtenir un permis de séjour. En de nombreux pays, l'étranger dépourvu de passeport n'est pas admis à séjourner. Il ne peut être reçu dans un hôtel, ni dans un hôpital. S'il a déjà une autorisation de séjour, celle-ci ne peut être renouvelée si le passeport n'est pas renouvelé.[1]

(1) POSSESSION OF A PASSPORT AS A CONDITION OF ADMISSION

The history of passports has been sufficiently considered elsewhere, and it is enough to note that the First World War witnessed the introduction of the passport system in its modern form.[2] A passport, in its current sense, came to mean a document of identity which a State will generally require alien travellers to have in their possession. As a general rule, it is for the municipal law of the State which the traveller seeks to enter to determine the form of the passport or visa that it requires.[3] In the United Kingdom the rules concerning the passport requirement for aliens are quite specific.[4] They require all passengers, whether Commonwealth citizens, E.E.C. or other nationals, to produce to the immigration officer on request either a valid passport or other document which indicates the holder's nationality and identity.[5]

[1] Reale, 'Le problème des passeports', 50 Hague *Recueil* (1934–IV), 89–187, at p. 171.

[2] Reale, art. cit. 89–187; Borella, 'Le Passeport', 64 *Rev. Gen. Dr. Int.* 301 (1960); Sibley and Elias, *The Aliens Act 1905* (1906), p. 44; Williams, 'British Passports and the Right to Travel', 23 I.C.L.Q. 642 (1974); 6 *B.D.I.L.* 10–11, 106–8; *Going Abroad*, Justice Report on Passports (1974); Jaconelli, 38 M.L.R. 314 (1975).

[3] There are certain exceptions, for example, where the matter is governed by treaty provisions such as those relating to the issue and validity of documents for refugees and stateless persons, and to the acceptance of alternative documents, including identity cards and collective passports.

[4] The current rules are made under the authority of the Immigration Act 1971. Formerly the situation was governed by the Aliens Order 1920 and the Aliens Order 1953, which were authorized by the Aliens Restriction Act 1914, which Act was itself continued in force for one year by the Aliens Restriction (Amendment) Act 1919 and subsequently re-enacted each year until 1971.

[5] 1973 H.C. No. 79 (Commonwealth Citizens), para. 3; 1973 H.C. No. 81 (E.E.C. and other Non-Commonwealth Nationals), para. 3. See also Immigration Act 1971, Sch. 2, paras. 2, 4; The Immigration (Landing and Embarkation Cards) Order 1975, S.I. 1975

It is a sufficient ground for refusal of entry that the passport produced is issued by an unrecognized government,[1] or by one which does not accept United Kingdom passports, or that the passport itself does not comply with international standards.[2] Other travel documents which may be tendered in lieu include collective passports,[3] 'non-national' travel documents issued to refugees and stateless persons,[4] and national identity cards.[5]

The principal purpose of the passport requirement is to establish the identity and nationality of those who seek admission to the State.[6] The second purpose is emphasized by those provisions which are common to immigration laws and which are concerned with what is inelegantly referred to as 'restricted returnability'. For example, any passenger who cannot satisfy the immigration officer that he will be admitted to another country after his stay in the United Kingdom may be excluded on that ground.[7] The passport, with its reference to returnability, is of crucial importance as indicating the destination to which the alien may be removed on his exclusion or subsequent deportation.[8]

No. 65. In any question whether a person is an alien or patrial, the onus lies on that person to prove any entitlement claimed: Immigration Act 1971, section 3(8); cf. Aliens Restriction Act 1914, section 1(4), applied in *R.* v. *Kaleko* [1923] 2 K.B. 793.

[1] Special provision is made for travellers from unrecognized States, so as to avoid any possibility of 'implied recognition'; see 387 H.C. Deb. (Written Answers), col. 424 (1972), reply by Mr. Kershaw, Under-Secretary of State. See also ECOSOC Doc. E/3438/Add. 1, p. 7, note 4 (27 Feb. 1961).

[2] 1973 H.C. No. 81, para. 4.

[3] Collective passport agreements exist with most States, other than those of the 'Eastern bloc': ECOSOC Doc. E/3438/Add. 1, p. 9, note 5. Seaman and aircrew are covered by their own particular regime, and the United Kingdom is party to the international agreements providing for the reciprocal recognition of their special travel documents: see, for example, Immigration Act 1971, section 8 (1); 1965 Convention on the Facilitation of Maritime Travel and Transport: 4 Int. Leg. Mat. 501, in force 1967; Merchant Shipping Act 1970, section 70; The Merchant Shipping (Seamen's Documents) Regulations 1972, Sch. 1 (S.I. 1972 No. 1295); below, pp. 156–9.

[4] See below, pp. 42–4.

[5] Under various bilateral arrangements, national identity cards in conjunction with British visitors' cards are acceptable: Turack, op. cit., pp. 60–3; for E.E.C. nationals, identity cards alone suffice: E.E.C. Directive 68/360 and below, pp. 40–1; 177.

[6] However, a passport will not necessarily be considered as conclusive of the holder's nationality: *R.* v. *Burke, Casey and Mullady*, 11 Cox C.C. 138 (1868); or as good evidence of the holder's whereabouts in a criminal trial: *U.S.* v. *Weiss* 491 F.2d 460 (1974).

[7] 1973 H.C. No. 79, para. 14; 1973 H.C. No. 81, para. 12. On applications for extension of stay by holders of restricted travel documents, see 1973 H.C. No. 80, para. 27; 1973 H.C. No. 82, para. 25.

[8] Immigration Act 1971, Sch. 2, para. 8; Sch. 3, para. 1. Cf. 1973 H.C. No. 79, para. 64; 1973 H.C. No. 81, para. 66; 1973 H.C. No. 80, para. 54; 1973 H.C. No. 82, para. 61. See further below, pp. 44–6.

Regulations similar to those in force in the United Kingdom can be found in other jurisdictions. In the Federal Republic of Germany, for example, Article 3 of the Ausländergesetz 1965 (AuslG.)[1] declares the 'Ausweispflict', which, interpreted literally, means the 'duty to identify oneself': 'Ausländer, die in den Geltungsbereich dieses Gesetzes einreisen, sich aufhalten oder aus ihm ausreisen wollen, müssen sich durch einen Pass ausweisen.' In fact this requirement is not strictly applied. The Minister of the Interior is empowered to authorize exceptions and, in particular, may free from the obligation those aliens whose return is guaranteed, or who produce other acceptable documents of identity.[2]

Some of the most detailed provisions of municipal law in respect of passports are to be found in the statutes and regulations of the United States. The Immigration and Nationality Act 1952 makes a first distinction between immigrant aliens and non-immigrant aliens. The passport requirement is imposed on both these classes, although with certain exceptions, limited primarily in favour of the nationals of contiguous territories. The statute defines a passport as 'any travel document issued by the competent authority showing the bearer's origin, identity, and nationality if any, which is valid for the entry of the bearer into a foreign country.'[3] In practice, this definition is not limited to a national passport and special provision is made for those who are unable to obtain such passport but who nevertheless manage to satisfy the documentary requirements in other ways.[4] Immigrant aliens will only be admitted to the United States if they are in possession of a valid unexpired immigrant visa, together with a valid unexpired passport 'or other suitable travel document, or document of identity and nationality'.[5] Similar provisions apply to non-immigrants, who require their own visa and a passport which

[1] BGBl. I, 353.

[2] *AuslG.* Article 3(2). Aliens who cannot establish their identity by a passport or other document may be issued with a 'Fremdenpass', but only after they have first entered the Federal Republic. Ibid., Article 4. See also Passverordnung vom 15 Feb. 1964, BGBl. I, 126, continued in force by *AuslG.* Article 55(4). For details of the further requirements of German law, see Schiedermair, *Handbuch des Ausländerrechts der Bundesrepublik Deutschland* (1968), pp. 110–15. Foreign passports must, *inter alia*, contain details of their area of validity and the Federal Republic must be included within such area; on United States practice in regard to 'area restrictions', see below, pp. 33–4.

[3] Immigration and Nationality Act 1952, section 101(a)(30), 8 U.S.C. s. 1101(a)(30).

[4] 22 C.F.R. 41.1.

[5] 8 U.S.C. s. 1182(a)(20); s. 1181(b) provides for certain exceptions in favour of returning resident aliens. Possession of a visa does *not* guarantee entry: s. 1201(h); below, p. 130.

is valid for a minimum of six months from the date of expiration of the initial period of admission, and which authorizes the holder to return whence he came or to proceed to another country.[1]

There are many exceptions to these requirements; for example, as regards immigrants, no passport is required if the alien is the spouse, parent, unmarried son or daughter of a United States citizen, or is stateless, or is an anti-Communist who for that reason is unable or unwilling to obtain a passport from the country of his nationality.[2] Certain non-immigrants are also exempt, including uniformed or documented members of the armed forces and American Indians born in Canada. In all other circumstances the passport obligation and the comprehensive visa system are strictly enforced. Indeed, the United States has only considered abolishing the visa requirement and admitting travel documents less than full passports for the nationals of contiguous States. One reason for this is to be found in the statutory definition of a passport, which requires that an alien have evidence of his right to enter another country. That this quality of 'returnability' plays an important part in United States law and practice is supported by official pronouncements. Thus, in answer to the recommendation of the Committee of Experts[3] in 1947 that bi- and multilateral agreements to waive the passport requirement on a basis of reciprocity should be encouraged, the United States limited its agreement to the case of States with common frontiers:

> Under such circumstances, the exclusion or deportation of an alien to his country of nationality, whenever . . . necessary . . . is relatively easy to accomplish . . . The current United States practice of requiring passports for aliens . . . from non-contiguous territories provides this country with a reasonable assurance that some foreign country will receive the alien whenever he becomes deportable. Any bilateral or multilateral agreement abolishing the passport requirement would have to provide the same assurance to the United States government.[4]

Such a policy explains in part why the United States did not ratify the General Convention on the Privileges and Immunities of the United Nations until 1970, and why it formerly did not recognize the validity of the United Nations *laissez-passer* as an international travel document. The United States would only accept such documents if

[1] Ibid., s. 1182(a)(26)(A).

[2] 8 C.F.R. 211.2; 22 C.F.R. 42.6; 42.112.

[3] The Committee was constituted after resolution passed by the Economic and Social Council. See U.N. Doc. E/436 for report and recommendations.

[4] U.N. Doc. E/2933, pp. 107–9.

presented with any other document such that, when considered together, they showed the origin of the official, his nationality if any, and his ability to enter some other country. However, consuls are now authorized to place visas in the *laissez-passer* for international officials employed by the United Nations. But the United States has also been reluctant to accept travel documents proposed to be issued to officials of the Organisation of American States, and has observed that if such documents were to be issued to United States nationals, this would constitute an infringement of sovereignty.[1]

(2) PASSPORTS AND THE 'RIGHT TO TRAVEL'

Given the almost universal acceptance of the passport requirement for aliens, it is clear that a refusal by the national State to issue such a document may seriously hamper the individual in his exercise of the 'right to travel'.[2] However, while such a right finds expression in a number of international instruments,[3] State practice in the municipal sphere tends to reflect a claim of absolute discretion, rather than any restrictive rule of general international law. Indeed, it may be that the provisions in question are not even potentially of a norm-creating character, in the sense employed by the International Court in the *North Sea Continental Shelf Cases*.[4] In so far as municipal

[1] Turack, op. cit., pp. 180–2. Generally on travel by international officials see ibid., chs. 16, 17, 18; Basdevant, *Les fonctionnaires internationaux* (1931), p. 53; Jenks, *The Headquarters of International Institutions* (1945), p. 37; Bowett, *The Law of International Institutions* (3rd ed., 1975), pp. 314–21; Brandon, 'The United Nations Laissez-passer', 27 B.Y.I.L. 448 (1950); General Convention on the Privileges and Immunities of the United Nations, Article IV, sections 11(d), 14, 17, 18(d); Article VII, sections 24–8; United Nations–United States Headquarters Agreement, 1947, Article III, section 9(b); Article IV, sections 11, 12, 13; Whiteman, *Digest*, vol. 8, p. 333; Convention on the Privileges and Immunities of the Specialised Agencies 1947, Article VIII, sections 26–30; Canada–I.C.A.O. Headquarters Agreement 1951, Article VIII, section 32; Switzerland–W.H.O. Agreement 1948, Article 14; Switzerland–I.L.O. Headquarters Agreement 1946, Article 14; United Kingdom International Organisations Act 1968; Immigration Act 1971, section 8(2); The Immigration (Exemption from Control) Order 1972, Article 4(g); 22 C.F.R. 41.12.

[2] This right or freedom may, of course, be hampered in other ways; witness the indirect effect of Exchange Control restrictions and the recent controversy over the Soviet 'education' or 'emigration tax': Williams, 'British Passports and the Right to Travel', 23 I.C.L.Q. 642, 651–52 (1974); Exchange between Secretary of State Kissinger and Senator Jackson, 69 A.J.I.L. 390–4 (1975).

[3] Universal Declaration of Human Rights, Article 13(2); International Covenant on Civil and Political Rights, Article 12(2); International Convention on the Elimination of All Forms of Racial Discrimination, Article 5 (d); European Convention on Human Rights, Fourth Protocol, Article 2(2).

[4] I.C.J. Rep., 1969, p. 3 at pp. 41–4.

systems do seek to limit any absolute discretion which the executive may claim in the issue of passports, then such developments probably owe more to local constitutionalism than to the impact of any burgeoning rule of international law.

In *Sawhney* v. *Assistant Passport Officer*,[1] for example, the Supreme Court of India held that the individual has a right to travel abroad, and that the refusal by the Government to issue him with a passport is a denial of the rights to personal liberty and equality before the law which are guaranteed by the Constitution of India. The Court referred to decisions of the United States courts which had accepted the right to travel, and it observed that the right was also recognized by Magna Carta and under the Common Law of England. The power claimed by the Government to issue passports at its discretion patently violated the doctrine of equality, for the differentia in the treatment of persons rested solely on the arbitrary selection of the executive, and such arbitrary power violated Article 14 of the Constitution.

The effect of this decision was not extensive, for within three months the Government had enacted the Passport Act 1967,[2] which forbids any citizen or alien to depart from, or attempt to depart from, India, unless he holds a valid passport or travel document. The right of an Indian citizen to be issued with a passport now stems from this statute,[3] which also lays down fairly wide grounds for refusal and withdrawal.[4]

In the United States, the issue of passports is governed by statute[5] and by extensive published regulations; the content of the latter owes much to decisions of the courts. In a series of cases between 1952 and 1967 there was a reaction against the Department of State's policy of refusing passports, withdrawing those already issued, and imposing so-called 'area restrictions'. The courts declared that the right to travel, and hence the right to a passport, was a right guaranteed by the Constitution. Consequently, it could only be restricted in accordance with the fundamental principle of due

[1] [1967] A.I.R. (S.C.) 1836.

[2] Printed in 7 *Indian Journal of International Law* (1967), 569–83; see also Nambiar, 'Right to a Passport', ibid., p. 526.

[3] Section 5.

[4] Sections 6, 10. A right of appeal is granted to persons aggrieved by such refusal or revocation (section 11), but no such appeal will lie against any order made by the Central Government, for example, that the issue of a passport is 'not in the public interest' (section 6 (2) (i)).

[5] Passport Act 1926, section 1 (44 Stat. 887).

process of law laid down in the Fifth Amendment. Under current regulations, passports are issued only to nationals, that is, to persons who owe permanent allegiance to the United States.[1] It is provided that a passport 'may be refused' where the applicant has not paid a repatriation loan, and where the Secretary of State determines that the national's activities abroad are causing or are likely to cause serious damage to the security or foreign policy of the United States.[2] There is also power to impose area restrictions.[3] However, any individual who is affected by an adverse decision regarding the issue, revocation, or restriction of a passport is entitled to make use of the system of administrative appeals provided.[4]

There is nothing in the legislative history to show that in passing the various passport Acts the United States Congress ever intended to authorize the executive to formulate substantive conditions in the issue of passports.[5] The intention appears to have been to enable the executive to lay down the necessary procedural rules. Nevertheless, the discretionary and political nature of the passport had been recognized as early as 1835 in the case of *Urtetiqui* v. *D'Arbel*,[6] and this character was presumed to continue into the very different circumstances of the twentieth century. By 1939, however, the discretionary authority of the Secretary of State was shown to be subject to the scrutiny of the courts,[7] but it was not until the enactment of three statutes, the Internal Security Act 1950, the Subversive Activities

[1] Cf. *United States* v. *Ushi Shiroma* 123 F. Supp. 145 (1954). The onus is on the applicant to prove his status: 22 C.F.R. 51. 40–1; cf. Federal Republic of Germany, Gesetz über das Passwesen, 1952 BGBl. I, 290, Article 6.

[2] 22 C.F.R. 51.70; 51.71.

[3] 22 C.F.R. 51.72. Special validation of passports for visits to restricted areas is possible, but is only considered where this is in the national interest of the United States; for example, where the applicant is an accredited journalist who intends to publish information about the restricted area: 22 C.F.R. 51.73. See further below, p. 34 n.4.

[4] 22 C.F.R. 51.80–105. Proceedings are heard before a single officer, from whom a further appeal may be made to the Board of Appellate Review. The decision of the Board is final, unless the matter is referred to the Secretary of State for decision. It is expressly provided that neither the hearing officer nor the Board may take into consideration any confidential information which is not part of the record: 22 C.F.R. 51.83; 51.95. In the Federal Republic of Germany the decision to refuse or to withdraw a passport is an administrative act (*Verwaltungsakt*), which can be challenged in the administrative courts. Although the passport authorities enjoy a certain amount of discretion, particularly in their appreciation of the relevant facts, this is subject to the controlling jurisdiction of the courts, and any unlawful or arbitrary exercise of their powers can be annulled: see Article 114, Verwaltungsgerichtsordnung 1960, BGBl. I, 17.

[5] Doman, 'Do Citizens have the Right to Travel?', 43 Amer. Bar Assoc. J. 307 (1957).

[6] 34 U.S. (9 Pet.), 692, 698 (1835).

[7] *Perkins* v. *Elg* 307 U.S. 325 (1939).

Control Act 1950, and the Immigration and Nationality Act 1952, that the most controversial cases occurred.

The first challenge to the effects of this legislation was raised in the case of *Bauer* v. *Acheson*.[1] The District Court of Columbia held, *inter alia*, that the denial of an American passport has a direct bearing on the applicant's personal liberty to travel outside the United States. It followed, therefore, that the discretion of the executive branch in such matters, although political, must be exercised with due regard to the constitutional rights of the citizen. The freedom to travel abroad, like other liberties guaranteed by the Constitution, is subject to reasonable regulation and control in the interests of public welfare, but the Constitution demands due process and equal protection of the laws in the exercise of that control.[2] Due process does not require a judicial hearing, but merely a procedure in which elements of 'fair play' are accorded, the essentials of which are notice and an opportunity to be heard before a judgment is reached. Consequently, the court found that in the present case the Secretary of State was without authority summarily to revoke a passport during the period for which it was valid, without prior notice or opportunity for a hearing, and on the bald statement that the citizen's activities were contrary to the best interests of the United States. There was, similarly, no authority to refuse to renew a passport under the same circumstances.

This decision was followed by a string of like cases,[3] and in *Schachtmann* v. *Dulles*[4] the court stated as a matter of principle that a passport is not simply a political document, so that its issue is not a purely political matter within the rule that purely political matters are non-justiciable.[5] This approach was affirmed by the Supreme Court in 1958 in its decision in *Kent* v. *Dulles*.[6] The Court here held that the pertinent statutes did not authorize the Secretary of State to withhold a passport for the reason stated, namely, that the plaintiffs had refused to file an affidavit concerning their membership of

[1] 106 F. Supp. 445 (1952).

[2] Cf. Article 2(2) and (3), Fourth Protocol, European Convention on Human Rights.

[3] See *Nathan* v. *Dulles* 129 F. Supp. 951 (1955); *Dulles* v. *Nathan* 225 F.2d 29 (1955); *Boudin* v. *Dulles* 136 F. Supp. 218 (1955); and compare now 22 C.F.R. 51.75 and 51.103.

[4] 225 F.2d 938 (1955).

[5] See Konvitz, *Civil Rights in Immigration* (1953), p. 44; also *Clark* v. *Dulles* 129 F. Supp. 950 (1955); *Robeson* v. *Dulles* 235 F.2d 810 (1956); *Communist Party of the United States* v. *Subversive Activities Control Board* 223 F.2d 531 (1955).

[6] 357 U.S. 116 (1958).

the Communist Party. The majority of the Court (the division was five to four) felt that Congress had not intended to give the Secretary of State an unbridled discretionary power. They were also of opinion that, while the issue of a passport carried some implication of an intention to extend diplomatic protection to the bearer, this was but one subordinate function. The primary purpose of the passport today was control over exit, and the right of exit was a personal right included within the word 'liberty' in the Fifth Amendment. While passport policy in general may involve foreign affairs judgments, it would appear that a refusal in an individual case has very little to do with foreign policy.[1]

The success of individual petitioners in asserting their right to be issued with a passport has not been matched by any similar success in regard to the legality of area restrictions. It was for long the policy of the United States not to issue passports for travel to countries which were not recognized or with which diplomatic relations were not maintained. Restrictions have also been placed on travel to areas of armed conflict and other areas where United States citizens might be in danger. The official attitude was explained in 1957, in regard to the denial of passports for travel to Communist China:

The United States does not recognise the Communist China régime and does not maintain diplomatic relations with it. The United States could not, therefore, extend normal diplomatic and consular protection to its citizens who travel in the area under Communist control. The fact that Communist China has engaged in the practice of taking, and are now holding, political hostages is clear evidence of the special need for such protection. As a matter of principle, the Government must extend such protection to every citizen to the limit of its capabilities whether or not the citizen would waive his right to protection.[2]

[1] See also *Aptheker* v. *Secretary of State* 378 U.S. 500 (1964) where the Supreme Court held that section 6 of the Subversive Activities Control Act 1950, which made it unlawful for members of any 'Communist organisation' to apply for or attempt to use a passport, was unconstitutional in that it restricted the right to travel too broadly and indiscriminately.

[2] Hearing before the Sub-Committee on the Far East and Pacific of the Committtee on Foreign Affairs, House of Representatives, 85th Congress, 1st Sess., 28 Mar. 1957, pp. 3–5. See also Hackworth, *Digest*, vol. III, 530; Whiteman, *Digest*, vol. 8, 288–306, 254. It is not illegal for a British subject and United Kingdom citizen to visit a State for which his passport is not valid. On the occasion of questions in the House of Commons concerning the visit of Mrs. Felton to North Korea during the currency of the Korean War, the Minister of State replied: 'The passport is a request to foreign governments to

Express judicial recognition of the power to restrict the travel of American citizens to certain countries or areas is to be found in the cases of *Worthy* v. *Herter*[1] and *Frank* v. *Herter*,[2] both dismissed by the Supreme Court in 1959.[3] Although the ruling in these cases may seem to be contrary to the view of the Court in *Kent* v. *Dulles* that the President has no inherent constitutional power to limit individual freedom to leave the country, it is apparent that the concept of area restriction is more of a political and foreign affairs matter than is the denial of a passport in an individual case.[4] Should the United States citizen decide to violate the area restrictions, then he will not generally make himself liable to criminal penalties, either under existing statutes or under the law of conspiracy.[5] Such activities may, however, be sufficient ground for the revocation or refusal of a passport.[6] In *Worthy* v. *United States* in 1964 the court declared unconstitutional section 215 of the Immigration and Nationality Act 1952, in so far as it purported to make it unlawful for a citizen to return to the United States without a valid passport. The court said:

> it is inherent in the concept of citizenship that the citizen, when absent from the country to which he owes allegiance, has a right to return, again to set foot on its soil . . . The Government cannot say to its citizen, standing beyond its border, that his re-entry into the land of his allegiance is a criminal offence.[7]

The comparatively settled passport regime of the United States stands in marked contrast to that current in the United Kingdom,

give certain facilities to the holder. If the passport is not valid for a particular country, then the Foreign Secretary cannot be said to have made that request in respect of that individual; but that does not stop the person going.' 489 H.C. Deb., cols. 3–4 (18 June 1951).

[1] 270 F.2d 905 (1959).

[2] 269 F.2d 245 (1959).

[3] 361 U.S. 918 (1959), cert. den.

[4] The decisions on area restrictions were upheld by the Supreme Court in *Zemel* v. *Rusk* 381 U.S. 1 (1965), in which the petitioner sought to challenge the refusal to issue passports valid for travel to Cuba. On 9 March 1977 President Carter announced the lifting of restrictions on travel to Vietnam, N. Korea, Cuba and Cambodia: 71 A.J.I.L. (1977), 512–4. See also Ehrlich, 'Passports', 19 Stan. L.R. 129 (1966–7); Sinderson, 'Executive Restrictions on Travel', 5 Houston L.R. 499 (1967–8).

[5] 8 U.S.C. s. 1185(b). *United States* v. *Laub* 385 U.S. 475 (1967); *Travis* v. *United States* 385 U.S. 491 (1967)—both cases involved prosecutions for travelling to Cuba.

[6] See amendments to Passport Regulations 1967, Whiteman, *Digest*, vol. 8, p. 286.

[7] 328 F.2d 386 (1964). See Article 7(3), Gesetz über das Passwesen, 1962, BGBl. 1952, I, 290, which provides that in no case is a passport to be refused to a German national who seeks to return to the Federal Republic. Cf. statement of United Kingdom practice, 475 H.C. Deb., cols. 28–9, now to be read subject to the Immigration Act 1971.

where there is no law which either declares the right to a passport or regulates its issue.[1] Technically, a citizen of the United Kingdom is under no obligation to carry a passport for the purposes of international travel and return to his own country. Thus, section 1 of the Immigration Act 1971 declares that patrials, those with the right of abode in the United Kingdom, 'shall be free to live in, and to come and go into and from, the United Kingdom without let or hindrance'.[2] But the appearance of an absolute right is substantially qualified by reference to those restrictions which may be required in order to enable this right to be established. The plain intention appears to be, that a United Kingdom passport, suitably endorsed, is the best evidence available in the matter. For the purposes of travel abroad there will be considerable practical difficulties, both in entering foreign countries and in finding a transport company which is willing to take the passenger without a passport.[3]

There are no published rules and regulations which set out the reasons which may justify the withdrawal or refusal of a passport, but these occasions have been the subject of various statements in Parliament.[4] Such declarations by the Government of the day are almost the only evidence of the 'law' of passports in the United Kingdom. The few decided cases tend to support the view that this is an area of prerogative and discretionary control, and only occasionally have the courts been called upon to consider the effect of possession of a passport.[5] In the notorious case of *Joyce* v. *D.P.P.* in 1946, for example, the House of Lords held that an alien abroad who holds a British passport enjoys the protection of the Crown and, so long as he has not renounced that protection, he is guilty of treason if he adheres to the King's enemies. The majority of the Court, Lord Porter dissenting, considered that the renewal of

[1] For an early example of the exercise of the discretionary power, see 5 *B.D.I.L.* 308 (*Snelling's* case).

[2] Williams, 'Without Let or Hindrance', 123 New L.J. 605–7 (1973); id., 'British Passports and the Right to Travel', 23 I.C.L.Q. 642 (1974).

[3] It is common immigration practice to make transportation companies liable for the expenses of removal of those refused entry; see *United States* v. *Norddeutscher Lloyd* 223 U.S. 512 (1912); 491 H.C. Deb., cols. 451–3 (25 July 1951).

[4] The grounds for refusal were set out in 1958 in a statement in the House of Lords and include the case of minors suspected of being taken illegally out of the jurisdiction, fugitives from justice, persons whose activities are notoriously undesirable or dangerous, and those who have not repaid repatriation loans: 209 H.L. Deb., col. 860. See also *Going Abroad* (1974), paras. 29, 46–7, 51–5; 985 H.C. Deb. (Written Answers), cols. 189–90.

[5] *R.* v. *Brailsford* [1905] 2 K.B. 730, 745.

Joyce's passport in 1939 was proof that the duty of allegiance continued until the passport ceased to be valid, or until some action on the part of the Crown or of the bearer put an end to the Crown's duty of protection. Counsel argued on behalf of the appellant that a passport is only a request to a foreign potentate and a command to a British representative abroad to afford the holder assistance; that no right to protection is derived from a British passport as such, and that a passport gives protection only in the colloquial sense and not that protection which is the counterpart of allegiance.[1] These views were not shared by the Court, which gave little weight to the general rule that the local allegiance of the alien is conterminous with his residence within the Realm,[2] or to the fact that the 'duty' of protection is not such as may be enforced at law.[3] The Lord Chancellor, Lord Jowitt, declared:

> possession of a passport by a British subject does not increase the Sovereign's duty of protection, though it will make his path easier. For him it serves as a voucher and means of identification. But the possession of a passport by one who is not a British subject gives him rights and imposes upon the Sovereign obligations which would not otherwise be given or imposed. It is immaterial that he has obtained it by misrepresentation and that he is not in law a British subject. By the possession of that document he is enabled to obtain in a foreign country the protection extended to British subjects. . . . [The] Crown in issuing a passport is assuming an onerous burden, and the holder of the passport is acquiring substantial privileges . . . [The] holder may demand from the State's representatives abroad and from the officials of foreign governments that he be treated as a British subject.[4]

The terminology is confused and fails to differentiate at any level between rights and duties and liberties or privileges, but the decision appears to be based on those benefits which may inure, in actual practice, to the holder of a British passport.[5] The most relevant of the dicta in this case simply affirms that the passport 'serves as a

[1] [1946] A.C. 347, at pp. 353–4. See also Lauterpacht, 9 Cam. L.J. 330 (1947); Glanville Williams, 10 Cam. L.J. 54 (1948).

[2] *Johnstone* v. *Pedlar* [1921] 2 A.C. 262.

[3] *China Navigation Co.* v. *Attorney-General* [1932] 2 K.B. 197.

[4] [1946] A.C. 347, at pp. 369, 370–1.

[5] Lord Porter dissented, *inter alia*, on the ground that the renewal of the passport was at best some evidence that allegiance continued. This was a question of fact for the jury to decide in view of the purpose for which the passport may have been retained: [1946] A.C. 347, at p. 381. Note, however, that the passport does guarantee the 'returnability' of the holder to the issuing State; see below, pp. 44–6.

voucher and means of identification', and that abroad it may be prima facie evidence of status and entitlement to the inchoate right of protection. From the point of view of the subject, however, neither the right to protection nor the correlative duty of allegiance flows from the possession of a passport. The correct position was stated by the Foreign Secretary, Sir Alec Douglas-Home, in 1972:

> The grant of a United Kingdom passport does not in itself confer a citizenship or other status on the holder. It recognises the status which he already has and is accepted internationally for travel purposes.[1]

It is from the personal status of the individual that his rights and duties are derived. From that status also there flows the right of the State in international law to exercise protection, and the obligation, which it owes to other States, to admit its nationals who may be expelled and who have nowhere else to go.[2]

Whereas in practice the possession of a United Kingdom passport may be accepted as prima facie evidence for the purpose of exercising protection and making representations, in other cases the legal significance of the passport will vary according to the context.[3] In 1962, the Commonwealth Immigrants Act imposed controls on Commonwealth citizens and on some classes of citizens of the United Kingdom and Colonies. The latter were identified as the holders of United Kingdom passports, whose passports were issued by the Government 'on behalf of the Government of any part of the Commonwealth outside the United Kingdom'.[4] The immigration controls were further extended in 1968 so as to include even the holders of 'full' United Kingdom passports, if they did not possess certain family connections with the United Kingdom.[5] This relation of the right of abode to the fact of 'belonging' to the United Kingdom is maintained by the patriality provisions of the Immigration Act 1971. Thus, the individual who holds a United Kingdom passport but who is not also patrial is subject to immigration control if he attempts to enter the country. At the same time, however, another set of rights

[1] 843 H.C. Deb. (Written Answers), col. 172.

[2] See further below, pp. 136–7.

[3] See 837 H.C. Deb. (Written Answers), col. 521.

[4] Commonwealth Immigrants Act 1962, section 1(3). Holders of United Kingdom passports 'issued to the holder by the Government of the United Kingdom' were otherwise exempt. This section was applied by the Court of Appeal in *R.* v. *Secretary of State, ex parte Bhurosah* [1968] 1 Q.B. 266 in respect of the holders of passports issued by the Governor of Mauritius; see also *Cheng* v. *Secretary of State* [1972] Imm. A.R. 5.

[5] Commonwealth Immigrants Acts 1962 and 1968, section 1(2A); *Mamacos* v. *Secretary of State* [1972] Imm. A.R. 11.

and duties is involved, which was described in 1972 by the Foreign Secretary, in relation to the expulsion of United Kingdom citizens from Uganda:

At the time of independence of the former British East African Territories, no specific undertakings were made either about the entry of East African Asians as such to the United Kingdom or about retention of citizenship. But this does not affect the obligation to admit nationals in certain circumstances if they are expelled and have nowhere else to go.[1]

The obligation which is here referred to is that obligation owed by the State of nationality to another State which has admitted its nationals, in circumstances in which the latter desires to exercise its powers of expulsion.[2] In such cases, the possession of a passport is an incident to, and some evidence of, the status which is conferred by municipal law. It is not constituent of that status, but may indicate to the receiving State the destination to which an alien once admitted can later be removed.[3]

The law and practice regarding passports in the United Kingdom is all that which remains after distilling various statements by Ministers in Parliament, various admissions to international conferences, the content of bilateral and multilateral treaties, and a few decisions of the courts. The aura of an absolute and arbitrary discretion hangs over the system, although there is little evidence of manifest abuse in practice.[4]

[1] 843 H.C. Deb. (Written Answers), col. 172. See further below, pp. 212–6.

[2] Schwarzenberger, *International Law* (3rd ed., 1957), vol. I, pp. 360–1; see also Oppenheim, *International Law* (8th ed., 1955), vol. I, pp. 645–6; *Nottebohm Case*, I.C.J. Rep., 1955, p. 4, per Judge Read, at pp. 47–8.

[3] The Foreign Secretary's reference above to the absence of any specific undertaking in regard to the retention of citizenship by East African Asians is not entirely correct; see, for example, Tanganyika Independence Act 1961, section 2, Uganda Independence Act 1962, section 2. The evidential role of the passport in the context of relations between the United Kingdom and East African countries must be considered in the light of such provisions.

[4] *Going Abroad* (1974), para. 46. See also 209 H.L. Deb., cols. 860 f.; case of Sir Frederick Crawford, whose passport was withdrawn after he entered the United Kingdom from Southern Rhodesia, where he had connections with the Smith regime: *The Times*, 9 May, 8, 19 June 1968; 764 H.C. Deb. (Written Answers), cols. 232–3, 270; ibid., cols. 1041–116; The Southern Rhodesia (Property in Passports) Order 1965 (S.I. 1965 No. 1955); *Ghani* v. *Jones* [1970] 1 Q.B. 693; Criminal Justice Act 1967, section 21; Parliamentary Commissioner Act 1967, section 4, Sch. 2, para. 4; Secretary of State for Foreign and Commonwealth Affairs Order 1968. For a similar system of executive discretion in France, see Dalloz, *Jurisprudence Générale*, 1949, 224–6; Borella, 'Le Passeport', 64 *Rev. Gen. Dr. Int.* 301, 315–17 (1960); *Annuaire Français de Droit International* (1961), 930; Cons. d'État, 11 mai 1960, Car, *Journal de Droit International* (1961), 404.

(3) LIBERALIZATION OF INTER-STATE TRAVEL: ALTERNATIVE TRAVEL DOCUMENTS

While the passport remains the universally acceptable travel document, municipal systems make frequent provision for the use of substitute documents. These exceptions reflect particularly the agreements entered into by contiguous and neighbouring States. In 1963 the United Nations Conference on International Travel and Tourism recommended in its Final Act that States should pursue the abolition of the passport through the conclusion of bi- and multilateral treaties. Yet it also noted that, while much had already been achieved on a regional basis, a valid passport was still the most suitable international travel document.[1] Where agreements do exist, they demonstrate the influence of the two most important functions of a full passport: the proof of identity and the guarantee of returnability.

Belgium was long a leading proponent of reciprocal arrangements designed to facilitate inter-State travel. In 1945, freedom of movement of persons was re-established with the Grand Duchy of Luxembourg by an exchange of notes. This agreement provided that Belgian nationals proceeding to Luxembourg, and Luxembourg nationals proceeding to Belgium, might be admitted to the two countries on production of an identity card issued by the competent local authorities.[2] In a similar agreement with the Netherlands, Belgium agreed to recognize a 'certificate of Netherlands nationality' as a valid travel document.[3] Dutch nationals are not required to carry identity cards, and this solution enabled the two States to abolish the obligation to carry a passport for nationals travelling between them.

Freedom of movement was further encouraged by the Benelux Agreement in 1960.[4] Passport control was eliminated at the internal frontiers and provision was made for the issue of a visa valid for

[1] See 562 H.C. Deb. (Written Answers), col. 111; also 1966 Report on Progress since the 1963 Conference: U.N. Doc. E/4145.

[2] 41 U.N.T.S. 265, cancelled and superseded by 65 U.N.T.S. 147, defining and extending the possible range of adequate identity documents, in turn supplemented by 79 U.N.T.S. 329. See also 23 U.N.T.S. 215, Franco-Belgian Agreement respecting Minor Frontier Traffic, which provided for the use of the 'carte frontalière' for frontier workers; and the Belgian Agreements with Monaco (51 U.N.T.S. 93) and Switzerland (71 U.N.T.S. 91).

[3] 68 U.N.T.S. 91.

[4] 374 U.N.T.S. 3; Turack, op. cit., pp. 89–100.

Benelux territory as a whole.[1] Sweden, Denmark, Finland, and Norway have established a 'common travel area' by similar agreements, and likewise a common policy regarding the entry and residence of aliens.[2] The United Kingdom, the Channel Islands, the Isle of Man, and the Republic of Ireland also form a common travel area, and passengers examined at any one point are thereafter free to travel to any other part without further examination. A common policy of control applies, and a passenger is to be excluded if there is reason to believe that he will attempt to enter a part of the travel area where he is not acceptable.[3]

The successful conclusion on a regional basis of agreements such as those considered above has resulted in localized travel regimes of remarkable freedom.[4] The acceptance of national identity cards may also have an indirect effect on the individual and on his 'right to travel', for he will often have a legal entitlement to such a card, where he has no enforceable right to a passport. In such cases, the right to travel will be limited spatially to a right to remove himself to those States which have agreed to recognize his identity card, but the area of administrative discretion and control is, to some extent, confined.

A further limitation of such powers is to be seen within the special regime existing in the E.E.C. Fundamental to the creation of a common market is the suppression of all obstacles which frustrate the free circulation of merchandise, people, services, and capital. Articles 48 to 57 of the Treaty of Rome propose the freedom of movement of workers and the right of establishment in the territory

[1] Convention on the Transfer of Control of Persons to the External Frontiers of Benelux Territory, Article 4; note also Article 5, which describes national security and 'ordre public' in terms of the whole territory.

[2] See 198 U.N.T.S. 37, 47; 199 U.N.T.S. 29.

[3] Immigration Act 1971, section 9; Immigration Rules for Control on Entry, 1973 H.C. No. 79, para. 8; 1973 H.C. No. 81, para. 6; The Immigration (Control of Entry through Republic of Ireland) Order 1972 (S.I. 1972 No. 1610); Turack, op. cit., p. 118. The United Kingdom also recognizes national identity cards in conjunction with visitors' cards in return for recognition being extended to the British Visitor's passport; entry in such cases is only permitted for visits of six months or less, and the privilege does not extend to those who are coming for employment: 1973 H.C. No. 81, para. 3 and note; E.E.C. nationals require only national identity cards. Collective passports may be accepted subject to certain conditions (Development of International Travel and Tourism, ECOSOC Doc. E33438/Add. I, p. 9, note 5, answer to question 41 (1961)), and the practice of 'no passport' excursions of one or two days' duration is supported (U.N. Doc. E/2933, Annex II, p. 104; The Immigration (Exemption from Control) Order 1972 (S.I. 1972 No. 1613), Article 5).

[4] For other examples, see Turack, op. cit., pp. 35–45, 49–50, 53–9, 67–77, 81–7.

of a Member State, for the purposes of employment, or involvement in the production or distribution of goods, or the provision of services. None of the rights accruing is absolute, and States may deny their exercise in certain circumstances, limited by reference to reasons of public health and security, and of 'ordre public'. The Treaty provisions have been given substantive effect by various Regulations and Directives of the European Commission, and by a number of recent decisions of the European Court of Justice.[1] Among those Regulations, No. 1612/68 declares the right of every national of a Member State[2] to take up and carry on a wage-paid occupation in the territory of another Member State.[3] The right for a national to leave his own State is necessarily implicit in this statement, but it is also laid down expressly in Directive 68/360:

> Member States recognise that [nationals] have the right to leave their territory with a view to taking up a wage-paid occupation and to carrying it on in the territory of another Member State. This right is exerciseable on simple production of a valid identity card or passport. Members of his family shall enjoy the same right as the national on whom they are dependent.[4]

The same Article also provides that Member States 'shall, in accordance with their own legislation, issue to their nationals' passports or identity cards showing, in particular, the nationality of the bearer.[5]

In theory, at least, the simple production of an identity card or national passport is sufficient formality for the nationals of one Member State who seek to exercise their treaty rights in the territory of another Member State.[6] Subsequent developments show that the exceptional powers allowed to State authorities by both the

[1] See further below, pp. 168–86; 299–306.

[2] For the definition of national, see below, pp. 173–6.

[3] Article 1(1); cf. European Social Charter 1961, Article 18(d).

[4] Article 2(1).

[5] Article 2(2). Note also Directive 64/220, Articles 6, 7; cf. United Kingdom law, *Secretary of State* v. *Lakdawalla* [1972] Imm. A.R. 26. Under Community law, where passports are the only documents valid for leaving the State, then they are to be valid for at least five years: Directive 68/360, Article 2(3). See France, loi du 9 juillet 1970, article 11, D. 1970. 182, extending to five years the validity of ordinary passports. By Directive 68/360, Article 2(4), no exit visa or equivalent obligation may be imposed on nationals.

[6] Directive 68/360, Article 3(1). See also the Standard Identity Card proposed by the Commission: Acts of the Organisation 1959 (1960), Doc. 60, pp. 175–7; Lyon-Caen, *Droit social européen* (1969), para. 333; Simmonds, 'Immigration Control and the Free Movement of Labour: A Problem of Harmonisation', 21 I.C.L.Q. 307 (1972).

Treaty and the subsidiary legislation are themselves subject to close control by the courts.[1]

(*a*) *Travel and Identity Documents for Refugees and Stateless Persons*

One other area in which States have agreed to issue travel and identity documents is that governed by the various instruments concerned with the status of refugees and stateless persons. The First World War and the Russian Revolution left Europe inundated with refugees and other displaced persons whose resettlement was hampered by the rigours of the new passport regime. The League of Nations took up the problem and in 1922 secured the agreement of States to the Arrangement with Regard to the Issue of Certificates of Identity to Russian Refugees.[2] The certificates in question were to be issued subject to various conditions, and would not, for example, imply the right for the refugee to return to the State of issue.[3] This defect was subsequently made good in part by an agreement in 1926 recommending the affixing of return visas, and thereafter Article 2 of the Convention of 28 October 1933[4] and Article 15 of the London Agreement of 15 October 1946 made the 'return clause' an integral part of the refugee's travel document.[5]

In the meantime, the benefit of the 'Nansen' agreements was extended to cover other categories of refugee, including all those generally who had ceased to enjoy the protection of their government.[6] Attempts were also made in the League of Nations to resolve the problems of those who were not refugees, but who were without nationality or whose nationality was in doubt. In 1927 the conference of the League proposed an identity document similar to that issued to refugees under the 1926 Agreement. Once again, this was

[1] Directive 68/360, Article 10; see also Directive 64/221; *Rutili* v. *Minister of the Interior* [1976] 1 C.M.L.R. 140. For criticism of the reserved powers as 'une sorte de survivance de la souverainété nationale', see Lyon-Caen, op. cit., para. 183. Cf. below, pp. 300–1. In the European context, consideration may also be given to the impact of the European Convention on Human Rights; see Articles 5, 8; Application 1076/61: *Recueil* (1963) i; Application 1438/62; *Recueil* (1963) i, cited in Fawcett, *The Application of the European Convention on Human Rights* (1969), pp. 62–3; Application 1012/61: *Recueil* (1961) ii; Application 1185/61; *Recueil* (1962) ii.

[2] 13 L.N.T.S. 238; Reale, 50 Hague *Recueil* (1934–IV), 89–187, at pp. 141–63.

[3] Reale, ibid., at p. 141. This document was the first of the 'Nansen' passports, introduced at the suggestion of Dr. Nansen, the High Commissioner for Refugees.

[4] Cmd. 534 (Treaty Series No. 4 of 1937).

[5] 11 U.N.T.S. 84; Turack, op. cit., pp. 123–36.

[6] Article 2 of the Recommendations made on 12 May 1926, cited by Reale, 50 Hague *Recueil* (1934–IV) 89–187, at p. 153.

hedged with limitations; for example, the issue of such document was not to give the holder any right to the protection of the diplomatic or consular authorities of the issuing State, nor was it to give to that State any right to exercise such protection. In the end, very few States adopted the recommendations on stateless persons.[1]

Today, both refugees and stateless persons are covered by multilateral conventions: the International Convention relating to the Status of Refugees 1951, and the International Convention relating to the Status of Stateless Persons 1954.[2] Articles 27 and 28, common to both conventions, provide (1) for the issue of identity papers to any refugee or stateless person in the territory of a State party, who does not possess a valid travel document; and (2) for the issue to resident refugees or stateless persons of travel documents for the purpose of foreign travel.[3] Contracting States may derogate from this obligation only where compelling reasons of national security or 'ordre public' require; to that extent, the refugee or stateless person may find himself better off than the local citizen. In format, this special travel document resembles the international-type passport,[4] but it recites expressly that it is issued,

> solely with a view to providing the holder with a travel document which can serve in lieu of a national passport. It is without prejudice to and in no way affects the holder's nationality.

The document also includes a 'return clause', which may be limited in respect of time by the issuing authority. In one Austrian case it was decided that the obligation to readmit terminated with the validity of the travel document.[5] In all other respects, travel documents for refugees and stateless persons fulfil the essential

[1] François, 'Le problème des apatrides', 53 Hague *Recueil* (1935–III), 358–69.

[2] 189 U.N.T.S. 137 and 360 U.N.T.S. 117, respectively.

[3] On United Kingdom practice see 681 H.C. Deb. (Written Answers), col. 221; *Going Abroad* (1974), paras. 38, 60; on United States practice, see amendment to 8 C.F.R. 223a.3, cited in 68 A.J.I.L. 506 (1974).

[4] See the specimen document in the Schedule to each convention; Turack, op. cit., pp. 128–34.

[5] *Re Spitzer* 24 I.L.R. 486 (1957); also United Kingdom Immigration Rules for Control on Entry, 1973 H.C. No. 79, para. 14; 1973 H.C. No. 81, para. 12. On practice in respect of visas for refugees, see European Convention on the Abolition of Visas for Refugees 1959; Article 5 provides expressly for the return of refugees, who 'shall be readmitted at any time to the territory of the Contracting Party by whom the travel document was issued, at the simple request' of the Party whose territory they have entered. On the latter point, compare Article 5, European Agreement on the Movement of Persons between Member States of the Council of Europe 1957.

function of providing evidence of identity and status, and a great number of States now recognize them as valid for the purpose of travel.

(4) THE INTERNATIONAL LAW OF PASSPORTS

Hitherto consideration has been given principally to the place of the passport in municipal law. Borella notes:

Le passeport est resté très largement un acte de droit interne, régi par le principe de la compétence exclusive des États . . . Quelque soit le système utilisé, la caractéristique générale des législations internes est que les autorités étatiques disposent d'un pouvoir très étendu, dans l'appréciation des conditions à remplir pour obtenir un passeport.[1]

Writing some thirty years earlier, Reale had expressed a similar view:

Étant un acte administratif qui ressortit au domain réservé et à la souveraineté nationale, elle est soustraite à tout contrôle et à tout appréciation.[2]

This character of the passport and the discretionary aspect of its issue are still favoured by State practice, although there is some tendency today to allow the procedural guarantees of due process in the case of refusal or withdrawal. The human rights aspect, the idea of the right to travel and hence the right to a passport as a right inherent in the individual, remains still within the realm of *lex ferenda*. Those conventions which propose the right have attracted few ratifications, and there is little evidence to suggest that it has established itself independently in customary international law. There is not yet sufficient and uniform activity over a period of time, such as to show a general recognition that a rule of law or legal obligation is involved. Municipal law has, however, begun to take note of the human rights aspect of travel, and it may be that this is some indication of the direction in which the law may be expected to develop.

(*a*) *Passports and 'Returnability'*

The fact that an alien is or is not returnable to some other State is frequently a crucial matter in the determination of whether he is to

[1] Borella, 64 *Rev. Gen. Dr. Int.* 301–34 (1960), at pp. 312, 315, 324.
[2] 50 Hague *Recueil* (1934–IV), 89–187, at p. 114.

be permitted to enter a foreign country. If it is subsequently found that the alien is 'undesirable', then the State will try to deport him elsewhere and practical difficulties may arise if he has no passport or if no other State is willing to issue him with one. So in one case, the Supreme Court of Brazil found that the expulsion of a Romanian national could not be implemented because of the Romanian Government's refusal to issue him with a passport.[1] Today there exists a strong body of authority for the proposition that the actual possession of a passport indicates the existence of a duty, binding on the issuing State, to readmit the holder if he is expelled from another State and has nowhere else to go.

This duty is often recognized in treaties and is even on occasion extended to cover those whose passports have expired, or who possess alternative documentary evidence of nationality. For example, by an agreement concluded in 1961, Austria and the Federal Republic of Germany agreed to accept each other's nationals if a presumption were established as to the individual's nationality.[2] Such presumption might be based on a passport, even if expired or wrongly issued, or on some other travel or identity document.[3] Expired passports also figure prominently in the 1957 European Agreement on the Movement of Persons as a sufficient guarantee of returnability, even if the nationality of the holder is under dispute.[4]

This issue of returnability is, furthermore, clearly related to the question of the passport as evidence of nationality. In fact there is no rule of customary international law which prohibits the issue of passports to non-nationals. Indeed, there are many precedents in favour of the practice, both political and humanitarian. Turack cites the example of Spain, France, and Italy after the Arab–Israeli war of 1967, whose flexible interpretation of nationality laws permitted the issue of passports to certain Jews in the United Arab Republic.[5] In other cases, passports may be issued to individuals who have been

[1] *Feldman* v. *Justica Publica*, Ann. Dig. 1938–40, Case No. 144.

[2] 414 U.N.T.S. 211.

[3] See also 1954 Agreement between Sweden and the Federal Republic of Germany: 200 U.N.T.S. 39; 1954 Agreement between Denmark and the Federal Republic of Germany: 200 U.N.T.S. 53; 1958 Agreement between Belgium and the Netherlands: 330 U.N.T.S. 84; 1962 Agreement between Austria and France: 463 U.N.T.S. 173.

[4] Article 5 of the European Agreement on the Movement of Persons between Member States of the Council of Europe (European Treaty Series, No. 25).

[5] Op. cit., p. 225. See also the cases involving the issue of British passports to the children of British subjects, who did not themselves hold British nationality: 5 *B.D.I.L.* 99–101, 277–8.

granted asylum or who, for political reasons, are unable to obtain one from their own government.[1] Clearly, such documents cannot declare the nationality of the holder with authority, but, if they are to be recognized by other States as valid travel documents, the guarantee of returnability is essential.

The importance of this requirement in customary international law is illustrated again by United Nations action in the matter of passports for Namibians. The Council for South West Africa decided in 1968 to arrange for the issue of travel documents in its own name.[2] However, it was accepted that a return clause was essential if such documents were to be recognized by other States. For this reason the Council attempted to secure the agreement of neighbouring countries to guarantee the returnability of passport holders to their respective territories. Such agreement was reached with Zambia in February, under which the right of Namibians to return to Zambia was to be granted initially for a period of two years.[3]

State practice, particularly in the form of the provisions of municipal law, insists upon returnability as essential to the validity of a travel document. It is accepted that the passport is itself sufficient evidence of this guarantee, even though it may be equivocal on the issue of nationality. Although the passport is primarily an instrument which emanates from municipal law, in this one respect at least its effect is dictated by a rule of customary international law.

(*b*) *The Passport as Evidence of Nationality*

That the passport may be equivocal on the question of nationality requires some qualification; for in day-to-day practice State authorities commonly look to the passport not only to ascertain returnability, but also as an indication of the holder's identity, nationality, and status. In the *Nottebohm Case* Liechtenstein argued that the 'acceptance' by Guatemala of Nottebohm's passport and the issue to him of a visa amounted, with other related administrative acts, to recognition of his status as a national of Liechtenstein.[4] This argument was denied by Guatemala:

il faudrait assurément que ces actes constituent de manière claire et non

[1] See the case of *Dr. Ramon Villeda Morales*, former president of Honduras, who found asylum in Costa Rica and was granted a diplomatic passport: Turack, op. cit., p. 225 n. 5.
[2] G.A. Res. 2372 (XXII), 12 June 1968, A/6716/Add. 1.
[3] See further 65 A.J.I.L. 571, 574–8 (1971); Turack, op. cit., pp. 244–5.
[4] *Nottebohm Case*, I.C.J. Pleadings, vol. I, pp. 25 f.

équivoque une reconnaissance définitive de la parfaite régularité et sincérité du changement de nationalité survenu.[1]

In the result, this view appears to have been accepted by the Court:

When Nottebohm . . . presented himself before the Guatemalan authorities, the latter had before them a private individual; there did not thus come into being any relationship between governments. There was nothing in all this to show that Guatemala then recognised that the naturalisation conferred upon Nottebohm gave Liechtenstein any title to the exercise of protection.[2]

The judgment thus appears to support the separation in law of passports and the right to exercise protection. This also is the view accepted in State practice, which relates protection to status, and not to the possession of a passport.[3] In the absence of special agreement, only the relation of nationality gives the State a right of protection.[4] On the question whether this relation exists in international law, the passport and acts affecting the passport are not conclusive.[5] In practice, States tend to insist that their passports be accepted as at least prima facie evidence of citizenship,[6] but the weight which an international tribunal gives to a passport will vary from case to case. In the *Mergé* claim, for example, the Commission relied to some extent on the use of a passport by a dual national in its determination that one rather than another nationality was dominant. But in this case there was, additionally, little evidence that the *de cuius* had otherwise established effective links with the second State.[7]

[1] Ibid., p. 196.

[2] *Nottebohm Case*, Judgment on the Merits, I.C.J. Rep., 1955, p. 4, at p. 18.

[3] Borchard, *The Diplomatic Protection of Citizens Abroad* (1915), pp. 493–4; Weis, *Nationality and Statelessness in International Law* (1956), p. 48; Diplock, 'Passports and Protection in International Law', 32 Grotius Society (1946), p. 42.

[4] *Panevezys-Saldutiskis Railways Case* P.C.I.J. (1939), Ser. A/B, No. 76; Hackworth, *Digest*, vol. III, p. 802.

[5] While passports frequently include a request for protection, this is purely formal and entails no legal consequences. Note that municipal courts have also taken the view that the passport is not conclusive proof of nationality; that it is not, as it were, to be recognized without more as a foreign act of State: *R.* v. *Burke, Casey and Mullady* 11 Cox C.C. 138 (1868); *Urtetiqui* v. *D'Arbel* 34 U.S. (9 Pet.) 692 (1835); *In re Gee Hop* 71 F. 274 (1895); *Scott* v. *McGrath* 104 F. Supp. 267 (1952); Hackworth, *Digest*, Vol. III, pp. 347, 435–6, 468; Moore, *Digest*, vol. IV, p. 492.

[6] Borchard, op. cit., pp. 488, 517; Hackworth, *Digest*, vol. III, p. 391, and see also at pp. 174–5, 178–9; *Lynch's* case, U.N. Rep., vol. V, p. 17, at p. 19 (1929). Cf. *Dawood Ali Arif* v. *Deputy Commissioner of Police* [1958] A.I.R. 565, 26 I.L.R. 364; *Noor Mohammed* v. *The State* [1956] A.I.R. 211; *Naziranbhai* v. *The State* [1957] A.I.R. 1.

[7] U.N. Rep., vol. XIV, pp. 236, 238–9 (1955). See also *Schmeichler-Pagh*, Clunet, vol. 92 (1965), p. 689 (Danish Supreme Court); *Wildermann* v. *Stinnes*, Ann. Dig. 1923–4,

Together with other factors, the possession and use of a passport may thus provide corroborative evidence of the status of the bearer. At other times it will be but one element in a given case which may, or may not, support the existence of an effective link. International tribunals retain jurisdiction to go behind the document in order to ascertain the true status. This general point was affirmed by the Italian–United States Claims Commission in the *Flegenheimer Case*,[1] where it was held that the tribunal might look beyond a certificate of nationality in order to determine whether the certificate was correct according to national and international law.

Although the possession of a passport is equivocal on the question of nationality, its acceptance by a foreign State raises other questions not fully explored by the Court in its judgment in the *Nottebohm Case*. The points at issue were stated succinctly by Judge Read in his dissenting opinion.[2] He noted that when an alien presents himself at the frontier, the State has an unfettered right to refuse admission. If, however, it permits the alien to enter, then, by its voluntary act, it brings into being a series of legal relationships with the State of which he is a national.[3] This relative relationship of rights and duties is the source of the receiving State's obligation to accord reasonable treatment[4] and of its right to terminate the matter by deporting the alien to his State of nationality. It is the source of the right of the State of nationality to exercise protection, and of that State's obligation to admit its nationals expelled from other States. In Judge Read's view, the original relationship which existed between Guatemala and Germany (Nottebohm's former State of nationality) came to an end with Nottebohm's naturalization in Liechtenstein: 'From that time on Guatemala had the right to deport Mr. Nottebohm to Liechtenstein, and Liechtenstein was under the correlative obligation to receive him on deportation.[5] The

Case No. 120; *Spaulding Claim*, 24 I.L.R. 452; *Zangrilli Claim*, 24 I.L.R. 459; Cf. *In re Bulla*, Ann. Dig. 1933–4, Case No. 111: 'the application for a passport for the purposes of enabling the applicant to obtain work cannot in the present case and having regard to the conditions of employment at the time, be regarded as prejudicing the question of nationality.'

[1] U.N. Rep., vol. XIV, pp. 327, 336–49 (1958). See also *Parker's* case, U.N. Rep., vol. IV, p. 35 at p. 38 (1926); and note *Gay* v. *Dulles* 248 F. 2d 421 (1957).

[2] I.C.J. Rep., 1955, p. 4 at pp. 34 ff.

[3] Ibid., p. 46. This analysis receives further support from the judgment of the International Court in the *Barcelona Traction Case*, I.C.J. Rep., 1970, p. 3 at p. 32 (para. 33), with respect to foreign investment and foreign nationals.

[4] *Barcelona Traction Case*, loc. cit.

[5] I.C.J. Rep., 1955, p. 4 at p. 48.

Court's judgment, however, does not deal with the question of how far Guatemala might have relied upon Nottebohm's Liechtenstein passport as a guarantee of returnability. Little significance was attached to the 'routine administrative acts' which characterized Guatemala's reaction to Nottebohm's purported change of nationality.[1] Guatemala was not estopped from subsequently denying the validity of that change, but at the same time it is not inconceivable that Liechtenstein would have been barred from avoiding its obligation to admit Nottebohm as the holder of one of its passports.

Similar issues arose at the time of the expulsions from Uganda in 1972.[2] While in many cases the United Kingdom citizens involved might not have satisfied the requirements of effective nationality, this would in no way have justified a refusal on the part of the United Kingdom Government to admit them. The principle of effective nationality does not operate in isolation, but must be applied in relation to other principles, such as estoppel, and in the light of international agreements. In this instance, passports played a crucial role. In United Kingdom law, the passports of the United Kingdom citizens in East Africa indicated that the holders were subject to immigration control. In international law, the same passports symbolized the substance of agreements entered into at the time of Ugandan independence, which expressly recognized the continuing status as United Kingdom citizens of those who did not exercise the right of option in favour of the local citizenship.[3] The continuing guarantee of returnability was to be implied as a consequence of those agreements and of the issue to the individuals concerned of United Kingdom passports.

(*c*) *Conclusions*

The general rule remains that the issue of passports is a matter within the reserved domain of domestic jurisdiction,[4] and an aspect of executive control over foreign affairs. States feel themselves free, therefore, to impose those conditions and restrictions which they deem fit, and it is apparent that the majority of States accept that the passport may be used to control the movement of their nationals.

[1] For an appreciation of such acts in another context, see the *Minquiers and Ecrehos Case*, I.C.J. Rep., 1953, p. 47 at pp. 68–70.

[2] On which see further below, pp. 212–6.

[3] See, for example, Uganda Independence Act 1962, section 2.

[4] Borella, 64 *Rev. Gen. Dr. Int.* 301–34 (1960), at p. 313; Reale, 50 Hague *Recueil* (1934–IV) 89–187, at p. 114.

The question of the right to travel as a fundamental freedom remains essentially a matter for local jurisdiction, as does the question whether any form of appeal is to be allowed against an adverse decision. If State discretion in this field is to be confined and structured, this will generally result from local developments, rather than from any direct impression by international law.

Assuming that there are no other restrictions, such as exit visas, the citizen holder of a national passport is thereby entitled to travel abroad. But his admission into another State is a different matter, and the simple possession of a passport entails rights only if the bearer can benefit from specific treaty provisions. Once admitted, however, the citizen may usually rely on his passport as prima facie evidence of status when seeking diplomatic or consular assistance. In the final analysis, protection flows from status itself, not from the document, and it is commonly accepted that there is no right, in the strict sense, to such protection. Similarly, the fact of possessing a passport in no way assures the entry of the *holder* into the State of issue; for the guarantee of returnability demanded by the rule of customary international law relates to obligations owed between States alone.

III

THE RELATION OF MATTERS OF IMMIGRATION TO THE RESERVED DOMAIN OF DOMESTIC JURISDICTION

QUESTIONS OF immigration, of the entry and expulsion of aliens, fall easily within traditional conceptions of domestic jurisdiction. It is still common to find expressed the view that such matters are for the local State alone to decide, 'in the plenitude of its sovereignty'.[1] In a similar way, it was for long argued that the only rule of international law concerning nationality was that the determination of nationality had nothing to do with international law. Yet that statement itself contains an implied reference to international law and today it is accepted that there are certain restrictions upon States' discretion, or freedom of decision,[2] in the field of nationality. It is well known that in the *Tunis and Morocco Nationality Decrees Case* the Permanent Court of International Justice described the delimitation of domestic jurisdiction as an essentially relative question, which was dependent upon the development of international relations.[3] Of perhaps greater significance is the reference in this case to States' powers which are *discretionary*. It will be argued below that this notion is particularly helpful, as indicating both the nature of a given power, and the limits within which it may be confined by rules of international law.

It is at the point at which seemingly unilateral acts are opposed to other States, and to the rights of other States, that the issue enters upon the international plane. In its Judgment in the *Anglo-Norwegian Fisheries Case*, the Court noted that,

> though it is true that the act of delimitation is necessarily a unilateral act, because only the coastal state is competent to undertake it, the

[1] *Ben Tillett's* case: 6 *B.D.I.L.* 124–50, at p. 147; see also *Expulsions from Zambia*: British Practice in International Law, 1966, p. 111; ibid. 1967, pp. 112–13.

[2] Cf. Schwarzenberger, *International Law* (3rd ed., 1957), vol. I, p. 359.

[3] (1923), Ser. B, No. 4, p. 24; see also Brownlie, *Principles of Public International Law* (2nd ed., 1973), pp. 284–5.

delimitation with regard to other States is dependent upon international law.[1]

Similarly, in asserting that the principle of effective nationality is a general principle of international law, and as such is a limitation upon the discretion of States, the International Court of Justice has declared that:

a State cannot claim that the rules it has . . . laid down are entitled to recognition by another State unless it has acted in conformity with this general aim of making the legal bond of nationality accord with the individual's genuine connection with the State which assumes the defence of its citizens by means of protection as against other States.[2]

Limitations in these two areas of local competence derive essentially from the fact that both institutions are opposable to third States. It is a matter for debate to what extent the subjects of the present inquiry, entry and expulsion, may also touch upon the rights of other States.

The reservation in regard to matters within domestic jurisdiction is of importance principally in two spheres, the political and the legal. In the political sphere, it operates as a bar to 'intervention' by the organs of international organizations, such as the United Nations. In the legal sphere, its effect is, similarly, to prevent adjudication of certain disputes by international tribunals and, incidentally, to serve as a sufficient justification for actions which may be the subject of protest by other States. The Charter of the United Nations declares that the Organization is based upon the principle of the 'sovereign equality' of its Members,[3] and that nothing in the Charter shall authorize the Organization to intervene in matters essentially within the domestic jurisdiction of any State or shall require Members to submit such matters to settlement under the Charter.[4] It is practically impossible to define sovereignty in isolation from any particular

[1] I.C.J. Rep., 1951, p. 116 at p. 132; see also Brownlie, 'The Relations of Nationality in Public International Law', 39 *B.Y.I.L.* (1963), 284.

[2] *Nottebohm Case*, I.C.J. Rep., 1955, p. 4 at p. 23.

[3] Article 2(1).

[4] Article 2(7). See the similar duty imposed on States and found in G.A. Resolution 1815 (XVII), 18 Dec. 1962; see also G.A. Res. 2131 (XX), 21 Dec. 1965, adopting a Declaration on the Inadmissibility of Intervention in the Domestic Affairs of States and the Protection of their Independence and Sovereignty, reaffirmed by G.A. Res. 2225 (XXI), 19 Dec. 1966. See generally, U.N. Doc. A/CN.4/209, 28 Feb. 1969, Proposals submitted to and Decisions of various United Nations Organs relating to the Question of State Responsibility (Supp. to Doc. A/CN.4/165).

context, and in Article 2(1) it serves to emphasize the political aspect of the independence and equal status of Members of the United Nations.[1] When linked with the principle of the reserved domain, however, it tends to become a barrier against the assumption of international obligations.[2]

In the debate around the constitutional competence of the organs of the United Nations, Lauterpacht concluded that matters essentially within the domestic jurisdiction of a State do not comprise matters which have become a subject of international obligations or which have become matters of 'international concern' by virtue of constituting an actual or potential threat to international peace and security.[3] For example, in so far as the Charter imposes a legal obligation upon Members to observe fundamental human rights and freedoms, such issues are therefore outside the reservation of Article 2(7). In consequence, the organs of the United Nations are not precluded from acts of implementation, such as investigation, study, report, and recommendation, which do not amount to 'intervention in the accepted legal connotation'.[4] Lauterpacht further affirmed that, in regard to the determination of matters of domestic jurisdiction, the power of interpretation belongs to the organ concerned, that is, to the General Assembly or the Economic and Social Council.

Although Article 2(7) contains no reference to international law or to the interpretative competence of a body such as the International Court of Justice, this does not entirely exclude legal criteria. It has been rightly pointed out that jurisdiction, whether of a political organ or a legal tribunal, is a legal concept which must, by its very nature, be a matter of law.[5] In practice, the General Assembly, while holding back from any formal interpretation of Article 2(7) which would limit its competence, has nevertheless proceeded to

[1] Brownlie, *Principles of Public International Law* (2nd ed., 1973), p. 281. See also the Principle of Sovereign Equality of States in the Declaration on Principles of International Law concerning Friendly Co-operation among States in accordance with the Charter of the United Nations: Annex to General Assembly Resolution 2625 (XXV), 24 Oct. 1970.

[2] Jenks, *A New World of Law* (1969), pp. 131, 133; cf. Brierly, *The Law of Nations* (6th ed., 1963), pp. 48–9.

[3] Lauterpacht, 'The International Protection of Human Rights', 70 Hague *Recueil* (1947–I), 5–108; id., *International Law and Human Rights* (1950); see also Higgins, *The Development of International Law through the Political Organs of the United Nations* (1963), pp. 77–81; Brownlie, *Principles of Public International Law*, p. 288.

[4] 70 Hague *Recueil* (1947—I), at p. 53.

[5] Waldock, 106 Hague *Recueil* (1962—II), at p. 180.

deal with specific matters concerned with economic, social, and colonial affairs. It does not appear to consider that Article 2(7) presents any obstacle to this practice.[1] In Waldock's view, the essential effect of Article 2(7) is twofold:

first, to preclude any intervention by the United Nations in a State's affairs except with reference to the State's international obligations either under the Charter or otherwise; and, secondly, even where international obligations of the State are involved, to preclude the United Nations from penetrating, without the State's consent, behind its authority over its own territory, nationals, ships and aircraft, except in cases of enforcement action for the maintenance or restoration of peace.[2]

It is not clear how far the qualified limitation on United Nations competence contained in the second limb of this conclusion should be taken.[3] It may be today that a State owes certain obligations towards the international community as a whole, and while a satisfactory theory of international responsibility in such matters remains to be defined, such obligations would go well beyond a State's prima facie exclusive authority over its territory, nationals, ships, and aircraft.

Indeed, Waldock is to be found among those writers who have emphasized the idea that human rights are 'matters of international concern':

the Charter provisions [on human rights], being treaty provisions, undoubtedly make the treatment by Member States of individuals, whether nationals or aliens, within their jurisdiction a matter of United Nations concern; but they do so only to the extent of the obligations which they contain and the jurisdiction which they confer upon the United Nations.[4]

Higgins, too, maintains that

the claim . . . that human rights questions cannot be essentially within the domestic jurisdiction . . . seems justified, for Articles 55 and 56 impose specific obligations by which all States are bound, Article 2(7) notwithstanding.[5]

[1] Rajan, *United Nations and Domestic Jurisdiction* (2nd ed., 1961), *passim.*

[2] Op. cit., at p. 190.

[3] See Schwelb, 19 I.C.L.Q. (1970), 483.

[4] Op. cit., at p. 198. See also Higgins, op. cit., pp. 77–81; she also points out that certain issues, principally those concerning the right of self-determination and the principle of non-discrimination, are regarded by the General Assembly as of 'international concern': ibid., pp. 90–104. Brownlie, *Principles of Public International Law* (2nd ed.), p. 288.

[5] Op. cit., p. 128. But note the objections raised by the United Kingdom before the

She is careful to point out, however, that the majority of Member States do not hold the view that Article 2(7) is entirely meaningless.[1] In her view, any limitation of that provision must be within the bounds of a reasonable interpretation, although she argues that the specific clauses on human rights do satisfy this qualification.[2]

The idea that the general field of competence comprised by the reserved domain is open to scrutiny and restriction is inherent in its nature as a concept, principally, of international law. Whether or not the present scope of Article 2(7) of the Charter is identical with the rule established in general international law, it is clear that the domestic jurisdiction exception may be confined in practice as a consequence of treaty obligations, as a result of the interpretations given to it by the organs of the United Nations, and by the progressive development of the customary law.

One example of the practical restriction of the sphere of domestic jurisdiction is to be found in a case which arose under the European Convention on Human Rights.[3] In its Second Memorial in preliminary proceedings to the *Belgian Linguistics Case*, the European Commission argued that the domain reserved to national jurisdiction depends upon each State's international commitments. It is not absolute and not invariable, but is a relative notion which varies with the development of international law and the extent of obligations imposed and undertaken.[4] In support of its argument the

Commission of Human Rights to the proposed draft of the International Convention on the Elimination of All Forms of Racial Discrimination. The first paragraph of the Preamble would have referred to the obligations imposed on all Members by the U.N. Charter in respect of human rights. The United Kingdom objected that the Charter did not, in fact, impose any such obligations: U.N. Docs. E/CN.4/SR 775, 779. The first paragraph to the Preamble now paraphrases Articles 55 and 56 and makes no reference to obligations.

[1] O'Connell takes the view that the prohibition on intervention in Article 2(7) has been emasculated as a result of the administrative measures taken by the Organization, which have had the effect of inducing Member States to conform to U.N. policies to which they are not, in strict law, required to conform: *International Law* (2nd ed., 1970), pp. 308 et seq.

[2] Op. cit., p. 130. Support for this view is to be found in the *Advisory Opinion on Namibia*, I.C.J. Rep., 1971, p. 16 at p. 57.

[3] On the plea of domestic jurisdiction before international tribunals generally, see Waldock, 31 *B.Y.I.L.* (1954), 96–142; O'Connell, *International Law* (2nd ed.), pp. 1082–1084; Brownlie, *Principles of Public International Law* (2nd ed.), pp. 289–90; *Peace Treaties Case*, I.C.J. Rep., 1950, p. 65. See also the Court's treatment of the 'vital interests' argument in the *Fisheries Jurisdiction Case*, I.C.J. Rep., 1973, p. 4 at pp. 19, 20.

[4] Second Memorial, Ser. B, p. 424 (14 July 1966).

Commission referred both to the *Nationality Decrees Case*[1] and to Resolutions adopted in 1954 by the Institute of International Law.[2] It concluded its argument as follows:

If States are . . . authorised by the Convention and Protocol to restrict the exercise of the rights and freedoms guaranteed where national security, the maintenance of order and the economic and fiscal spheres are affected, it seems reasonable to conclude that no field of governmental activity lies *a priori* outside the scope of the Convention, thus constituting a domain reserved to States.[3]

The Commission also called attention to the fact that the Belgian Government had not exercised the option open to it of making express reservations under Article 64 of the Convention.

For its part, the Belgian Government argued that the complaints referred to the Court were not covered by the Convention and the Protocol, but formed part of the reserved domain of the Belgian legal order.[4] However, in its Judgment on this preliminary objection in 1967, the European Court of Human Rights unanimously rejected any possibility of resort to the notion of the reserved domain. It declared:

the Convention and Protocol which relate to matters normally falling within the domestic legal order of the Contracting States, are international instruments whose main purpose is to lay down certain international standards to be observed by the Contracting States in their relations with persons under their jurisdiction . . . [The] jurisdiction of the Court extends to all cases concerning the interpretation and application of those instruments . . . [and] . . . the Court cannot in the circumstances regard the plea based upon the notion of the reserved domain as possessing the character of a preliminary objection of incompetence.[5]

[1] P.C.I.J. (1923), Ser. B, No. 4.

[2] *Annuaire de l'Inst. de droit inter.*, vol. 45, II, pp. 292, 293: 'Art. I: The reserved domain is the domain of State activities where the jurisdiction of the State is not bound by international law. The extent of this domain depends on international law and varies according to its development. Art. 3: The contracting of an international obligation in a matter within the reserved domain debars a party to that obligation from invoking the objection of the reserved domain with regard to any problem of interpretation or application of the obligation in question.'

[3] Second Memorial, Ser. B, p. 436.

[4] Acts of the Court, No. 5, Summary at p. 16. Cf. *Guardianship of Infants Case*, I.C.J. Rep., 1958, p. 53; below, pp. 295–7.

[5] Acts of the Court, No. 5, p. 19. Cf. *Peace Treaties Case*, I.C.J. Rep., 1950, p. 65 at pp. 70–1; Lauterpacht, *International Law and Human Rights*, p. 174; see also the case against Greece: 12 *Yearbook* 72; 7 Int. Leg. Mat. 833.

Apart from cases of inter-State treaties, where nations agree to surrender 'sovereign rights' in terms, it will always be difficult to establish legal principles applicable to the reserved domain. The example of the European Convention shows that the most significant developments are likely to result from regional arrangements, where States can be persuaded to limit the exercise of their rights in detail, by reference to the aims and purposes of a given treaty, and to submit themselves to the jurisdiction of an international tribunal.

Issues arising from the exercise of powers of exclusion and expulsion are commonly affected by matters such as nationality and fundamental human rights. For this reason, any claimed presumption that such powers are sealed within the reserved domain requires close scrutiny. Proposed grounds for rejecting such a presumption in relation to the treatment of aliens in general and the principle of non-discrimination in particular are examined more fully below.[1]

[1] See pp. 75–87.

IV

THE IMPRESSION OF HUMAN RIGHTS STANDARDS ON THE TREATMENT OF FOREIGN NATIONALS

(1) INTERNATIONAL MINIMUM STANDARD OR NATIONAL TREATMENT

THE STANDARD of treatment to be accorded to foreign nationals continues to be a fruitful source of conflict and controversy. In the past, much was made of the difference between what was commonly described as the international minimum standard on the one hand, and the standard of national, or equal, treatment, on the other hand. The 'international minimum standard' was known by a variety of names, which included the 'standards of the more advanced States', the 'ordinary standards of justice', the 'standard of civilized justice', and so forth. Indeed, the variety of the terminology was matched with as little agreement regarding the content of the proposed standard.[1]

The origins of the standard may be found in the practice of the economically more powerful nations of Western Europe which, together with the United States of America, were most interested in securing the position of their nationals abroad. Not only did these States apply the standard between themselves, but they sought also to impose it upon other nations, particularly those with less well developed or inefficient judicial and administrative systems. The reaction which duly followed expressed itself in the doctrine of the equality of treatment of nationals and aliens, and in the contention that aliens could not acquire, through any principle of international law, a position more privileged than that of nationals.

Both 'standards' have enjoyed a measure of general support. Thus,

[1] In 1931 Borchard was inspired to castigate the standard as 'vague, deceiving and confused, properly calculated to produce error, for it pretends to express a conception which in reality seldom if ever exists': *Annuaire de l'Inst. de droit inter.*, vol. 1, p. 265. Cf. his earlier views: *Diplomatic Protection of Citizens Abroad* (1915), pp. 179, 345.

it was for long accepted that the individual who removed himself to a foreign State must take the local law and local conditions as he found them. His entry was an entry within the jurisdiction and, as Phillimore observed: 'Every individual who enters a foreign country, binds himself, by a tacit contract, to obey the laws enacted in it for the maintenance of the good order and tranquillity of the realm.'[1] This view was, however, extended in support of the argument that the alien had no right to expect anything more than equal treatment.[2] Such an approach is very much in line with traditional conceptions of sovereignty and with the entrenched presumption that the ordering of persons within the limits of its territory is an aspect of the domestic jurisdiction of a State.[3] It may be readily admitted that the theory of national treatment looks reasonable, especially if an alien has long been resident in a foreign State, enjoying its advantages and the protection of its government. There is then some basis for maintaining that he should in corresponding degree become assimilated to a national of that State.[4] Nevertheless, there has been concerted opposition to extreme versions of the doctrine of equality. For example, in a reply to Mexico in 1938, the United States Secretary of State, Hull, declared:

> the Mexican doctrine of risk . . . presupposes the maintenance of law and order consistent with the principles of international law; that is to say, when aliens are admitted into a country the country is obligated to accord them that degree of protection of life and property consistent with the standards of justice recognised by the law of nations.[5]

The established principle that a State may not invoke its municipal law as a sufficient justification for avoiding its international obligations[6] is also commonly adduced in opposition to the doctrine of equal treatment; and yet equality, in its widest sense, would seem to offer more than an alien or his government can reasonably

[1] *Commentaries on International Law* (1st ed., 1855), vol. II, ss. 2, cited in 6 *B.D.I.L.* 322. See also Vattel, *Droit des gens*, ii, 8, 101, 102; Wolff, *Jus Gentium*, ss. 156, 163, 299, 300, 301.

[2] Calvo, *Le droit international* (5th ed.), vol. VI, p. 231; Montevideo Convention on Rights and Duties of States 1933, Article 9: 165 L.N.T.S. 19.

[3] See Brownlie, *Principles of Public International Law* (2nd ed., 1973), p. 508.

[4] Thus, in the *Nottebohm Case* the Court found that Nottebohm's effective nationality was that of Guatemala: I.C.J. Rep., 1955, p. 4 at pp. 25–6.

[5] 32 A.J.I.L., Supp. (1938), pp. 181–207.

[6] *Treatment of Polish Nationals and other Persons of Polish Origin or Speech in the Danzig Territory*, P.C.I.J. (1932), Ser. A/B, No. 44, at p. 24.

request. In the absence of treaty, international law expressly permits certain inequalities in regard to foreign nationals, for example, in the matters of ownership of property or the holding of certain jobs.[1] In 1949, the most that Roth could affirm was that international law assured to the alien 'a certain juridical situation',[2] but the problem remains to determine the quality of this certain situation in any given case. The local law is clearly relevant on this point. That was admitted by the U.S.A.–Mexico Claims Commission in the *Roberts Case* in 1925, where it was further affirmed that equality of treatment of aliens and nationals did not constitute, in the light of international law, the *ultimate* test of the propriety of acts of the authorities in regard to aliens.[3]

In 1962, however, the Inter-American Juridical Committee, in the Contribution of the American Continent to the Principles of International Law that govern the Responsibility of the State, proposed the following Article:

> The State is not responsible for acts or omissions with respect to foreigners except in those same cases and conditions where, according to its own laws, it has such responsibility toward its own nationals.[4]

The United States voted against this proposal and, in a separate opinion, included the following as its position on the proper standard of treatment due to aliens:

> When a State admits foreigners to its territory, it has an international duty to protect their life and property according to a minimum standard of rights determined by international law. Neither the receiving State nor the foreigner's State can, by its own law, determine this international standard. It is determined by international law. A State which fails to comply with the applicable international law, as regards the person or property of foreigners in its territory, incurs international responsibility and must make reparation in such form as may be appropriate.[5]

The alien's position remains anomalous and controversial. While he binds himself to obey the local law, he still continues to enjoy the diplomatic protection of his own State. But that there is a presumption in favour of the local jurisdiction is apparent from the reluctance of governments to pursue diplomatic claims on behalf of nationals

[1] Borchard, 'The Minimum Standard of the Treatment of Aliens', A.S.I.L. Proc. (1939), pp. 51, 56; 6 *B.D.I.L.* 327–30.

[2] Roth, *Minimum Standard of International Law applied to Aliens* (1949), pp. 82–3.

[3] U.N. Rep., vol. IV, p. 77; Ann. Dig. 1925–6, p. 227.

[4] Whiteman, *Digest*, vol. 8, pp. 885–6.

[5] Ibid.

long settled abroad.[1] While the corollary of the alien's duty to submit to the local law may be his right to the protection of that law,[2] attempts by jurists to establish and to list the minimum rights required to be recognized have not met with any general success.[3] Borchard's view, that international responsibility would be incurred in the event of violation by a State of 'a somewhat indefinite standard of treatment',[4] perhaps most closely represents the substance of the views of such jurists.

However, despite its vagueness, the general notion of a minimum standard found some support in various decisions of the Mexico–U.S.A. General Claims Commission.[5] The *locus classicus* is the *Neer Case* in 1926, in which Commissioner Nielsen observed:

it is . . . clear that the domestic law and the measures employed to execute it must conform to the requirements of the supreme law of members of the family of nations, which is international law, and that any failure to meet these requirements is a failure to perform a legal duty, and as such an international delinquency . . . The treatment of an alien, in order to constitute an international delinquency, should amount to an outrage, to bad faith, to wilful neglect of duty, or to an insufficiency of governmental action so far short of international standards that every reasonable and impartial man would recognise its insufficiency. Whether this insufficiency proceeds from the deficient execution of a reasonable law or from the fact that the laws of a country do not empower the authorities to measure up to international standards, is immaterial.[6]

[1] Phillimore, op. cit., vol. II, s. iv; 6 *B.D.I.L.* 247; see also the opinion of the Law Officers in *Mr. Patel's Case* (1897): 6 *B.D.I.L.* 323.

[2] O'Connell, *International Law* (2nd ed., 1970), p. 941; 6 *B.D.I.L.* 322 ff.; Briggs, *The Law of Nations* (2nd ed., 1952), pp. 561–70; see also *Nottebohm Case*, I.C.J. Rep., 1955, per Judge Read, dissenting, at p. 47.

[3] See Anzilotti, R.G.D.I.P., vol. 13 (1906); Cavaglieri, 26 Hague *Recueil* (1929—I), 213, 454; Verdross, 37 Hague *Recueil* (1931—III), 353; *Les règles internationales concernant le traitement des étrangers* (1932), p. 31; Kaufmann, 54 Hague *Recueil* (1935—IV), 427; Roth, op. cit., pp. 182 f.

[4] *Diplomatic Protection of Citizens Abroad*, pp. 179, 345. It is frequently argued that the standard is like any other standard, for example, the standard of reasonable care in the law of negligence, and that it can only be defined or quantified in a set of concrete circumstances; see O'Connell, op. cit., p. 943; Law Officers' opinion, *Alexandria Riots 1882*: 6 *B.D.I.L.* 322–3. Cf. Brownlie's suggestion of a variable standard, such as *diligentia quam in suis*: op. cit., p. 512.

[5] By Article I of the General Claims Convention 1923, claims were to be decided in accordance with principles of international law, justice, and equity: U.N. Rep., vol. IV, p. 11. See also Italy–Venezuela Mixed Claims Commission 1903, Protocol: U.N. Rep., vol. X, p. 479; Netherlands–Venezuela Mixed Claims Commission 1903, Protocol, Article I: ibid., p. 709.

[6] U.N. Rep., vol. IV, p. 60 (1926).

It may also be noted that, while the standard might be indefinite when considered in the abstract, both customary law and treaty had for long set out specific exceptions to the absoluteness of territorial competence.[1] Customary law prescribed rights and privileges for diplomatic agents, and treaties were the instruments by which States agreed to guarantee to each other's nationals particular standards of treatment, for example, in respect of access to the courts and of freedom and security in the enjoyment of property and trade.[2] From the seventeenth century onwards there was also a progressive development in the standards of most-favoured-nation and national treatment,[3] which set further limits to territorial jurisdiction over foreigners. While the standards prescribed were restricted in scope and were primarily those of equal or non-discriminatory treatment, they did good service as the basis for the later development of a broader, objective standard.[4]

Today neither the international minimum standard nor the doctrine of equal treatment provides an adequate solution to the problems raised by the presence of foreign nationals on a State's territory. While the international minimum standard is unconscionably vague, the doctrine of equal treatment tends to restrict the freedom of aliens to the same degree as that of nationals, and often to an extent which other States find unacceptable. Brownlie draws a useful distinction between, on the one hand, the question of what is the actual content of any proposed standard and the mode of its application and, on the other hand, the core principle, which is that the territorial sovereign cannot in all circumstances avoid responsibility by pleading that aliens and nationals have received equal treatment.[5] This distinction underlines the fact that international law, while it has long permitted certain discriminations against aliens (for example, in the matter of political rights), now also prohibits even certain actions by States against their own nationals. Developments in the latter respect raise particularly pertinent issues concerning the reserved domain of domestic jurisdiction, and the extent to which confinement of this area by rules of international law will affect the entry and expulsion of aliens. Immigration is still viewed

[1] Brownlie, op. cit., pp. 507–9.

[2] Neufeld, *The International Protection of Private Creditors from the Treaties of Westphalia to the Congress of Vienna (1648–1815)* (1971), pp. 97–100; 6 *B.D.I.L.* 330–2.

[3] Neufeld, op. cit., pp. 110–12.

[4] See Schwarzenberger, *International Law* (3rd ed., 1957), vol. I, p. 207.

[5] Brownlie, op. cit., p. 511.

as essentially a domestic matter,[1] but it may be that this otherwise simple issue will yet impinge upon established and fundamental human rights.

(2) PROPOSALS FOR A 'STANDARD OF HUMANITY'

One solution to the conflict between the international minimum standard and the doctrine of equal treatment was proposed by García-Amador, during his time as Special Rapporteur to the International Law Commission on the subject of State Responsibility. In his view, the solution was to be found in a synthesis of the two principles, founded upon the development of the international recognition of the essential rights of man. With the Charter of the United Nations as a basis for a standard of humanity, García-Amador suggested that whether an individual was a citizen or an alien was henceforth immaterial. The human being, as such, would now come under the direct protection of international law.[2]

In his Third Report, García-Amador expressed the view that,

> the conflict and antagonism formerly existing between the 'international standard' and the principle of equality of nationals and aliens have become obsolete in consequence of the political and juridical phenomenon in the post-war world of the recognition of fundamental human rights, and hence it would be useless to continue to hope that either the 'international standard' or the principle of equality will prevail.[3]

These submissions met with two principal objections. The first was that an individual, whether an alien or a national, could not be regarded as a direct subject of international law. The second was that fundamental human rights had not yet been recognized by positive international law. The Special Rapporteur was unable to produce any very satisfactory answer to these objections, and barely conceded the difficulties obstructing the subsumption of human rights provisions within a coherent theory of international obligation.[4]

[1] Verdross, citing President Wilson, in *Les règles internationales concernant le traitement des étrangers* (1932), p. 24. See also the response of the Australian Government to the suggestion that its assisted-passage scheme for immigrants violated anti-discrimination provisions of United Kingdom law: the *Guardian*, 8 Jan. 1971.

[2] For a useful summary of García-Amador's efforts, and reaction thereto, see *First Report on State Responsibility* by Roberto Ago, Special Rapporteur: U.N. Doc. A/CN.4/217; Yearbook of I.L.C., 1969—II.

[3] U.N. Doc. A/CN.4/111; Yearbook of I.L.C., 1958—II, para. 8; see also Yearbook of I.L.C., 1956—II; ibid. 1957—I, pp. 155 ff.; ibid. 1957—II; Whiteman, *Digest*, vol. 8, p. 376.

[4] Yearbook of I.L.C., 1958—II, para. 10.

In 1961, in his Sixth Report, García-Amador submitted a revised draft on State Responsibility, Article 1 of which sought to define the new standard, now to be based on the international recognition of human rights and fundamental freedoms. In paragraph (1) it declared:

For the purpose of the application of the provisions of this draft, aliens shall enjoy the same rights and legal guarantees as nationals, but these rights and guarantees shall in no case be less than 'the human rights and fundamental freedoms' recognised and defined in contemporary international instruments.[1]

The second paragraph of this proposed Article attempted to enumerate the 'human rights and fundamental freedoms', including specifically the right to life, to liberty, and to security of the person. Other provisions referred to the right to a remedy and to redress for any violation of the said rights, and laid down certain procedural and other guaranteees for those accused of crime.[2] Although the remainder of the revised draft followed fairly uncontroversial lines, it was not well received. In so far as it attempted a synthesis of the international minimum standard and the principle of equal treatment, it was defective in that it continued to reflect overmuch the principles enunciated in arbitral decisions of the past. In particular, the prominence given to the right to own property was heavily criticized, and would appear to be even less acceptable to States today.[3]

For, in discussion on the general issue of standards of treatment, two tendencies have been especially apparent in the practice of States. The first reflects the keen desire of many States to see further developments within the field of human rights; the second is to be seen in the continuing and vociferous insistence upon permanent sovereignty over natural resources. In the latter area, the institution of diplomatic protection has been strongly attacked by traditional and newly recruited adherents of the Calvo Doctrine.[4] In

[1] Ibid. 1961—II, pp. 1 et seq.

[2] Paragraph (3) permitted substantial derogation from the obligation otherwise assumed to protect the individual's right to life, liberty, and security of the person, and to the ownership of property. Cf. Article 15(1), European Convention on Human Rights; Applications 3321/67, 3322/67, 3323/67, 3344/67 (Denmark, Norway, Sweden, the Netherlands *v.* Greece); *The Greece Case:* 12 *Yearbook* 72.

[3] The "right" in question is criticized by Brownlie as an attempt to raise a practice of economic life into a principle of human rights: op. cit., pp. 513–14.

[4] See the Separate Opinions of Judges Padilla Nervo and Ammoun in the *Barcelona Traction Case*, I.C.J. Rep., 1970, p. 3, at pp. 247, 294.

matters of 'wealth deprivation',[1] the principle of national treatment is firmly entrenched, with an increasing number of States now insisting that disputes relating to nationalization measures fall to be considered by local courts alone.[2] It may be that, in the future, while the foreign national will benefit from the generality of human rights standards, he will no longer enjoy that security of property which was so often and successfully insisted upon in the past. For present purposes it is necessary to examine the degree of influence exerted by developments in human rights standards generally, together also with the practical operation of powers of exclusion and expulsion; in this way light may be shed on the circumstances in which the exercise of power amounts to the breach of an international obligation.

Human rights standards have in general made considerable progress since the end of the Second World War and the positive declaration of principles in the Preamble and Article I of the United Nations Charter. Within the Organization itself, interest in human rights issues has been demonstrated by Articles 55 and 56 of the Charter,[3] resolutions of the General Assembly, by the adoption of instruments such as the Universal Declaration of Human Rights in 1948,[4] and by the conclusion of multilateral treaties such as the Genocide Convention.[5]

[1] See Lillich, 'The Diplomatic Protection of Nationals Abroad: An Elementary Principle of International Law under Attack', 69 A.J.I.L. (1975), 359 at p. 360 n. 11, for the meaning of 'wealth deprivation'.

[2] See Lillich, op. cit., for a discussion of UNCTAD Res. 88 (XII), U.N. General Assembly Res. 3171 (XXVIII) and, in particular, Article 2(2)(c) of the Charter of Economic Rights and Duties 1974.

[3] Article 55 requires the United Nations to 'promote', *inter alia*, 'universal respect for, and observance of, human rights and fundamental freedoms'. Article 56 declares: 'All Members pledge themselves to take joint and separate action in co-operation with the Organization for the achievement of the purposes set forth in Article 55.' There has been considerable debate on whether this Article imposes any legal obligation upon Member States, but the political and judicial organs of the U.N. have tended to accept the premiss. See *Advisory Opinion on Namibia*, I.C.J. Rep., 1971, pp. 56–7; Schwelb, 66 A.J.I.L. (1972), 337, 350–1; cf. United Kingdom objections to the proposed draft preamble to the International Convention on the Elimination of All Forms of Racial Discrimination: U.N. Docs. E/CN.4/SR 775, 779.

[4] U.N. Doc. A/811; Brownlie, *Basic Documents on Human Rights* (1971), p. 106. See also Waldock, 106 Hague *Recueil* (1962—II), pp. 33, 199; Introduction to the Annual Report of the Secretary-General on the Work of the Organization, Aug. 1958, A/3844, Add. I, p. 5.

[5] 78 U.N.T.S. 277. Forty-three States signed the Genocide Convention and there have been over seventy ratifications and accessions. It came into force in 1961. See also United Kingdom Genocide Act 1969; Schwelb, 9 I.C.L.Q. (1960), 654, 657–8.

The constitutions of other international organizations, such as UNESCO and the International Labour Organization, have also played a part. In particular, the constitution of the I.L.O. emphasizes the need for 'social justice' in its Preamble, and in Article 41 the Organization is authorized to suspend any Member 'found by the United Nations to be flagrantly and persistently pursuing by its legislation a declared policy of racial discrimination such as apartheid'.[1] The Annex to the Constitution prescribes the aims and purposes of the Organization and affirms that,

> all human beings, irrespective of race, creed, or sex, have the right to pursue both their material well-being and their spiritual development in conditions of freedom and dignity, of economic security and of equal opportunity.[2]

The generality of these sentiments has been transformed by treaty into a series of detailed obligations owed by signatory States in respect of two classes in particular. The 1951 Convention Relating to the Status of Refugees[3] and the similar 1954 Convention on Stateless Persons[4] not only set out substantive rights, such as the right not to be expelled save on the most serious grounds, but also call for certain standards of treatment. The general rule is that the refugee or stateless person is to receive non-discriminatory or at least most-favoured-nation treatment in his enjoyment of basic rights, such as access to the courts or to employment.[5]

(3) THE 1966 CONVENTIONS

It was only in the mid-sixties that some success was achieved in securing a broader-based and more elaborate recognition of certain kinds of basic rights and freedoms. In 1965, the United Nations General Assembly adopted the International Convention on the

[1] Instrument of Amendment (No. 2), 1964, adopted on 9 July 1964. This new Article is not yet in force: Brownlie, *Basic Documents in International Law* (2nd ed., 1972), p. 64.

[2] Constitution of the International Labour Organization, Annex, Declaration concerning the Aims and Purposes of the I.L.O., Part II(a): U.K.T.S., No. 59 (1961), Cmnd. 1428; Brownlie, *Basic Documents in International Law* (2nd ed.), p. 66.

[3] 189 U.N.T.S. 137. This Convention has been amended by the Protocol of 1967: 606 U.N.T.S. 267.

[4] 360 U.N.T.S. 117.

[5] Common to both Conventions, Articles 13, 15, 17, 18, 19, 21, and 26 call for most-favoured-nation treatment, and Articles 14, 16, 20, 22, 23, 24, and 29 for national treatment.

Elimination of All Forms of Racial Discrimination,[1] the importance of which lay in its enunciation of a principle of non-discrimination which had been developing over the years.[2] Article 1 of the Convention defines racial discrimination as:

> any distinction, exclusion, restriction or preference based on race, colour, descent, or national or ethnic origin, which has the purpose or effect of nullifying or impairing the recognition, enjoyment or exercise of human rights and fundamental freedoms in the political, economic, social, cultural or any other field of public life.[3]

Yet this broad statement of principle is at once followed by an exception clause providing that the Convention is not to apply to distinctions, exclusions, etc. which a State Party may make between its nationals and others.[4] Clearly, however, this exceptional privilege of the State to differentiate between the national and the alien would not justify what was effectively a policy of racial discrimination. While certain rights, such as the right to participate in elections and to vote,[5] will be limited to nationals, the one fundamental rule contained in Article 6 is to be applied without distinction. This rule requires States Parties to assure to *everyone within their jurisdiction* effective protection against acts of racial discrimination.

In 1966, the General Assembly adopted two instruments of wider import: the Covenant on Economic, Social and Cultural Rights and the Covenant on Civil and Political Rights. Both Covenants entered into force in the first months of 1976, but it is a matter for debate to what extent they may be said to reflect, or even to crystallize, existing rules of general international law. It may be that they continue to represent only desirable standards,[6] although there is much to be said for the view which sees them as 'authoritative evidence of the content of the concept of human rights as it appears in the Charter of the United Nations'.[7]

Both Covenants are incidentally relevant to the treatment of aliens. For example, Article 2(2) of the Covenant on Economic,

[1] U.K.T.S. Misc. No. 77 (1969), Cmnd. 4108. As of August 1977 this Convention had received 93 ratifications and accessions.

[2] See Schwelb, 15 I.C.L.Q. (1966), 996–1059; Vierdag, *The Concept of Discrimination in International Law* (1973).

[3] On alienage as a sufficient ground for discrimination, see further below, pp. 83–7.

[4] Article 1(2).

[5] Article 5(c).

[6] Robertson, *Human Rights in the World* (1972), pp. 33–4. See further below, pp. 71–4.

[7] Brownlie, *Basic Documents in International Law* (2nd ed.), p. 150; O'Connell, *International Law* (2nd ed.), p. 747.

Social and Cultural Rights declares that States Parties undertake to guarantee that the various rights set out will be exercised without discrimination of any kind, including specifically discrimination as to 'birth or other status'. This would appear to be wide enough to limit the circumstances in which discrimination against aliens is justified but the following paragraph provides:

Developing countries, with due regard to human rights and their national economy, may determine to what extent they would guarantee the economic rights recognised in the present Covenant to non-nationals.

This provision was the object of a certain hostility from the United States, which advanced the view that it was contrary to many existing treaties and inconsistent with generally recognized principles of international law.[1] While there is some weight behind this argument, the tendencies which it seeks to oppose are now fairly well established, for example, in a number of General Assembly Resolutions.[2]

Objections of a different kind may be raised to Article 4, which permits States to apply certain restrictions to the exercise of rights generally. It declares that rights may be made subject to 'such limitations as are determined by law only in so far as this may be compatible with the nature of these rights and solely for the purpose of promoting the general welfare in a democratic society.' Permissible grounds for derogation of this nature are so vague as to be nearly meaningless. While the 'general welfare in a democratic society' may embrace those matters often described in terms of national security, 'ordre public', and public health,[3] the provisions of the Covenant make no attempt to be more specific or to introduce an element of objectivity.[4]

Apart from Article 2(3) considered above, no special limitation upon the rights of foreign nationals is apparent in other articles of the Covenant. These recognize, for example, the right of everyone to the opportunity to gain his living by work which he freely chooses

[1] Whiteman, *Digest*, vol. 8, p. 378. Compare Article 2, Charter of Economic Rights and Duties of States 1974, and note the amendment to that Article proposed by the United States and the United Kingdom, among others: 14 Int. Leg. Mat. 253, 262.

[2] See General Assembly Resolution 1803 (XVII) of 1962 on Permanent Sovereignty over Natural Resources; Resolution 3281 (XXIX) of 1974, adopting the Charter of Economic Rights and Duties.

[3] See Inglés, *Study of Discrimination in respect of the Right of Everyone to leave any Country, including his own, and to return to his Country*: U.N. Doc. E/CN.4/Sub.2/229/Rev. 1 (1963), pp. 36–7.

[4] On the inherent limits to such terms, see further below, pp. 293–5.

or accepts,[1] and the right of everyone to the enjoyment of just and favourable conditions of work.[2] The framing of these provisions suggests that, while Article 2(3) imposes no obligation upon States to permit aliens to work within their jurisdiction, if such privilege is granted, then they must be treated according to the same standard as is applicable to nationals.

It is the Covenant on Civil and Political Rights, however, which is perhaps most relevant to the status of aliens. Article 2(1) declares:

> Each State Party . . . undertakes to respect and to ensure to *all individuals within its territory and subject to its jurisdiction* the rights recognised in the present Covenant, without distinction of any kind, such as race, colour, sex, language, religion, political or other opinion, *national or social origin*, property, *birth or other status*.[3]

This is clearly wider and more explicit than the provision contained in Article 2(2) of the Covenant on Economic, Social and Cultural Rights. Article 4(1) of the Covenant on Civil and Political Rights enlarges on the prohibition against any form of discrimination, with particular reference to the permitted measures of derogation:

> In time of public emergency which threatens the life of the nation and the existence of which is officially proclaimed, the States Parties . . . may take measures derogating from their obligations under the present Covenant to the extent strictly required by the exigencies of the situation, provided that such measures are not inconsistent with their other obligations under international law and do not involve discrimination solely on the ground of race, colour, sex, language, religion, or social origin.

The anti-discrimination provision here is not so widely drawn as that in Article 2(1) of this same instrument, but measures taken against a particular class of aliens which was determinable solely by reference to race or colour would not be justified.[4] In addition, the measures of derogation must be consistent with a State's other obligations under international law. It is to be remarked that paragraph 2 expressly forbids any derogation from those provisions which guarantee the right to life,[5] or which forbid torture or inhuman treatment,[6] slavery, servitude,[7] conviction, or punishment

[1] Article 6. [2] Article 7.

[3] Emphasis supplied. Compare Article 1, European Convention on Human Rights.

[4] On the expulsions from Uganda in 1972, see below, pp. 212–6.

[5] Article 6. [6] Article 7. [7] Article 8(1), (2).

under retroactive laws,[1] and also from those articles which guarantee the right to recognition as a person before the law[2] and the right to freedom of thought, conscience, and religion.[3]

The content of the articles which follow elaborates many of the rights and freedoms first set out in the Universal Declaration, and to a certain extent reflects the principles already incorporated in the European Convention. Thus, Article 9 declares the right of everyone to liberty and security of the person, and to freedom from arbitrary arrest and detention. Article 10 prescribes that all persons deprived of their liberty shall be treated with humanity and with respect for the inherent dignity of the human person. Article 12 calls for freedom of movement for everyone lawfully within the territory of a State, and for the right to leave any country. Emphasis is also placed on the fact that, while these rights may be restricted, the power of the State in the matter is essentially discretionary and confined by reference to its purpose and to the requirement that decisions be taken according to law.

Further rights are set out in subsequent articles, which include the right of aliens not to be arbitrarily expelled,[4] the right to equality before courts and tribunals,[5] the right to privacy, honour, and reputation,[6] and the right of the family to protection by the State.[7] The content of Article 26 is becoming increasingly familiar:

> All persons are equal before the law and are entitled without discrimination to the equal protection of the law. In this respect, the law shall prohibit any discrimination and guarantee to all persons equal and effective protection against any discrimination on any ground such as race, colour, sex, language, religion, political or other opinion, national or social origin, property, birth or other status.

So it is that the limitations on the competence of States generally may also confer specific benefits upon the alien.

Nevertheless, some caution remains necessary in the evaluation of these recent conventional provisions, particularly in the light of the Judgment of the International Court of Justice in the *North Sea*

[1] Article 15; also Article 11, which prohibits imprisonment solely for inability to fulfil a contractual obligation.

[2] Article 16. [3] Article 18. [4] Article 13.

[5] Article 14(1). [6] Article 17(1).

[7] Article 23(1). The rights in question are more in the nature of qualified, rather than absolute, rights; see Marshall, 'Rights, Options and Entitlements', *Oxford Essays in Jurisprudence*, ed. Simpson, Second Series (1973), 228–41.

Continental Shelf Cases.[1] The Covenants have entered into force only in the early part of 1976, and it may be that the details of the provisions in question still fail to qualify as rules of customary international law. Nevertheless they do serve as a most important source of standards.[2]

(4) HUMAN RIGHTS STANDARDS AND GENERAL INTERNATIONAL LAW

It is no longer necessary to appeal to natural law in order to support the proposition that basic human rights are established within the realm of positive international law.[3] In its decision in the *Barcelona Traction Case* the International Court of Justice referred to a category of international obligations which are owed towards the community of States as a whole.[4] The Court observed that some of these obligations derive from general international law, while others spring from international instruments of a universal or quasi-universal character.[5] Much remains to be done, however, if any coherent theory is to emerge from these dicta. Certainly, the prohibition on genocide may now be located within the area of law referred to as *jus cogens*, or international public policy,[6] from which no derogation is permitted. Implicit in the prohibition, of course, is the idea of universality, so that, to take an extreme example, no programme of genocide could be justified on the basis of a distinction drawn between nationals and aliens.

The status of other rules relating to fundamental human rights is not so clear. The Court itself referred to protection from slavery, in respect of which there is a long history of international action and

[1] I.C.J. Rep., 1969, p. 3.

[2] On the question of applying human rights standards, see the dissenting judgment of Judge Jessup in the *South West Africa Cases* (Second Phase), I.C.J. Rep., 1966, p. 5 at p. 441; *Advisory Opinion on Namibia*, I.C.J. Rep., 1971, p. 16 at p. 57.

[3] Cf. Dissenting Opinion of Judge Tanaka in the *South West Africa Cases* (Second Phase), I.C.J. Rep., 1966, p. 5 at p. 297. See also Inglés, op. cit., pp. 1–4, where the right under study is said to be founded on natural law.

[4] I.C.J. Rep., 1970, p. 3 at p. 32.

[5] Note also the impact of regional instruments, such as the European and American Conventions on Human Rights.

[6] See Articles 53, 64, Vienna Convention on the Law of Treaties 1969; Brownlie, *Principles of Public International Law* (2nd ed.), pp. 499–502; cf. O'Connell, *International Law* (2nd ed.), pp. 244–5; Schwarzenberger, 43 Texas L.R. (1965), 455–78; id., *International Law and Order* (1971), ch. 4; Verdross, 60 A.J.I.L. (1966), 55–63.

agreement,[1] and to the prohibition on racial discrimination. It is to be remarked that both these rights figure in conventions among those from which no derogation is permitted, even in exceptional circumstances.[2] If this criterion of 'no derogation' is applied to the rights enumerated generally in international conventions, then three other rights stand out as future candidates for inclusion within a category of *jus cogens*. These are the right to life, in so far as the individual is protected against 'arbitrary' deprivation of life;[3] the right to be protected against torture or cruel or inhuman treatment or punishment; and the right not to be subjected to retroactive criminal penalties.[4] Additionally, one may propose the right of everyone to be recognized as a person before the law,[5] a right sometimes expressed indirectly in terms of the right of everyone to an effective remedy, coupled with the rule of non-discrimination.[6]

Now whether general international law requires the protection of any of these rights remains an open question. Certainly they are included within the provisions of many international instruments, and are reflected also in national legal systems. The latter fact is by no means conclusive evidence of a sufficient *opinio juris*, although it does perhaps indicate the limits to what States seek to claim for themselves. Similarly, the mere fact that rights are included in international covenants is not conclusive evidence of the status of those rights within the body of international law. In the *North Sea Continental Shelf Cases* in 1969 the International Court of Justice stated that treaty rules might well emerge as rules of customary international law. But its Judgment is a model of caution and strongly advises against the making of any general assumptions in the matter.

In this case, the 'equidistance/special circumstances' principle for delimiting the continental shelf failed to meet the three criteria held

[1] See Slavery Convention 1926: 60 L.N.T.S. 253; Protocol 1953: 212 U.N.T.S. 17; Supplementary Convention on the Abolition of Slavery, the Slave Trade, and Institutions and Practices similar to Slavery 1956: 266 U.N.T.S. 3; I.L.O. Convention concerning Forced or Compulsory Labour 1930: 39 U.N.T.S. 53; I.L.O. Convention concerning the Abolition of Forced Labour 1957: 320 U.N.T.S. 291; Universal Declaration of Human Rights, Article 4; Covenant on Civil and Political Rights, Article 8; European Convention, Article 4; American Convention, Article 6.

[2] e.g. European Convention, Article 15(2); Covenant on Civil and Political Rights, Article 4; American Convention, Article 27.

[3] The inadequacy of this description is manifest.

[4] European Convention, Article 15(2); Covenant on Civil and Political Rights, Article 4; American Convention, Article 27.

[5] Covenant on Civil and Political Rights, Article 16; American Convention, Article 3.

[6] Cf. European Convention, Articles 13 and 14.

to be essential to the process. The Court found that Article 6 was not essentially norm-creating,[1] that the number of States participating in the Convention, although respectable, was hardly sufficient,[2] and finally, that subsequent State practice did not provide conclusive evidence of an *opinio juris sive necessitatis*. Earlier in its Judgment the Court had also observed that there was both a positive law and a fundamentalist aspect to the arguments advanced by Denmark and the Netherlands. The former was supported by reference to the work already done in the field of delimitation by international legal bodies, to State practice, and to the influence of the Geneva Convention. The fundamentalist aspect related to the so-called 'natural law' of the continental shelf, and looked to equidistance as having the *a priori* character of a legal norm.[3] Very similar arguments can be mustered in support of human rights standards and in support of the view that international covenants have merely reflected or crystallized existing norms of customary international law. The Court also noted that Article 6 of the Continental Shelf Convention was one of those provisions open to reservation; it observed:

> this cannot be so in the case of general or customary rules and obligations which, by their very nature, must have equal force for all members of the international community, and cannot therefore be the subject of unilateral exclusion exerciseable at will by any one of them in its own favour.[4]

A further analogy may here be drawn between the privilege of a State to make reservations to certain terms of a treaty, and its privilege to derogate from certain obligations in human rights conventions. Where reservation or derogation is barred, then this may support a finding that a treaty stipulation embodies or crystallizes a pre-existing or emergent rule of customary international law.

It is no straightforward matter, however, to apply the general principles favoured by the Court to the human rights and fundamental freedoms now set out in, for example, the Covenant on Civil and Political Rights. Problems derive not only from the difference in the nature of the subject-matter, but also from the absence of an effective basis of responsibility. While some recognition has been

[1] Article 6 refers in the first place to delimitation by agreement.

[2] At the date of Judgment the Convention had been in force for five years and had received thirty-nine ratifications and accessions. By 1977, the number of Parties had increased to fifty-three.

[3] I.C.J. Rep., 1969, p. 3 at p. 28.

[4] Ibid., pp. 38–9. See also Padilla Nervo, Separate Opinion, at p. 98; but note Baxter, 129 Hague *Recueil* (1970—I), pp. 48–51.

extended to human rights over very many years, their role in raising the individual to the level of subject of international law is comparatively new, as is their reduction to a set of finite rules. The Racial Discrimination Convention has been widely ratified,[1] but States have adopted a more cautious approach to the two 1966 Covenants.[2] This may suggest a desire on their part to adhere to the prima facie exclusive authority over territory and inhabitants which seems to follow from theories of sovereignty and the doctrine of the reserved domain.

Nevertheless, today there can be little doubt that acts of genocide or the implementation of a policy of racial discrimination are unlawful; they affect the interests of other States and also constitute matters of international concern sufficient to justify action by organs of the United Nations. As the corpus of human rights law builds up, the detailed provisions of recent conventions will move into the foreground, to impose specific obligations upon States. During this evolutionary period, however, there can be little doubt that such detailed provisions will continue to indicate the content of *general* obligations already assumed by States[3] and to set out standards of treatment to be accorded to both nationals and aliens. An example of this slow but progressive limitation of States' powers is evident in the history and development of the principle of non-discrimination.

[1] By August 1977 93 States were parties to the Convention.

[2] By August 1977 44 States had ratified or acceded to the Covenant on Civil and Political Rights and 46 States were party to the Covenant on Economic, Social and Cultural Rights. Each Covenant required 35 ratifications to come into force. The Optional Protocol to the Covenant on Civil and Political Rights required 10 ratifications and had also entered into force.

[3] For example, by way of Articles 55 and 56 of the United Nations Charter; see above, p. 65.

V

THE PRINCIPLE OF NON-DISCRIMINATION AND ITS APPLICATION TO FOREIGN NATIONALS

(1) THE MEANING OF DISCRIMINATION

THE PRINCIPLE or norm of non-discrimination has figured prominently in modern attempts to secure the better protection of fundamental human rights. Rights such as the right to life, liberty, and security of the person and the right to equality before, and equal protection of the law, clearly allow for no distinction between nationals and aliens. Yet it is apparent that both general international law and recent conventions foresee continued distinctions between these two groups.[1] The 'basic rights' of the alien may be assured, but it is a matter for debate to what extent his other rights and interests may be restricted. While it can be argued that non-discrimination as a general principle or rule is confined to distinctions drawn on the basis of race alone, there is now considerable evidence for the view that, as a standard of international law, non-discrimination is drawn on a wider scale.[2]

International instruments most frequently define discrimination in terms of some exclusion or restriction, or alternatively as some privilege or preference, which operates to nullify the particular rights which it is intended to entrench. As an element in many theories of justice, the principle of equality imposes upon those who wish to treat individuals differently the duty of showing cause for such differential treatment.[3] Such a formal approach to the character

[1] e.g. Article 1(2), International Convention on the Elimination of All Forms of Racial Discrimination 1966; Article 2(3), Covenant on Economic, Social and Cultural Rights 1966; Articles 13 and 25, Covenant on Civil and Political Rights 1966.

[2] See Convention on the Political Rights of Women 1953; Declaration on Elimination of Discrimination against Women 1967; Draft Convention on the Elimination of All Forms of Religious Intolerance 1967.

[3] Ginsberg, *On Justice in Society* (1965), pp. 11, 42. Equality, be it of rights or treatment, is here employed as equivalent to non-discrimination.

of justice offers little guidance to the necessary content of that concept and, by itself, suggests few restrictions upon those grounds which may be raised to support inequalities. Justice itself may not be equality alone,[1] and a distinction must be maintained between what has been described as, 'the concept of justice as meaning a proper balance between competing claims [and] a conception of justice as a set of related principles for identifying the *relevant considerations* which determine the balance'.[2] It is to the content of these principles that one must look in order to obtain the assurance of equality.[3]

(*a*) *Non-Discrimination in the Jurisprudence of International Tribunals*

In practice, international tribunals have stepped determinedly beyond simple appearances of equality. The Permanent Court of International Justice observed, for example, that equality in fact may well demand different treatment in order to attain a result which establishes an equilibrium between different situations. In the *Minority Schools in Albania Case*,[4] the Court was called upon to interpret the provision in the Albanian Declaration 1921, Article 5 (1), that 'minorities will enjoy the same treatment and security in law and in fact as other Albanian nationals'.[5] In rejecting Albania's plea that the abolition of private schools constituted a general measure applicable to the majority as well as to the minority, the Court adopted its earlier ruling in the *German Settlers in Poland Case*: 'There must be equality in fact . . . as well as ostensible legal equality . . . in the sense of absence of discrimination in the words of the law.'[6]

More recently the European Court of Justice has developed and applied the prohibition on discrimination based on nationality as that is laid down in Articles 7, 48, and 59 of the Treaty of Rome.

[1] See the criticism of Aristotle's formal description (following Plato, *Laws*, Bk. VI, p. 757) in Lucas, *The Principles of Politics* (1966), pp. 242 f.

[2] Rawls, *A Theory of Justice* (1971), p. 10, emphasis supplied. Ginsberg similarly refutes discrimination based on 'irrelevant differences' (op. cit., pp. 57, 58), and Lucas also on 'irrelevant distinctions' (op. cit., pp. 238–9).

[3] Rawls, op. cit., pp. 507 f.

[4] P.C.I.J. (1935), Ser. A/B, No. 64.

[5] Compare Article 38, Lausanne Peace Treaty 1923 (28 L.N.T.S. 11): 'The Turkish Government undertakes to assure full and complete protection of life and liberty to all inhabitants of Turkey without distinction of birth, nationality, language, race or religion.'

[6] P.C.I.J. (1923), Ser. B, No. 6, at p. 24; and see the decision in *Acquisition of Polish Nationality*, P.C.I.J. (1923), Ser. B, No. 7, p. 14.

The Court has not only ruled against overt discrimination,[1] but has also shown itself ready to strike at such measures of covert discrimination as, by the application of other criteria of differentiation, lead *in fact* to discrimination on the basis of nationality. Such alternative criteria may include requirements relating to origin, place of birth, residence within the territory of the State, or other matters, applied in any way so as to reserve benefits to nationals of the particular Member State.[2]

In their joint dissenting opinion in the *Minority Schools Case*, Judges Hurst, Rostworowski, and Negulesco also proposed a more specific approach. They stated:

> The word 'equal' implies that the right so enjoyed must be equal in measure to the right enjoyed by somebody else. . . A right which is unconditional and independent of that enjoyed by other people cannot with accuracy be described as an 'equal right'. 'Equality' necessarily implies the existence of some extraneous criterion by reference to which the content is to be determined.[3]

That extraneous criterion may be the treatment which is accorded to other groups similarly situated, so that discrimination and equality are essentially relational terms. Alternatively, it may be possible to review the validity of distinctions in the light of more general propositions. The dissenting opinion of Judge Tanaka in the *South West Africa Cases* (Second Phase) is of particular assistance in the latter respect.[4] That this was a minority Judgment in no way detracts from its value; the Court did not deal with the merits of the case and the majority Judgment neither supports nor challenges the reasoning upon which Judge Tanaka based his dissenting views. In referring to the idea of equality, Judge Tanaka states that it

> does not exclude the different treatment of persons from the consideration of the differences of factual circumstances such as sex, age, language, religion, economic condition, education, etc. To treat different matters equally in a mechanical way would be as unjust as to treat equal matters differently . . . If individuals differ one from another and societies also,

[1] See, for example, *Re French Merchant Seamen* [1974] 2 C.M.L.R. 216; *Reyners* v. *Belgian State* [1974] 2 C.M.L.R. 305.

[2] *Sotgui* v. *Deutsches Bundespost* [1974] E.C.R. 153, 164; *Van Binsbergen* v. *Bestuur van de Bedrijfsvereniging voor de Metaalnijverheid* [1975] 1 C.M.L.R. 298. Cf. *Prais* v. *Council of the European Communities* [1976] 2 C.M.L.R. 708; Article 4 Directive 77/249.

[3] P.C.I.J. (1935), Ser. A/B, No. 64, at p. 25.

[4] I.C.J. Rep., 1966, p. 6 at pp. 284–316; also printed in Brownlie, *Basic Documents on Human Rights* (1971), pp. 455 ff.

their needs will be different, and accordingly, the content of law may not be identical. Hence is derived the relativity of law to individual circumstances . . . A different treatment comes into question only when and to the extent that it corresponds to the nature of the difference. To treat unequal matters differently according to their inequality is not only permitted but required. The issue is whether the difference exists.[1]

From this restatement of the requirement of relevant differences, Judge Tanaka goes on to affirm that different treatment must be assessed according to the criterion of justice or reasonableness.

Different treatment must not be given arbitrarily; it requires reasonableness, or must be in conformity with justice, as in the treatment of minorities, different treatment of the sexes regarding public conveniences, etc. . . . Discrimination according to the criterion of 'race, colour, national or tribal origin' in establishing the rights and duties of the inhabitants of the territory is not considered reasonable and just. Race, colour, etc., do not constitute in themselves factors which can influence the rights and duties of the inhabitants as in the case of sex, age, language, religion, etc. If differentiation be required, it would be derived from the difference of language, custom, etc., not from the racial difference itself.[2]

Discrimination is not synonymous with differential treatment. The concept of discrimination, as employed in international law, connotes distinctions which are unfair, unjustifiable, or arbitrary.[3] From Judge Tanaka's Judgment in the *South West Africa Cases* and from that of the European Court of Human Rights in the *Belgian Linguistics Case*,[4] certain propositions emerge. Differential treatment is not unlawful (1) if the distinction is made in pursuit of a legitimate aim;[5] (2) if the distinction does not lack an 'objective justification'; (3) provided that a reasonable proportionality exists between the means employed and the aims sought to be realized.

[1] I.C.J. Rep., 1966, pp. 305, 306.

[2] I.C.J. Rep., 1966, p. 313.

[3] McKean, 'The Meaning of Discrimination in International and Municipal Law', 44 *B.Y.I.L.* (1970), 177. For criticism of the definition adopted in the United Kingdom Race Relations Act 1968, see Hepple, *Race, Jobs and the Law in Britain* (2nd ed., 1970), pp. 42–8, 49–57, 85–111. See now Race Relations Act 1976, section 1 and *passim*.

[4] See further below, pp. 81–2.

[5] Note the differential treatment ('positive discrimination') which is permitted by Article 1(4) of the International Convention on the Elimination of All Forms of Racial Discrimination 1966. A suggestion that certain governments may not be bound by international standards of non-racial treatment because that would be 'unfair' (Ghai, 67 A.S.I.L. Proc. (1973), 125) receives no support from the Convention.

Whether or not there is discrimination will thus depend upon a consideration of all the relevant circumstances.[1]

(b) Non-Discrimination as required by the European Convention on Human Rights

Some indication of current developments can be obtained from an examination of the provisions of the European Convention on Human Rights and of the jurisprudence of the European Commission and the European Court. Article I of the Convention declares: 'The High Contracting Parties shall secure to *every one within their jurisdiction* the rights and freedoms defined in Section 1 of this Convention.'[2] Thereafter the rights and freedoms laid down are all expressed broadly and apply equally to both aliens and nationals. Article 16 provides the only explicit exception, and permits restrictions to be imposed on the political activities of the former.[3] Article 15 makes provision for general and wider powers of derogation in time of war or other public emergency, but in no case is derogation permitted from Article 2 (which guarantees the right to life), Article 3 (which prohibits torture), Article 4(1) (which prohibits slavery or servitude), and Article 7 (which prohibits retroactive criminal legislation). Furthermore, any State Party which resorts to this right of derogation is obliged to keep the Secretary-General of the Council of Europe informed of the measures taken and the reasons for them. The right, or privilege, is thus limited by reference to the criterion of war or serious threat to the nation and exists as a controlled discretion. It has been characterized by the European Court of Human Rights as an 'exceptional right', in a case in which it was also held that it was for the Court to decide whether the derogation was warranted by the extent of the alleged emergency.[4]

The overriding principle of non-discrimination is set out in Article 14:

> The enjoyment of the rights and freedoms set forth in this Convention shall be secured without discrimination on any ground such as sex, race,

[1] *Treatment of Polish Nationals and other Persons of Polish Origin or Speech in the Danzig Territory*, P.C.I.J. (1932), Ser. A/B, No. 44, at p. 28.

[2] Emphasis supplied. The European Convention and Protocols may be found in European Treaty Series, Nos. 5, 9, 44, 45, 46. See further Jacobs, *The European Convention on Human Rights* (1975), pp. 188 ff. and *passim*.

[3] Note the relation of this Article to Article 14; see Fawcett, *The Application of the European Convention on Human Rights* (1969), p. 251.

[4] *Lawless Case*, 4 *Yearbook* 470, 472–5 (1961). Cf. *Guardianship of Infants Case*, I.C.J. Rep., 1958, p. 55.

colour, language, religion, political or other opinion, national or social origin, association with a national minority, property, birth or other status.

A number of decisions of the European Commission have supported the limitation of this principle to the rights and freedoms set forth in the Convention,[1] but in other cases Article 14 has been accorded a much more independent role.[2]

The Commission has also enlarged, perhaps haltingly, upon the meaning of unlawful discrimination.[3] In one case, for example, the applicant had been convicted and sentenced in the Federal Republic of Germany for homosexual activities.[4] He contended, *inter alia*, that repression of the crimes in question was a violation of the Convention not only in principle, in that it infringed the right to respect for family life guaranteed by Article 8, but also in its application, in that it was confined to offences by men, thus contravening the principle of non-discrimination as to sex which was protected by Article 8 in conjunction with Article 14. However, in the Commission's view, the Convention expressly permitted the regulation of private and family life, within the prescribed limits, and the 'margin of appreciation' left to States had not been exceeded in this case.[5] The Commission in effect balanced the interests of the individual against the interests of public health and morality, to conclude that the discrimination was not unreasonable.

Different treatment was also upheld in the case of *Gudmundsson* v. *The Republic of Iceland* in 1960.[6] The applicant complained of the differential treatment accorded to co-operative societies and joint-stock companies in the matter of taxation. The Commission took the view that different treatment was a common factor in taxation laws and that there was, therefore, no sufficient basis for calling in question the character of those laws as a legitimate means of taxation.

[1] See Application 86/55: 1 *Yearbook* 199; Application 673/59: 4 *Yearbook* 286.

[2] Application 238/56: 1 *Yearbook* 205; Application 434/58: 2 *Yearbook* 354; Application 1465/62: 5 *Yearbook* 256; and see below, pp. 164–6.

[3] Cf. Jacobs, *The European Convention on Human Rights*, pp. 188–93.

[4] Application 104/55: 1 *Yearbook* 228.

[5] On the margin of appreciation in expulsion cases, see Application 3170/67 *v.* Belgium and United Kingdom; Application 3898/68 *v.* United Kingdom; and below, pp. 290–1. In later decisions the Commission has dropped any express reference to a margin of appreciation for the reason that such a principle was implicit, in the sense that the Commission always considers the particular circumstances of the parties in each case. See *Case Law Topics No. 4*, 'Human Rights and their Limitations', p. 2 and *passim*.

[6] Application 511/59: 3 *Yearbook* 394.

Additionally, the right to equal application of the tax laws was not such a right as was guaranteed by either the Convention or the First Protocol.[1]

Further progress in the development of the concept of discrimination was made in the case of *Grandrath* v. *The Federal Republic of Germany*,[2] which involved a possible violation of Article 14 in conjunction with either Article 4 or Article 9. By a majority of 8:5, the Commission adopted the following interpretation of Article 14:

> The application of Article 14 does not depend upon a previous finding of the Commission that a violation of another Article . . . already exists. . . . Consequently, if a restriction which is in itself permissible [under the Convention] is imposed in a discriminatory manner, there would be a violation of Article 14 in conjunction with the other Article concerned.[3]

Such progressive elaboration of the conventional principle of non-discrimination is of importance to the general issue. In the context of movements across frontiers, for example, it suggests itself as an inherent qualification upon the right of States to exclude aliens.[4] It may be that the prospective entrant, while still retaining a precarious position, is entitled nevertheless to demand that he shall not be excluded on any of the prohibited grounds alone, such as sex, race, or colour.

To date, the leading case to involve Article 14 is that relating to certain aspects of the laws on the use of languages in education in Belgium.[5] The applicants in this case alleged violations of Articles 8 and 14 of the Convention and of Article 2 of the First Protocol. On the question of admissibility, the Commission expressed in detail its views on the application of Article 14 in relation to the rights and freedoms guaranteed by the Convention. It declared that Article 14 did not impose a purely negative obligation on States. Enjoyment of the rights and freedoms must be assured, or guaranteed, without discrimination. The Commission envisaged the possibility that different measures taken by a State Party in respect of different parts of its territory or groups of its population could, while not on their face violating the article defining the right in question,

[1] 3 *Yearbook* 394, 424.
[2] Application 2299/64: 10 *Yearbook* 636.
[3] Ibid., p. 678; see also at p. 680 for examples of unlawful discrimination.
[4] See Application 1465/62: 5 *Yearbook* 256. Cf. Application 7729/76.
[5] On admissibility and the question of the reserved domain, see above, pp. 55–6.

nevertheless amount to such violation if that article were read in conjunction with Article 14.[1]

In view of the Commission's espousal of an independent role for Article 14, the Belgian Government's arguments before the Court were concentrated principally on the scope of that Article. The Court did, in fact, adopt the views of the Commission and, while accepting that the guarantee in Article 14 was not capable of a separate existence, agreed that a measure itself in conformity with a particular article might nevertheless be unlawful if that article were read together with Article 14. In the present case, the applicants could not claim the right, under Article 2 of the Protocol, to obtain from the public authorities the creation of a special kind of educational establishment. However, a State which had set up such an establishment could not, in laying down entrance requirements, introduce discriminatory measures within the meaning of Article 14.

In spite of the very general wording of the French version of Article 14 ('sans distinction aucune'), the Court held that that Article did not forbid every difference in treatment in the exercise of the rights and freedoms guaranteed. Those words had to be read in the light of the more restrictive text of the English version. A wide interpretation would lead to absurd results and the Court therefore proposed a number of guiding principles:

> the principle of equality of treatment is violated if the distinction has no objective and reasonable justification. The existence of such a justification must be assessed in relation to the aim and effects of the measure under consideration, regard being had to the principles which normally prevail in democratic societies. A difference in treatment in the exercise of a right laid down in the Convention must not only pursue a legitimate aim; Article 14 is likewise violated when it is clearly established that there is no reasonable relationship of proportionality between the means employed and the aim sought to be realised.[2]

[1] Report of the Commission, 24 June 1965, paras. 400, 401. See also, Eissen, 'L'Autonomie de l'Article 14 de la Convention Européenne des Droits de l'Homme dans la Jurisprudence de la Commission', in *Mélanges offerts à Polys Modinos* (1968), pp. 122–45.

[2] Judgment of the European Court of Human Rights, 23 July 1968, p. 34; see also the findings on the particular questions submitted to the Court at pp. 44 ff. A recent municipal decision of note is that of the Judicial Committee of the Privy Council in *Akar* v. *Attorney-General of Sierra Leone* [1970] A.C. 853. The Board was faced with a proposed constitutional amendment which purported to restrict citizenship to persons 'of Negro African descent'. The Board held (Lord Guest dissenting) that this new condition of citizenship was essentially racial and offended the constitutional guarantees of fundamental rights and non-discrimination. It may be noted that these guarantees themselves owed much to the influence of the European Convention on Human Rights; see de

(2) DISCRIMINATION ON THE BASIS OF NATIONALITY

In developing his conclusion that the norm of non-discrimination had become a rule of customary international law, Judge Tanaka observed that the concept of equality before the law and equal protection of the law was a feature common to many constitutions.[1] This fact alone is some evidence of the acceptance of equality as a general principle of law, and it is additionally remarkable that many States do guarantee fundamental rights without distinction between citizens and aliens.[2]

It has been seen that modern covenants and conventions tend to propose three distinct elements as incidents of unlawful discrimination. There must be (1) a distinction, exclusion, restriction, or preference, which is (2) based on one or more of the specific grounds, such as race, colour, or religion, and which (3) has the purpose or effect of nullifying or impairing the enjoyment or exercise on an equal footing of the rights and freedoms which are guaranteed. Yet, despite the general wording of recent conventions, discrimination which is based on nationality alone may still be permissible, at least within certain limits.[3] For example, the State's duty to admit individuals is usually limited in favour of those who are its nationals,

Smith, *The New Commonwealth and its Constitutions* (1964), pp. 180–99. See also *Guinn and Beal* v. *United States* 238 U.S. 347 (1915), and compare generally the decision of the Privy Council to opposite effect in *Pillai* v. *Mudanayake* [1953] A.C. 514, upholding legislation which barred a large number of Indian Tamils from becoming citizens of Ceylon because neither their fathers nor grandfathers were born there (especially at p. 530). See further on the status of the Tamils 4 *Indian Journal of International Law* (1964), 522–6, 637–40; *The Tamils of Sri Lanka* (1975), Minority Rights Group, Report No. 25.

[1] I.C.J. Rep., 1966, at p. 300. Equality as a norm of general international law was also accepted by Judge Wellington Koo (ibid., p. 234) and Judge Padilla Nervo (ibid., pp. 455, 464–8). Peaslee, *Constitutions of the Nations* (1965), vol. I, p. 7, estimates that some 75 per cent of the world's constitutions acknowledge the principle of equality.

[2] See, for example, the availability of habeas corpus in the law of the United Kingdom and the United States: *R.* v. *Home Secretary, ex parte Soblen* [1963] 1 Q.B. 829; *Yick Wo* v. *Hopkins* 118 U.S. 356 (1886); *Fong Yue Ting* v. *U.S.* 149 U.S. 698 (1893); United States Constitution, Article I(1)(9). The remedy is, however, limited to alien friends: *Netz* v. *Ede* [1946] Ch. 224; *R.* v. *Bottrill, ex parte Küchenmeister* [1947] K.B. 41; *Ludeck* v. *Watkins* 335 U.S. 160 (1941). See also Article 3, Constitution of the Federal Republic of Germany; Articles 14 and 15, Constitution of the Republic of India; de Smith, *The New Commonwealth and its Constitutions*, pp. 183 ff.

[3] Note the exclusion of nationality from the generic term 'national origins' by the House of Lords in *London Borough of Ealing* v. *Race Relations Board* [1972] A.C. 342. Compare the similar result in *Espinoza* v. *Farah Manufacturing Co. Inc.* 94 S. Ct. 334 (1973), Douglas J. dissenting at pp. 340 ff. See now Race Relations Act 1976, sections 1 (1)(b)(ii), 3(1)

and it is widely accepted that aliens may be barred from the exercise of political rights,[1] the ownership of certain property, and the holding of public office.[2] State practice supports the lawfulness of such discriminations,[3] although there is a tendency for States to accord each other's nationals greater equality in fact, as a result of extensive treaty obligations. The disadvantages of alienage were significantly reduced through the development of the standards of most-favoured-nation and national treatment in the commercial treaties of the seventeenth century and onwards,[4] and here in the underlying principle of equality lie the origins of the norm of non-discrimination. Even in the absence of treaty, certain measures which discriminated against foreigners alone were unacceptable. In matters of taxation, for example, the view generally held was that the alien was liable 'in the manner and to the same extent as the native subjects'.[5] Such a rule readily follows from the principle that the alien is subject to the laws of the State in which he is resident.[6] But, as Phillimore noted in 1855:

> Foreigners, whom a State has once admitted unconditionally into its territories, are entitled not only to freedom from injury, but to the execution of justice in respect of their transactions with the subjects of that State. No State has a right to set, as it were, a snare for foreigners . . .[7]

[1] Batiffol and Lagarde, *Droit international privé* (1970), p. 198, citing Domat. See also proposals for franchise reform in Aden, in *British Practice in International Law*, 1964—I, at pp. 66–7; Article 16, European Convention on Human Rights.

[2] For example, no alien may own a British ship: Status of Aliens Act 1914, section17; nor may he generally take Crown employment: Aliens Employment Act 1955. Cf. *In re Griffiths* 93 S. Ct. 2851 (1973); *Sugarman* v. *Dougal* 93 S. Ct. 2842 (1973).

[3] See *Mrs. Stevenson's* case (landholding), 6 *B.D.I.L.* 327–8; *Grant's* case (exercise of certain trades), ibid., pp. 328–9; *Mrs. Thompson's* case (establishment of schools), ibid., p. 329.

[4] See treaties cited in 6 B.D.I.L. at pp. 330–2; Neufeld, *The International Protection of Private Creditors from the Treaties of Westphalia to the Congress of Vienna (1648–1815)* (1971), pp. 97–8, 110–13.

[5] 6 *B.D.I.L.* 405, 406, 408; case involving the Treaty with Colombia of 1825: ibid., p. 333. It has also been suggested that if alien property is included within nationalization measures while national property is excluded, then this may be a discrimination prohibited by international law; see White, *The Nationalization of Foreign Property* (1961), ch. 6; *Anglo-Iranian Oil Case*, I.C.J. Pleadings, pp. 93–7. But compare Covenant on Economic, Social and Cultural Rights 1966, Article 2 (3); Charter of Economic Rights and Duties 1974, Article 2; *Gudmundsson* v. *Iceland*: 3 *Yearbook* 394.

[6] Cf. case involving the Colombian transit tax on mail: 6 *B.D.I.L.* 414–18; case concerning the Treaty with Brazil of 1827: ibid., p. 419; Albrecht, 'Taxation of Aliens in International Law', 29 *B.Y.I.L.* (1952), 145, 172. On 'confiscatory taxation', see *British Practice in International Law*, 1964—II, 202–6.

[7] *Commentaries on International Law* (1st ed., 1855), vol. II, s. 2, cited in 6 *B.D.I.L.*,

In the past, the right of access to the courts was commonly granted to aliens by treaty,[1] but today it may more readily be argued that rights such as that to life, to liberty, to security of the person, and to the equal protection of the law, exist independently of the status of the individual. There can be no objective justification for denying their application to the alien *qua* alien.

This view is supported by developments in the field of human rights treaties. In the Covenant on Civil and Political Rights 1966, for example, the rights are guaranteed without distinction to all individuals within the territory of a Contracting State and subject to its jurisdiction.[2] Article 4 provides for a right of derogation in time of public emergency which itself would probably justify distinctions between nationals and aliens; it is to be noted that the anti-discrimination provision in the first paragraph is narrower than the general provision in Article 2(1), and that it does not include 'property, birth or other status' within the prohibited grounds. However, it is expressly stated that there must be no derogation from those rights and freedoms which guarantee life, which prohibit torture and slavery, which secure the recognition of every one as a person before the law, which forbid retroactive legislation, etc.[3] In addition, the exercise of the exceptional right of derogation is subject to the overriding principle which requires that it should not be used to effect discrimination solely on the ground of race, colour, sex, religion, language, or social origin.[4]

The principle of non-discrimination imposes distinct limitations upon the liberty of States to deal with aliens. In racial matters, non-discrimination has a normative character and may be adjudged a part of *jus cogens*. In other matters involving distinctions against aliens in regard to property, to access to the courts, to entry, exclusion, and expulsion, the question to be asked is whether there is now

at p. 322; on submission to the local law, see 6 *B.D.I.L.* 278 ff. See also O'Connell, *International Law* (2nd ed., 1970), p. 941.

[1] Neufeld, op. cit., pp. 100–1; 6 *B.D.I.L.* 186–7. See also *Johnstone* v. *Pedlar* [1921] 2 A.C. 262, per Lord Phillimore at p. 296; Draft Principles on Equality in the Administration of Justice, ECOSOC Doc. E/CN.4/1077, 7 Oct. 1971 (Commission on Human Rights—Sub-Commission on Prevention of Discrimination and Protection of Minorities), especially Principles 3, 13, and 14.

[2] Article 2 (1). The exercise of 'political rights' is expressly confined to citizens by Article 25.

[3] Article 4(2); Oppenheim, *International Law* (8th ed., 1955), vol. I, p. 688.

[4] Article 4(1). Compare the similar provision on derogation in Article 15 of the European Convention on Human Rights; see also *Lawless Case*, 4 *Yearbook* 470, 472–5.

a sufficient body of rules by which to determine whether the State's exercise of discretion is justifiable, or whether it amounts to unlawful discrimination. Distinctions in these areas purportedly based on alienage, or on the competence to deal with aliens at will, but which are in reality founded on racial grounds, are clearly barred by the general principle set out above. Even in other matters, alienage as the sole basis for distinctions must remain questionable, and it has been the object of both treaties and international practice to prevent injurious discriminations against aliens generally.[1] In a United States case in 1970, the District Court of Arizona struck down a fifteen-year residency requirement for aliens as a condition of eligibility for welfare assistance. Such a condition was held to amount to a denial of equal protection and, in the court's view, alienage was an inherently suspect basis of classification.[2]

Further amelioration of the position of the alien will, most probably, be accomplished through the medium of bi- and multilateral treaties. Over and above the basic human rights, such treaties will seek to assure, for example, national treatment or equality of opportunity or treatment in employment,[3] equal rights to trade union membership,[4] and to the benefits of social security.[5] Article 7 of the E.E.C. Treaty declares that within the scope of application of the Treaty, and without prejudice to special provisions, 'any discrimination on the grounds of nationality shall be prohibited'.

[1] *Hines* v. *Davidowitz* 312 U.S. 52 (1941), per Black J. at p. 65.

[2] *Richardson* v. *Graham* 313 F. Supp. 34 (1970), affirmed 403 U.S. 365 (1971). It may be that this case is limited to aliens admitted for permanent residence, but see *Sailer* v. *Tonkin* 356 F. Supp. 72 (1973). See also *Guerra* v. *Manchester Terminal Corporation* 350 F. Supp. 529 (1972); *Mohamed* v. *Parks* 352 F. Supp. 518 (1973); *Cuk* v. *Brian* 355 F. Supp. 133 (1972); *Chapman* v. *Gerard* 456 F.2d 577 (1972); compare *Gonzales* v. *Shea* 318 F. Supp. 572 (1970), in which the District Court of Colorado held that United States citizenship as a condition of eligibility under Colorado's 'unique pension program' did not violate the equal protection clause of the Fourteenth Amendment; *Perkins* v. *Smith* 370 F. Supp. 134 (1974), in which alienage as a bar to jury service was upheld. In his dissenting opinion in *Espinoza* v. *Farah Manufacturing Co. Inc.* 94 S.Ct. 334 (1973), Douglas J. expressed the view that any policy of preferring those born in the United States necessarily involved a discrimination based on birth outside the United States, which was equivalent to discrimination on the (prohibited) basis of national origin (at pp. 340–1). See also *Mow Sun Wong* v. *Hampton* 500 F.2d 1031; 96 S. Ct. 1895 (1976); *Matthews* v. *Diaz* 96 S. Ct. 1883 (1976); *National Labor Relations Board* v. *International Longshoremen's Association, Local No. 1581 AFL-CIO* 489 F.2d 635 (1974).

[3] e.g. I.L.O. Convention on Discrimination (Employment and Occupation) 1958; European Convention on Establishment 1955; European Social Charter 1961; I.L.O. Employment Policy Convention 1964.

[4] e.g. I.L.O. Migration for Employment Convention (Revised) 1949.

[5] e.g. I.L.O. Equality of Treatment (Social Security) Convention 1962.

Advocate-General Lagrange submitted before the European Court of Justice that 'non-discrimination . . . reaches beyond the limits of the establishment of a Common Market',[1] but it will be seen that in practice the E.E.C. national may still be subjected to the discriminatory measure of expulsion. None the less while Member States do retain certain reserve powers, their exercise is limited by the controlling provisions of Community law.[2]

On the general issue of equality, it remains for international law to answer the question whether alienage is, in the circumstances, a 'relevant difference' justifying differential treatment. The principle of non-discrimination expressly rules out certain types of distinction, and raises a very strong presumption of equality. The burden of proof lies on the party seeking to invoke exceptions to show objective justification and proportionality.[3] It is this manner of proceeding which is prescribed by the general rule of international law, and an indication has been given of the way in which this and more detailed rules control the discretion which States may otherwise enjoy in their treatment of aliens. The content of these more detailed rules is explored below, in relation to the powers claimed by States to exclude and to expel aliens.

[1] *Re Electric Refrigerators* [1963] C.M.L.R. 289, 294; see also *Reyners* v. *Belgian State* [1974] 2 C.M.L.R. 305; *Casagrande* v. *Landeshauptstadt Munich* [1974] 2 C.M.L.R. 423; *Alaimo* v. *Prefect of the Rhône* [1975] 1 C.M.L.R. 262; *Van Binsbergen* v. *Bestuur van de Bedrijfsvereniging voor de Metaalnijvereheid* [1975] I C.M.L.R. 298; *Walrave* v. *Association Union Cycliste Internationale* [1975] 1 C.M.L.R. 320, 333, at paras. 28 and 29.

[2] See further below, pp. 181–6; 300–6.

[3] See above, pp. 77–8.

PART II

THE ENTRY AND EXCLUSION OF FOREIGN NATIONALS

INTRODUCTION

It is in policies of admission and exclusion that one sees clearly the discriminations practised by States in the choice of those whom they will admit. Where those who seek entry desire to settle permanently, it is not uncommon for the host State to weight the balance more favourably for those who, as near as can be, reflect the ethnic and cultural origins of the indigenous population. Until 1965, for example, the United States pursued what was known as the 'national origins' quota system. An over-all numerical maximum of immigrants was set and that figure was broken down into percentages corresponding to the racial geography of the country. It naturally operated to secure the position of the principally North European majority and to preserve the minority status of many South European and Asian groups.

Homogeneity can be maintained in other ways as well. For many years Australia adhered to the so-called 'white Australia' policy. When colour alone as a bar to eligibility for permanent immigration was abandoned, the policy was continued in practice by confining the benefits of assisted passage to those of European origin. The Race Relations Board challenged the validity of this policy under United Kingdom anti-discrimination laws in 1970. The Government of Australia replied that the question of who was to receive assisted passage was a matter for the Government alone to determine, and that it would be 'an infringement of Australia's rights as a sovereign State if its immigration authorities overseas were subject to the application of the laws of other countries'.[1]

States are commonly unable or unwilling to treat permanent immigration in other than a racial context. Stringent controls will often be justified in the name of national identity and self-preservation. In defence of the national-origins system, Senator McCarran declared in 1952: 'Assimilation is the key to a sound immigration system.'[2] But the practice of racial discrimination in matters of immigration is not always overt. The provisions of the law of the United Kingdom do not specify colour as a ground of exclusion, but

[1] The *Guardian*, 8 Jan. 1971; see also ibid. 18 Nov. 1970; *The Times*, 5 Jan. 1973.

[2] Quoted in Konvitz, *Civil Rights in Immigration* (1953), p. 59.

sanction discrimination in reverse, by granting special privileges to those 'connected' with the United Kingdom. This benefits the citizens of the 'white Commonwealth' countries to the detriment of large numbers of the coloured citizens of the United Kingdom. The general tendency in recent years, however, has been to abandon racial grounds as the principal basis for immigration control. In 1965 the United States replaced the former system of population-related quotas by over-all numerical limits.[1] However, prospective immigrants from Eastern Hemisphere countries must still qualify under certain preferences in order to gain admission to the United States.[2] Each of the preferences is restricted to a certain percentage of the maximum and, for example, while 10 per cent are reserved for skilled or unskilled workers, 74 per cent of available preferences are reserved in favour of relatives either of citizens or of aliens admitted for permanent settlement. In this way the existing balance of population is maintained, although not so rigidly as before.

By comparison, the Canadian system of immigration control appears somewhat more objective. It is based on points, with account being taken of fluency in English and French, adaptability, resourcefulness, etc. An independent applicant must obtain a minimum score, while others may secure credits by virtue of having relatives or sponsors in Canada or adequate resources to set up in business.[3]

The immigration laws of the United States, Canada, and the United Kingdom all contain discriminatory provisions. The question in each case is whether that discrimination can be justified on any reasonable grounds. The United States and Canada are still primarily countries of immigration; the United Kingdom is not. Some attempt to rationalize the immigration policy of the United Kingdom was made in 1972 by the Home Secretary, Mr. Carr, who based the Government's policy on three declared principles:

The first principle is the recognition that Britain is an overcrowded island with a labour force which, for the moment at least, appears ample for her

[1] 170,000 immigrant visas for the natives of independent countries of the Eastern Hemisphere; 120,000 for natives of Western Hemisphere countries: 8 U.S.C. s. 1152, in force in 1968. [2] 8 U.S.C. s. 1153.

[3] Immigration Act 1952; Immigration Appeal Board Act 1967; Immigration Regulations 1967: P.C. 1967—1616; Hawkins, *Canada and Immigration: Public Policy and Public Concern* (1972). Following publication of the 1974 Green Paper on Immigration Policy the law has now been substantially reformed. See the Immigration Act 1977, and in particular the statement of 'Immigration Objectives' in section 3.

needs, and, therefore, that there must be restriction of all permanent immigration to . . . the 'inescapable minimum' . . . The second principle is to recognise, within this overall need, a continuing responsibility to those in various parts of the world who remain entitled to United Kingdom citizenship. Hence the decision to reserve for these people as large a proportion as possible of the limited numbers we are able to admit year by year, and to do so in a controlled and orderly way. The third principle is the recognition that it is both right and natural to give easy access to Britain to all those with close and recent ties with this country, provided they create no significant pressure for permanent settlement.[1]

It is out of the conflict of the second and third principles that there have arisen the racially objectionable provisions of the current law. The State's obligations to its own citizens have been compromised in the dubious concept of patriality. The distinction drawn between citizens operates in fact as a racial one, and would appear to be contrary not only to the particular provisions of the European Convention on Human Rights,[2] but also to the compelling principle of non-discrimination examined above.

The discriminations practised in immigration control by Canada and the United States are of a different kind. First, each of these States gives substantial preferences to those related to, or sponsored by, people already established within national boundaries. Secondly, and this is especially apparent in the Canadian system, significant advantages are granted to those who speak the local language and who, culturally, are most likely to settle down. Thirdly, each State looks most favourably upon those immigrants who will be of greatest value to itself, either in terms of special skill or other achievement. In its way, each of these preferred categories may produce discrimination on racial grounds. The first classification ensures that a high proportion of future immigrants will reflect the established population. The second classification likewise ensures the reception of those most easily assimilable; and the third indirectly encourages immigration from those more highly developed countries in which applicants will have had an opportunity to acquire the necessary skills.

For the moment these discriminations will be justified on the ground that they are broadly based and that a man is not excluded by reason of his race or colour alone. There is some weight in the

[1] 851 H.C. Deb., col. 598.

[2] See below, pp. 163–6.

argument that it is just and reasonable to treat relatives differently from independent applicants, and that this amounts simply to the effective recognition of legitimate interests. To such an extent, discriminatory provisions may escape characterization as unfair, improper, or arbitrary, while those present in the law of the United Kingdom would not. It is apparent that the encouragement of immigration is not a purely altruistic activity: the State is looking to its own interests, and to that end will find more acceptable the economically, socially, and culturally tractable. For these reasons, and with additional reference to its 'inalienable rights', the State will continue to claim a very wide margin of discretion in regard to control over entry. It will seek to leave itself free to decide upon the grounds of exclusion, both for immigrants and non-immigrants, to decide whether these shall relate to personal qualities such as criminal record or physical or mental disability, or to more general grounds such as race, religion, and colour. In 1932, Verdross observed: 'Les questions d'immigration ne sont pas du tout laissées à la compétence arbitraire d'un État seul, car le droit international limite sa compétence en la matière, en vue du bien commun de l'humanité.'[1] However, except in those areas in which treaties or peremptory norms operate, such as that of non-discrimination, it is not easy to bring matters of entry and exclusion within the bounds of international law. The preponderant view remains that these are matters essentially within the reserved domain of domestic jurisdiction, although in the past there was some consensus as to the existence of a general duty to admit aliens. Thus, Vittoria noted: '[It] was permissible, from the beginnings of the world (where everything was in common) for anyone to set forth and travel wheresoever he would.'[2] This idealized view, it was said, entailed the consequence that the Spaniards might lawfully carry on trade with foreign nations, provided that they did no harm.

Grotius accepted that the right to engage in commerce pertains equally to all peoples,[3] that temporary sojourn should be accorded to all those who pass through a country, and permanent sojourn to

[1] Verdross, *Les règles internationales concernant le traitement des étrangers* (1932), p. 25. Cf. President Roosevelt (1906): 'Whether they are Catholic or Protestant, Jew or Gentile; whether they come from England or Germany, Russia, Japan or Italy, matters nothing. All we have a right to question is a man's conduct.' Cited in Konvitz, op. cit., p. 20.

[2] *De Indis*, III. 1 (1696; Carnegie Inst. 1917).

[3] *De Jure Praedae* (1604; Clarendon Press, 1950), pp. 218–19.

the exile.[1] Wolff, however, proposed certain limits to the freedom of movement. Thus, while the exile might request admittance, he had no right in the matter and entry could be refused for good reasons, where

there is fear lest the morals of the subjects may be corrupted, or lest prejudice may be aroused against religion, or even lest criminals be admitted because of whom injury threatens the State, and other things which are detrimental to public welfare . . . [Moreover,] since nations are free, the decision in these matters must be left to the nations themselves and that decision must be respected.[2]

Vattel was of the same view, that entry could be denied in the case of danger to the nation: 'It belongs to the nation to judge whether her circumstances will or will not justify the admission of the foreigner.'[3] The sovereign was free to forbid the entrance of foreigners in general or in particular cases,[4] and to impose conditions upon the grant of permission to enter.[5]

It was Vattel who proved to be the inspiration behind the decisions in two important exclusion cases in the late nineteenth century. In *Musgrove* v. *Chun Teeong Toy* the Privy Council upheld the validity of a statute designed to exclude the Chinese from the state of Victoria.[6] On the question whether an alien had any right to enter British territory, it was noted:

No authority exists for the proposition that an alien has any such right. Circumstances may occur in which the refusal to permit an alien to land might be such an interference with international comity as would properly give rise to diplomatic remonstrance from the country of which he was a native, but it is quite another thing to assert that an alien excluded from any part of Her Majesty's dominions by the executive government there, can maintain an action in a British court.[7]

[1] *De Jure Belli ac Pacis*, II. 2, XV, XVI (1646; Carnegie Inst. 1913).
[2] *Jus Gentium Methodo Scientifica Pertractatum* (1764; Clarendon Press, 1934), ss. 148, 149.
[3] Ed. Chitty (1834), I. 19, 230.
[4] *Ibid.* II. 7, 94.
[5] Ibid. II. 8, 100; the right to impose conditions ought to be exercised 'with regard to the duties of humanity'. See also ibid. II. 10, 135: 'A difference in religion is not a sufficient reason to exclude him, provided he does not engage in controversial disputes with a view to disseminate his tenets.'
[6] [1891] A.C. 272; 6 *B.D.I.L.* 9–77.
[7] [1891] A.C. 272, 282.

In a United States decision on similar facts, it was declared:

> It is an accepted maxim of international law, that every sovereign nation has the power, as inherent in sovereignty, and essential to its self-preservation, to forbid the entrance of foreigners within its dominions, or to admit them only in such cases and upon such conditions as it may see fit to prescribe.[1]

The twentieth century has been witness to substantial developments in immigration law and control. States have pressed on, assuming the right of exclusion to be 'inherent in their sovereign powers', although the exercise of this right is necessarily tempered by the exigencies of modern intercourse. An alien on the threshold of initial entry has, effectively, no definable right: he awaits the discretionary grant of the privilege of entry and an arbitrary or unjust exclusion entails uncertain consequences.

In the *Nottebohm Case*, Judge Read observed as part of his dissenting opinion: 'When an alien comes to the frontier, seeking admission . . . the State has *an unfettered right* to refuse (it) . . .'[2] O'Connell, writing in 1970, concluded:

> A general right of entry is too abstract to permit a tribunal to say that a specific individual has been wrongfully excluded. The appreciation of him as a security or racial or moral contamination risk is essentially subjective, and it is difficult to conceive of an occasion when one could with confidence say that the faculty of appreciation has been misused.[3]

It is the purpose of what follows to show the manner in which this 'subjective faculty of appreciation' does come under the control of, first, developed principles of municipal law, and, secondly, the rules and standards of international law, the latter deriving from the general law and from specific treaty obligations.

[1] *Nishimura Ekiu* v. *United States* 142 U.S. 651, 659 (1892), per Gray J. See also Hackworth, *Digest*, Vol. III, pp. 549–52, 690–707, 717 ff.

[2] I.C.J. Rep., 1955, p. 4, at p. 46.

[3] *International Law*, p. 696; see also Ryan, 'Immigration, Aliens and Naturalization in Australian Law', in O'Connell, ed., *International Law in Australia* (1965), pp. 465–99.

VI

ENTRY AND EXCLUSION UNDER THE LAW OF THE UNITED KINGDOM

(1) HISTORY OF CONTROL OVER ALIENS AND COMMONWEALTH CITIZENS

FROM SHORTLY after the end of the Napoleonic Wars until 1905 no foreigners were excluded or expelled from Great Britain. The various Aliens Acts passed during this period dealt principally with registration and were not in fact applied with any vigour.[1] It had never been very clear whether the Crown enjoyed any prerogative powers in matters of entry and exclusion, and in 1890 it was argued that such powers existed only with reference to foreign sovereigns, their ambassadors, and forces.[2] In the following year, however, the Privy Council decided in the case of *Musgrove* v. *Chun Teeong Toy* that the Crown did have the power to *legislate* to prevent any alien from entering British territory.[3] Since 1905 Aliens Acts of one sort or another have been continually in force, and it is doubtful whether the prerogative powers are still relevant in time of peace. Nevertheless, the most recent legislation proclaims that the statutory powers shall not be taken to supersede or impair Her Majesty's prerogative powers in respect of aliens.[4]

The first of the modern generation of alien statutes was the Aliens Act 1905, passed to restrict Jewish immigration from East Europe.[5]

[1] 6 *B.D.I.L.* 100. See the statutes cited in Holdsworth, 9 *H.E.L.*, pp. 90 ff. Convicted aliens could be effectively removed from the realm by way of conditional pardon: Higgins, 'Voluntary Deportation', [1963] Crim. L.R. 680.

[2] Craies, 'The Right of Aliens to enter British Territory', 6 L.Q.R. (1890), 27. Cf. Haycraft, 'Aliens Legislation and the Prerogative of the Crown', 13 L.Q.R. (1897), 165. For a modern view of the prerogative, see Macdonald, *The New Immigration Law* (1972), pp. 8–9.

[3] [1891] A. C. 272. Cf. *Attorney-General for Canada* v. *Cain* [1906] A. C. 542.

[4] Immigration Act 1971, section 33(5). See also remarks of Lord Denning M.R., in *Schmidt* v. *Secretary of State* [1969] 2 Ch. 149, at p. 168; *R.* v. *Bottrill, ex parte Küchenmeister* [1947] K.B. 41.

[5] The Act was passed following the *Report of the Royal Commission on Alien Immigration* 1903 (Cd. 1741). See also S.R. & O. 1905, No. 1325, 1326; Gainer, *The Alien Invasion* (1972); Garrard, *The English and Immigration, 1880–1910* (1971).

The Act required inspection only for 'alien steerage passengers' carried on 'immigrant ships'.[1] Provision was made for such passengers to disembark at specified immigration ports.[2] and for the making of returns in respect of all such passengers.[3] On landing, alien steerage passengers came before an immigration officer and a medical inspector.[4] Pending consideration of their case, and providing suitable arrangements had been made, would-be entrants might be conditionally disembarked, although securities were required by those responsible for transportation.

The exclusion provisions of the 1905 Act were aimed at the one generic class, 'undesirable immigrants'. The declared purpose of the Act was to reduce the social cost of immigration, and thus the class was identifiable principally by lack of funds or inability to work. An immigrant was deemed to be undesirable (*a*) if he did not have, or was not in a position to obtain, the means of decently supporting himself and any dependants: (*b*) if he was insane or was likely to become a public charge owing to disease or infirmity; (*c*) if he had been sentenced in a foreign country for an extradition crime not being an offence of a political character; (*d*) if an expulsion order under the Act had been made against him.[5] In the last three cases exclusion was mandatory, irrespective of means. As regards the 'means' themselves, there was some room for appreciation, but the burden was on the applicant to satisfy the immigration officer either of his present position or of his future prospects.[6]

Where granted, leave to land was given orally to the immigrant by the immigration officer—there was no question of landing conditions—and the immigrant was free to go. In the case of a refusal, notice was given to the alien in writing, setting out the grounds of

[1] Aliens Act 1905, section 8. An 'immigrant ship' was defined as any ship carrying more than 20 (reduced to 12 by the Conservatives, then raised again to 20 by the Liberals) alien steerage passengers. This class was in turn defined to include all passengers other than those travelling first class; there were some exemptions in favour of second-class passengers, but where there was only one class, they were all reckoned as alien steerage passengers.

[2] Ibid., section 6.

[3] Ibid., section 5.

[4] A less detailed inspection procedure was applied to alien seamen and 'transmigrants': ibid., section 8(1).

[5] Aliens Act 1905, section 1(3).

[6] It was expressly provided that leave to land should not be refused, on the ground of want of means or the probability of the alien becoming a charge on the rates, to any immigrant who proved that he was seeking to enter the country solely to avoid persecution or punishment on religious or political grounds.

his undesirability and informing him of the right of appeal to the Immigration Board established by the Act.[1]

This statute remained in force until 1919, although it was in practice superseded by the emergency legislation of the First World War. It is debatable how effective the Act was, for any alien who could raise enough money to travel first class escaped inspection, and the statutory guarantees of asylum were generous by any modern standard. However, the very existence of the Act and its somewhat cumbrous machinery seem to have achieved some over-all numerical control over those admitted, and to that extent to have reduced the 'costs' of immigration.[2]

Additional powers of control were rushed through Parliament in one day at the outbreak of the First World War. These were contained in the Aliens Restriction Act 1914, introduced as a temporary measure for time of war or 'other occasion of imminent national danger'. At the conclusion of hostilities they were continued in force from year to year under the authority of the Aliens Restriction (Amendment) Act 1919 and the annual Expiring Laws Continuance Acts.[3] The Aliens Restriction Acts 1914 and 1919, and the Aliens Orders made thereunder, regulated the entry and expulsion of aliens until the entry into force of the Immigration Act 1971 on 1 January 1973. For most of this period the only entrants subject to control were aliens, defined by the [British Nationality and] Status of Aliens Act 1914 as persons who were not British subjects.[4] There existed then throughout the Empire one common nationality, derived from the common allegiance to the Crown. British subjects, wherever they came from, enjoyed an unrestricted right of entry into the United Kingdom until 1962.[5] Aliens, on the other hand, were not permitted to land or embark in the United Kingdom save with the leave of an immigration officer and at an approved port or place.[6]

Certain exceptions again applied to passengers in transit and alien

[1] Aliens Act 1905, section 1(2).

[2] Gainer, *The Alien Invasion*, ch. 9.

[3] The 1905 Act was repealed by the Act of 1919.

[4] Section 27. Cf. British Nationality Act 1948, section 32(1).

[5] This was not the case throughout the Commonwealth. For example, the Australian Immigration Restriction Act 1901 (No. 17) effectively reduced all immigration from South East Asia by way of a dictation test (section 3). See also *Re Munshi Singh* 6 W.W.R. 1347 (1914); *Thornton* v. *The Police* [1962] A.C. 339 (P.C.).

[6] Aliens Order 1953, Article 1(1); Cmnd. 4296, para. 3.

crewmembers,[1] but otherwise the grant of leave to land was conditional on the alien being able to maintain himself and any dependants in the United Kingdom,[2] or, if he entered to work, on condition that he was in possession of a work permit issued for engagement to a particular employer and by the appropriate authority.[3] It was further provided that leave to land might be granted subject to any conditions of which notice was given to the alien by the immigration officer.[4] Like the 1905 Act, the Aliens Orders also prescribed the grounds for exclusion, and included an additional ground for exclusion in the case of an alien arriving for the purposes of controlled employment, but without a work permit.[5] Over and above the specific grounds, a wide discretionary power was granted to immigration officers to refuse admission wherever it appeared that the alien's presence in the United Kingdom was undesirable, for example, on account of his character, conduct, or associations, or if he was a danger to the national security, or if he would not be returnable to another country.[6] This final, reserve power of decision on the question of the alien's desirability is common to the immigration laws of most States. It is still extant in the law of the United Kingdom, an area of discretion for which it is difficult to establish, with any precision, the boundaries of control.[7]

[1] Ibid., Article 2(1)(2). Cf. *Küchenmeister* v. *Home Office* [1958] 1 Q.B. 496.

[2] Aliens Order 1953, Article 4(1)(a); Cmnd. 4296, paras. 11–14.

[3] Aliens Order 1953, Article 4(1)(b); Cmnd. 4296, paras. 22–4. The 'appropriate authority' in employment matters was formerly the Ministry of Labour, and is now the Department of Employment. See Hepple, *Race, Jobs and the Law in Britain* (2nd ed., 1970), pp. 50–2 and *passim*. Work permits were generally valid for one year, but might be extended on an annual basis; after four years the restrictions were usually removed: Cmnd. 4296, para. 34. Certain permit-free categories were also admitted, e.g. doctors and dentists: Cmnd. 4296, para. 25; and there were special provisions for businessmen (ibid., paras. 28–30), and persons of independent means (ibid., paras. 31–3).

[4] Aliens Order 1953, Article 5; Cmnd. 4296, para. 5. Such conditions might limit the length of stay, for example, or require the alien to register with the police.

[5] Ibid., Article 4; Cmnd. 4296, para. 58.

[6] Cmnd. 4296, para. 59. Cf. 649 H.C. Deb., cols. 423–4.

[7] Following the enactment of the Immigration Appeals Act 1969, aliens were granted certain rights of appeal, although not all those anticipated were ever brought into force. The alien might appeal, for example, against the refusal to issue him with a visa, but not against a refusal to admit him; see Aliens (Appeals) Order 1970 (S.I. 1970 No. 151); Immigration Appeals (Notices) Regulations 1970 (S.I. 1970 No. 793); Immigration Appeals (Procedure) Rules 1970 (S.I. 1970 No. 794). See now Immigration Act 1971. See also *Annual Report of the Council on Tribunals* (1970–1), paras. 30–2; *Annual Report* for 1971–2, paras. 25, 63–5; *Annual Report* for 1972–3, paras. 52–6; *Annual Report* for 1973–4, paras. 70–2; Hepple, 'Aliens and Administrative Justice: The *Dutschke* Case', 34 M.L.R. (1971), 501.

Only in 1962 was any control over the entry of British subjects/Commonwealth citizens into the United Kingdom introduced. For many reasons, including the practical inconvenience of a labour shortage in the 1950s, the United Kingdom had stood alone among Commonwealth countries in not imposing any such restrictions. The ideal of the common status of British subjecthood was maintained, and recognized in favour of those who possessed either citizenship of the United Kingdom and Colonies or citizenship of any independent State of the Commonwealth.[1] The right of entry into the British Isles was incidental to the status of British subject,[2] but in the wake of a campaign against coloured immigration and declared fears about unresolved social problems, this right was abolished by the Commonwealth Immigrants Act 1962.

This piece of legislation drew a first distinction between citizens of the United Kingdom and Colonies and citizens of independent Commonwealth countries. But a further distinction was also made among United Kingdom citizens themselves, which depended upon whether their passports were issued by the United Kingdom Government or 'on behalf of the Government of any part of the Commonwealth outside the United Kingdom'. The holders of passports in the latter class were made subject to control.[3]

Additional restrictions were brought in by the Commonwealth Immigrants Act 1968, which was intended primarily to bring under control large numbers of United Kingdom *citizens* resident in East and Central Africa.[4] Hitherto such citizens had continued to enjoy the unrestricted right of entry into the United Kingdom by virtue of their citizenship and the fact that, after the independence of their countries of residence, their passports were issued by the United Kingdom authorities. In most cases the resident Asian population

[1] British Nationality Act 1948, section 1.

[2] *D.P.P.* v. *Bhagwan* [1972] A.C. 60.

[3] Commonwealth Immigrants Act 1962, section 1(2), (3); *R.* v. *Secretary of State, ex parte Bhurosah* [1967] 3 All E. R. 831; *Secretary of State* v. *Lakdawalla* [1972] Imm. A.R. 26; *Mamacos* v. *Secretary of State* [1972] Imm. A.R. 11; *Cheng* v. *Secretary of State* [1972] Imm. A.R. 5. For a general survey, see Bottomley and Sinclair, *Control of Commonwealth Immigration* (1970); Hepple, *Race, Jobs and the Law in Britain* (2nd ed.), pp. 19–24.

[4] Entry was to be restricted to 1,500 heads of families per annum, plus dependants. In 1971, this was raised to 3,000 'special vouchers', with an additional allocation that year of an extra 1,500: 818 H.C. Deb., col. 380. The number of vouchers has again been increased, and this may owe something to international pressure and to the various applications made to the European Commission on Human Rights, complaining about the operation of the law; see further below, pp. 163–6.

UNIV. DUNELM

did not acquire local citizenship by operation of law at independence.[1] Instead, a statutory right of option was provided, and local citizenship could be obtained by registration; but if this right were not exercised, then the laws of the United Kingdom ensured that the former national status was retained, as it were, by default.[2] Many among the Asian population preferred to retain what at the time appeared to be the more preferable status of United Kingdom citizen.[3] In the late sixties, however, local policies of 'Africanization' were accelerated, and many non-citizens found themselves unable to obtain the requisite trade licences, and, in consequence, a living.[4] In anticipation of mass immigration from East Africa, the Government of the United Kingdom decided to act.

Citizens of the United Kingdom and Colonies who held United Kingdom passports, but who had no substantial connection with that country, were immediately brought under control. 'Substantial connection' was established if the applicant for entry could show that he or she, or at least one parent or grandparent, (*a*) was born in the United Kingdom; or (*b*) was naturalized in the United Kingdom; or (*c*) became a citizen of the United Kingdom and Colonies by virtue of adoption in the United Kingdom; or (*d*) became such citizen by registration under the British Nationality Act 1948 or the British Nationality Act 1964.[5] In cases of no substantial connection the admission of United Kingdom citizens was dependent upon

[1] For a general view of the position of Asians see Ghai and Ghai, *The Asian Minorities of East and Central Africa* (Minority Rights Group, Report No. 4, 1971). See also *Whither Kenyan Asians?* (Young Fabian Pamphlet, 1969).

[2] e.g. Zambia Independence Act 1964, sections 3(4), 4; Uganda Independence Act 1962, section 2; Kenya Independence Act 1963, sections 2(3), 3; Tanganyika Independence Act 1961, section 2; Malawi Independence Act 1964, sections 2(3), 3.

[3] Ghai and Ghai, op. cit., pp. 13–17.

[4] Ibid., pp. 18–22.

[5] Commonwealth Immigrants Act 1968, section 1. The wording of condition (*d*) above excludes, for example, persons who became citizens by such registration in Kenya, Tanganyika, or Uganda before those countries became independent. The 1968 Act also removed the right of a child to join a single parent (other than a sole surviving parent), although such child would be admitted where family or other considerations made exclusion undesirable: section 2 of the Act of 1962, as amended by section 2 of the Act of 1968; Cmmd. 3566, paras. 1–4. In addition, the minimum age for admission of dependent fathers was raised to 65: Cmn. 3566, para. 5; and it was made a criminal offence to land in the United Kingdom without examination by an immigration officer: section 4A(1), (2), (4), Commonwealth Immigrants Acts 1962 and 1968. The period within which an entrant must be examined was extended from 24 hours to 28 days; see *R.* v. *Governor of Brixton Prison, ex parte Ahsan* [1969] 2 Q.B. 222; *R.* v. *Governor of Pentonville Prison, ex parte Azam* [1973] 2 W.L.R. 949 (C.A.); [1973] 2 All E.R. 765 (H.L.).

possession of a 'special quota voucher'. While there was nothing overtly discriminatory in the statute itself, the fact that exemption from control was granted to those whose parents or whose grandparents were born in the United Kingdom underscored the contemporary view that the entry of United Kingdom citizens from East Africa was a racial problem, and not a purely immigration problem.[1] Very few white settlers would be caught by these provisions, which have been repeated in the Immigration Act 1971 by the introduction of the concept of 'patriality'.

The new law, which was intended to bring together the separate regimes governing entry and residence for aliens and Commonwealth citizens, introduces no significant reforms; the immigration law of the United Kingdom is still without one essential foundation —a comprehensive, and comprehensible, law of citizenship.[2]

(2) THE IMMIGRATION ACT 1971

The Immigration Act 1971 employs the concept of 'patriality' to describe the status of those who possess the 'right of abode' in the United Kingdom and who thereby 'shall be free to come and go into and from the United Kingdom without let or hindrance except such as may be required . . . to enable their right to be established'.[3] All those who are not patrial, and who therefore do not have the

[1] In the course of debate on the Immigration Rules made under the 1971 Act, it was estimated that a 'grandparents provision' would give a right of entry to somebody, one of whose grandparents left the United Kingdom as a babe in arms in about the year 1800. It was argued that people in this category could not honestly be described as having close family ties with this country: 851 H.C. Deb., col. 600 (David Steel, M.P.). Under the Fifteenth Amendment to the Constitution of the United States there is a prohibition on the passing of laws which discriminate in the franchise and, in particular, which seek to bar Negro voters. A number of states attempted to circumvent this provision by employing a 'grandfather clause' in laws which imposed a literacy test as a condition of the right to vote. The effect of these laws was that an illiterate white was entitled to vote, because his grandfather could vote, while an illiterate Negro was barred because his grandfather would have been a slave. In *Guinn and Beal* v. *United States* 238 U.S. 347 (1915) the Supreme Court held that such clauses were contrary to the Fifteenth Amendment, which guaranteed the right to vote without distinction as to race, colour, or previous condition of servitude. On proceedings before the European Commission on Human Rights and the application of the 1968 Act, see below, pp. 163–6.

[2] Reform of the law of citizenship was announced in 1973: 849 H.C. Deb., cols. 635–4.

[3] Immigration Act 1971, section 1(1); a patrial may therefore be questioned or detained in order to establish his status; see Williams, 'Without Let or Hindrance', 123 New L.J. 605–7 and 'British Passports and the Right to Travel', 23 I.C.L.Q. (1974), 642; cf. United States law, below, p. 130.

right of abode, are subject to control and to the rules which may regulate the conditions of their entry and stay.[1]

Section 2 of the Act lays down the conditions for the acquisition of patriality.[2] This new status was intended to represent the fact of attachment to or substantial connection with the United Kingdom and, in view of this premiss, it is perhaps not surprising to find that it excludes that same class of United Kingdom citizens which was distinguished by the 1968 Act. But patriality does not only divide and exclude among United Kingdom citizens; it goes much farther and extends the right of abode to numbers of the citizens of independent Commonwealth countries who, previously, were caught by the 1962 and 1968 provisions.[3] For the most part these newly qualified entrants are to be found in the independent countries of the 'old', or white Commonwealth, such as Canada, Australia, New Zealand, and even South Africa. A necessary consequence of patriality in its application to the citizens of these countries is that distinctions must be drawn among them also. For example, a New Zealander of 'British stock' might qualify as a patrial, whereas it is most unlikely that a New Zealander of Maori extraction would so qualify.[4]

For those who do not benefit from the status of patrial, the Immigration Act makes it unlawful to enter the United Kingdom without leave. It is further provided that such leave to enter or remain may be either for a limited or for an indefinite period.[5] If such leave to

[1] Immigration Act 1971, section 1 (4). Four sets of Immigration Rules were laid before Parliament on 25 January 1973 under section 3(2) of the Act; these had been revised in the light of Parliament's rejection of the first set of Rules on 22 November 1972. The new rules revert to the primary distinction between Commonwealth citizens on the one hand, and E.E.C. and other non-Commonwealth nationals on the other hand. See *Statement of Immigration Rules for Control on Entry* (Commonwealth Citizens) 1973 H.C. No. 79; (E.E.C. and other Non-Commonwealth Nationals) 1973 H.C. No. 81; *Statement of Immigration Rules for Control after Entry* (Commonwealth Citizens) 1973 H.C. No. 80; (E.C.C. and other Non-Commonwealth Nationals) 1973 H.C. No. 82. A motion to disapprove the Rules as laid was negatived on 21 February 1973 by 283 votes to 240: 851 H.C. Deb., cols. 577–646.

[2] See above, pp. 13–4.

[3] Macdonald, *The New Immigration Law* (1972), pp. 35–6. 'United Kingdom ancestry', expressed in terms of the grandparent clause, is an additional ground for privileged treatment under the Immigration Rules for those who are not quite patrials: 1973 H.C. No. 79, paras. 27–8.

[4] See the views expressed by Lord Porritt, former Governor-General of New Zealand, in debate in the House of Lords on the Immigration Bill in 1971: 339 H.L. Deb., cols. 548–51; see also 851 H.C. Deb., cols. 580–1, 591–3, 604–5, 618–19. 626–7, 630–2.

[5] Immigration Act 1971, section 3(1). To enter without leave is punishable on sum-

enter is limited, then it may also be made subject to conditions, for example, restricting employment or requiring registration with the police.[1] The power to give or refuse leave to enter the United Kingdom is to be exercised by immigration officers, and the power to give leave to remain or vary the duration of stay or the conditions of entry, by the Secretary of State.[2] The Immigration Appeals Tribunal and the adjudicators provided for by the Immigration Appeals Act 1969 are continued under the new Act, and members of the Tribunal are appointed by the Lord Chancellor, adjudicators by the Secretary of State.[3]

Although it is the Immigration Act which lays down the basic principles of control, it is to the immigration rules that one must turn in order to understand the working of these principles in any given context. The statute anticipates that the rules made will regulate the admission and stay of persons coming for employment, for study, as visitors, or as dependants.[4] For these and other purposes, the Secretary of State may take account of citizenship or nationality,[5] and this has enabled the rules to be framed with some regard for the United Kingdom's obligations as a member of the E.E.C.[6]

mary conviction with a fine of not more than £200 or with imprisonment for six months or with both such fine and imprisonment: section 24(1)(a). There is an extended time limit for prosecutions, which may be tried if an information is laid within six months of the commission of the offence, or if it is laid within three years of the commission of the offence and not more than two months after the date certified by a chief officer of police to be the date on which evidence sufficient to justify proceedings came to the notice of an officer of his police force: sections 24(3) and 28(1). Police constables or immigration officers are empowered to arrest without warrant anyone who has, or who there is reasonable cause to suspect has committed such an offence: section 24 (2).

[1] Ibid., section 3(1)(c). Under the current Rules, registration with the police may only be required of non-Commonwealth nationals, although this could be changed in the future: 1973 H.C. No. 81, paras. 56–7. See also section 4(3) and The Immigration (Registration with Police) Regulations 1972 (S.I. 1972 No. 1758); and section 4(4) and The Immigration (Hotel Records) Order 1972 (S.I. 1972 No. 1689).

[2] Immigration Act 1971, section 4(1); Sch. 2, para. 1. The Secretary of State is also empowered to provide for the regulation of a variety of other topics by statutory instrument.

[3] Ibid., section 12; Sch. 5.

[4] Immigration Act 1971, section 1(4). The status of the Rules, whether as 'rules of practice' only or 'rules of law' is somewhat uncertain. See section 19(1)(a)(i); cf. per Roskill L. J. in *R.* v. *Chief Immigration Officer, ex parte Bibi* [1976] 1 W.L.R. 979, 985.

[5] Ibid., section 3(2). *N.B.* section 3(7) which empowers the Secretary of State by Order in Council to prohibit or restrict the embarkation of non-patrial foreign nationals as a measure of retaliation for restrictions imposed on United Kingdom citizens seeking to leave the countries of which those non-patrials are nationals.

[6] See further below, pp. 119–20.

(*a*) *Pre-entry Procedures*

A patrial may enter the United Kingdom without leave, and to that extent he is not bound to undergo any form of examination abroad, although in some circumstances he may need a 'certificate of patriality' as proof of his right of abode.[1] For non-patrials, however, the documentary requirements have been tightened up. Any non-patrial who now comes to settle in the United Kingdom must possess an 'entry clearance' in the form of a visa, or an entry certificate, or a Home Office 'letter of consent', the precise document depending on his national status.[2]

For some time visas have been, and still are, required by the nationals of most East European countries, some Asian and African countries, and now Cuba.[3] They are also needed by stateless persons and other holders of non-national travel documents, for example, refugees.[4] The Home Office 'letter of consent' is an innovation; it is not compulsory except for those coming for settlement, but otherwise it is available to any non-visa foreign national who wishes to ascertain in advance whether he is admissible to the United Kingdom.[5] Finally, a non-patrial United Kingdom citizen who holds a United Kingdom passport must produce either a special voucher or an entry clearance in lieu. If he arrives without such a document, his exclusion is mandatory,[6] and it is this provision in particular which

[1] Immigration Act 1971, section 3(9); 1973 H.C. No. 79, para. 4. Such certificates may be issued by a British Government representative abroad or directly, on application to the Home Office. A woman who claims patriality by virtue of marriage to a United Kingdom citizen is not obliged to apply for a certificate abroad: *R.* v. *Secretary of State, ex parte Phansopkar* [1975] 3 All E.R. 497.

[2] Immigration Act 1971, section 33(1). E.E.C. Nationals are exempt: 1973 H.C. No. 81, paras. 49–54. Under earlier law, entry certificates were compulsory only for Commonwealth wives and children under 16: Immigration Appeals Act 1969, section 20.

[3] For the full list, see Appendix to 1973 H.C. No. 81.

[4] 1973 H.C. No. 81, para. 8. Refugees who hold such travel documents issued by States which have signed the 1959 European Convention on the Abolition of Visas for Refugees (E.T.S., No. 31) do not require visas if coming for visits of three months or less: ibid., footnote to para. 8. See above, pp. 42–4.

[5] 1973 H.C. No. 81, para. 8.

[6] 1973 H.C. No. 79, para. 38: 'such passenger *is* to be refused leave to enter'. In *Shah* v. *Secretary of State* [1972] Imm. A.R. 56 the Immigration Appeals Tribunal held that the method of issue of special vouchers in East Africa was outside the appeals system and under the control of the Foreign and Commonwealth Office. In other cases an appeal can be brought against the refusal to issue any entry clearance, whether visa, entry certificate, or other document which is evidence of a person's eligibility for entry into the United Kingdom: Immigration Act 1971, sections 13(2), 33(1). Cf. Immigration Appeals Act 1969, section 24(1).

accounts for the practice of 'shuttlecocking', that is, continually deporting those without proper documents to their point of embarkation.[1]

So far consideration has been given only to those documents which are required by passengers coming for settlement in the United Kingdom, and by the dependants of such passengers or of persons already settled. This does not include what is perhaps the most important category of entrants, namely, those coming to work. Under the earlier legislation, work permits were issued to aliens, employment vouchers to Commonwealth immigrants. Work permits were subject to a number of restrictions, and were usually tied to a specific job with a specific employer and for a specified time.[2] The numbers issued were entirely a matter for the Ministry of Labour or the Department of Employment. Employment vouchers for Commonwealth citizens, on the other hand, although restricted to a maximum of 8,500 in 1965,[3] did not carry the same restrictions as work permits.[4] A Commonwealth citizen who entered with an employment voucher had an automatic right to settle,[5] while the alien was obliged to seek renewal of his permit from year to year and enjoyed no such right.

The Immigration Act now imposes on all non-patrials subject to the requirement of a work permit the same uniform restrictions as previously applied only to aliens. Any passenger subject to control who comes to the United Kingdom to take employment is to be mandatorily excluded if he does not have a work permit, unless he comes within one of the exempted categories.[6] The holder of a cur-

[1] 1973 H.C. No. 79, para. 40.

[2] Aliens Order 1953, Article 4(1)(b); the maximum time was twelve months, but this could be extended.

[3] None had in fact been issued since September 1964; see Hepple, *Race, Jobs and the Law in Britain* (2nd ed.), pp. 19–24.

[4] But an employment voucher was mandatory for a Commonwealth citizen wishing to enter the United Kingdom 'for the purpose of taking up or looking for employment': Cmnd. 4298, para. 28. In *Baldacchino* v. *Secretary of State* [1972] Imm. A.R. 14 the appellant held an entry certificate endorsed 'visitor'. The Tribunal held that he was rightly excluded on the basis of evidence that his secondary purpose in coming was to look for employment. A work permit is not included in the statutory definition of 'entry clearance' (above, p. 106 n. 2) and there is no appeal against refusal of issue: *Latiff* v. *Secretary of State* [1972] Imm. A.R. 76; Immigration Appeals Act 1969, section 24 (1); Immigration Act 1971, sections 13(2), 33(1).

[5] Commonwealth Immigrants Act 1962, section 2(3)(a). He might be deported only during the first five years, after conviction.

[6] 1973 H.C. No. 79, para. 25; 1973 H.C. No. 81, para. 23. A work permit does not exempt the holder from complying with visa requirements. See also 1973 H.C. No. 79,

rent work permit is normally to be admitted for the period specified in the permit, subject to conditions permitting him to change his employment only with the permission of the Department of Employment.[1] Work permits are issued by the Department in respect of a specific post with a specific employer,[2] and considerable governmental control is thus retained over the movements of the migrant work force.

(*b*) *Procedure on Arrival*

Only non-patrials require leave to land in the United Kingdom, but the Immigration Act expressly declares that it shall lie on the person who claims patriality to prove his entitlement.[3] Immigration officers are empowered to examine any person arriving in the United Kingdom, in order to determine whether he is patrial, whether leave to land is to be granted to a non-patrial and, if so, on what conditions.[4] In the course of any such examination, every person is obliged to furnish the immigration officer with whatever information may be required to establish his identity, nationality, etc.[5] For many patrials there will be no particular problems, and a certificate of patriality will only generally be required in the case of someone who claims the right of abode other than under section 2(1)(a) or (b) of the Act or by virtue of marriage to a man to whom section 2(1)(a) or (b) applies.[6] This provision, however, entails further conse-

paras. 37, 39–46; 1973 H.C. No. 81, paras. 33, 34–41. On the permit-free categories, see below, p. 111.

[1] 1973 H.C. No. 79, para. 26; 1973 H.C. No. 81, para. 24.

[2] 1973 H.C. No. 79, para. 25: 1973 H.C. No. 81, para. 23. A worker may apply for an extension of stay beyond the first maximum of twelve months. Such extension 'may' be granted if the worker is still engaged in the employment specified in the permit or in other employment approved by the Department of Employment, and the employer confirms that he wishes to continue to employ him: 1973 H.C. No. 80, para. 19; 1973 H.C. No. 82, para. 17. Cf. the provisions in favour of E.E.C. nationals, paras. 32–9; The Immigration (Revocation of Employment Restrictions) Order 1972 (S.I. 1972 No. 1647).

[3] Immigration Act 1971, section 3(8).

[4] Ibid., section 4; Sch. 2, para. 2; see also para. 3 for similar powers in respect of departing passengers. Detention pending examination may be ordered: para. 16.

[5] Ibid., Sch. 2, para. 4.

[6] Ibid., section 3(9); 1973 H.C. No. 79, para. 4. Section 2(1) (a), (b) declares to be patrial those who have acquired United Kingdom citizenship through birth, adoption, naturalization, or registration in the United Kingdom, either in their own right or through a parent. In October 1971 it was stated that both entry certificates and certificates of patriality would probably take the form of a stamp in the passport: 324 H.L. Deb., col. 430.

quences for the holders of United Kingdom passports. The Immigration Rules provide that a passenger holding a passport issued in the United Kingdom or Ireland is to be admitted freely without proof of patriality, unless the passport carries an endorsement to the effect that the bearer is subject to immigration control.[1] Passports issued to United Kingdom citizens in the United Kingdom will now distinguish between patrials and non-patrials, although it is provided that a citizen of the United Kingdom and Colonies who holds a United Kingdom passport, wherever issued, and who satisfies the immigration officer that he has previously been settled in the United Kingdom, should be freely admitted.[2]

When considering an applicant's case for admission, immigration officers are under a duty to act fairly and honestly, letting the applicant know the impressions he has made and giving him a fair opportunity to rebut any unfavourable impression. To this limited extent only do the rules of natural justice apply, and before the introduction of a statutory appeals system it was difficult successfully to challenge the actions of immigration officers in the courts. In one case,[3] Lord Denning drew a distinction between two decisions involving actions by Commonwealth immigrants.[4] In his Lordship's view, the restricted rules of natural justice applied only in the one case where the immigrant had a right to enter if he satisfied certain conditions. In the second case there was no such right, but admission might be granted in the complete discretion of the immigration officer. Natural justice did not apply at all and the authorities were under no duty either to give reasons for exclusion or to permit an opportunity to make representations. The immigrant from the Commonwealth was in the same position as the alien, seeking the privilege of entry which was within 'the licence of the Crown'.[5] The statutory appeals

[1] 1973 H.C. No. 79, para. 5. United Kingdom passports issued after 1 January 1973 indicate whether or not the holder has the right of abode in the United Kingdom. Holders of passports issued before that date are entitled to readmission unless the passports carry endorsements which show that the bearer is subject to immigration control. The bearer of an unendorsed passport issued before 1 January 1973 who intends to take advantage of the free movement provisions of the E.E.C. may apply for the endorsement 'Holder has the right of abode in the United Kingdom': see Passport Office Leaflet P1.

[2] 1973 H.C. No. 79, para. 5; Immigration Act 1971, section 1(2).

[3] *Schmidt* v. *Secretary of State* [1969] 2 Ch. 149.

[4] *Re H.K.* (*an infant*) [1967] 2 Q.B. 617, and *R.* v. *Secretary of State*, *ex parte Avtar Singh* (1967, unreported), cited by Lord Denning in [1969] 2 Ch. 149, at p. 170.

[5] See also *Re A* (*an infant*) [1968] 2 All E. R. 145; *Padmore* v. *Secretary of State* [1972] Imm. A.R. 1; *Secretary of State* v. *Alibhai* [1972] Imm. A.R. 127.

system has gone some way towards remedying this situation, but even here the courts have on occasion carried over the presumption of procedural incapacity.[1]

As is so often the case, possession of an entry clearance may facilitate the holder's admission, but is itself no guarantee; it stands merely as evidence of eligibility for entry. However, in most cases, admission will only be refused if the immigration officer is satisfied that (*a*) false representations were made or material facts concealed for the purpose of obtaining the clearance, whether or not to the holder's knowledge; or (*b*) if a change of circumstances since issue has removed the basis of the holder's claim to be admitted.[2] The holder of an entry clearance is also liable to be excluded on the general grounds of inadmissibility, such as medical reasons, restricted returnability, criminal record, the existence of a deportation order against him, or if exclusion would be conducive to the public good. In examining the holder of an entry clearance the immigration officer is entitled to act on reasonable inferences and any other information available to him, although there continues to be a limited presumption in favour of eligibility.[3]

Similar provisions apply to the examination of the holders of work permits. Again, the presumption is in favour of eligibility for admission, but the immigration officer may nevertheless order exclusion if his examination reveals good reason for doing so, for example, in the case of false representations made to obtain the permit, or if the holder's true age puts him outside the limits for employment, or if the holder does not intend to do, or is incapable of doing, the employment specified.[4] A passenger who comes for employment without a work permit is mandatorily excluded, unless he comes within one of the permit-free categories, or benefits from the privileges granted to those with 'United Kingdom ancestry' and to those who come on 'working holidays'. The permit-free categories are set

[1] *R.* v. *Chief Immigration Officer, London (Heathrow) Airport, ex parte Hazari*, reported in *The Times*, 25 Nov. 1975.

[2] 1973 H.C. No. 79, para. 12; 1973 H.C. No. 81, para. 10.

[3] 1973 H.C. No. 79, para. 13; 1973 H.C. No. 81, para. 11. The holder of an entry clearance who is refused admission can appeal against that decision without first having to leave the country.

[4] 1973 H.C. No. 79, para. 26; 1973 H.C. No. 81, para. 24. The immigration officer has a discretion to admit a passenger whose work permit is out of date if satisfied that circumstances beyond his control prevented his timely arrival and that the job is still open: ibid.

out at length in the Immigration Rules,[1] and include ministers of religion, doctors, dentists, private servants of members of diplomatic missions,[2] teachers and others on approved schemes, seamen under contract to join a ship in British waters,[3] and various others. Privileges in employment are granted to those with United Kingdom ancestry, and an entry clearance is granted expressly for this purpose. No work permit is required in addition, and those who qualify under this head are given indefinite leave to enter.[4] Commonwealth citizens on working holidays are permitted to take employment 'incidental to their holiday', and they may be admitted for a period of twelve months, extendable within a maximum of five years.[5]

Passengers may also be admitted as businessmen, as persons of independent means, or as self-employed. Businessmen who have secured an entry clearance are to be admitted for a period not exceeding twelve months, while those without an entry clearance are to be admitted first for two months, but with the prospect of extension. In both cases, any leave to enter will be granted subject to a condition restricting the freedom to take employment.[6] In order to prevent the use of this category to circumvent the controls, it is provided that the applicant for an entry clearance shall show, if he is joining an established business, that he will be investing his money in it, that he will receive an adequate share of the profits, and that he will be able to bear his share of the liabilities.[7] If he intends to start his own business, then he must present evidence of sufficient funds. In neither case is it permitted for the applicant to supplement his income by additional employment for which a work permit would otherwise be required.[8]

A passenger of independent means is to be admitted if he is in a position to maintain himself and his dependants indefinitely in the

[1] 1973 H.C. No. 79, para. 29; 1973 H.C. No. 81, para. 25.

[2] See the Immigration (Exemption from Control) Order 1972 (S.I. 1972 No. 1613).

[3] On entry by crewmembers, see below, pp. 156–9.

[4] 1973 H.C. No. 79, para. 27.

[5] Ibid., para. 28; see also 851 H.C. Deb., cols. 596–7.

[6] 1973 H.C. No. 79, paras. 31–2; 1973 H.C. No. 81, paras. 27–8.

[7] 1973 H.C. No. 79, para. 33; 1973 H.C. No. 81, para. 29. See *Pritpal Singh* v. *Secretary of State* [1972] Imm. A.R. 154; *Secretary of State* v. *Stawczykowska*, [1972] Imm. A.R. 220. Cf. *Secretary of State* v. *Martin*, [1972] Imm. A.R. 146 and note the comment of the Queen's Bench Division, ibid., p. 275 f.

[8] 1973 H.C. No. 79, para. 34; 1973 H.C. No. 81, para. 30. The Immigration Rules make no express reference to a class of 'treaty aliens' or 'treaty investors'; see below, pp. 192–5.

United Kingdom without working, and he may satisfy the immigration officer on this count by producing evidence of funds available.[1] Where an entry clearance has been obtained in advance, leave to land may be for twelve months, and for two months in other cases. In *Randhawa* v. *Secretary of State* the Immigration Appeals Tribunal held that it was not permissible to consider the appellant's own means in conjunction with the support which he received from partial dependence on his family, in this case the provision of free board and lodging. In the circumstances, the claim to remain permanently in the United Kingdom was rejected.[2] Similar provisions apply in respect of self-employed persons, such as artists and writers, who may also be admitted if the immigration officer is satisfied that they can maintain themselves and their dependants without engaging in controlled employment.[3]

Wives and children under 18 of any of the above categories may enter and be admitted for the same period as the passenger in whose behalf they claim admission. If the latter is prohibited from taking employment, then a similar condition is to be imposed on the dependants. No further dependants may be admitted until that passenger is 'settled' in the United Kingdom within the meaning of the Act, but it is expressly provided that no dependants at all shall be admitted in behalf of seasonal workers or of those admitted for resident domestic employment.[4] Wives and children must also fulfil the requirements of further rules applicable to the dependants of those admitted for settlement.[5] In every case apart from that of a Commonwealth citizen who is patrial or who was settled in the United Kingdom on 1 January 1973, the person concerned must be able and willing to support his dependants without recourse to public funds. The Immigration Rules do not expressly recognize the problems which may arise in the case of polygamous marriages, and the word 'wife' is not qualified in any way. It is declared, however, that a woman who has been living in permanent association with a man has no claim to enter, but that she may be admitted after due consideration has been given to local customs and traditions tending to estab-

[1] 1973 H.C. No. 79, para. 35; 1973 H.C. No. 81, para. 31.

[2] [1972] Imm. A.R. 158.

[3] 1973 H.C. No. 79, para. 36; 1973 H.C. No. 81, para. 32. The way is again made easier for those who have obtained entry clearances in advance.

[4] 1973 H.C. No. 79, para. 37; 1973 H.C. No. 81, para. 33. See also Macdonald, *The New Immigration Law*, pp. 66–71.

[5] 1973 H.C. No. 79, paras. 39–46; 1973 H.C. No. 81, paras. 34–41. In all cases dependants seeking admission must come provided with an entry clearance: ibid.

lish the permanency of the association.[1] This might suggest that a similar discretion would apply in regard to polygamous marriages. The significance of such marriages in other contexts tends to vary with the circumstances. For example, there is no title to benefit in matters of national insurance, industrial injuries, and family allowances in the case of a marriage which is actually polygamous.[2] On the other hand, in the case of a claim for supplementary benefits, provision for a man's requirements takes account of and includes any wife living with him and of any of their children in the household.[3] Since 1972 English law has extended recognition to foreign marriages valid in form under the *lex loci celebrationis* and, in respect of capacity, under the law of domicil.[4] For the purposes of entry into the United Kingdom, it is apparent that the word 'wife' must include a party to a polygamous marriage which is thus recognized. In one case no doubt was raised on this point, the only question being whether the husband had acquired a domicil of choice in England so as to render him incapable of contracting a valid polygamous marriage.[5]

As a general rule, children under 18 are entitled to settle in the United Kingdom with their parents, but interpretation of the rules in the past has produced inconsistency and hardship.[6] Difficulties have arisen over the proof of age, a problem particularly apparent in the case of children arriving from countries with insufficiently developed systems of registration. In *Aftab Miah* v. *Secretary of State* the Immigration Appeals Tribunal came face to face with the problems of assessment of age on the basis of X-ray photographs.[7] It was presented with different determinations from four equally highly qualified doctors and, in the end, concluded that the appellant must be accepted, 'on the balance of probabilities', as the son of the sponsor.

Further problems arise in cases where a child seeks admission to

[1] 1973 H.C. No. 79, para. 42; 1973 H.C. No. 81, para. 37.

[2] As opposed to a marriage which is only potentially polygamous at the time of a claim.

[3] 845 H.C. Deb. (Written Answers), cols. 277–8.

[4] Matrimonial Proceedings (Polygamous Marriages) Act 1972.

[5] *Afza Mussarat* [1972] Imm. A.R. 45; *Ishiodu* [1975] Imm. A.R. 56.

[6] The new rules do not differ appreciably or materially from those previously applicable: see now 1973 H.C. No. 79, paras. 43–4; 1973 H.C. No. 81, paras. 38–9.

[7] [1972] Imm. A.R. 185. See also *Iqbal Haque* v. *Entry Certificate Officer, Dacca* [1974] Imm. A.R. 51, where the Tribunal took into account environmental factors in Bangladesh as a reason for rejecting Western standards in assessing age by reference to bone growth.

join one parent only. Consideration must then be given to the question of who has had the 'sole responsibility' for bringing up the child, and whether there are family or other circumstances which make exclusion undesirable. Appeals on the first point show little consistency, and it is not clear how the criterion of 'sole responsibility' is to be satisfied. Sometimes the determination will be based on evidence of money sent for the support of the child abroad, and sometimes on evidence of the absence of the other parent. None of these factors, however, is conclusive, and a decision may well go against a child who is being satisfactorily cared for by a grandparent or other relative.[1] As regards the second point, it has been held by the Tribunal that the conditions under which the child is living in the home country are not to be weighed against the conditions available for the child in the United Kingdom. The situation in this country is only to be taken into account if the conditions overseas show that exclusion is undesirable.[2]

By contrast, the position of the children, wives, and other dependants of nationals of E.E.C. States is considerably better. For example, the family of the E.E.C. entrant, which is entitled to enter with him as of right,[3] is to be regarded as consisting not only of his wife, but also his children under 21, other children if still dependent, and dependent parents and grandparents.[4] The general rule in non-E.E.C. cases is that children over 18 must qualify for admission in their own right. Thus, while in certain circumstances an unmarried and fully dependent son under 21 or an unmarried daughter under 21 may be admitted if the whole family is settled in the United Kingdom or is being admitted for settlement, there is no right in the matter.[5]

[1] Compare *Emmanuel* v. *Secretary of State* [1972] Imm. A.R. 69 with *Martin* v. *Secretary of State* [1972] Imm. 69; see also *McGillivary* [1972] Imm. A.R. 63; *Williams* [1972] Imm. A.R. 207; *Pusey* [1972] Imm. A.R. 240; *Sloley* v. *Entry Certificate Officer, Kingston* [1973] Imm. A.R. 54; *Bovell* v. *E.C.O., Georgetown* [1973] Imm. A.R. 37; *Manzar Alam* v. *E.C.O., Lahore* [1973] Imm. A.R. 79; *Pinnock* v. *E.C.O., Kingston* [1974] Imm. A.R. 22; *Ravat* v. *E.C.O., Bombay* [1974] Imm. A.R. 79; *E.C.O., Kingston* v. *Holmes* [1975] Imm. A.R. 20; *Eugene* v. *E.C.O., Bridgetown* [1975] Imm. A.R. 111.

[2] *Howard* v. *Secretary of State* [1972] Imm. A.R. 93, as applied in *Secretary of State* v *Campbell*, ibid., p. 115. In *Campbell* the adjudicator's decision in favour of two Jamaican children against the refusal of entry certificates to join their mother was upheld on the facts.

[3] See Regulation 1612/68, Article 10(1).

[4] 1973 H.C. No. 81, paras. 53–4.

[5] Cf. *Patel* v. *Secretary of State* [1972] Imm. A.R. 59; *Tarsem Singh* v. *Secretary of State* [1972] Imm. A.R. 265. Compare *Pereira* v. *Secretary of State* [1972] Imm. A.R. 224.

Provision is also made for the admission of certain other dependants of persons settled in the United Kingdom, including parents, grandparents, and distressed relatives.[1] In addition, leave to land may be granted to those who wish to enter the country in order to get married, although formerly the rules looked more favourably upon women who sought to enter, than upon men.[2] The latter were only granted permission to enter for settlement if a substantial degree of hardship would be caused to the woman in having to live outside the United Kingdom in order to be with her husband.[3] Here the law struck at the woman who was herself a patrial or settled in the country, and the Government maintained the view that 'international custom' in immigration matters placed responsibility with the head of the household, that is, with the husband.[4] After much pressure, the rules were finally changed in 1974, although the right of entry now conferred on the husband or fiancé is not an absolute right.[5]

Those already settled in the United Kingdom on 1 January 1973 are given a limited protection under the Act,[6] but other residents not so 'settled' are less well off. Under section 3(4) of the Act a person's leave to enter and remain in the country lapses on his going to any State or territory outside the common travel area, whether or not he lands there. The Immigration Rules further provide that a person whose stay in the United Kingdom was subject to a time limit and who returns after a temporary absence abroad has no claim to be admitted as a returning resident.[7]

[1] 1973 H.C. No. 79, paras. 45–6; 1973 H.C. No. 81, paras. 40–1. Relatives may qualify if they are isolated, i.e. living alone with no relatives to turn to, and distressed, i.e. living at a standard substantially below that of their own country; entry is only exceptionally granted to those under 65. See further, 851 H.C. Deb., col. 594.

[2] 1973 H.C. No. 79, paras. 48–50; 1973 H.C. No. 81, paras. 43–5.

[3] *Kuldip Singh* v. *Secretary of State* [1972] Imm. A.R. 211; *Ahmet* [1973] Imm. A.R. 1; *Sadhu Singh* v. *E.C.O., New Delhi* [1973] Imm. A.R. 67; *Papayianni* [1974] Imm. A.R. 1; *Constantinides* [1974] Imm. A.R. 30; *Papadopoulous* [1974] Imm. A.R. 46.

[4] See further below, pp. 165–6.

[5] Cmnd. 5715–18; *Vasiljevic* [1975] Imm. A.R. 100, [1976] Imm. A.R. 44.

[6] Immigration Act 1971, section 1(2), (5); *Shahbaz Khan* [1972] Imm. A.R. 172; *Tosir Khan* [1974] Imm. A.R. 55; *Hashim* [1974] Imm. A.R. 75; *Costa* [1974] Imm. A.R. 69; *Joshi* [1975] Imm. A.R. 1; *R.* v. *Secretary of State, ex parte Mughal* [1973] 3 All E. R. 797; *Bashir* v. *Immigration Officer, Dover* [1976] Imm. A.R. 96.

[7] 1973 H.C. No. 79, para. 53; 1973 H.C. No. 81, para. 48. There are a few exceptions to this rule; section 3(4) provides that leave to enter or remain shall not lapse if the person concerned returns to the United Kingdom in circumstances in which he is not required to obtain leave to enter: see the examples in The Immigration (Exemption from Control) Order 1972 (S.I. 1972 No. 1613), Article 5.

Finally, in addition to the regulations which govern those coming for settlement, express provision is made for those who seek only temporary admission, for example, as visitors,[1] students,[2] or 'au pair girls'.[3]

(*c*) *General Grounds for Exclusion*

A passenger who does not fall within any of the admissible categories considered above is to be refused entry,[4] but even if he does so qualify, leave to enter may still be denied on any of a number of additional grounds set out in the Immigration Rules.[5] In each case the authority of a Chief Immigration Officer must always be obtained before a final decision to exclude is taken. However, any passenger, whether he holds an entry clearance or not, may be refused admission for medical reasons, on the basis of criminal record, because he is subject to a deportation order, or because his exclusion is 'conducive to the public good'. The general rule is that no appeal may be entered against exclusion while the passenger remains in the United Kingdom, unless he is the holder of an entry clearance or is named in a current work permit.[6]

Medical examinations may be required of passengers, and medical inspectors are appointed by the Secretary of State.[7] Normally, any passenger who intends to remain in the United Kingdom longer than six months will be examined, as also any passenger who appears to be mentally or physically abnormal, or who mentions medical treatment as a reason for his visit.[8] The medical inspector may advise that admission is undesirable for medical reasons, in which case the

[1] 1973 H.C. No. 79, paras. 15–17; 1973 H.C. No. 81, paras. 13–15.

[2] 1973 H.C. No. 79, paras. 16–20; 1973 H.C. No. 81, paras. 18–22; *Amusu* [1974] Imm. A.R. 16; *Kpoma* [1973] Imm. A.R. 25; *Juma* [1974] Imm. A.R. 96; *Perween Khan* [1972] Imm. A.R. 245, 268; *Khan (S.G.H.)* [1975] Imm. A.R. 26, 64.

[3] 1973 H.C. No. 79, paras. 23–4; 1973 H.C. No. 81, paras. 21–2; *Ramjane* [1973] Imm. A.R. 84. The United Kingdom provisions are in accordance with the European Agreement on Au Pair Placement 1969; see Articles 2, 3, 4, and the *Explanatory Report* (Council of Europe, 1972). For criticisms of the present state of au pair arrangements, see 851 H.C. Deb., cols. 620–1.

[4] Only limited recognition is given to the 'right of asylum': 1973 H.C. No. 79, para. 54; 1973 H.C. No. 81, para. 55; see further below, pp. 137–42.

[5] 1973 H.C. No. 79, paras. 55–66; 1973 H.C. No. 81, paras. 58–68. Admission may also be refused to a passenger who produces an unacceptable passport or travel document; see above, pp. 25–9.

[6] Immigration Act 1971, section 13(3).

[7] Immigration Act 1971, Sch. 2, para. 1(2); Macdonald, *The New Immigration Law*, pp. 72–5, 77–80.

[8] 1973 H.C. No. 79, para. 58; 1973 H.C. No. 81, para. 60; Immigration Act 1971, Sch. 2, para. 2(2), (3).

immigration officer 'should' refuse leave to enter, unless there are strong compassionate circumstances.[1] The immigration officer is also required to take account of specified diseases or conditions brought to his attention by the medical inspector which might interfere with the passenger's ability to support himself and any dependants. There is no published list of undesirable diseases or conditions, although presumably guidance is given in the unpublished instructions from the Secretary of State. Returning residents and the wives and children under 18 of persons settled in the United Kingdom are not to be refused admission on medical grounds, but the immigration officer is empowered to require further examination or necessary treatment after admission.[2]

Exclusion on the ground of criminal record may be ordered in the case of any passenger other than the wife or child under 18 of a person settled in the United Kingdom, where that passenger has been convicted in any country, including the United Kingdom of an extradition crime. The immigration officer has a discretion to grant leave to enter where this is justified by strong compassionate reasons.[3]

A passenger currently subject to a deportation order is mandatorily excluded and if he wishes to make representations in the matter, he must first return to his own country from where he may apply for revocation of the order. If the revocation is refused, then he will generally have a right of appeal.[4]

Finally, there is a general discretionary power to order exclusion on the ground that this is conducive to the public good. Any passenger, other than the wife or child under 18 of a person settled in the United Kingdom, may be so excluded where (*a*) the Secretary of State has personally directed exclusion; or (*b*) from information available to the immigration officer it seems right to refuse leave to

[1] Admission may be refused where the passenger declines to undergo medical examination. As interpreted, the word 'should' in the Rules implies an imperative: *Al-Tuwaidji* v. *Chief Immigration Officer*, *London* (*Heathrow*) *Airport* [1974] Imm. A.R. 34; *E.C.O.*, *Bombay* v. *Sacha* [1973] Imm. A.R. 5.

[2] 1973 H.C. No. 79, para. 60; 1973 H.C. No. 81, para. 62; Immigration Act 1971, Sch. 2, para. 7.

[3] 1973 H.C. No. 79, para. 61; 1973 H.C. No. 81, para. 63; offences of a political character are not, therefore, to be taken into account. Cf. *R.* v. *Governor of Brixton Prison*, *ex parte Soblen* [1963] 2 Q.B. 243; below, pp. 226–8. On appreciation of compassionate grounds, see *Langridge* [1972] Imm. A.R. 38; *Liberto* [1975] Imm. A.R. 61.

[4] 1973 H.C. No. 79, para. 62; 1973 H.C. No. 81, para. 64. Cf. *Dervish* [1972] Imm. A.R. 48; *Sanusi* [1975] Imm. A.R. 114.

enter, for example, in the light of the passenger's character, conduct, or associations.[1] Where exclusion or the refusal of an entry clearance is ordered personally by the Secretary of State, 'and not by a person acting under his authority', the individual affected is barred from any appeal within the statutory system, whether he is in the United Kingdom or abroad.[2] It is clearly intended that this power of the Secretary of State will be exercised primarily in 'security' and political cases, and it is apparent that appeals against exclusion simply on the basis of a man's character or associations were more acceptable to the government of the day. Nevertheless, it may be that recourse to the courts is still open. Unlike the law of the United States, no express mention is made of the alternative remedies, but in other contexts, including deportation and the removal of illegal immigrants, the courts have declared their competence to go behind the orders in question to see whether the statutory powers have been abused.[3] The practical difficulties, however, are considerable: a very heavy burden of proof will lie on the individual affected, and in many cases he will have been removed from the jurisdiction and beyond the writ of habeas corpus. But if manifest abuse could be shown, then without doubt the courts would be free to intervene.

(*d*) *Rights of Appeal*

Where a passenger is excluded, steps may be taken to secure his removal and, as a general rule, he will be returned to that State in which he embarked for the United Kingdom.[4]

First, however, he must be handed a written notice of the decision, informing him of the reasons for the decision and indicating his

[1] 1973 H.C. No. 79, para. 63; 1973 H.C. No. 81, para. 65. Note also the very wide powers of inquiry and examination granted to the immigration officer, including the power to search for and detain documentary evidence, and the duty incumbent on the passenger to provide information: Immigration Act 1971, Sch. 2, para. 4. Cf. *Rice* v. *Connolly* [1966] 3 W.L.R. 17. A passenger who is detained under Sch. 2, paras. 16 and 18 pending a decision on his admissibility may apply for bail after seven days: 1973 H.C. No. 79, para. 66; 1973 H.C. No. 81, para. 68; Immigration Act 1971, Sch. 2, paras. 21–5.

[2] Immigration Act 1971, section 13(5). Compare 'security' exclusions in the United States, below, pp. 126–8. Cf. Immigration Appeals Act 1969, section 2 (1), now repealed.

[3] *R.* v. *Governor of Brixton Prison, ex parte Soblen* [1963] 2 Q.B. 243; *R.* v. *Governor of Pentonville Prison, ex parte Azam* [1973] 2 W.L.R. 949 (C.A.).

[4] 1973 H.C. No. 79, paras. 64–5; 1973 H.C. No. 81, paras. 66–7; cf. *Küchenmeister* v. *Home Office* [1958] 1 Q.B. 496, 509–11. Directions to secure removal can be given to the captain of the ship or aircraft on which the passenger arrived, or to the owners or agents of such ship or aircraft: Immigration Act 1971, Sch. 2, para. 8; see also paras. 12, 13, 19, 20, 26, 27.

rights of appeal, if any.[1] As noted above, there is no statutory right of appeal in 'security' cases, and in many other cases the passenger will only be able to exercise his right after he has left the United Kingdom.[2]

The right to appeal against directions for removal to a particular country is very limited; it applies only to the case of one who is also appealing against a decision that he requires leave to enter, that is, one who is claiming to be patrial, and to the case of one who was refused admission while he held a current entry clearance or work permit.[3] There is thus no right of appeal against 'refoulement', the immediate return of a refugee who arrives without an entry clearance.[4]

The provisions which require the exercise of rights of appeal from abroad,[5] in common with other parts of the Immigration Rules, do not fully reflect the extent of the United Kingdom's obligations within the E.E.C. in regard to free movement. It was said at the time in the House of Commons:

> An E.E.C. national cannot enter this country without leave. He must have a passport or visa and we have the right to refuse entry on a number of grounds . . . on medical grounds, on a criminal record, on grounds of personal undesirability and on conducive grounds.[6]

This statement, and the Immigration Rules to which it refers, fails to take fully into account the Regulations and Directives which are already in force within the E.E.C. In particular, detailed provision has been made concerning those diseases and afflictions which justify exclusion. It has also been declared that conviction for a criminal offence is not itself a sufficient ground for exclusion, and

[1] See The Immigration Appeals (Notices) Regulations 1972 (S.I. 1972 No. 1683); such notice may also be handed to someone authorized by the passenger to receive it, e.g. a solicitor or adviser: *R.* v. *Chief Immigration Officer, Manchester Airport, ex parte Insah Begum* [1973] 1 W.L.R. 141 (C.A.).

[2] Cf. *R. v. Secretary of State, ex parte Azam* [1973] 2 W.L.R. 949; (C.A.); [1973] 2 All E.R. 765 (H.L.), in which the applicants employed the habeas corpus procedure to challenge the legality of their detention and of directions for their removal as illegal immigrants. There is only a very limited right of appeal under the Immigration Act 1971, section 16; see also *ex parte Hassan* [1976] 1 W.L.R. 971 and cf. *ex parte Badaike*, *The Times*, 4 May 1977.

[3] Immigration Act 1971, Section 17(5).

[4] See below, pp. 137–42.

[5] Immigration Act 1971, section 13(3); 1973 H.C. No. 79, paras. 68–9; 1973 H.C. No. 81, paras. 70–1.

[6] 851 H.C. Deb., col. 588.

the so-called 'conducive grounds' do not coincide at all with the concept of 'ordre public' which has been elaborated and defined in Directive 64/221.[1] Article 5 of this Directive creates a presumption in favour of the E.E.C. national and makes provision for 'conditional entry'. This may in certain circumstances be allowed under the Immigration Act,[2] but detention as the general rule pending the decision on admission is ruled out by the Directive. The same applies to any provision requiring the E.E.C. national to leave the country before exercising his right of appeal. The entry of E.E.C. nationals is a matter now for Community law; to the extent that United Kingdom statutes and regulations imperfectly reflect that law, they stand to be disregarded.[3]

The new Immigration Act contains stringent provisions applicable to illegal entrants and to all intents and purposes such persons are considered as stopped at the port of entry. If they are apprehended, they may be dealt with in exclusion proceedings and their removal ordered without the additional requirement of a deportation order.[4] Prior to 1968, it was no offence to enter the United Kingdom without being examined by an immigration officer, and any Commonwealth citizen who entered and remained free for more than twenty-four hours became, in effect, a lawful immigrant.[5] In the leading case of *D.P.P.* v. *Bhagwan*[6] it was held that evasion of the Commonwealth Immigrants Act 1962 in this way was not a criminal offence, and it was not until 1968 that entry without examination was made criminal. Thereafter any person who entered without examination entered in breach of the immigration laws; he was an illegal entrant and could never become ordinarily resident or settled in the United Kingdom.[7] However, it was only the clandestine landing which was made an offence,[8] and the illegal entrant had to be prosecuted within

[1] See below, pp. 182–4; 300–6.

[2] Sch. 2, para. 21.

[3] *Van Duyn* v. *Home Office* [1975] 1 C.M.L.R. 1; below, pp. 302–4.

[4] Immigration Act 1971, sections 4(2), 16(1), (2); Sch. 2, para. 9.

[5] *R.* v. *Governor of Brixton Prison, ex parte Ahsan* [1969] 2 Q.B. 222. The same rule did not apply to aliens, who were only permitted to land with the leave of an immigration officer: Aliens Order 1953, Article 1(1); for removal of aliens who landed unlawfully, see Article 9.

[6] [1972] A.C. 60. The 'Bhagwan Gap', as it was known, only benefited those who came in clandestinely, without examination, and not those who had previously been refused admission.

[7] *Re Abdul Manan* [1971] 1 W. L. R. 859 (C.A.). See now Immigration Act 1971, section 33(1).

[8] Commonwealth Immigrants Acts 1962 and 1968, section 4A.

six months of that landing.[1] As Lord Denning pointed out in the case of *R.* v. *Secretary of State, ex parte Azam*,[2] after six months the illegal entrant was virtually untouchable, but that did not mean that he was here as of right. His presence continued to be unlawful, although he could not be prosecuted for it. The entry into force of the Immigration Act 1971 brought new provisions for the removal of all those in the United Kingdom in breach of the immigration laws. In effect the Act imposes a retrospective penalty on such entrants and renders them liable to removal for an offence which was not previously punishable in this way. In *Azam's* case the Court of Appeal upheld the retrospective effect of the law in three applications for habeas corpus, and their decision was affirmed by the House of Lords.[3] Criticism of these aspects of the Act prompted the Home Secretary to announce an amnesty in 1974, in favour of all those who entered illegally between 9 March 1968 and 28 January 1973.[4]

Within the statutory system, adjudicators will generally meet two types of exclusion appeal. Section 13 (1) of the Act provides for appeals against the decision that a passenger requires leave to land, or against the refusal of leave to enter itself. Section 13(2) provides for appeals against the refusal of a certificate of patriality or an entry clearance.[5] The statute declares that the adjudicator shall allow the appeal if he considers (1) that the decision or action was not in accordance with law or any applicable immigration rules;[6] or

[1] Magistrates Courts Act 1952, section 104.

[2] [1973] 2 W.L.R. 949.

[3] [1973] 2 All E.R. 765. Cf. European Convention on Human Rights, Articles 6, 7. For a decision the other way in respect of the criminal provisions of the Act, see *Waddington* v. *Miah* [1974] 1 W.L.R. 683.

[4] 872 H.C. Deb., cols. 637–46.

[5] There is no appeal against the decision by the Department of Employment not to issue a work permit: *Latiff* [1972] Imm. A.R. 76. For appeals decided under the earlier, but analogous legislation, see *Padmore* [1972] Imm. A.R. 1 (entry certificate obtained by misrepresentation); *Mustun* [1972] Imm. A.R. 97 (entry certificate obtained by concealment of material facts); *Georgiou* [1972] Imm. A.R. 179 (reconsideration and appreciation of the question, whether applicant a 'genuine visitor'); *Perween Khan* [1972] Imm. A.R. 245 (untrue statement invalidating entry certificate); *Idowu* [1972] Imm. A.R. 197 (presumption in favour of eligibility displaced by agent's failure to disclose that he was applying on holder's behalf).

[6] Immigration Act 1971, section 19(1)(a)(i). For this purpose the adjudicator may review any determination of a question of fact on which the decision or action was based: section 19(2). The adjudicator is required to dismiss an appeal against refusal of leave to enter if satisfied that at the time of the refusal the appellant was an illegal entrant; and to dismiss any appeal against the refusal of an entry clearance if satisfied that a deportation order was in force in respect of the appellant at the relevant time: section 13(4), and note section 16(4).

(2) where the decision or action involves the exercise of discretion by the Secretary of State or by an immigration officer and that discretion should have been exercised differently.[1] In every other case the appeal is to be dismissed.

If the appeal is allowed, the adjudicator may give such directions as he thinks necessary for giving effect to his decision. For example, he may order release from detention and he may also make recommendations in respect of any other relevant matters, including conditions of admission.[2] The decision and directions are binding on the Secretary of State and immigration officers, although their implementation may be suspended so long as an appeal can be brought against the adjudicator's determination, and so long as that appeal is pending.[3]

[1] Immigration Act 1971, section 19(1)(a)(ii). A refusal to depart from the immigration rules shall not itself be taken to involve the exercise of discretion: section 19(2); see also *Glean* [1972] Imm. A.R. 84; cf. *R.* v. *Peterkin* (*Adjudicator*), *ex parte Soni* [1972] Imm. A.R. 253 (Q.B.D.).

[2] Immigration Act 1971, section 19(3).

[3] Ibid., section 20(2). Appeals from the decisions of adjudicators to the Immigration Appeals Tribunal are governed by section 20(1) and the rules of procedure regulating the grant of leave to appeal: The Immigration Appeals (Procedure) Rules 1972 (S.I. 1972 No. 1684), Part III. The Secretary of State also benefits from section 21 of the Act, under which he may at any time refer any matter to an adjudicator or to the Tribunal which relates to an appeal already heard and which was not dealt with at the original hearing.

VII

ENTRY AND EXCLUSION UNDER THE LAW OF THE UNITED STATES OF AMERICA

ALTHOUGH FOR many years immigration into the United States was restricted by laws directed to the exclusion of certain racial groups,[1] a most significant amendment now declares that no person shall be discriminated against in the issue of an immigrant's visa because of his race, sex, nationality, place of birth, or place of residence.[2] Admittedly, there are certain exceptions to this general rule in favour of 'special immigrants' and immediate relatives, but these in no way detract from the strong recognition which is here given to the mandatory rule of non-discrimination.

As amended, the Immigration and Nationality Act 1952 is the principal statute governing the entry of aliens, both immigrants and non-immigrants. Numerical control and the issue of visas etc. are dealt with by the Department of State through consular officers abroad, while practical control at the borders of the United States is exercised by officers of the Immigration and Nationality Service. Deportation and exclusion proceedings are conducted locally by immigration judges,[3] and the Attorney General has delegated his authority to hear appeals from the decisions of such judges to the Board of Immigration Appeals, which is established as part of the Attorney General's office.

United States law makes a first distinction between immigrants and non-immigrants.[4] The latter are further reduced into distinct categories, such as aliens in transit, treaty aliens, alien students, international organization aliens, representatives of foreign information media, exchange workers, and so forth.[5] The 1952 Act also

[1] Konvitz, *Civil Rights in Immigration* (1953), pp. 3–20.

[2] 8 U.S.C. s.1152(a), enacted in 1965.

[3] Formerly known as 'special inquiry officers'.

[4] 8 U.S.C. s. 1101(a)(15).

[5] An Act of 7 April 1971, 84 Stat. 116, introduced additonal categories, including fiancées, fiancés, and 'business executives'. Classification determines the class of visa which will be granted.

elaborates the classes of aliens which are to be excluded from the United States, whether prospective immigrants or non-immigrants, but these classes are exclusive and cannot be enlarged at the discretion of the executive.[1] Although the grounds for exclusion are numerous, the number of aliens actually excluded is small; in 1960, for example, less than 1 per cent of all applicants for entry were barred.[2]

(1) THE IMMIGRATION AND NATIONALITY ACT 1952, AS AMENDED

The Act forbids the entry of those previously deported, excluded, or removed. Thus, an alien against whom a final order of exclusion has been made is barred for a year, and one against whom an expulsion order has been executed or who has been removed from the United States at government expense is perpetually barred, unless in each case the Attorney General has consented to their re-applying for admission.[3] Stowaways always were excluded, but since 1952 the Attorney General's discretion to admit has been eliminated and alien stowaways are now excluded absolutely.[4] The Act also bars those who arrive without documents or with improper documents, and those who have made wilful misrepresentations in seeking entry.[5]

The next category of grounds for exclusion is that dealing with personal qualifications, and first among these grounds are those concerning physical and mental defectives. Exclusion is frequently mandatory when a specific disease or affliction is found, and this may occur either at the border or at the time of visa application.[6] As re-

[1] *Gegiow* v. *Uhl* 239 U.S. 3 (1915). The grounds for exclusion may not be disregarded either by executive officers or the courts, although the Act does empower the Attorney General, in certain circumstances, to waive an applicant's inadmissibility: Immigration and Nationality Act 1952, section 211(b); section 212(d)(3), (4), (5), (6); 8 U.S.C. s. 1181 (b); s. 1182(d)(3), (4), (5), (6).

[2] This figure does not include the number of aliens refused visas by consular officers. See generally, Gordon and Rosenfield, *Immigration Law and Procedure* (rev. ed., 1974), ch. 2.

[3] 8 U.S.C. s. 1182(a)(16), (17).

[4] Ibid., s. 1182(a)(18).

[5] e.g. s.1182(a)(19) bars from entry 'any alien who seeks to procure, or has sought to procure a visa or other documentation, or seeks to enter the United States by fraud, or by wilfully misrepresenting a material fact'.

[6] In the latter case the consul's determination is not appealable and the frustrations which result from the medical rejection at this stage seldom come to public view.

gards mental defects or disabilities, the Act requires the exclusion of those who are insane, or who have had one or more attacks of insanity, or who are afflicted with psychopathic personality or sexual deviation;[1] these are vague terms which are intended to be made concrete in the light of medical judgments. Chronic alcoholism and narcotic drug addiction also justify exclusion, although the latter disability does not include a person who uses drugs solely for the relief of pain or for some other medical reason.[2] One ground which has been much criticized is that which excludes aliens, other than non-immigrants, who are ineligible for citizenship.[3] This class includes many aliens who at one time or another have claimed exemption from military service under the provisions of treaties between their own countries and the United States.[4]

Physical defects or disabilities may result in refusal of entry, as, for example, in the case of any dangerous contagious disease. Other physical conditions may also bar an alien if they are such as to impair his earning capacity and unless he can satisfy the consul or immigration officer that he will not have to earn a living.[5] Paupers, professional beggars, and vagrants are specifically barred, as are those who, in the opinion of the consular officer or immigration officer, are likely to become public charges.[6] While statutory use of the word 'opinion' appears to limit the possibilities of judicial review, it has been held that the exercise of this discretion, by an immigration officer, must be based on some tangible evidence which produces a reasonable probability that the alien will become a public charge after entry.[7] In the case of *Gegiow* v. *Uhl* the Supreme Court overruled the determination of an immigration officer that an alien was excludable as a prospective public charge simply because he was destined to Portland, Oregon, where the labour market at the time was overcrowded. The Court held that a person is likely to become a public charge if he is one whose anticipated dependence on public

[1] Epilepsy as a mandatory bar was abolished by section 15(b), Act of 1965, 79 Stat. 911. See generally, 8 U.S.C. s. 1182(a)(1), (2), (3), (4).

[2] 8 U.S.C. s. 1182(a)(5).

[3] Ibid., s. 1182(a)(22).

[4] *Lapenieks* v. *INS* 389 F.2d 393 (1968); *Colombo* v. *INS* 531 F.2d 943 (1975). Non-immigrant aliens are no longer required to register for military service and are not liable to be drafted while non-immigrant status is maintained: 88 Stat. 348; 50 U.S.C. App. 451(a).

[5] 8 U.S.C. s. 1182(a)(6).

[6] Ibid., s. 1182(a)(8), (15).

[7] 22 C.F.R. 42.91(a)(15)(i).

aid is due to poverty and to physical or mental afflictions.[1] The Act of 1952 also bars illiterates,[2] and aliens accompanying excluded aliens.[3]

The next important category of grounds for exclusion deals with cases of misconduct by the applicant. For example, the Act bars aliens who have been convicted, or who admit the commission, of a crime involving moral turpitude.[4] Other convicted aliens are also excluded,[5] although there are certain exceptions in favour of those convicted of purely political offences, for juvenile offenders, and in respect of petty offences.[6] The law is particularly strict, however, in its attitude to so-called 'immoral aliens', such as prostitutes, polygamists, those convicted of drug offences,[7] and the smugglers of aliens.[8]

One class of aliens that is of particular interest is that of 'subversives'. As long ago as 1901, after the assassination of President McKinley by Leon Czolgosz, an 'anarchist terrorist', an Act was passed to bar from the United States aliens who advocated or who belonged to organizations which advocated the violent overthrow of the Government.[9] In 1904, the Supreme Court declared that this law was not open to constitutional objection.[10] Even if the term 'anarchist' were interpreted to cover the simple philosopher possessed of no evil intention, the law was still valid. The Court based its decision, in part, on the 'accepted principle' of international law that every sovereign nation had the inherent power to forbid the entry of foreigners.[11]

[1] 239 U.S. 3 (1915). See also *Gabriel* v. *Johnson* 29 F.2d 347 (1928); *Berman* v. *Curran* 13 F.2d 96 (1926). As yet there is no right of judicial review by which to challenge comparable determinations by consular officers; *Colombo* v. *INS* 531 F.2d 678 (1976).

[2] 8 U.S.C. s. 1182(a)(25) bars aliens 'over sixteen years of age physically capable of reading who cannot read or understand some language or dialect'. There are certain exceptions.

[3] Ibid., s. 1182(a)(30).

[4] Ibid., s. 1182(a)(9). 'Moral turpitude' is an extremely vague categorization usually defended for its flexibility and adaptability to changing *mores*.

[5] 8 U.S.C. s. 1182(a)(10) applies to offenders who have been convicted of two or more offences and actually sentenced to imprisonment for five years or more.

[6] Ibid., s. 1182(a)(9), as amended.

[7] In *Lennon* v. *INS* 527 F.2d 187 (1975), however, it was held that conviction for possession of marijuana was no bar to admissibility because, under the relevant United Kingdom law, knowledge was not a necessary element in the offence.

[8] Ibid., s. 1182(a)(11), (12), (23), (31).

[9] 32 Stat. 1213 (1903).

[10] *U.S., ex rel. Turner* v. *Williams* 194 U.S. 279 (1904).

[11] Ibid., at p. 290. See also per Fuller C.J., at p. 294. For later developments, see 39 Stat. 889 (1917); 40 Stat. 1012 (1908); 41 Stat. 1008 (1920); 54 Stat. 673 (1940); *Kesler* v. *Strecker* 307 U.S. 22 (1939).

The prohibition on past as well as present members of subversive organizations has been a dominant feature of modern legislation; the Internal Security Act 1950, for example, specifically named the Communist Party as such an organization, and banned aliens who at any time had been party members. The Immigration and Nationality Act 1952 deals with subversives in three ways: (1) it bars aliens who, in the judgment of consular officers or of the Attorney General, are coming to the United States to engage in activities prejudicial to the public interest or safety;[1] (2) it orders the exclusion of those who would probably engage in such activities after entry;[2] and (3) it imposes additional restrictions on aliens who advocate or have advocated 'proscribed' doctrines. These provisions are aimed primarily at the Communist Party, but would also apply to adherents of the Nazi Party or any other non-Communist totalitarian regime.[3] In 1971, in the case of *Mandel* v. *Mitchell*, a new attempt was made to challenge the validity of these rules, after a refusal to grant waiver of inadmissibility to the plaintiff, a prominent Marxist.[4] The latter, together with a number of American scholars who had invited him to speak in the United States, applied for judgment declaring that section 212(a)(28) of the Act of 1952 was invalid. The problem of *locus standi* was dismissed by the District Court, which held that the plaintiff's status as a party did not rest on any individual right to enter the country, but on the American citizens' 'right to hear' and the constitutional guarantees of the First Amendment.[5]

[1] 8 U.S.C. s. 1182(a)(27). One who was entering temporarily to advocate and lecture on pacifism and legal opposition to conscription was held not to be coming to engage in prejudicial activity within the meaning of this restriction: *Matter of M.* 5 I.N. 248 (1953); Gordon and Rosenfield, op. cit., pp. 2–221 f.

[2] 8 U.S.C. s. 1182(a)(29). Exercise of this power may result in exclusion without a hearing. Those excludable on this ground cannot be granted a waiver of inadmissibility for the purpose of temporary entry.

[3] 8 U.S.C. s. 1182(a)(28). These provisions were originally enacted in the Internal Security Act 1950. In order to clarify their purpose, Congress declared in 1951 that the exclusion of subversives related only to those whose membership or affiliation was voluntary; see now, s. 1182(a)(28)(I). Section 8 of an Act of 1949 (63 Stat. 212) authorizes the Director of the Central Intelligence Agency, the Attorney General, and the Commissioner of Immigration to determine that the admission of a particular alien for permanent residence is in the interests of national security or essential to furtherance of the national intelligence mission. Entry is permitted without regard to the general requirements of immigration and other laws, up to a maximum of 100 persons each year. There are no published regulations or procedures.

[4] 325 F. Supp. 620 (1971); 8 U.S.C. s. 1182(d)(3), (6).

[5] 325 F. Supp. 620, at pp. 630–1.

The statutory provisions were aimed directly at the belief and advocacy of proscribed doctrines. Such a law would certainly have been unconstitutional as regards citizens of the United States, but the question in this case was, whether the same test could apply to the alien. The majority of the Court found that certain earlier decisions and dicta were no longer binding.[1] The proper test to be applied where restrictions on freedom of speech were in issue was that of 'clear and present danger',[2] and this was equally applicable to aliens and to citizens.[3] On appeal to the Supreme Court, however, this judgment was reversed.[4] The Court reasserted the traditional doctrine of plenary and unqualified power which Congress has been held to enjoy in the regulation of entry into the United States.[5] It held that the alien could not challenge the statute which required his exclusion, and that the First Amendment rights of United States citizens could not overcome the paramount authority of Congress *vis-à-vis* the alien.

(*a*) *Pre-Entry Procedures*

With the exception of the inhabitants of certain countries in the Western Hemisphere, all aliens who seek to enter the United States are required to be in possession of a valid visa, either as an immigrant or as a non-immigrant.

(*i*) *Immigrants* The 1952 Act confers on consular officers exclusive authority to pass on applications for immigrant visas, and these determinations are not subject to direct control by the Secretary of State.[6] The latter has, however, issued regulations to which consular officers must adhere,[7] and he is expressly empowered to

[1] e.g. *Turner* v. *Williams* 194 U.S. 279, 292: 'Those who are excluded cannot assert the rights in general obtaining in a land to which they do not belong as citizens'; *Bridges* v. *Wixon* 326 U.S. 135, 161: 'The Bill of Rights is a futile authority for the alien seeking admission for the first time to these shores'.

[2] *Dennis* v. *United States* 341 U.S. 494 (1951).

[3] 325 F. Supp. 620, at p. 628. The dissenting judge based his reasoning on the fact of the alien's presence in the country, at which point only he becomes vested with the rights which the Constitution guarantees to all people within the borders. Reference was also made to essential matters of national security and foreign policy, the so-called 'political question doctrine', on which see Konvitz, *Civil Rights in Immigration*, p. 44.

[4] Sub. nom. *Kleindienst* v. *Mitchell* 408 U.S. 753 (1972).

[5] See *Harisiades* v. *Shaughnessy* 342 U.S. 580 (1952); *Galvan* v. *Press* 347 U.S. 522 (1954); *Rowoldt* v. *Perfetto* 355 U.S. 115 (1957); *Perdroza-Sandoval* v. *INS* 488 F.2d 899 (1974).

[6] 8 U.S.C. s. 1201(a).

[7] 22 C.F.R. 42; see also 22 C.F.R. 42.1; 8 U.S.C. s. 1101(a)(9).

instruct such officers to discontinue issuing visas to nationals or residents of States which refuse to accept deportees.[1] In respect of visa applications, no formal hearing or proceeding is authorized, either by statute or regulation. The resulting unreviewable authority of consuls to deny visa applications has been much criticized,[2] and this has led to the adoption of procedures for supervision and review by the Department of State.[3] In practice, upon a request made by members of Congress, lawyers, or other interested parties, the Visa Office of the Department will often re-examine consular action and, if it is found to be erroneous, will submit an advisory opinion which the consular officer will generally follow.[4]

Assuming that the immigrant visa is issued, it is ordinarily valid for a maximum period of four months. In effect, it is a prima facie determination of eligibility to enter the United States, but it does not ensure the holder's entry. The question of admissibility can be raised again by an immigration officer, and exclusion ordered if it is then found that the holder does not qualify.[5]

(*ii*) *Non-immigrants.* The non-immigrant who seeks to enter the United States must be in possession of a valid non-immigrant visa or, for some purposes, a valid border-crossing card. As is the case with prospective immigrants, alien visitors must show that they do not fall into any of the proscribed and excludable classes described above. They are not, however, subject to numerical restrictions and they may enjoy additional benefits under treaty.[6] The procedure for application is less detailed and shorter, although the consul may request any supplementary information wherever he deems this to be necessary. In the case of a refusal to issue a visa there is once more no established review procedure, although in practice reconsideration may be secured along the same lines as for immigrants.

Non-immigrant visas are normally valid according to reciprocal arrangements with the State where they are issued. In some cases,

[1] 8 U.S.C. s. 1253(g). This often occurs in respect of 'Iron Curtain' countries, although exceptions may be granted in individual cases or specified classes of cases.

[2] Cf. United Kingdom law, which permits an appeal against the refusal to issue an 'entry clearance': Immigration Act 1971, section 13(2).

[3] 22 C.F.R. 42.130.

[4] A court could not compel the issue of a visa even if it were possible to obtain jurisdiction over the consul abroad: *United States, ex rel. Ulrich* v. *Kellogg* 30 F.2d 984; *United States, ex rel. London* v. *Phelps* 22 F.2d 288.

[5] 8 U.S.C. s. 1201(h). A visa may also be revoked by a consular officer or by the Secretary of State: ibid., s. 1201(i).

[6] See further below, pp. 192–5.

visas may be issued which are valid indefinitely and for an indefinite number of entries, while others may be restricted to a limited number of admissions. Unlike immigrant visas, the non-immigrant visa is not a document but a stamp in the applicant's passport in which dates, validity, restrictions, and the like are inscribed. Non-immigrant visas may be extended or revalidated either by the issuing office or by any other consular office, but only if the applicant has been maintaining *bona fide* non-immigrant status and is otherwise still eligible.

(*b*) *Procedure on Arrival*

Whether an individual has the right to enter the United States must always be determined at the border, and everyone seeking to enter the country is presumed to be an alien until he shows otherwise.[1] Mere possession of a visa, of either class, is no guarantee of admission, and the process of checking is repeated at the border.[2] The final authority and responsibility for administering the immigration laws, manning the borders, and preventing the illegal entry of aliens is vested in the Attorney General, and this he has mostly delegated to immigration officers and other officials of the Immigration and Nationality Service.[3] The Service has the power to scrutinize the qualifications of each applicant for entry at the frontier,[4] and with this there goes an extensive power to conduct interrogations and to take evidence, where necessary, under oath and in writing.[5]

The first examination which a person arriving at the borders of the United States may be required to undergo is the medical inspection. This will establish whether there is any need for a period of quarantine, and it may settle the particular question of the admissibility of the individual. The inspection is carried out by medical officers of the United States Public Health Service; they have no

[1] *U.S.* v. *Sing Tuck* 194 U.S. 161 (1904); *Pan Am* v. *U.S.* 122 F. Supp. 682 (1954).

[2] Obligations also devolve on transportation lines generally, and, for example, the owners and masters of such lines are under a duty to prevent landings at other than designated ports of entry: 8 U.S.C. s. 1229; they are also obliged to prevent the embarkation of obviously inadmissible passengers and must, therefore, ensure that their passengers are in possession of valid visas: ibid., ss. 1223, 1227. Cf. *U.S.* v. *Norddeutscher Lloyd* 223 U.S. 512 (1912).

[3] 8 U.S.C. s. 1101(a)(18).

[4] Any alien who enters without inspection is liable to be deported: 8 U.S.C. s. 1251 (a)(2).

[5] Immigration officers also have the power to issue subpoenas, to board, search, and arrest: 8 U.S.C. s. 1225(a).

direct authority to exclude any individual, but it is for them to issue the medical certificates upon which immigration officers will normally base their decisions. In certain circumstances, such as cases of mental affliction, the individual has the right of appeal to a board of medical officers, at which he may introduce an alternative opinion.

The immigration inspection proper is concerned directly with the admissibility of the applicant. Not only are visas no guarantee of admission, but even the bearer of a United States passport may be subjected to inquiry and rejection by the immigration officer if he finds that the citizenship claim is not substantiated.[1] These broad powers are emphasized by the Act itself;[2] any prospective entrant may be required to declare under oath the purpose for which he comes, how long he intends to remain, and, if an alien, whether he intends to become a citizen.[3]

Most applicants are admitted directly, but in cases of doubt the law permits temporary detention pending a final determination. This detention may be ordered by an immigration officer, but it does not constitute a 'landing'; in the eyes of the law, the alien is regarded as stopped at the frontier. In practice, only those who are considered likely to abscond or those whose freedom of movement might threaten national security or public safety will be detained in custody. The others are usually released on conditional parole, with reasonable restrictions to ensure their availability. Again, this is not an 'entry' and any subsequent proceedings relate to entry and exclusion, not to expulsion.[4]

While an immigration officer has the authority to admit an alien, he has no power acting alone finally to bar the applicant or to waive

[1] *Yee* v. *Barber* 225 F.2d 707; 347 U.S. 988 (1954). A prior administrative declaration of status is not *res judicata* and does not preclude a subsequent reappraisal at the time of entry. Although the immigration officer's jurisdiction may depend on alienage, he has the right to question and to detain anyone claiming citizenship, and to determine whether that claim is justified: *U.S.* v. *Sing Tuck* 194 U.S. 161 (1904).

[2] 8 U.S.C. s. 1225(a). Inspection takes place at the time and place designated, although in certain circumstances the practice of 'pre-inspection' may be employed. In such cases, the applicant is inspected once and for all in a foreign country, and this procedure was much used for those entering under the Displaced Persons and Refugee Relief Acts.

[3] The applicant may also be called on to supply any other information which will aid the immigration officer in determining whether he is admissible: 8 U.S.C. s. 1225(a). At the same time immigration officers will scrutinize the applicant's identity and documents, and check that his name is not noted in the so-called 'look-out' books.

[4] See below, p. 132. Cf. United Kingdom Immigration Act 1971, section 11.

the statutory grounds for exclusion. In such situations he must refer the matter to other officers, and, generally, where the officer is not fully satisfied, to an immigration judge for a hearing. In cases of the last class the alien is detained or released on parole, and he is informed of the proceedings and of his right to be represented by counsel.

(*c*) *Rights of Appeal*

There is a marked conceptual difference between proceedings for exclusion and proceedings for expulsion. Once an alien is actually admitted to the United States, even if his stay is quite brief, he can be dealt with only in expulsion proceedings.[1] An applicant for entry has the burden of proving his admissibility; in deportation proceedings, on the other hand, it is the government which must satisfy the burden of proof. Furthermore, the constitutional requirements of 'due process' give greater protection to the alien who is already in the United States. Nevertheless, the Supreme Court has held that an alien who is excluded from the United States must be given a fair hearing, with an opportunity to establish his right to enter.[2] The Court has further held that there is a manifest lack of due process where the proceedings are blatantly unfair, or such as to prevent a proper investigation, or reveal a manifest abuse of the discretion committed by statute to the administrative officer in charge of the proceedings, or where it appears that the authority of such officer was not fairly exercised.[3]

The conduct of proceedings is in the charge of an immigration judge, who is himself appointed out of the ranks of the Immigration Service by the Attorney General.[4] The hearing before him is a more informal affair than a trial in court, but still the basic ingredients of fair play must be followed. The alien is seeking a privilege and he must establish his claim. On the other hand, he must be given a chance to bring forward his proof, and a reasonable opportunity to examine, cross-examine, and to present evidence. In addition, the decision of the immigration judge must be based on evidence in the

[1] This rule applies also to the alien who has entered the country illegally.

[2] *Chin Yow* v. *U.S.* 208 U.S. 8 (1908).

[3] *Kwock Jan Fat* v. *White* 253 U.S. 454 (1920). Cf. *Ekiu* v. *United States* 142 U.S. 651 (1892), in which it was held that the fair-hearing requirement was satisfied by an administrative hearing, and that immigration statutes which make administrative findings in such cases final and not subject to judical review are valid. See now, 8 U.S.C. s. 1105(a).

[4] 8 U.S.C. s. 1101(b)(4).

record of the hearing. Any departure from this basic procedure may lead to challenge in the courts. Hearings have been ruled unfair where there was a refusal to admit competent evidence,[1] where there was no adequate support in the record for the order of exclusion,[2] and where there was a denial of an opportunity of appeal afforded by the statute and by regulations.[3] The impartiality of the proceedings is aided by statutory provisions which declare that an officer may not conduct a case in which he has previously participated in an investigating or prosecuting capacity, that there shall be an administrative appeal from the finding of an immigration judge, and that such findings may be brought before the courts on application for habeas corpus.[4]

The applicant has the privilege of representation by counsel or by any other representative of his choice who is entitled to practise in such proceedings.[5] The proceedings are quite informal, but although the judicial rules of evidence do not generally apply, the decision itself must be reasoned and include discussion of the evidence and the findings,[6] together with notice of the applicant's right of appeal.[7] The Board of Immigration Appeals hears appeals from the decisions of immigration judges, and in so doing it exercises the authority and discretion of the Attorney General.[8]

[1] *You* v. *Nagle* 34 F.2d 848 (1929).

[2] *Tod* v. *Waldman* 266 U.S. 113 (1924).

[3] *Kwock Jan Fat* v. *White* 253 U.S. 454 (1920). Curtailment of the right to a fair hearing has been vigorously opposed (for example, in dissenting opinions in *Knauff* v. *Shaughnessy* 338 U.S. 537 (1950): Konvitz, *Civil Rights in Immigration*, pp. 48–51), but limitations were upheld by a bare majority in *Shaughnessy* v. *Mezei* 345 U.S. 212 (1953). Some alien entrants may be better off than others, for example, lawful residents returning after a brief absence abroad; see below, pp. 259–61.

[4] 8 U.S.C. s. 1105a(b); s. 1226(a), (b), (c). The immigration judge has the power to conduct exclusion proceedings, to administer oaths, to present and receive evidence, to interrogate, examine, and cross-examine the alien and witnesses, and to determine whether the applicant for entry shall be admitted or excluded. He may also issue subpoenas and order the taking of depositions in cases pending before him: ibid., s. 1225 (a); 8 C.F.R. 287.4.

[5] 8 U.S.C. s. 1362. On the work of voluntary agencies, see Lowenstein, *The Alien and the Immigration Law* (1957).

[6] 8 U.S.C. s. 1226(a); *Chun* v. *Proctor* 84 F.2d 763 (1936); *Jelic* v. *District Director* 106 F.2d 14 (1939).

[7] 8 C.F.R. 263.3. Where the decision is to admit the alien, the District Director has a similar right of appeal. The alien's right is not absolute, and it does not apply if he is excluded for security reasons on confidential information or if he is mandatorily excludable for physical or mental infirmity: 8 U.S.C. s. 1226(b), (d). An exclusion order will not be enforced where an appeal is pending.

[8] 8 C.F.R. 3.1(d)(1), (2); *Jarecha* v. *INS* 417 F.2d 220 (1969).

It has already been observed that the alien at the frontier does not enjoy the full benefits of the constitutional right to a hearing. Indeed, there are certain situations in which the right is absolutely excluded, for example, in the case of alien stowaways.[1] Special rules apply also to alien crewmembers[2] and to security cases. If it appears that the alien is inadmissible on security grounds, he is normally excluded and no further hearing may be held except as expressly authorized.[3]

Any alien who is ordered to be excluded is usually immediately conveyed back to the country whence he came, in accommodation of the same class and in the same vessel or aircraft, unless the Attorney General, in his discretion, orders otherwise.[4] Unlike expulsion proceedings, there are no alternatives possible in fixing the place of removal, and the excluded alien is given no say in regard to the country to which he would like to go.[5] An alien cannot apply for suspension of deportation, as this relief is available only to those who are within the United States. He may seek a stay of execution, but this is wholly within the discretion of the District Director.[6]

(*d*) *Conclusions*

The system of immigration control in the United States is elaborate and complex,[7] but in many ways it is remarkable for the extent to which it permits appeal against and review of the exercise of executive discretion. The statute and the regulations made thereunder are highly detailed and such definition helps to confine and structure the powers in question. Two areas stand out, however, as beyond effective control: (1) the authority of consular officers to

[1] This does not apply in the case of a resident of the United States, if the stowaway claims United States citizenship, or if he manages to get into the country.

[2] See below, pp. 156–9.

[3] 8 U.S.C. s. 1225(c); 8 C.F.R. 235.6.

[4] 8 C.F.R. 236.6.

[5] *Wah* v. *Shaughnessy* 190 F.2d 488 (1951). Consent of the country of destination is not a prerequisite to execution of the order of removal. Cf. *Stacher* v. *Rosenberg* 216 F. Supp. 511 (1963), where the court ruled that in the case of a long-term resident of the United States returning after a temporary absence abroad, the United States was the only country which qualified as the country whence he came, and that he could not be removed under an exclusion order to any other State.

[6] See 8 U.S.C. s. 1227(a), (c) on the obligations of transportation lines. Carriers are liable for the expenses of detention and removal in exclusion proceedings, and this obligation is enforceable by civil suit.

[7] But see Wasserman, 'The Undemocratic, Illogical and Arbitrary Immigration Laws of the United States', 3 *International Lawyer* (1969), 254.

deny visas; and (2) the procedure in 'security' cases. The former raises, essentially, problems of jurisdiction which would not be insuperable. The latter represents retention by the State of its powers of appreciation in matters deemed by it to touch the national interest. But even here the powers remain discretionary and, providing that the evidentiary burden could be satisfied, cases of manifest abuse would be corrected by the courts.

In regard to the system of appeals, the municipal law of the United States is probably in advance of international law requirements, although there is clear and abundant evidence to support the view that, generally, a certain standard of treatment is due even to the alien on the point of initial entry. The statutory prohibition on discrimination, however, and its local effect of confining the limits of executive discretion, clearly embodies the rule of international law.

VIII

OBLIGATIONS TO GRANT ADMISSION IMPOSED BY GENERAL INTERNATIONAL LAW

(1) NATIONALS

REFERENCE HAS already been made in different contexts to the obligation of the State to admit its own nationals.[1] This obligation is most traditionally stated as correlative to the 'right' of expulsion. Schwarzenberger observes:

> To make the right of expulsion effective, the practice of States has insisted on the duty of the home State to receive back any national expelled from a foreign State.[2]

Oppenheim is also specific, and describes the function of nationality as involving one particular right and one particular duty:

> The right is that of protection over its citizens abroad which every State holds . . . The duty is that of receiving such of its citizens as are not allowed to remain on the territory of other States.[3]

However, it remains a matter for debate[4] to what extent a State is free to expel persons long established on its territory, who may be considered to have acquired the effective nationality of that State. Moreover, it is far from clear that a State is under a duty to receive those of its nationals who have been *unlawfully* expelled from another State, at least in so far as the duty to admit is one which is owed between States alone.

Recently, the view has been canvassed that the State's duty to admit its nationals may be owed not only to a second State which wishes to repatriate them, but to any legal person with a recognized

[1] See above, pp. 20–1, 44–6.

[2] *International Law* (3rd ed., 1957), vol. I, p. 361.

[3] *International Law* (8th ed., 1955), vol. I, pp. 645–6. See also the *Nottebohm Case*, I.C.J. Rep., 1955, p. 4, per Judge Read, dissenting, at pp. 34, 47–8; *R.* v. *Secretary of State, ex parte Thakrah* [1974] 2 W.L.R. 593.

[4] On which see further below, pp. 255–61.

interest in the preservation of the human right of an individual to enter his own State.[1] Whatever view is taken of the notion of *actio popularis*, the specific issue of the right of entry as a human right must not pass unconsidered. It features in many international instruments,[2] and it underlay the controversy over the admission of United Kingdom citizens from East Africa. However, the duty of admission as an obligation owed at large and to the international community as a whole is another matter entirely, and suffers from all the doubts and uncertainties which adhere to the notion of obligations *erga omnes*. Of course, this does not mean that States may not agree among themselves to recognize such a right as incidental to obligations assumed within some regional organization.[3]

Considered simply as an obligation between States, the duty to admit *nationals*[4] is firmly fixed within the corpus of general international law. So in a decision of the European Court of Justice in 1975 it was said:

[22] . . . it is a principle of international law, which the E.E.C. Treaty cannot be assumed to disregard in the relations between Member States, that a State is precluded from refusing to its own nationals the right of entry or residence.[5]

(2) REFUGEES AND ASYLUM

The position of refugees and of others who seek asylum has long been of concern. There have been many who have argued in favour of the individual's 'right of asylum', of his right to secure entry to some State other than his own.[6] However, the practice of States

[1] Plender, *International Migration Law* (1972), p. 74; Higgins, 'The Right in International Law of an Individual to enter, stay in and leave a Country', 49 *International Affairs* (1973), 341–57; *Patel et al.* v. *United Kingdom* (Application 4403/70), Decision of the European Commission on Admissibility, October 1970.

[2] See Article 5(d), International Convention on the Elimination of All Forms of Racial Discrimination 1966; Article 12, International Convenant on Civil and Political Rights 1966, Articles 2, 3, Fourth Protocol, European Convention on Human Rights 1950.

[3] See *Second Report on State Responsibility*, Roberto Ago, Special Rapporteur, Yearbook of the I.L.C., 1970—II, p. 177 at 184–6.

[4] It is conceded that this term alone begs many questions.

[5] *Van Duyn* v. *Home Office* [1975] 1 C.M.L.R. 1, 18. See also Weis, *Nationality and Statelessness in International Law* (1956), pp. 49–50; and below, pp. 302–4.

[6] Wolff, *Jus Gentium Methodo Scientifica Pertractatum* (1764), ss. 147–9. See the original draft of Article 14, Universal Declaration of Human Rights: U.N. Doc. A/C.3/285, Rev. 1; the objections raised, particularly by the United Kingdom: U.N. Doc. A/C.3/SR 121, pp. 4–6; and the French proposal which was rejected: U.N. Doc. A/C.3/244.

tends more to the support of that view which Morgenstern affirmed in 1949, namely, that the right of asylum is the right of the State to grant protection, which in turn is founded on the 'undisputed rule of international law' that every State has exclusive control over the individuals within its territory.[1] Today, this exclusively jurisdictional approach has been mitigated somewhat by increased recognition of protection as a humanitarian duty.[2] Progressive developments in the laws of extradition, in the concept of political offence, in the notion of persecution, and in the principle of non-discrimination have all tended to improve the over-all lot of the individual. Nevertheless, it is still to be doubted whether there is any rule which obliges States to admit those fleeing from persecution, although, as will be presently argued, admission or continued residence may be secured in roundabout fashion.

International action and co-operation over the last sixty years have endowed the word 'refugee' with the status of a term of art. In treaties designed to secure the status of refugees and concluded in the inter-war years, the criterion generally adopted to distinguish the refugee was the fact of his not actually enjoying the protection of the government of his State of origin, whether or not he was 'legally' entitled to such protection.[3] It was emphasized in a contemporary work that there could never be a satisfactory and comprehensive definition of 'political refugee', and that those hitherto adopted were, at best, technical definitions for legal and administrative purposes. In the view of the writer, Simpson, it was important not to lose sight of the 'essential quality' of the refugee as one

> who has sought refuge in a territory other than that in which he was formerly resident as a result of political events which rendered his continued residence in his former territory impossible or intolerable.[4]

The notion of the intolerability of continued residence caused by

[1] Morgenstern, 'The Right of Asylum', 26 *B.Y.I.L.* (1949), 327. See also Moore, *Digest*, vol. II, 757; Hackworth, *Digest*, vol. II, 623; Weis, 'Legal Aspects of the Convention of 25th July 1951 Relating to the Status of Refugees', 30 *B.Y.I.L.* (1953), 478, 481.

[2] Sinha, *Asylum and International Law* (1971), pp. 280–2.

[3] Jennings, 'International Law and the Refugee Question', 20 *B.Y.I.L.* (1939), 98; see also Convention concerning the International Status of Refugees 1933: 159 L.N.T.S. 199.

[4] Simpson, *Refugees—A Preliminary Report of a Survey* (1938), p. 1. The preliminary report was consolidated into the same author's *The Refugee Problem* (1939), which recounts the measures both national and international which were taken to deal with the problem.

political conditions goes to the heart of the problem, and it predates the broad criteria adopted after the Second World War.

These criteria were comprehensively described in the 1951 Convention Relating to the Status of Refugees.[1] As amended by the 1967 Protocol, this Convention defines as a refugee a person who,

> owing to well-founded fear of being persecuted for reasons of race, religion, nationality, membership of a particular social group or political opinion, is outside the country of his nationality and is unable or, owing to such fear, is unwilling to avail himself of the protection of that country, or who, not having a nationality and being outside the country of his former residence is unable or, owing to such fear, is unwilling to return to it.[2]

The Convention does *not* guarantee a right of entry in so many words, but it does oblige States parties not to impose penalties for illegal entry on refugees, provided that they report to the authorities without delay and show good cause for their actions.[3] Articles 32 and 33 are of particular importance. The former declares that a refugee lawfully within a State shall be expelled only on grounds of national security or public order, and that he shall be permitted a hearing and appeal against such order of expulsion, 'except where compelling reasons of national security otherwise require'.[4] Article 33 declares again the rule prohibiting the expulsion or return of a refugee to the frontiers of a territory where his life or freedom would be threatened on account of his race, religion, etc. The normative quality of this rule is emphasized by the terms of the second paragraph, circumscribing the exceptional privilege of derogation. Thus, it is expressly provided that the benefit of non-refoulement may not be claimed by a refugee, 'whom there are *reasonable grounds* for regarding as a

[1] The United Nations General Assembly, by Res. 429(v) of 14 December 1950, decided to convene in Geneva a conference of Plenipotentiaries to complete the drafting of, and to sign, the Convention. Text of Convention: 189 U.N.T.S. 150.

[2] Article I A(2), as amended by Article I(2) of the 1967 Protocol: 606 U.N.T.S. 267. See also United States, *Policy Guidelines on Asylum Requests 1972*: 11 Int. Leg. Mat. 228; United Kingdom, *Statement of Immigration Rules for Control on Entry* (Commonwealth Citizens), 1973 H.C. No. 79, para. 54; (E.E.C. and other Non-Commonwealth Nationals), 1973 H.C. No. 81, para. 55.

[3] Article 31(1).

[4] The Contracting States also agree to allow such refugee a reasonable period in which to seek legal admission to another State: Article 32(3); *Expulsion of an Alien* (*Austria*) *Case*, 28 I.L.R. 310. During that period the Contracting States have the right to apply such internal measures of control as they deem appropriate; see, for example, article 28, ordonnance du 2 nov. 1945; Kiss, *Répertoire de la pratique française en matière de droit international public*, vol. IV, p. 462.

danger to the security of the country . . . or who, *having been convicted by a final judgment of a particularly serious crime*, constitutes a danger to the community of that country'.[1] Moreover, it is to be noted that no State party to the Convention is entitled to make any reservation to this Article,[2] and, as has been argued above, this element of 'no derogation' lends additional weight to the view of non-refoulement as a rule of general international law.[3]

The efficacy of these provisions within certain local jurisdictions is well illustrated by the *Refugee (Germany) Case*. Here the court held that a refugee who had obtained an extension of his residence permit on the basis of untruthful statements was not 'lawfully' within the Federal Republic. The restriction on permissible grounds of expulsion did not, therefore, apply to him in the manner foreseen by Article 32. However, the court also held that the right inherent in Article 33 was not similarly tied to lawful presence, and it had to be interpreted to mean that no refugee, whether lawfully or unlawfully within the territory, may be expelled to a place of persecution.[4] An almost identical conclusion was reached in the United States case, *Chim Ming* v. *Marks*, in 1974.[5]

The definition of 'refugee' provided by the 1951 Convention, as amended, has been adopted in Article I of the O.A.U. Convention on Refugee Problems in Africa.[6] Article II deals specifically with 'asylum' and provides that Member States shall use their best endeavours to receive or to secure the settlement of refugees defined in Article I.[7] It affirms that the grant of asylum is a peaceful and

[1] Article 33(2), emphasis supplied.

[2] Article 42. Reservations are also forbidden in respect of Articles 1 (definition of refugee), 3 (non-discrimination), 4 (national treatment on religion), 16 (1)(free access to courts), and 36–46. See also the 1967 Protocol, Article VII.

[3] See above, pp. 71–4.

[4] 28 I.L.R. 297. In the *Yugoslav Refugee (Germany) Case*, 26 I.L.R. 496, the court held that lawful residence in the State could be established even if preceded by an illegal entry. See also *Homeless Alien (Germany) Case*, 26 I.L.R. 503.

[5] 505 F.2d 1170 (1974).

[6] 8 Int. Leg. Mat. 1288 (1969).

[7] The 1951 definition originally qualified refugee status by reference to flight 'as a result of events occurring before 1st January 1951'. In *Molefi* v. *Principal Legal Adviser* [1971] A.C. 182, the Judicial Committee of the Privy Council, on an appeal from Lesotho, considered that the events contemplated were happenings of major importance involving territorial or profound political changes. In this case the appellant claimed the benefit of the Convention and the right not to be expelled to South Africa. It was conceded that he was outside his country and that he had a well-founded fear of persecution (at p. 195), but the Privy Council agreed with the Lesotho Court of Appeal that the 1948 elections which brought the Nationalists to power in South Africa, and the pre-1951 legislation

humanitarian act and restates the prohibition on measures which would compel a refugee to return to or remain in a territory where he faces persecution.[1] No express concession is made to overriding considerations of national security, although if a Member State finds difficulty 'in continuing to grant asylum to refugees', then recourse is to be had to other Member States and through the O.A.U.[2]

Regional conventions of this nature,[3] together with developments in municipal law, provide substantial evidence of the current position in general international law. It may be affirmed that the prohibition on the return of refugees to countries of persecution has established itself as a general principle of international law, binding on States automatically and independently of any specific assent.[4] Earlier State practice supports the contention that, for example, Articles 32 and 33 of the 1951 Convention reflected or crystallized a rule of customary international law at the time of their formulation, and practice since that date reaffirms this conclusion. The high standard of proof which is required on the issue of *opinio juris* can in this case be satisfied. The relevant provisions are of a 'fundamentally norm-creating character',[5] and the fact that expulsion or return may be permitted in exceptional circumstances does not deny this premiss, but serves simply to indicate the boundaries to the exercise of discretion. Furthermore, and as has already been noted, no State is entitled to make any reservation to the obligation of non-refoulement contained in Article 33.

Both the 1951 Convention and the 1967 Protocol have enjoyed widespread and representative participation,[6] and the time factor also operates in favour of the rule against return as a rule of

and repressive government policy, were merely the background to later events (at p. 197). Because the appellant had remained in South Africa until 1961, it was the view of the court that it could not be said that he was outside his country 'as a result of events occurring before 1951'. The 1967 Protocol will avoid strictly legal interpretations of this nature, and the O.A.U. Convention goes further, to provide that the benefits of refugee status shall also apply to those forced to leave on account of external aggression, occupation, foreign domination, or events seriously disturbing public order: Article I(2).

[1] Article II(2), (3),

[2] Article II(4), (5). In such cases, provision is to be made for temporary residence.

[3] See also Article 22(7), (8) of the 1969 American Convention on Human Rights, which approximate the political offender to the persecuted and emphasize the status of individual rights. Text: 65 A.J.I.L. (1971), 679; 9 Int. Leg. Mat. 101; Brownlie, *Basic Documents on Human Rights* (1971), p. 399.

[4] See *North Sea Continental Shelf Cases*, I.C.J. Rep., 1969, p. 3, at pp. 37–8.

[5] Ibid., p. 42. Cf. Part IV, Final Act, U.N. Conference on Stateless Persons 1954.

[6] As of August 1977 the 1957 Convention had 68 parties, and the 1967 Protocol 63.

customary international law. It is a rule which has its effects beyond the conventional relationship. In the particular circumstances, its breach may therefore involve international responsibility towards other contracting parties, towards some regional institution, or, given further development of the concept of obligations *erga omnes*, towards the international community as a whole.

(*a*) '*Asylum*' *and* '*political offence*'

The position in general international law of the related category, those accused or convicted of 'political' offences, is far less clear.[1] Both refugees and political offenders are peculiarly susceptible of a violation of basic human rights, and it is these considerations which dominate questions concerning their admission or removal from State territory. Political offence is one small part of the wider topic of asylum, but it is evidently the one part in which political considerations, strictly speaking, will vie with humanitarian considerations.

The difficulty of defining 'political' offence with any precision can be gathered from an examination of any municipal system. Courts approach the problem from a number of different angles, and interpretations vary from the somewhat rigid views of the courts of the United States and the United Kingdom, to the broader, approach of the courts of the Federal Republic of Germany, where strict categorizations are rejected in favour of the application of the general criteria of persecution.[2]

It may still be argued, however, that the rule of non-extradition of the political offender is a rule of municipal law and not of international law.[3] The political offender who is extradited will thus generally be barred from pleading that he has a right not to be tried before the court of the requesting State,[4] unless he otherwise bene-

[1] The divergence in State practice can be readily appreciated from a consideration of Article 3 of the European Convention on Extradition 1957 (European Treaty Series No. 24), and the reservations thereto.

[2] See *VerwRspr*. Bd. 20, S. 332, decision of the OVG, Münster, 1968.

[3] O'Connell, *International Law* (2nd ed., 1970), p. 729.

[4] In the *Delivery without Extradition* (*Germany*) *Case*, Ann. Dig., 1919–22, Case No. 185, the court held that where a Dutch policeman had brought the accused to the frontier and there handed him over to the German authorities, the extradition treaty did not contain any provision conferring upon an accused person the right to invoke the absence of extradition proceedings as a reason preventing prosecution. The general principle was more recently affirmed in a case in which it was said that generally rights and duties deriving from an extradition treaty benefit only States: *BGHSt*. Bd. 18, S. 218 (1963).

fits under the rule of speciality.[1] Nevertheless, this does not remove the possibility that the State which orders the extradition is acting in violation of an international obligation.

However, if municipal law condones the surrender of political offenders,[2] the individual may be additionally prejudiced by the fact that there is no other State in a position, or interested, to claim that there has been a breach of international law. The political offence is manifestly one area which involves political considerations, and the traditional view has been that, while international law permits and favours the non-extradition of political offenders, it leaves it to individual States to interpret this competence more or less after their own fashion. Developments in the last quarter-century have introduced limitations to the permissible content of political offence, and it is clear that a State is no longer free, for example, to refuse extradition in respect of the crime of genocide.[3] Possible future limitations may exclude the hijacking of civil aircraft and offences against diplomats, but it seems likely that it will be necessary to

See also *Katz* v. *Officer Commanding the Polish Military Prison, Jerusalem* Ann. Dig., 1943–5, Case No. 45; *Cook* v. *United States* 288 U.S. 102 (1933). More recently in the United States the courts have indicated that the authorities no longer enjoy *carte blanche* in regard to the irregular recovery of fugitive offenders: *U.S.* v. *Toscanino* 500 F.2d 267 (1974). While not every irregularity will vitiate proceedings (see *U.S.* v. *Gengler* 510 F.2d 62 (1975)), due process will now protect against extraterritorial government conduct of the most outrageous and shocking character.

[1] See, for example, *Fiscal* v. *Samper*, decision of the Spanish Supreme Court (1934), Ann. Dig., 1938–40, Case No. 52; *United States* v. *Rauscher* 119 U.S. 407 (1886); *R.* v. *Smith (Derrick)*, *Law Society's Gazette*, 7 Jan. 1976, p. 15.

[2] There are a number of precedents for the mutual surrender of political offenders; see *The State (Duggan)* v. *Tapley* [1952] I.R. 62 (Irish Supreme Court); also, the procedure for rendition under the Fugitive Offenders Act 1881: 6 *B.D.I.L.* 765 ff.; Article 10, Treaty of Great Britain with the Shah of Persia 1814: Aitchison, *Treaties, Engagements and Sanads* (1909), vol. XII, p. 54. Notice also the exclusion of particular offences, such as assassination of a Head of State, from the political offence exception: European Convention on Extradition, Article 3(3); United Kingdom Fugitive Offenders Act 1967, section 4(5); and cf. the modern tendency to 'depoliticize' such offences as hijacking, offences against internationally protected persons (U.S.A.-Canada Extradition Treaty 1971, Article 4(2)(i), (ii)), the taking of hostages and bomb attacks (European Convention on the Suppression of Terrorism 1977, Articles 1, 2).

After the Second World War, Belgium and France agreed by an Exchange of Notes, on the mutual surrender of collaborators; see *Colman*, Cour de Paris, Ch. des mises en accusation, arrêt du 5 déc. 1947; *Nothomb*, Cour d'Amiens, arrêt du 20 mai 1953: Kiss, *Répertoire de la pratique française en matière de droit international public*, vol. II, pp. 217–18. Cf. the refusal of extradition by the Supreme Court of Brazil in the *Denmark (Collaboration with the Enemy) Case*, Ann. Dig., 1947, Case No. 71; *Spiessens*, Cour de Colmar, arrêt du 7 mai 1953: Kiss, op. cit., vol. II, p. 219.

[3] See Article VII, Genocide Convention 1948.

view each offence within a broader context, and with due consideration given to humanitarian issues and the fundamental rights of the individual. That these matters remain of principal concern is evidenced by the fact that proposals to remove offences from the political exception are generally balanced by reference to the right, and the duty, of the 'receiving State' to institute proceedings in the alternative, where extradition is denied. It is precisely at the point where persecution begins or basic human rights are violated that international law is involved. Although the International Court of Justice has opened the way for the development of a theory of obligations on a scale transcending normal bilateral, or even multilateral, relationships, the principles of responsibility in such circumstances remain to be worked out. The general notion suggests limits to the competence of States, as also the class of case in which even refusal of entry might constitute the violation of an international obligation, even though no other State has a direct interest, in the traditional sense, in the individual affected.

In the meantime, it may be that these developments in general international law will bear their first fruits in municipal systems and will exert a formative influence on both the content and the interpretations of laws. In the Federal Republic of Germany, for example, the 'right of asylum' is expressed in the 1949 Constitution, Article 16 of which declares, 'politisch Verfolgte geniessen Asylrecht'. What is remarkable, however, is the substantive effect which has been given to this otherwise vaguely expressed right both by the courts and by the legislature. The result is that there is embraced within the one class of 'Asylberechtigten' not only the refugee and the stateless person, but also the political offender and the politically persecuted.[1] In addition to the Constitution, the Aliens Law (Ausländergesetz) of 1965 introduces specific benefits. It provides that aliens who enjoy the right of asylum and who are lawfully within the Federal Republic may only be expelled for the most serious reasons.[2] Article 14 of this law provides that no alien shall be deported to any country in which his life or freedom is threatened on account of his race, religion, nationality, or political opinion.[3] These rights are not without

[1] Weissmann, *Ausländergesetz* (1966), p. 159. See also *BGHSt.* Bd. 3, S. 393, 395 (1953); *BVerfGE.* Bd. 9, S. 174 (1954); *BGHSt.* Bd. 15, S. 297 (1961).

[2] Article 11(2), *AuslG.* 1965: 'schwerwiegenden Gründen der öffentlichen Sicherheit und Ordnung'.

[3] There are some exceptions in cases involving national security. See also Schiedermair, *Handbuch des Ausländerrechts der Bundesrepublik Deutschland* (1968), pp. 105 ff.

qualification, however, and may be denied to those who use their asylum to fight against democratic freedoms.[1]

Despite the provisions of the constitution, it has been argued that the grant of asylum remains a privilege which can be refused at any time in the interests of national security.[2] In practice, however, the tendency of decided cases is to emphasize the subjective nature of the right of the individual and to control executive discretion, rather than to express recognition of some precarious privilege. At the same time, the courts have widened the class of the politically persecuted who are entitled to benefit from that right.[3] The phrase 'politisch Verfolgte' is clearly wider than the related phrase 'politisch Verbrecher', and in order to qualify under the Constitution the refugee is not required either to commit any offence or to wait upon the beginnings of a programme of persecution.[4] In one case decided in 1971 it was held that the possibility of punishment for 'Republikflucht'[5] was a sufficient ground for the grant of refugee status.[6] In the view of the court, the punishment for absence abroad amounted to political persecution and not to a purely criminal punishment, as the refugee authorities and the lower tribunals had held:

> [Die Bestrafung wegen Republikflucht] diente dem Zweck, die politische Herrschaft des Kommunismus zu sichern. Sie ist nicht vergleicher mit Strafen, durch die auch in Rechtsstaaten dem unerlaubten Grenzübertritt gewehrt wird.[7]

The court here also took into account evidence of the applicant's opposition to the Hungarian regime, his refusal to join the party,

[1] Article 18, Grundgesetz: 'gegen die freiheitlich demokratische Grundordnung'. Cf. Article 17, European Convention on Human Rights.

[2] Schiedermair, op. cit., p. 248.

[3] *BGHSt.* Bd. 8, S. 61 (1953): '[Asylrecht] ist ein Grundrecht, das allen politischen Verfolgten ohne Rücksicht auf ihre Staatsangehörigkeit zusteht.'

[4] *BVerfGE.* Bd. 9, S. 174 (1954), in which the court took into account the possibility of persecution resulting from the refugee's overstaying his visa and his contacts with exile groups. See also Weissmann, op. cit., p. 403.

[5] 'Republikflucht'—the crime of fleeing from the State, often to be found in the penal codes of totalitarian regimes.

[6] *BVerwGE.* Bd. 39, S. 27 (1971); see also, *Yugoslav Refugee (Germany) Case* 26 I.L.R. 496; *Homeless Alien (Germany) Case*, 26 I.L.R. 503; *Refugee (Germany) Case*, 28 I.L.R. 297.

[7] '[Punishment for the crime of flight from the Republic] serves the goal of securing the political sovereign authority of communism. It is not comparable with the penalties with which, even in "constitutional states", unauthorized border crossing is punished.' *BVerwGE.* Bd. 39, S. 27, 28–9. The nature of such penalties was to be distinguished by reference to their purpose, which should not be to hinder or prevent journeys abroad.

and the fact of assistance given to another refugee. In all the circumstances, he could not be described simply as a 'Wirtschaftsflüchtling'.[1]

Despite these developments, the fact remains that the protection of the law will only generally be available *after* admission. In the United States, for example, there is only a limited right to apply for the discretionary grant of parole existing in favour of the alien on the point of initial entry, and he must show that he would be subject to persecution if returned to the country whence he came.[2] Similarly, in the United Kingdom, there is no statutory right of appeal while still in the country for any person refused admission, unless at the time he is in possession of a valid entry clearance.[3] State practice still denies to the 'right of asylum' the character of an interest enforceable in law, at the instance of the individual. And yet the influence of the rule of non-return is apparent; no State today claims the right to send an individual back to a place of persecution, and even the 'straightforward application of immigration laws' is tempered by recognition of the international obligation.[4]

[1] Ibid., pp. 30–1: 'Politisch Verfolgte geniessen Asylrecht ohne Rücksicht auf ihre Zahl.'

[2] 8 U.S.C. s. 1182(d)(5). For the plea of 'anticipated persecution' as a ground of appeal in deportation proceedings (8 U.S.C. s. 1254(h), as amended), see *Fu* v. *INS* 386 F.2d 750 (1967); *Mercer* v. *Esperdy* 234 F. Supp. 611 (1964); *Blazina* v. *Bouchard* 286 F.2d 510 (1961); *Glavic* v. *Beechie* 225 F. Supp. 24 (1963); *Kovac* v. *INS* 407 F.2d 102 (1969); cf. *Berdo* v. *INS* 432 F.2d 824 (1970); *Chim Ming* v. *Marks* 505 F.2d 1170 (1974). See also Evans, 'The Political Refugee in United States Immigration Law and Practice', 3 *International Lawyer* (1969), 204; *Pierre* v. *United States* 547 F.2d 1281 (1977).

[3] Immigration Act 1971, sections 13(5), 17(5).

[4] See further below, pp. 218–21.

IX

OBLIGATIONS TO GRANT ADMISSION TO CERTAIN OTHER EXCEPTIONAL CATEGORIES

THERE ARE a number of categories of people who, by virtue of the rules of general international law, or of treaty, or as the result of practice, enjoy privileges and exemptions in the matter of entry into foreign States. Included within these exceptional categories one finds diplomats, special missions, the officials of international organizations, crewmembers, refugees, and stateless persons, The position of the last two categories has been discussed above; consideration will now be given briefly to those remaining.

(1) DIPLOMATS AND CONSULS

The privileges and immunities of diplomats have long been based on customary international law, and those of consuls most frequently on bilateral treaties. It is recognized that the 'right of legation' is founded essentially on necessity, the practical convenience of maintaining normal contact, and the mutual consent of States.[1] Privileges and immunities follow as essential to the successful performance of diplomatic functions, and it is apparent that a foreign diplomat who arrives at the frontier of the State to which he has been accredited is to be admitted.[1] The Vienna Convention on Diplomatic Relations 1961 provides that those entitled to diplomatic privileges and immunities are to enjoy them as from the moment of entry.[2] This presumably admits of at least a formal submission to immigration control,[3] but it is now clearly established that objections to the appointment of any particular individual as head of a mission should be raised before he is dispatched to take up

[1] Article 2, Vienna Convention on Diplomatic Relations 1961: 500 U.N.T.S. 95. See also Hackworth, *Digest*, vol. IV, p. 393.

[1] Plender, *International Migration Law*, p. 99.

[2] Article 39. Cf. *Harvard Research Draft Convention on Diplomatic Privileges and Immunities* 1932, 26 A.J.I.L. (1932), Supp., 67, Article 16 at pp. 89–90.

[3] Cf. Article 41, Vienna Convention.

his appointment. The Vienna Convention declares the customary rule that the sending State must make certain that the *agrément* of the receiving State has been given in respect of the person whom it proposes to accredit.[1] It is further provided, and generally recognized in practice, that the receiving State is not obliged to give reasons for the refusal of *agrément*, so that in effect it exercises a totally discretionary power in the first matter of admission.[2]

Once admitted, the diplomatic agent[3] enjoys personal inviolability and general immunity from criminal and most civil and administrative jurisdiction.[4] He is not, therefore, subject to alien registration laws or to deportation. However, the receiving State may declare the head of a mission, or any member of the diplomatic staff, to be *persona non grata* at any time.[5] The sending State is then obliged to recall the person concerned or to terminate his functions with the mission. If it refuses to do so, or fails to act within a reasonable time, then the receiving State may itself refuse to recognize that person as a member of the mission. The provisions of immigration and other laws would then apply, although before that moment the diplomat must be given a reasonable time in which to effect his own departure.[6] On the question of the personal acceptability of diplomats, it is clear that the receiving State has absolute powers of judgment. This is primarily a political matter, but the diplomat is generally guaranteed treatment in accordance with his status.

Recently, there has been a movement towards raising consuls more or less to the level of diplomatic agents,[7] and in many respects they now enjoy similar privileges. Because of the predominance of certain established practices, the International Law Commission

[1] Article 4; cf. *Harvard Research*, Article 9(1)(a).

[2] Article 4(2); cf. *Harvard Research*, Article 9(1)(b).

[3] Defined in Article 1, Vienna Convention.

[4] Articles 29–36. These immunities cover also members of his family forming part of his household and, within limitations, administrative, technical, and service staff: Article 37; cf. *Harvard Research*, Article 19. See also Vienna Convention, Article 27(5), inviolability of the diplomatic courier; Article 40, diplomats in transit. Cf. *Harvard Research*, Article 15; United Kingdom Diplomatic Privileges Act 1964, section 2(5).

[5] Article 9. Other members of the mission staff may also be declared unacceptable and the receiving State is in no case obliged to give reasons. A person may be declared *non grata* or not acceptable prior to arrival. Cf. *Harvard Research*, Article 12.

[6] Privileges and immunities normally run until the diplomat has left the country: Article 39(2).

[7] Brownlie, *Principles of Public International Law* (2nd ed., 1973), pp. 348–9.

proposed draft articles on Consular Relations in 1963.[1] These subsequently formed the basis of the Vienna Convention on Consular Relations of the same year.[2] Article 46 of this Convention provides that consulate members, their families, and private staff shall be exempt from aliens registration laws and any residence permit requirement. This immunity does not extend, however, where the consular employee is not employed full-time, or where he engages in some private occupation.[3]

Many municipal systems reflect either the express provisions of these conventions or the customary rules upon which they are based. For example, the Vienna Convention on Diplomatic Relations has been enacted in the United Kingdom by the Diplomatic Privileges Act 1964, and it is further expressly provided in the Immigration Act 1971 that the laws affecting non-patrials shall not apply to any person so long as he is a member of a diplomatic mission.[4] Members of his family who form part of his household are likewise entirely exempt from control, as are those who have similar immunity from jurisdiction as is conferred on a diplomatic agent. The Immigration Act empowers the Secretary of State to exempt other classes from control, and this power has been exercised in application of the Consular Relations Act 1968.[5] Consular officers in the service of States with which consular conventions have been concluded[6] are exempted from any provisions of the Immigration Act relating to non-patrials. They do not, therefore, require leave to land, nor are they subject to registration or deportation.[7] Consular officers and employees of States with which no convention exists are exempted from all control except those provisions which relate to deportation.[8] In the United States, accredited diplomats and the like come within the class of 'non-immigrants', together with members of their families. Other diplomatic staff, employees, and

[1] U.N. Doc. A/CONF. 25 (23 Apr. 1963).

[2] The Convention came into force on 19 March 1967: 596 U.N.T.S. 261; Do Mascimento e Silva, 13 I.C.L.Q. (1964), 1214. See also United Kingdom Consular Relations Act 1968.

[3] See Vienna Convention on Consular Relations, Articles 53, 54, and note the restricted immunity from arrest given by Article 41.

[4] Immigration Act 1971, section 8(3).

[5] Ibid., section 8(2); see also The Immigration (Exemption from Control) Order 1972, Article 3 (S.I. 1972 No. 1613).

[6] See the Schedule to S.I. 1972 No. 1613.

[7] This exemption extends also to consular employees and family members.

[8] S.I. 1972 No. 1613, Article 4(h), (i), (j).

servants are likewise admitted on a basis of reciprocity.[1] Ambassadors, public ministers, career diplomats, and consular officers are exempted from deportation, and even if they fail to maintain their status they are not to be required to depart from the United States save with the approval of the Secretary of State, unless they fall within the provisions aimed at anarchists and subversives.[2]

The identification of diplomats and others is facilitated by the practice of issuing diplomatic passports and diplomatic visas, and possession of one or other of these documents would constitute prima facie evidence of status.[3] However, it should be noted that accreditation and acceptability are essentially political matters, and that the resolution of any dispute as to whether a given individual is entitled to diplomatic immunity is within the hands of the receiving State.[4] In *United States* v. *Coplon and Gubitchev*,[5] the District Court had to consider whether any effect was to be given to the fact of possession by Gubitchev of a diplomatic passport and visa. In an *aide-mémoire* submitted to the court, the U.S.S.R. argued that, the United States having formally admitted Gubitchev to the United States on a diplomatic visa, the official organs of that country had thereby recognized his diplomatic status.[6] The court preferred the views of the United States Government, and declared:

The visa which was affixed to the defendant's passport did not of itself constitute a grant of diplomatic immunity for all of his activities in this country . . . That diplomatic visas are on occasion granted . . . as a matter of courtesy and do not thereby constitute a recognition of diplomatic status has been [the Government's] proclaimed policy and is set forth in its promulgated and published regulations.

[1] Immigration and Nationality Act 1952, 8 U.S.C. s. 1101(a)(15)(i), (ii), (iii).

[2] 8 U.S.C. s. 1251(e). Adjustment to the status of permanent resident may be granted under s. 1255b(a). For analogous provisions of French law, see ordonnance du 2 nov. 1945, especially article 4; and for the law of the Federal Republic of Germany, see Ausländergesetz 1965, BGBl. I, 353, Article 49; Verordnung über Reiseausweise als Passersatz und über die Befreiung vom Pass- und Sichtvermerkszwang 1952, BGBl. I, 295, Article 2.

[3] Cf. 8 U.S.C. s. 1101(a)(11). There seems to be no rule, either of general international law or of practice, by which diplomats are exempt from visa requirements. Privileges and immunities do not commence until entry, but international comity would demand that visas be issued promptly and that documentary requirements be reduced to a minimum.

[4] *N.B.* Diplomatic Privileges Act 1964, section 4.

[5] 88 F. Supp. 915 (1950); *United States* v. *Melekh* 190 F. Supp. 67 (1960).

[6] Gubitchev was in fact an employee of the United Nations Secretariat. On the status of international officials generally, see below, pp. 152–5.

In order to ground a claim of immunity it was necessary that the defendant was not only 'in an intimate association with the work of a permanent diplomatic mission', but also that his accreditation to the United States Government should be certified by the Department of State.[1]

(2) SPECIAL MISSIONS

Ad hoc diplomacy and the use of special missions are phenomena of increasing importance.[2] They may be employed even in the absence of diplomatic relations, but once again their status depends in the first place upon the consent of the receiving State. It is generally assumed that special missions have no special status in customary international law, but that they benefit from the ordinary principles of sovereign immunity and the express or implied conditions of the invitation received by the sending State.[3] Indeed, at the 1965 Senate Hearing on the Vienna Convention of Diplomatic Relations, the Legal Adviser affirmed that the conventional privileges and immunities did not apply to the 'personal rank of ambassador accorded by the President to a United States representative'.[4] The application of such privileges would depend upon the nature of the representative's assignment abroad and, by implication, upon the consent of the receiving State.

Although special missions may have no special status in customary international law, in 1965 the International Law Commission referred specifically to the 'modern rules of international law' concerning the practice of using such missions.[5] As a result of its further endeavours in this field, the United Nations General Assembly in 1969 adopted and opened for signature the Convention on Special Missions.[6] This is in large measure based upon the principles contained in the Vienna Convention on Diplomatic Relations. Thus,

[1] In *R.* v. *Governor of Pentonville Prison, ex parte Teja* [1971] 2 Q.B. 274, the Divisional Court held that a foreign State's unilateral action in appointing a diplomatic agent, apparently to prevent his extradition, did not confer diplomatic immunity on the representative and, until the United Kingdom had accepted and received the intended representative as a *persona grata*, the diplomatic agent was not immune from proceedings in English courts.

[2] Brownlie, *Principles of Public International Law* (2nd ed.), pp. 349–50; O'Connell, *International Law* (2nd ed.), p. 913.

[3] Brownlie, op. cit., p. 350.

[4] Whiteman, *Digest*, vol. 7, pp. 33–47, at p. 41.

[5] Yearbook of I.L.C., 1965—II, p. 109; Whiteman, *Digest*, vol. 7, pp. 42–5.

[6] G.A. Res. 2530 (XXIV), 8 Dec. 1969, Annex: (a) Convention (b) Optional Protocol concerning the Compulsory Settlement of Disputes.

Article 2 emphasizes the importance of the consent of the receiving State, although Article 7 notes that the existence of diplomatic relations is itself irrelevant. The appointment of the members of missions is, like that of diplomats, subject to the right of the receiving State to decline to admit any individual without giving reasons.[1] Privileges and immunities are generally co-extensive with the entry of the mission into the State and its departure therefrom.[2] Heads of State and 'persons of high rank' are to enjoy the facilities, privileges, and immunities accorded by international law,[3] while privileges and immunities in other cases are extended by analogy with the corresponding provisions of the Vienna Convention.[4] However, it is expressly provided that the severance of diplomatic relations shall not *ipso facto* operate to terminate the functions of the special mission.[5]

There is sufficient in common between the provisions of the General Assembly Convention and those of the Vienna Convention to warrant the conclusion that similar principles apply to the admission of special missions as to that of diplomats.[6]

(3) INTERNATIONAL OFFICIALS

The privileges and immunities of diplomats are well founded in customary law and have since been codified and developed in international conventions. The status of officials of and representatives to international organizations is not so well settled and is largely dependent on treaty. Previously, international officials were treated by analogy with diplomats,[7] although this practice could clearly compromise their independent status by subjecting them to the vagaries of national passport regimes and to the personal objections of receiving States.[8] Article 105(2) of the United Nations Charter declares that the representatives of Members and the officials of the Organization are to enjoy such privileges and immunities as are necessary for the independent exercise of their

[1] Articles 8, 12. [2] Article 43. [3] Article 21.

[4] Articles 24–7, 29, 31, 39, 42; note Article 46.

[5] Article 20.

[6] See, for example, The Immigration (Exemption from Control) Order 1972 (S.I. 1972 No. 1613), Article 4(a).

[7] e.g. Article 7(4), Covenant of the League of Nations; see also Basdevant, *Les fonctionnaires internationaux* (1931), p. 53.

[8] Jenks, *The Headquarters of International Institutions* (1945), p. 37.

functions in connection with the Organization.[1] The content of the said privileges and immunities has been amplified in the General Convention on the Privileges and Immunities of the United Nations, and supplemented in agreements concluded by the United Nations and the specialized agencies with those States in which they are situated.

The General Convention provides that the representatives of Member States, while exercising their functions, are to be exempt in respect of themselves and their spouses from immigration restrictions and aliens registration.[2] This same privilege is to apply to the classes of officials of the United Nations specified by the Secretary-General.[3] The status of representatives and officials thus depends on treaty and on the provisions of local law.[4] The agreement between the United States and the United Nations regarding the headquarters of the United Nations of 1947 deals specifically with the question of access.[5] The United Nations undertakes to prevent the headquarters district from becoming a haven for criminals,[6] and the United States guarantees that federal, state, and local authorities will not impede transit to and from the headquarters.[7] This guarantee is assumed irrespective of the relations which may exist between the United States and the governments of the individuals concerned.[8] Laws and regulations continue to apply in respect of entry into the United States and visas may be required. However, these are to be issued promptly, without charge, and the

[1] See also Articles 19, 42(3), Statute of the International Court of Justice; Turack, *The Passport in International Law* (1972), ch. 18; *Zoernsch* v. *Waldock* [1964] 1 W.L.R. 675.

[2] General Convention on the Privileges and Immunities of the United Nations, Article IV, section 11(d); see also, ibid., section 14. Such exemptions are to apply both in the States being visited and in those through which the representative passes in transit. The principal representatives of Members are entitled to diplomatic privileges and immunities generally. Cf. United Nations–United States Headquarters Agreement, Article 15.

[3] General Convention, Article V, sections 17, 18(d); Bowett, *The Law of International Institutions* (3rd ed., 1975), pp. 308–21.

[4] e.g. United Kingdom International Organisations Act 1968; Immigration Act 1971, section 8(2), (3); The Immigration (Exemption from Control) Order 1972 (S.I. 1972 No. 1613), Article 4(g); United States Immigration and Nationality Act 1952, 8 U.S.C. s. 1101(a)(15)(G)(i)–(v), referring to the International Organisations Immunities Act 1945, 59 Stat. 669.

[5] Text in 11 U.N.T.S. 11; T.I.A.S. 1676.

[6] U.N.–U.S.A. Headquarters Agreement, Article III, section 9(b).

[7] Ibid., Article IV, section 11; see also Immigration and Nationality Act 1952, 8 U.S.C. s. 1101(a)(15)(C).

[8] U.N.–U.S.A. Headquarters Agreement, Article IV, section 12.

laws are to be applied so as not to interfere with the privileges conferred.[1] Should any individual abuse his privileges, the removal of the alien in question may be effected in accordance with the special procedure laid down.[2]

Article VII of the General Convention makes provision for the issue of United Nations 'laissez-passer',[3] to be recognized by Member States as valid travel documents. This has been described as a 'privilege of dubious value',[4] but in practice it is recognized by a large number of States Parties to agreements with the specialized agencies.[5] The major exception was for long the United States, which insisted on the possession of national passports and visas. The former attitude of the United States Government towards section 24 of the General Convention was stated by the Secretary of State, Marshall, in 1947:

> The language does not authorise or require, and is not interpreted by the Department of State as authorising or requiring the United Nations or any Member State to issue or accept a document which is a substitute for a passport or other document of nationality; it provides only for a certificate attesting to the United Nations affiliation of the bearer in respect to travel and will be accepted by the United States as such.[6]

[1] Ibid., section 13(a). Except as provided, the United States retains 'full control and authority over the entry of persons . . . into the territory of the United States and the conditions under which persons may remain or reside there': section 13(d). Cf. Article IX, section 27.

[2] Ibid., Article IV, section 13(b)(1), (2), (3). It is declared that the Headquarters Agreement is to complement the General Convention.

[3] Sections 24–8. For a brief history of the original proposals for a United Nations passport, see Turack, *The Passport in International Law*, pp. 158–61; Brandon, 'The United Nations Laissez-passer', 27 *B.Y.I.L.* (1950), 448.

[4] Bowett, *The Law of International Institutions* (3rd ed.), p. 319.

[5] Turack, *The Passport in International Law*, pp. 165–6; Convention on the Privileges and Immunities of the Specialized Agencies 1947, Article VIII, sections 26–30: 33 U.N.T.S. 261. See also Canada–I.C.A.O. Headquarters Agreement 1951, Article VIII, section 32: 96 U.N.T.S. 156; Switzerland–W.H.O. Agreement 1948, Article 14: 26 U.N.T.S. 331; Switzerland–I.L.O. Headquarters Agreement 1946, Article 14: 15 U.N.T.S. 383. Federal Republic of Germany, Verordnung über Reiseausweise als Passersatz . . . , 1952 BGBl. I, 295, Article 1(1)9.

[6] Whiteman, *Digest*, vol. 8, p. 333. Cf. Headquarters Agreement with Switzerland 1946, Article VII, sections 21–5: 1 U.N.T.S. 164. United Kingdom law does not deal expressly with the United Nations *laissez-passer*, but U.N. officials generally are not subject to immigration control and do not require leave to land: International Organisations Act 1968; Immigration Act 1971, section 8 (2); The Immigration (Exemption from Control) Order 1972, Article 4 (g). The Immigration Rules require the production of a passport, 'or other document satisfactorily establishing . . . identity and nationality'; this would presumably include the *laissez-passer*: *Immigration Rules for Control on Entry*, 1973 H.C. No. 79, para. 3; 1973 H.C. No. 81, para. 3.

At the same time the United States admitted that passport and visa requirements should not be imposed so as to prevent the proper exercise of the functions of international officials, any renewed insistence upon national travel documents would tend to perpetuate notions of national dependence.[1] For most purposes international officials are not to be confused with government representatives and there are sound arguments in favour of extending the exceptional regime which applies to them. Bowett has observed that,

> It follows from the fact that international officials are not accredited to States (as diplomats are) that the principle of *persona non grata* is not applicable to them. The proper procedure is for the host State to make its representations to the Secretary-General who alone can decide whether they shall be withdrawn from the territory.[2]

The General Convention affirms that the basis for the grant of privileges and immunities is not the personal benefit of individuals, but the safeguarding of the independent exercise of their functions.[3] The United States has guaranteed to admit representatives from States with which it does not maintain diplomatic relations or which it does not recognize,[4] but there have been a number of cases in which host States have refused to permit the entry of the representatives of States with which they do not have normal relations.[5] Such action is probably inconsistent with treaty obligations, particularly those assumed under Article 105 of the United Nations Charter and under the General Convention. Once a State has consented to the presence on its territory of the United Nations, in whatever form, then it would seem to be obliged, by the principle of good faith at least, to extend all those privileges and immunities anticipated by Article 105 and by the particular treaties.[6] Refusal to permit entry would thus constitute the breach of an international obligation.[7]

[1] The *laissez-passer* is now accepted for visa purposes: 22 C.F.R. 41.12; above, pp. 28–9.

[2] Op. cit., p. 319.

[3] Article IV, section 14; Bowett, op. cit., p. 314.

[4] Cf. Switzerland–W.H.O. Agreement 1948, Article 14(b).

[5] This has arisen particularly out of the Arab–Israeli conflict; see the examples cited in Plender, *International Migration Law*, at p. 111.

[6] Cf. Bowett, op. cit., p. 310.

[7] For details of international regional organizations and their travel documents, see Turack, op. cit., ch. 17. On the problems raised by the entry of armed forces, see Plender, op. cit., pp. 115–20; Bowett, *United Nations Forces* (1964), at pp. 79–8.

(4) CREWMEMBERS

Although not at first sight within the same class as diplomats and international officials, the crewmembers of ships and aircraft also benefit from their own travel regime. The International Civil Aviation Organization and the Intergovernmental Maritime Consultative Organization have both pioneered the widespread adoption of international standards and practices regarding the movement of seamen and aircrews. Most of the progress has been accomplished in the years since 1950 and, as with many such developments, the process began through the medium of the bilateral treaty. For example, in 1950 Italy and Belgium agreed, by an exchange of notes, to admit each other's nationals without visas if they were the holders of valid seamen's books.[1]

In 1955 the International Labour Organization Joint Maritime Conference proposed the meeting which led eventually to the 1958 Seafarers' National Identity Documents Convention.[2] The provisions of this Convention apply to all seamen engaged in any capacity aboard any vessel other than a warship, which is employed in maritime navigation and is registered in a territory for which the convention is operative. Seamen's cards may in addition be issued to non-national seamen serving on board the issuing State's ships, and no statement of the holder's nationality is required,[3] although he is to be entitled to readmission to the State of issue. States Parties to the Convention are obliged to admit the holder of a seaman's card for temporary shore leave, to enable him to join a ship or to transfer to another ship, to pass in transit to join a ship in another State or for repatriation, or for any other purpose approved by the host State. However, each Contracting State retains the right to exclude any particular individual or to prevent his remaining in its territory.

Further progress towards the adoption of international standards was made in the 1965 Convention on the Facilitation of Maritime

[1] 68 U.N.T.S. 283. See also United Kingdom–France Agreement 1953: 186 U.N.T.S. 151 (entry for up to fifteen days was permitted, although the right to exclude 'undesirables' was expressly retained); U.S.A.–Greece Treaty of Friendship, Commerce and Navigation 1951, Article XXII(6): 224 U.N.T.S. 151.

[2] 389 U.N.T.S. 277. The Convention entered into force in 1961. Turack, op. cit., ch. 14.

[3] If any such statement on nationality is included, it is not to be regarded as conclusive: Turack, op. cit., p. 140.

Travel and Transport.[1] The Annex to this Convention provides that a valid seafarer's identity card or a passport shall be the basic document providing public authorities with information relating to the individual member of the crew on the arrival or departure of a ship.[2] Such document is to be accepted as standard, in lieu of a passport, when it is necessary for the seaman to enter or leave a country generally for the purposes of his employment.[3]

The 1958 Convention has been ratified or acceded to by over twenty States, which now issue and recognize a standardized seaman's identity document on the basis of reciprocity. Similar standardization has been made in respect of aircraft personnel,[4] and the I.C.A.O. has been active in encouraging recognition of crew-members' licences as sufficient travel documents.[5] Municipal systems frequently recognize the peculiar status of crewmembers and local provision is made in respect of the treaties and conventions considered. The United Kingdom Immigration Act 1971 declares that the members of ship's crew may enter and remain without leave until the departure of the ship or ships on which they are engaged.[6] Aircraft personnel also do not require leave where they enter on engagement to leave on the same or another aircraft as a crewmember within seven days.[7] However, a crewmember may not enter without leave if (*a*) there is a deportation order in force against him; or (*b*) he has at any time been refused leave to enter the United Kingdom and has not since been given leave to enter and remain; or

[1] 4 Int. Leg. Mat. 501, in force 1967.

[2] Section 3(10). Limitations are also placed on the information which public authorities can require the document to contain: section 3(10)(1). British Seamen's Cards are issued under regulations made by virtue of section 70, Merchant Shipping Act 1970, which came into force on 1 January 1973. See the form set out in Schedule 1, The Merchant Shipping (Seamen's Documents) Regulations 1972 (S.I. 1972 No. 1295).

[3] Additional information may be obtained from the 'crew list', which many States require captains to produce to local immigration authorities. See, for example, the form set out in the Schedule to the Immigration (Particulars of Passengers and Crew) Order 1972 (S.I. 1972 No. 1667); Immigration Act 1971, Sch. 2, para. 27.

[4] Turack, op. cit., ch. 15.

[5] In order to be recognized, such licences must contain, at the very least, a certification of re-entry to the State of issue, a photograph of the bearer, and a record of his date and place of birth: Turack, op. cit., p. 150. Note the provisions of the United Kingdom–Yugoslavia Air Service Agreement 1959: 359 U.N.T.S. 339, discussed in Turack, op. cit., pp. 151 f.

[6] Immigration Act 1971, section 8(1). Cf. United States Immigration and Nationality Act 1952, 8 U.S.C. ss. 1281–2.

[7] Immigration Act 1971, section 8(1).

(*c*) an immigration officer requires him to submit to examination under Schedule 2 of the Act.[1]

Although crewmembers enjoy certain privileges in matters of entry, if they remain longer than their permitted time they can be dealt with under the same procedure as applies to illegal entrants and those refused leave to land. Immigration officers are empowered to order the summary removal of such crewmembers,[2] although there is a limited but practically meaningless right of appeal on the ground that there was in law no power to give the directions for removal. It is of little use because it cannot be exercised while the appellant is in the United Kingdom.[3] The right of appeal against removal on objection to destination is also limited and will not apply to the ordinary case of the man who jumps ship.[4] In much the same way, the provisions which permit the United States authorities to suspend deportation or to adjust the status of non-immigrant aliens to that of permanent resident do not apply in the case of crewmembers.[5]

International organizations have done much to establish a rational regime facilitating the temporary entry and sojourn of crewmembers. The primary intention has been to expedite international travel and to prevent unnecessary delays owing to immigration procedures.[6] Seen in this light, it is perhaps not surprising that entry facilities for crewmembers have been balanced by rigorous measures for the removal of those who remain behind.

One area which has not yet been made the object of regulation is that dealing with installations on the Continental Shelf. The question is, whether immigration laws can touch the alien who arrives directly on such an installation from another State. In the

[1] Section 8(1). It is apparent that both seamen's cards and aircrew licences would constitute sufficient documents of identity within the Immigration Rules. Cf. Federal Republic of Germany, Verordnung über Reiseausweise als Passersatz . . . , 1952 BGBl. I, 295, Article 1(1)3, 8.

[2] Immigration Act 1971, Sch. 2, paras. 12–15.

[3] Ibid., section 16(1), (2). The appeal is in any case to be dismissed, notwithstanding that the ground of appeal is made out, if the adjudicator is satisfied that there was power to give the like directions on the ground that the appellant was an illegal entrant. It remains possible to challenge the legality of any detention prior to removal, and hence the removal itself, by way of habeas corpus; see per Lord Denning, M.R., in *R.* v. *Governor of Pentonville Prison, ex parte Azam* [1973] 2 W.L.R. 949, at pp. 960–1.

[4] Immigration Act 1971, section 17. Curiously, there is an appeal only if the crewmember who jumps ship enters in breach of a deportation order.

[5] Immigration and Nationality Act 1952, 8 U.S.C. ss. 1254(f), 1255(a).

[6] Cf. Articles 22, 23, 27(j), I.C.A.O. Chicago Convention 1947: 15 U.N.T.S. 295.

United Kingdom the Continental Shelf Act 1964 provides for the application of civil and criminal law to structures on the shelf, which are thereby effectively assimilated to State territory.[1] Offences may be prosecuted and the offence may for all incidental purposes be treated as having been committed in any place in the United Kingdom. It appears that a landing on such a structure without the leave of an immigration officer could constitute an offence under section 24 of the Immigration Act 1971. Section 11(3) of the Continental Shelf Act declares that a 'constable' on any such installation shall have all the powers, protection, and privileges which he has in the area for which he acts as constable. It is questionable whether this includes an immigration officer, who may well be barred from exercising his functions on Continental Shelf installations. However, in 1974 it was said in response to a question in Parliament that passports are required for journeys from Scotland to oil rigs in the Scottish sector, because of the existence of direct travel links to the rigs from foreign ports.[2]

[1] Section 3. The Act also declares that provision may be made for treating as insurable employment any prescribed employment which is directed towards the exploitation of the resources of the Continental Shelf. Presumably this employment may also be made subject to the regime of work permits.

[2] 877 H.C. Deb. (Written Answers), col. 343 (July 1974).

X

OBLIGATIONS TO GRANT ADMISSION ARISING FROM TREATY

AN EXAMINATION of municipal law controls and a first consideration of international obligations well illustrate the thesis that States retain a wide margin of appreciation in the matter of entry to their territory. No State today adheres to the 'free movement' school, although there is a degree of similarity between local regimes and grounds of control. In principle, the entry of aliens is within the reserved domain of domestic jurisdiction, but it has already been noted that there are certain limits to the State's competence in this area. The major difficulty in any case will be to characterize the refusal of entry as the breach of an international obligation, such as to involve the State in international responsibility. Obligations do exist in respect of those fleeing from persecution, and these obligations, it has been argued, derive both from treaty and from customary international law. At the same time it was admitted that it will often be unclear to whom the relevant obligations are owed. In his dissenting opinion in the *Nottebohm Case*, Judge Read expressed the general rule that an exercise of the 'unfettered right' to refuse admission prevents any legal relationship from coming into existence between the 'receiving State' and the State of the alien's nationality.[1] This general rule is particularly relevant to the fulfilment of conditions for the exercise of diplomatic protection, but today account must also be taken of that burgeoning corpus of obligations transcending the confines of this traditional institution.

Treaties, whether bilateral or multilateral, are a primary source of obligations and, by their terms, may indicate more precisely the limits to State discretion in matters of entry and exclusion. The number of agreements and instruments which directly or indirectly bear upon the status of foreigners is legion, and their role has a long history. Early treaties of great significance were the 'capitulations', under which complete and separate legal regimes

[1] I.C.J. Rep., 1955, p. 4, at pp. 47–8.

were set up for the benefit of foreign nationals. During the seventeenth, eighteenth, and nineteenth centuries, bilateral treaties of friendship and commerce were concluded to regulate the status of the individual merchant in particular, to recognize his legal personality, and to secure minimum rights.[1] Modern treaties have progressed still farther, and tend to accord greater protection to the alien and to approximate his rights to those of the national.

Since the Second World War it has been common to find, for example, that treaties make provision for a hearing in the case of refusal of a residence permit, for the right to counsel, to an interpreter, and to communicate with one's consul, and for restrictions on the power to expel, particularly in favour of the long-term resident.[2] Other treaties have confirmed the status of particular groups; for example, by a Treaty of May 1945 Belgium agreed with France on the regulation of minor frontier traffic and on the issue and recognition of frontier permits.[3] In the same year, Belgium and Luxembourg furthered the re-establishment of freedom of movement by suspending the passport requirement and accepting national identity cards as sufficient evidence of status for their nationals passing between the two countries.[4] In addition to the limited regimes set up by treaties of this nature, due consideration must also be given, particularly in the European context, to broader based, multilateral agreements concerned with the rights of the individual.

(1) THE EUROPEAN CONVENTION ON HUMAN RIGHTS

The European Convention does not, in the main body of its provisions, protect a right of entry as such.[5] This was underlined in an early decision of the European Commission on Human Rights where it noted, in regard to the particular case:

[1] Neufeld, *The International Protection of Private Creditors from the Treaties of Westphalia to the Congress of Vienna (1648–1815)* (1971), pp. 96–8, 100–1, 110–12, and *passim*. See also 6 *B.D.I.L.* 330–2.

[2] See, for example, the Treaty of Establishment between the Federal Republic of Germany and Italy 1957, considered in *Re Expulsion of an Italian Worker* [1965] C.M.L.R. 53.

[3] 23 U.N.T.S. 215.

[4] 41 U.N.T.S. 13, 265.

[5] Article 3 of the Fourth Protocol does proclaim such right for nationals, but the Protocol is as yet unratified by Cyprus, Greece, Italy, Malta, the Netherlands, Switzerland, Turkey, and the United Kingdom. See Jacobs, *The European Convention on Human Rights* (1975), pp. 182–8; and below, pp. 286–90,

que la requérante semble revendiquer pour son mari le droit de se fixer sa résidence sur le territoire d'un État autre que son État national . . . qu'aux termes de ses articles 1 et 25(1), la Convention garantit les seuls droits et libertés définis en son titre premier; que seule la violation alléguée d'un de ces droits et libertés peut faire l'objet d'une requête recevable devant la Commission; que le droit susmentionné ne figure pas, quant à son principe, parmi lesdits droits et libertés; que le principe de non-discrimination consacré à l'article 14 de la Convention ne vaut que dans la jouissance des droits et libertés reconnus dans la Convention . . .[1]

So it follows that, unless another right or freedom guaranteed by the Convention is in issue, a complaint by a foreigner that entry to a Contracting State has been refused him is inadmissible. Nevertheless, there are a number of provisions under which the foreigner denied admission may be able to bring himself before the European Commission. For example, Article 3 of the Convention forbids degrading treatment; Article 5 defines the right to security of the person; Article 8 provides for respect for family life; and Article 14 protects individuals from discrimination.

A number of decisions of the Commision have brought these rights into play in matters of entry and exclusion. Thus, where an alien was refused entry to Sweden to take part in custody proceedings, the Commission decided that there existed the possibility of a violation of Article 6 of the Convention, which guarantees a fair hearing in the determination of civil rights and obligations. This reasoning was supported by reference to the fact that in the case in hand the personal character and manner of life of the applicant appeared to be a matter directly relevant to the formation of the Swedish court's opinion on the merits of the claim. In addition, the applicant's ex-wife was in a position to attend the hearings and to impugn in court the applicant's personal qualities. The Commission noted further:

a State which signs and ratifies the [Convention] must be understood as agreeing to restrict the free exercise of its rights under general international law, including its right to control the entry and exit of foreigners to the extent and within the limits of the obligations which it has accepted under that Convention.[2]

In another case, brought this time under the provisions of Article 8, the Commission held that, although the Austrian Government

[1] Application 238/56: 1 *Yearbook* 205.
[2] Application 434/58: 2 *Yearbook* 354.

had refused to readmit a deported German national, they had in no way prevented his wife, who had remained behind, from crossing into Germany to see or live with the applicant. On the facts, there had been no such interference with family life as was prohibited by Article 8.[1] The substance of this view has been repeated in a more recent decision, in which the Commission observed, first, that there were no legal obstacles to the family effectively establishing their life in the husband's home State, and secondly, that a decision by the wife to remain, as she was entitled to do, in the United Kingdom, did not thereby mean that there had been an interference by the authorities with the applicant's family life, within the meaning of Article 8(1) of the Convention.[2] In other applications which have involved the question of admission of those convicted of crimes, the Commission, while noting the principle that domestic authorities had a 'considerable measure of discretion in taking into account factors in the case which might appear to them to be critical for the prevention of disorder or crime', has nevertheless affirmed that it is the Commission itself which is the final judge of whether the measures taken are in breach of the Convention.[3]

The Commission retained for further examination the case of *Mohamed Khan* v. *United Kingdom*, which concerned a refusal of admission by immigration authorities acting under the Commonwealth Immigrants Act 1962.[4] The applicants alleged violation of the right to respect for family life and the right to receive a fair and impartial hearing before an independent tribunal in a determination of their civil rights under Article 6(1). The United Kingdom Government argued, *inter alia*, that the rights concerned were not

[1] Application 411/58 (unpublished), cited in *Case Law Topics*, No. 2, *Family Life* (1972), p. 7. See also Applications 1855/63 *v.* Denmark (*Recueil* 16, p. 50); 2535/65 *v.* Federal Republic of Germany (*Recueil* 17, p. 28); 3325/67 *v.* United Kingdom (*Recueil* 25, pp. 117, 121).

[2] Application 5269/71 (*Papayianni* v. *United Kingdom*), Decision of the European Commission on Admissibility, 8 Feb. 1972, printed at [1974] Imm. A.R. 7. Application to the European Commission followed on the decision of the Immigration Appeals Tribunal in *Secretary of State* v. *Papayianni* [1974] Imm. A.R. 1.

[3] In Application 3170/67 *v.* United Kingdom the Commission held that, in considering the background, character, and unfavourable criminal record of the applicant, the decision of the United Kingdom authorities to refuse admission was 'reasonable' and in no way exceeded the 'margin of appreciation'. See also Application 3898/68; both decisions are reported in *Case Law Topics* No. 2, pp. 10–11.

[4] Application 2991/66: 10 *Yearbook* 478. Cf. Application 2992/66 *Harbhajan Singh* v. *United Kingdom*, where the complaint was rejected when the applicant failed to show such a family link to exist as would establish family life within Article 8.

'civil rights' within the meaning of the Convention, but this was rejected by the Commission. In its view it was necessary to examine the merits of the applicants' case as regards a possible breach of the provisions of Article 8, and a Sub-Commission set up for this purpose achieved a friendly settlement at the end of 1968. The United Kingdom agreed to issue the requisite entry certificate and to make an *ex gratia* payment to cover the airfare from Pakistan.

Although those provisions of the European Convention which have been ratified by the United Kingdom do not include the right of a national to enter his own State, it has been argued that the 1968 legislation in fact infringed other related provisions. Between February 1970 and July 1972 a total of 255 applications by East African Asians against the United Kingdom Government were registered by the Europran Commission on Human Rights. These were originally placed in thirteen groups, and in October and December 1970 the Commission declared admissible respectively Groups I (12 applications) and II (6 applications), in so far as they raised issues under Articles 3, 5, and 14, whose determination should depend upon an examination of the merits of the cases. In respect of three of the applications, the complaints were also declared to be admissible under Articles 8 and 14.[1] Notice of the other groups was given at intervals to the United Kingdom Government, but further proceedings were suspended pending the outcome of the proceedings in Groups I and II.[2]

In argument before the Commission on the applications in Group I, the United Kingdom Government found it difficult to deny the discriminatory effect of the 1968 legislation. As regards the rights protected under Article 3, the Government alleged that there was no discrimination and that the applicants had at all times enjoyed the same rights as every other person seeking to reside in the United

[1] Applications 4478/70 and 4486/70 of Group I, and Application 4501/70 of Group II. See further below, pp. 165–6. All other complaints under Articles 8 and 14 were declared inadmissible, as being manifestly ill-founded.

[2] Of the 255 cases considered, by August 1972 at least 201 applicants had been admitted to the United Kingdom: *Press Release*, Council of Europe, C (72) 24, 25 Aug. 1972. The Commission's Report on Groups I and II under Article 31 of the Convention ('if a solution is not reached') was transmitted to the Committee of Ministers in 1974, but publication was delayed, apparently indefinitely, in the hope of achieving a friendly settlement. Of the applications in the remaining Groups nearly half had been struck off the list by the end of May 1977, as the individuals, having been admitted to the United Kingdom, failed to pursue their petitions: *Press Release*, Council of Europe, B (77) 26, 27 May 1977.

Kingdom. At the same time, however, the Government accepted that, had the United Kingdom been bound by the Fourth Protocol to the Convention, then the 1968 Act *was* discriminatory, and that, if this issue ever became relevant, the Government would have to justify that discrimination. In the meantime, and without prejudice to its alternative submissions, the Government admitted that the legislation was discriminatory in so far as its object was to exclude more than a limited number of East African Asians from entering the United Kingdom at any one period. The basis of the Government's case was that this still did not amount to discrimination *in the enjoyment of those rights and freedoms guaranteed by the Convention.* This argument was rejected by the Commission, which concluded:[1]

> Quite apart from any consideration of Article 14, discrimination based on race could, in certain circumstances, of itself amount to degrading treatment within the meaning of Article 3 . . . it is generally recognised that a special importance should be attached to discrimination based on race and that publicly to single out a group of persons for differential treatment on the basis of race might . . . constitute a special form of affront to human dignity.[1]

In respect of those applications which were based on an alleged breach of Article 8 of the Convention, the United Kingdom Government argued that, where a person has no right to enter or remain in a particular country, he cannot obtain such a right by having his wife change her residence to that country and then invoking Article 8.[2] It was further submitted that the place of residence of a family is normally the place of residence of the husband,[3] and that in so far as Article 8 safeguards a right for husband and wife to live together permanently in any particular place, it does not safeguard such right at a place other than the place of residence of the husband. In the opinion of the United Kingdom Government, the separation of husband and wife was not attributable to the Government, but to the voluntary actions of the applicants.[4] However, the Commission

[1] Decision of the Commission as to the admissibility of 25 applications by *S.M.L. Patel* (Application 4403/70) and others against the United Kingdom, Oct. 1970, p. 36.

[2] Cf. Application 238/56: 1 *Yearbook* 205.

[3] 846 H.C. Deb., cols. 37, 40–1; 849 H.C. Deb., col. 663. See now the change in the Immigration Rules introduced by Command Papers 5715–18, in respect to the entry of husbands and fiancés of women settled in the United Kingdom, and amending 1973 H.C. No. 79, para. 47; 1973 H.C. No. 81, para. 42. Cf. *Vasiljevic* v. *Secretary of State* [1975] Imm. A.R. 100; and below, p. 270.

[4] Compare Application 5269/71, *Papayianni* v. *United Kingdom*, above, p. 163.

noted that it was unlikely that, in the circumstances, the applicants would have been able effectively to establish their family life in Uganda, and the substance of the Government's submissions was rejected. Applications 4478/70, 4486/70, and 4501/70 were declared admissible in that the actions of the United Kingdom Government were capable of constituting an interference with the right to respect for family life within Article 8, or of raising an issue under Article 14 in conjunction with Article 8.[1]

The law of 1968 was criticized not only on the ground of racial discrimination, but also as being in breach of the duty in international law which a State has to admit its nationals.[2] Before the European Commission the United Kingdom Government maintained that it was never the intention that United Kingdom citizens resident in East Africa should be permanently prevented from entering the United Kingdom. In the view of the Government, the purpose of the Act was to regulate the flow of entrants at a level which the United Kingdom was capable of absorbing at any one time. The allocation of special vouchers was designed to implement this regulatory purpose and, while no voucher was ever refused to an eligible applicant, the system of priorities which was based on the individual's immediate needs might delay the issue of a voucher to a particular person.

The Government's view of its final obligation to United Kingdom citizens in East Africa and elsewhere has, to a certain extent, been vindicated by subsequent events. At the time of the mass expulsion of such citizens from Uganda in late 1972, the United Kingdom Government affirmed that it was under a duty to take in its nationals.[3]

[1] Even under the new rules it remains possible for a woman to be obliged to quit her own country in order to be with her husband (see *Vasiljevic* v. *Secretary of State* [1975] Imm. A.R. 100), and this is possibly inconsistent with developments in other fields affecting women's rights; see, for example, the Guardianship of Minors Acts 1971 and 1973, section 1(1); Sex Discrimination Act 1975.

[2] For the view of the Court of Appeal on the international obligation, see *R.* v. *Secretary of State*, *ex parte Thakrah* [1974] 2 W.L.R. 593; see also, *Bulletin of the International Commission of Jurists*, No. 34 (June 1968), p. 35; 759 H.C. Deb., col. 1501. Cf. the view expressed by Wilson, that the United Kingdom's regulatory measures are reasonable and justifiable under presently accepted general international law: *International Law and Contemporary Commonwealth Issues* (1971), ch. 5, at p. 165.

[3] See the statement by the Foreign Secretary, Sir Alec Douglas-Home, in a television broadcast reported in *The Times*, 1 Sept. 1972: 'successive British governments have made clear that in the last resort if these people were ever expelled we accepted an obligation to take them in . . . . Under international law a State has a duty to accept those of its nationals who have nowhere else to go.' See also *The Times*, 21 Sept. 1972, letter from the Prime Minister, Mr. Heath, to the Monday Club.

Thereafter, the official attitude became somewhat equivocal. In a statement made on the introduction of revised Immigration Rules in January 1973, the Home Secretary, Mr. Carr, explained to the House of Commons that the Uganda expulsions had created a new situation. He said:

The Government consider that to have a similar burden thrust on us again would impose unacceptable strains and stresses in our society and, not least, endanger our ability to carry out our duty to those immigrants already resident here. The Government therefore think it is right at this time . . . when there is no threat to United Kingdom passport holders elsewhere, to make it clear that while we shall continue to accept our responsibility to United Kingdom passport holders by admitting them in a controlled and orderly manner through the special voucher scheme, this as much as it is reasonable and realistic for us to do if good community relations are to be maintained in Britain.[1]

It may be that this was only a political statement for local digestion and it is probably unwise to speculate on the basis of some future and hypothetical mass expulsion. There remains, at base, the acceptance of responsibility for United Kingdom citizens; regulatory controls remain, but their restrictive effect has been offset to some extent by a further increase in the number of special vouchers.

This policy reflects the traditional view of many governments, that the entry of aliens and some classes of nationals is not a right which may be enforced by the individual. However, discretion in such matters is clearly limited for those States which are parties to the European Convention. In the protection which it extends to individual rights, the Convention sets the boundaries of State competence. It indicates with some precision the circumstances in which an exercise of lawful powers may nevertheless constitute an abuse. This effect has the additional consequence of raising the individual from the confines of his nationality and, by impinging on the traditional areas of State competence, the Convention places obligations in respect of fundamental rights and freedoms in an area of regional control. A similar process also occurs in respect of other treaties of more limited application and intention. As will presently be seen, State powers in such cases are confined by reference both to the terms of the treaty and to its object and purpose.

[1] 849 H.C. Deb., cols. 655–6; see also statement by Mr. Thorpe, ibid., col. 660; and further, 851 H.C. Deb., cols. 577–646, especially at cols. 589–91, 602–4, 608–10, 637–8.

(2) THE EUROPEAN CONVENTION ON ESTABLISHMENT 1955 AND THE TREATY OF ROME 1957

Article 1 of the European Convention on Establishment provides:

Each Contracting State shall facilitate the entry into its territory by nationals of the other Parties for the purpose of temporary visits and shall permit them to travel freely within its territory except when this would be contrary to 'ordre public', national security, public health or morality.[1]

Prolonged or permanent residence is also to be facilitated,[2] although this may be limited in accordance with the social and economic conditions of the States Parties. Moreover, the Protocol expressly provides that each Contracting State shall have the right to judge by national criteria the reasons of 'ordre public', national security, and so forth, which may justify exclusion,[3] and it is apparent that this concession may amount to a very wide power of derogation. Of the Convention as a whole, it has been said:

En l'absence de dispositions spécifiques imposant l'abolition d'une législation nationale discriminatoire, et considérant les larges clauses échappatoires contenues dans le traité, aussi bien que son objectif limité, on peut dire que la Convention n'a qu'un intérêt pratique réduit.[4]

This conclusion is not entirely justified in the light of other provisions of the treaty and of the principles of general international law which apply to its interpretation. For example, the treaty expressly declares that a Contracting Party may only restrict the rights of nationals of other Parties for the reasons set forth in the Convention, and to the extent compatible with the obligations otherwise assumed.[5] The object of the treaty is to facilitate establishment. The obligations assumed by States may not be very extensive, but an exercise of powers of derogation which frustrated the declared object and purpose would clearly be in breach of those obligations. The reservation of 'ordre public' certainly represents a

[1] European Treaty Series No. 19. See also Article 1, European Agreement on the Movement of Persons 1957, which makes provision for the reciprocal acceptance of informal documents of identity for those entering for periods of less than three months. This Agreement also permits derogation on grounds relating to 'ordre public': Articles 6, 7 (E.T.S. No. 25).

[2] Article 2.

[3] Section I; see also Section III.

[4] *Droit des Communautés Européennes*, para. 1861.

[5] Protocol, Section I(c).

reservation of discretionary power, but that is not equivalent to a reservation of arbitrary power. In the context of the specific treaty obligations, it must be understood as an exceptional right which, in the final analysis, is subject to impartial adjudication.[1]

The Convention on Establishment appears from its terms to be wider even that the Treaty of Rome, but it espouses generalities rather than details, and so must be considered of lesser effect. As the first multilateral treaty in an area traditionally governed by bilateral agreements, it purports to be a complete charter of the rights and duties of States in their relationship with the nationals of other Contracting Parties.[2] But the problems of entry and residence are approached with excessive caution—the obligation assumed is merely to 'facilitate' these ends. The analogous provisions of the Treaty of Rome offer an illuminating contrast; there can be little doubt that the agreements most effective in achieving freedom of movement between States are those which concern themselves with detail, and which envisage a local plan to be fulfilled by the co-ordination of national regimes. It has been observed that,

> entre les États européens le problème que pose la présence d'étrangers est moins l'octroi du standard minimum de civilisation que celui des conditions de participation à la vie économique.[3]

This conclusion is particularly pertinent in regard to the fundamental economic basis of the Treaty of Rome, and in relation to its provisions as to the right of establishment.[4] Moreover, where the stated aim is to establish a community with free movement of labour, services, and capital, it becomes no longer possible to leave the interpretation of the relevant provisions to individual governments, for these are matters which will have important repercussions on the 'sovereignty' of each Member State.

Article 48 of the Treaty of Rome called for free movement of

[1] *Guardianship of Infants Case*, I.C.J. Rep., 1958, p. 55. The importance of this case, and its relevance to the reservation of 'ordre public', is discussed in detail, below, pp. 295–7.

[2] It is doubtful whether non-signatory States could obtain the advantages of the European Convention on Establishment through the operation of the most-favoured-nation clause in existing or future bilateral treaties. The Convention is not an ordinary treaty, but was promoted by a regional institution to achieve certain regional objectives. See further, Kiss, 'La Convention européenne et la Clause de la Nation la plus favorisée', *Ann. Fr.* (1957), 478–89.

[3] Bastid, 'L'Organisation européenne et le traitement réciproque des nationaux', *Rev. Cr.* (1953), 467, 474.

[4] Articles 48–56.

labour to be achieved by the end of the transition period, and it emphasizes that this entails the abolition of all discrimination based on nationality, in respect of employment, pay, and conditions.[1] This article applies to wage-earners, whether skilled or unskilled,[2] and the notion of 'Community worker' has been shown to be itself a concept of Community law; it does not arise from, and is not governed by, national law. It embraces not only manual workers, but all employees;[3] not only a present worker, but also one who, having left his job, is capable of taking another.[4]

The meaning of free movement of labour is prescribed in some detail, as also is the action to be taken by organs of the Community and by Member States themselves.[5] Free movement entails the abolition of all discrimination based on nationality *vis-à-vis* Community workers.[6] It entails, further, the existence of rights in favour of the individual, and of limitations on the circumstances in which an exercise of those rights may be restricted. The rights declared in Article 48(3) include (i) the right to accept offers of employment actually made;[7] (ii) the right to move freely for this purpose within the territory of Member States;[8] (iii) the right to remain in a Member State in order to work in accordance with the law governing the

[1] Article 48(1), (2).

[2] Cf. Article 69, European Coal and Steel Community Treaty, in which Member States undertook to remove nationality restrictions on employment in the coal and steel industries in favour of workers nationals of Member States who had recognized qualifications. Article 96, Euratom Treaty, anticipated similar steps to liberalize access to skilled employment in the field of nuclear energy.

[3] *Vaasen-Goebbels* v. *Beamtenfonds vor het Mijnbedriff* [1966] C.M.L.R. 508, 521.

[4] *Unger* v. *Bestuur der Bedrijfsvereniging voor Detailhandel en Anbachten* [1964] C.M.L.R. 319: 'The Treaty, having by Articles 48–51 instituted the free circulation of workers, has thereby conferred on this term a Community meaning. If this could arise from internal law, each State would then have the power to modify the content of the concept of "migrant worker" and to eliminate certain categories of persons at will from the protection of the Treaty.' See also *Re Expulsion of an Italian National* [1965] C.M.L.R. 285; *City of Wiesbaden* v. *Barulli* [1968] C.M.L.R. 239, 242; *R.* v. *Secchi* [1975] 1 C.M.L.R. 383; below, pp. 300–6.

[5] Freedom of movement was in fact established in November 1968. The free-movement provisions became directly binding on the United Kingdom at the date of accession, 1 January 1973, except in respect of Northern Ireland for which a five-year transitional period was negotiated: *The United Kingdom and the European Communities*, Cmnd. 4715, para. 144.

[6] Article 48(2); see also Articles 3, 7.

[7] Regulation 1612/68, Articles 1, 5, 7. The provisions of Article 48 do not extend to employment in the civil service, or to the policy- and decision-making levels of nationalized industries. Cf. *Reyners* v. *Belgian State* [1974] 2 C.M.L.R. 305.

[8] Since Regulation 1612/68, Article 1, free movement is no longer tied to the taking of jobs notified to the employment exchange. Mégret, *Le Droit de la CEE*, vol. III, p. 21.

employment of nationals of that State; and (iv) to right to remain in another Member State after having been employed there.[1] Restriction on the exercise of these rights must be justified by reference to concepts of 'ordre public', public security, and public health, specified in Article 48(3), and since developed in secondary legislation and the jurisprudence of the European Court.[2]

Under the authority of Article 49, a three-stage plan for the realization of free movement of labour was implemented. The first stage, in the years 1961–4, involved the retention of national priorities in the labour market, with certain exceptions in favour of E.E.C. nationals.[3] In the years 1964–8 priority for Community workers was introduced, with certain exceptions retained in favour of national workers.[4] Finally, in 1968, the regime of free movement was established, with the entry into force of Regulation 1612/68 and Directive 68/360 which provided for *de jure* free movement in the six States, together with equality and the principle of non-discrimination. Since then, substantial provision has also been made in respect of social security, so that under Community law the Community worker has established rights to social security benefits in respect of the periods spent by him working in any of the Member States.[5] The migrant worker is not placed at a disadvantage, and wherever he goes within the Community he takes with him his social security entitlements.[6]

These, then, are the basic provisions governing freedom of movement of labour within the E.E.C.[7] In practice, it is debatable to what extent they are relevant to the European worker. In the years 1958–70 the European Community suffered from a shortage of manpower, and this led to the importation of labour from States outside the Community. For example, it has been estimated that of

[1] Regulation 1251/70. It is not clear whether this right to remain includes a 'right to return' to a State where a worker has at some time been employed, or whether it is limited to the State where he is last employed. Article 8(2) of this Regulation only provides that States shall look favourably on workers in this position: Mégret, op. cit., vol. III, p. 5.

[2] See Directive 64/221 and further below, pp. 181–6, 300–6.

[3] See Regulation 15/61.

[4] See Regulation 38/64.

[5] See Article 51, E.E.C.; Regulations 1408/71 and 574/72, as amended: J.O. L 2, 1973; J.O. L 86, 1973. These Regulations came into force throughout the enlarged Community on 1 April 1973.

[6] *Bestuur der Sociale Verzekeringsbank* v. *Smieja* [1974] 1 C.M.L.R. 620.

[7] Matters of detail are dealt with in Regulation 1612/68 and Directives 64/221 and 68/360; see further below, pp. 181–6.

the 3·7 million migrant workers in the Community, between 2·3 and 2·7 million came from third States such as Greece, Turkey, Yugoslavia, Spain, etc. Indeed, the Community concluded agreements with such States, particularly in respect of the importation of labour.[1] However, it was never very clear to what extent workers from third States might enjoy the benefits which accrue to the E.E.C. migrant worker. It is possible that Article 48(1) is wider than Article 48(2), and that the general objectives of the E.E.C. Treaty would be best advanced by permitting free movement of labour regardless of nationality.[2]

In one case in 1968 it was held by a Belgian court that Treaty references to workers or their dependants were limited to workers who were *ressortissants* of Member States, or who are stateless persons or refugees resident in Member States, and their dependants.[3] But whether a worker must always be within these categories in order to come under the Treaty is less settled. There has been a tendency to maintain the restrictive approach, so that, for example, in times of recession, the worker from a third State will find himself at a particular disadvantage in social security and related matters. The fact that Community law obliges a Member State to keep its labour market open to workers from other Member States was used as the basis for a German decision that nationals from other States,

[1] Cf. Articles 12–14 of the 1964 Agreement with Turkey, which anticipate the gradual removal of restrictions on the movement of labour, establishment, and the supply of services; see also Regulations 1232–5/71. A similar agreement with Greece was suspended during the time of the Colonels; Greece applied for full membership of the E.E.C. on 12 June 1975. These agreements are in addition to the association agreements permitted by Articles 131–6 with those non-European countries and territories which have special relations with the Member States. Article 135 permits the establishment of free movement with these territories, subject to the provisions of 'ordre public', public security, and public health, and to the unanimous approval of Member States.

[2] Cf. Articles 3(c), 7. Böhning, 'The Scope of the E.E.C. System of Free Movement of Workers', 10 C.M.L. Rev. (1973), 81; a rejoinder to Edens and Patyn, 9 C.M.L. Rev. (1972), 322–8. In 1976 the Council of Ministers resolved on an action programme for migrant workers and members of their families. The necessity of improving the lot of migrant workers from third States was emphasized and the goal of equality was proposed in regard to living and working conditions, wages, and economic rights. The realization of this aim is intended to be matched by joint action to suppress illegal immigration. See Council Resolution, 9 Feb. 1976: O.J., vol. 19, No. C34, p. 2 (14 Feb. 1976); cf. European Convention on the Legal Status of Migrant Workers 1977.

[3] *Sociale des Mutualités Chrétiennes à Bruxelles* v. *H.D.C.* reported in *Cahiers de droit européen* (1970), 210. Cf. Council Declaration 64/305, 25 Mar. 1964, J.O., 22 May 1964, No. 78: the entry of refugees established in the territory of another Member State 'doit être examinée avec une faveur particulière'.

in this case an Egyptian student, have no right to find employment in the Federal Republic.[1]

The fact remains, however, that such conclusions are by no means the necessary consequence of the Community provisions. Regulation 1612/68 merely prohibits discrimination as between nationals of Member States,[2] and simply reaffirms the provision originally laid down in Regulation 38/64, namely, that the nationals of other Member States shall enjoy *priority* over others as regards access to employment.[3] In certain other areas, a broader definition of the concept of worker may be in order. Thus, in Regulation 1408/71, Article 1 lays first emphasis on the fact of being insured as the indicator for social security entitlements. Article 2, which sets down the scope of the Regulation *ratione personae*, enlarges the traditional limitation to nationals of Member States and admits refugees and stateless persons resident within a Member State.[4] The survivors of insured workers are also included irrespective of such workers' nationality, but provided that the survivors themselves are nationals of Member States, or stateless persons or refugees residing within the territory of one of the Member States.

(*a*) '*Nationals*' *of Member States*

Although there may be some variation in the content of the term 'worker', the general rule remains that Treaty benefits accrue to those who are nationals (*ressortissants*) of the Member States.[5] The category of nationals is determined by reference to the local law of the State concerned, and that status will be evidenced by a passport or other national identity card. Certain problems emerge, however, from the respective nationality laws of France, the Netherlands, Germany, and the United Kingdom.

[1] *VerwRspr*. Bd. 19, S. 958 (OVG, Münster, 1968); see also *Re Residence Permit for an Egyptian National* [1975] 2 C.M.L.R. 402 (OVG, Rheinland-Pfalz, 1972).

[2] Articles 1, 2, 4, 5, 6. In its Opinion on the proposal for a Council Directive on education of children of migrant workers, the Economic and Social Committee described equality of opportunity in education as a fundamental principle of European society. Although Regulation 1612/68 was, strictly speaking, applicable only to nationals of Member States, the social action programme was intended for all migrant workers. It was noted that migrant workers from non-Member States now accounted for approximately 70 per cent of the total: O.J., vol. 19, No. C45, p. 6 (27 Feb. 1976).

[3] Article 1(2); see also Lipstein, *The Law of the European Economic Community* (1974), pp. 84–6; *Fracas* v. *Belgian State* [1975] 2 C.M.L.R. 442.

[4] Article 2(1), (2).

[5] Regulation 1612/68, Article 1(1): 'Any national of a Member State, irrespective of his place of permanent residence, shall be entitled to take up and carry on a wage paid occupation in the territory of another Member State.'

According to the law of the Federal Republic of Germany, and to a declaration made at the time of accession to Euratom and the E.E.C., German nationals include citizens of the German Democratic Republic.[1] The status of French national embraces citizens of the French overseas territories from the date at which they establish their permanent residence in France.[2] Furthermore, the status of Dutch national includes those who enjoy that status solely by birth in or relation or connection with certain dependent territories. The latter, and French nationals who are not permanently resident in France and who derive their status from connection with an overseas territory, are not E.E.C. nationals for the purposes of Articles 48 and 49, even though they may enjoy the privilege of unrestricted entry into Holland or France.[3]

These somewhat anomalous classifications have much in common with the situation and circumstances of Commonwealth citizens and non-patrial United Kingdom citizens. When the United Kingdom signed the Treaty of Accession it made a declaration on the meaning to be given to the phrase 'United Kingdom national' for the purposes of the Treaty.[4] Basically, this definition includes citizens of the United Kingdom and Colonies and British subjects without that citizenship or the citizenship of any other Commonwealth country, who have the right of abode in the United Kingdom.[5] In addition, United Kingdom citizens from Gibraltar, even though not 'patrials', also enjoy the benefits of Articles 48 and 49.

The British Declaration, in particular, has been the object of considerable criticism. Böhning, for example, invokes the composite status of British subject, derived now from the British Nationality Act 1948, as a ground for holding that it is 'incompatible with the Treaty of Rome and its derivative legislation to have one nationality definition for domestic purposes, but to exclude from it certain sections of the population for E.E.C. purposes'.[6] He relies further

[1] See above, pp. 16–20.

[2] Loi du 28 juillet 1960; cf. loi no. 73-42 du 9 janv. 1973, Titre VIII.

[3] Böhning and Stephen, *The E.E.C. and the Migration of Workers* (1971), p. 27; ibid., Supplement (1972), pp. 3–4. *Statement of Immigration Rules for Control on Entry* (E.E.C. and other non-Commonwealth Citizens), 1973 H.C. No. 81, para. 50.

[4] Cmnd. 4862–1, p. 118.

[5] i.e. they are 'patrial' and not subject to control under the Immigration Act 1971. United Kingdom nationals and patrials are not co-extensive; see Immigration Act 1971, section 2(1)(d).

[6] 10 C.M.L. Rev. (1973), 81, at pp. 83–4; see also by the same author, *The Migration of Workers in the United Kingdom and the European Community* (1972), pp. 153 ff.

on the fact that immigrants admitted to the United Kingdom from the new Commonwealth countries enjoy certain material benefits, political, economic, and social, as a reason for assimilating them to nationals of the United Kingdom, thereby entitled to freedom of movement. This is, in many ways, an interesting and attractive argument, but it is based finally on incorrect premisses. Commonwealth immigrants may be broadly divided into two classes: (*a*) Citizens of the United Kingdom and Colonies; and (*b*) Citizens of the independent States of the Commonwealth. It happens that both are assimilated within the term Commonwealth citizen/British subject, and that to both are accorded the right to vote and other social and economic privileges. These consequences follow from thc British Nationality Act 1948, but nevertheless differences remain between the two classes. Thus, the citizens of independent States of the Commonwealth do not cease to be such citizens. Certainly, they may enjoy the 'material rights' of United Kingdom citizenship, but for the United Kingdom to go farther and to treat them as its citizens for all purposes would be a breach of the obligations owed in international law to their own States of nationality. After five years in the United Kingdom, the individuals involved may opt for United Kingdom citizenship, but until such time they do not form part of the body politic; local allegiance may be owed, but the principal tie remains with their own State.

The full force of the discriminatory measure, and indeed the main objection, is to be found in its application to those who are United Kingdom citizens, and yet who have no 'right of abode'. Such citizens, in the full sense of the word, are denied the rights of free movement until such time as they shall have acquired the status of patrials, i.e. generally, after five years' residence in the United Kingdom. An indication of the grounds which lie behind the distinctions[1] forced into the definition of 'nationals' is to be found in the Joint Declaration on free movement attached by the 'Six' to the Final Act of the Treaty of Accession. By this Declaration it was noted that 'the enlargement of the Community could give rise to certain difficulties for the social situation in one or more Member States', and the Member States therefore reserved the right to bring such matters for settlement before the institutions of the Community.[2]

[1] The existence of the various distinctions may be compared with the expressed objectives of the Community; see Articles 2, 3(c), (i), (k), 5, 7; Regulation 1612/68, Preamble.

[2] Cmnd. 4862–1, p. 117.

It is manifest that this Declaration was made expressly in order to permit later restrictions upon the movement of black citizens, particularly from the United Kingdom. Nevertheless, it would still not be possible for any single Member State to impose such restrictions unilaterally.[1] Furthermore, in view of the Treaty's objectives, it is open to doubt whether a sufficient consensus could be obtained either to cut back the fundamental tenet of free movement, or to run counter to the general norm of non-discrimination.[2] Certainly, the European Court of Justice has set itself against allowing measures incompatible with fundamental rights recognized and guaranteed by the constitutions of Member States, and indicated in the various international treaties to which Member States are parties.[3]

The criterion of nationality finishes as hardly a satisfactory basis for the free-movement provisions, and it is unlikely that it could ever be successfully reduced to an absolute concept for the purposes of the Treaty of Rome. Although declared as the basic qualification for participation in the benefits, nationality is continually displaced by provisions intended to benefit refugees and stateless persons, and the families and dependants of nationals.[4]

(*b*) *Rights Incidental to Free Movement*

In addition to the generality of rights described above, the migrant worker also enjoys specific rights which bear particularly on his entry into the territory of another Member State. The Regulations made under Article 48 confer enforceable rights on the individual, and in one case in 1962 the court declared:

> The legal position . . . by which the grant of a residence permit is in the discretion of the authorities has been altered in favour of those workers who are nationals of the E.E.C. Member States to the effect . . . that there exists a legal right to the grant of a residence permit, unless reasons of safety or public order or public health stand against it.[5]

[1] Note the exceptional safeguard measures permitted under Regulation 38/64, Article 2, and compare with the Community procedure which has replaced it: Regulation 1612/68, Article 20; Mégret, op. cit., p. 26.

[2] Cf. Article 49(d); and see above, pp. 75–87.

[3] *J. Nold K.G.* v. *European Commission* [1974] 2 C.M.L.R. 338; and see *Rutili* v. *Minister of the Interior* [1976] 1 C.M.L.R. 140, para. 32. See also *Prais* v. *Council of the European Communities* [1976] 2 C.M.L.R. 708.

[4] See Regulation 1612/68, Article 10(1); Directive 68/360, Article 4(4).

[5] *Re Residence Permits* [1964] C.M.L.R. 5 (decision of the Berlin Verwaltungsgericht,

Directive 68/360 requires the suppression of the remaining restrictions on the movement and residence of the E.E.C. nationals referred to in Regulation 1612/68.[1] A most important provision is contained in Article 2, by which States Members recognize the right of their nationals to leave the country 'en vue d'accéder à une activité salariée et de l'exercer sur le territoire d'un autre État membre'. This right is exercisable on simple presentation of a valid passport or identity card, which States are in turn obliged to issue.[2] Similarly, entry to other Member States is to be permitted on production of the relevant travel document, and visas may only be demanded of family members who are not E.E.C. nationals.[3] Once admitted, the E.E.C. national is entitled to a residence permit, and again the only formality required is that he show the travel document with which he entered the territory, together with a declaration of engagement from his employer.[4] Members of his family must also show their travel documents, and a certificate from the competent authority of the State of origin showing their relationship to the worker and, where necessary, their dependence on that worker.[5] Residence permits will

1962); this decision was based upon Regulation 15, and the right to be issued with a residence permit today is no longer tied to a labour permit. See also *Re Expulsion of an Italian National* [1965] C.M.L.R. 285. Regulation 1612/68 lays down specific rights on non-discrimination in access to employment (Articles 2, 3, 4, 5, 6; see *Re French Merchant Seamen* [1974] 2 C.M.L.R. 216); equality of treatment concerning conditions of employment (Article 7); equality of treatment as regards membership of trade unions and the exercise of trade union rights (Article 8); and non-discrimination in housing (Article 9). Article 10 declares the right of the worker's family to join him, and family is defined to include the spouse, children under 21 or, if older, dependent children; dependent relatives of the worker and his spouse in the ascending line. States are also required to look favourably on the admission of other dependent relatives. The exercise of the right of settlement is made conditional upon provision by the worker of adequate housing (Article 10(3)): Mégret, op. cit., p. 24. Once admitted for settlement, spouse and children under 21 are entitled to take up employment (Article 11; *Ministère Public* v. *Scarabel* [1968] C.M.L.R. 264), and children are to be admitted to schools etc. on the same terms as nationals (Article 12; see *Casagrande* v. *Landeshauptstadt, Munich* [1974] 2 C.M.L.R. 423; followed in *Alaimo* v. *Prefect of the Rhône* [1975] 1 C.M.L.R. 262).

[1] Directive 68/360, Article 1: J.O., 19 Oct. 1968, No. L257.

[2] Ibid., Article 2(1), (2). Where a passport is the only valid exit document, then it must be valid for at least five years: Article 2(3). No exit permit or visa may be required: Article 2(4). See above, pp. 34–8, for United Kingdom practice, which continues to be governed by the royal prerogative.

[3] Directive 68/360, Article 3. Cf. France, décret du 5 janv. 1970, art. 2.

[4] Directive 68/360, Article 4(3)(a), (b). This article creates the 'carte de séjour de ressortissant d'un État de la CEE'. Cf. France, décret du 5 janv. 1970, articles 3, 4, 10; article 4 of this law also requires the E.E.C. national to produce a medical certificate. See Directive 64/221, Annex, list of diseases which justify exclusion.

[5] Directive 68/360, Article 4(3)(c), (d), (e).

generally be valid for five years and are automatically renewable and valid for the whole territory.[1]

The holder of a residence permit enjoys the right to take up and carry on wage-paid occupations in the territory concerned under the same conditions as local nationals. Such a permit is not tied to a specific job,[2] and the E.E.C. national is free to move around at will. Moreover, the permit may not be withdrawn merely because the holder is out of work, either because of temporary incapacity from illness or accident, or because he is 'involuntarily unemployed'.[3] However, the permit's duration may be reduced to a period of not less than one year if the holder is involuntarily unemployed for more than twelve consecutive months.[4] Otherwise, States Members may only derogate from the provisions of this Directive on grounds of 'ordre public', public security, or public health.[5]

More recently, Regulation 1251/70 has emphasized that the right of residence which accrues to active workers, 'a pour corollaire le droit reconnu par le traité de demeurer sur le territoire d'un État membre après y avoir occupé un emploi.'[6] In effect, this Regulation recognizes, and gives practical meaning to, acquired rights of residence in favour of the migrant worker. Certain conditions are laid down, but the privilege of continued residence is granted not only to the worker, but also to his family.[7] Where a worker qualifies, then

[1] Directive 68/360, Article 6(1). Cf. France, décret du 5 janv. 1970, articles 5, 6. Permits of shorter duration may be issued to those whose stay is only temporary: Directive 68/360, Article 6(3), and in certain circumstances no permit is required: ibid., Article 8. Cf. décret du 5 janv. 1970, articles 7, 8, 9.

[2] Compare United Kingdom practice, Böhning and Stephen, *The E.E.C. and the Migration of Workers*, Suppl. (1972), p. 1; and see above, p. 108. Cf. Federal Republic of Germany, Arbeitserlaubnisverordnung, 1971, BGBl. I, p. 152, which makes provision for the issue of work permits to foreign workers either for a particular job or without restriction: Article 1. Such unrestricted permits are also available, for example, where the individual has spent five years working in the Federal Republic, or is married to a German national, or has been accorded refugee status: ibid., Article 2.

[3] *City of Wiesbaden* v. *Barulli* [1968] C.M.L.R. 239, 246. The court held, *inter alia*, that the Treaty and Regulation 38/64, in referring to freedom of residence of E.E.C. nationals in E.E.C. States, only confer such freedom in furtherance of the movement of workers in the Community labour market. An idle alien layabout not intending to take work may not rely on these provisions to avoid expulsion from the E.E.C. country of which he is not a national. See also *R.* v. *Secchi* [1975] 1 C.M.L.R. 383; *The State* v. *Royer* [1976] 2 C.M.L.R. 619.

[4] Directive 68/360, Article 7; *Williams* v. *Secretary of State for Justice* [1977] 1 C.M.L.R. 669.

[5] Ibid., Article 10. See below, pp. 300–6.

[6] J.O., 30 June 1970, No. L142/24; on the self-employed, see now Directive 75/34.

[7] The term 'worker' includes (*a*) the worker who has reached pensionable age, has

his family may remain even if the worker has died,[1] and those who come within the Regulation have the right to a residence permit valid for five years and automatically renewable.[2]

(*c*) *Freedom of Establishment*

In addition to the special rules applicable to the wage-earner, treaty provisions and subordinate legislation also deal with the individual who wishes to set up in business on his own account, or to engage in some other non-salaried activity. These provisions fall under the general rubric of the 'right of establishment', and are covered by Articles 52–8 of the Treaty of Rome. The general principle, stated in Article 52, is that

> Freedom of establishment shall include the right to take up and pursue activities as self-employed persons and to set up and manage undertakings . . . under the conditions laid down for its own nationals by the law of the country where such establishment is effected.

This concept of establishment is by no means new, and already it figures in a multitude of bilateral and multilateral treaties, so much so that it can be looked upon as a term of art. Generally, the provisions of such treaties aim to equate the alien with the national in respect of professional and commercial activities, although none so far concluded goes quite the whole way towards creating the effective and practical regime anticipated within the European Community. The potential scope of the E.E.C. provisions is vast, and Directives already issued cover activities ranging from agriculture to the film industry, from the wholesale trade to forestry and logging. In other areas, such as banking and the mutual recognition of diplomas and qualifications, progress was not at first so fast.[3] However, in 1974,

been employed for at least twelve months in the State concerned and has resided there for more than three years; (*b*) the worker with two years' residence in the State of his employment, who becomes incapacitated; (*c*) the worker who lives and works in one State, and then works in another State while continuing to reside in the first State: Article 2(1)(a), (b), (c). In certain circumstances the residence qualification is inapplicable, for example, if the worker's spouse is a national of the State of residence or lost that nationality on marriage: Article 2(2). Directive 72/194 extends to this class of workers the benefits of Directive 64/221.

[1] Regulation 1251/70, Article 3(1). In some circumstances, for example, death from industrial disease, the family may remain even though the worker dies before qualifying: Article 3(2).

[2] Ibid., Article 6.

[3] Mégret, op. cit., vol. III, pp. 90, 104–6; the *Times Higher Education Supplement*, 15 June 1973.

the European Court held that Article 52, in so far as it prescribed non-discrimination on the ground of nationality, was legally perfect, taking direct effect at the end of the transitional period. Directives, as the medium for liberalizing or opening-up the various professions no longer played a necessary role, although they would facilitate the exercise of the right of establishment.[1] The Court went on to apply the same reasoning to those Articles which deal with the provision of services, holding that Articles 59(1) and 60(3) have direct effect, and can be relied on before national courts as source of the rule against discrimination.[2]

Article 53 of the Treaty, which prohibited Member States from introducing any new restrictions on establishment, was itself held by the Court in 1964 to be complete and legally perfect.[3] But it was also noted that the right of establishment guaranteed by the Treaty was the right to 'national' treatment only, and that it did not confer an absolute right to engage in any occupation, It is in this light that one can the better understand the movement to achieve greater harmonization of procedures and regulations, and wider recognition of diplomas and qualifications. It is precisely this process which the Court had in mind in the *Reyners Case*, when it referred to the important and continuing role of Directives in making easier the path of those who seek to exercise the right of establishment. In this way the effectiveness of 'national treatment' as an *exclusionary* principle can be overcome. One commentator has noted that,

> the disparity in the systems applicable to nationals in the matter of the exercise of professions makes the clause of national treatment totally ineffective for the setting up of an equitable régime of the right of establishment on the international plane.[4]

For this reason, Article 57 of the Treaty of Rome is of major importance, in that it forecasts co-ordination of requirements based,

[1] *Reyners* v. *Belgian State* [1974] 2 C.M.L.R. 305, 324, paras. 26–7, 30–2.

[2] *Van Binsbergen* v. *Bestuur van de Bedrijfsvereniging voor de Metaalnijverheid* [1975] 1 C.M.L.R. 298; *Walrave* v. *Association Union Cycliste Internationale* [1975] 1 C.M.L.R. 320.

[3] *Costa* v. *E.N.E.L.* [1964] C.M.L.R. 425, 458.

[4] Piot, 'Of Realism in Conventions of Establishment', *Clunet* (1961), 38–84. Cf. Article 10, European Convention on Establishment, which requires non-discrimination in employment between nationals of the Contracting Parties. For details of local efforts in this field, and for an indication of the limited benefits accruing from 'national treatment', see *First Periodical Report by the Standing Committee on Establishment (Individuals)* (1971), pp. 31–43.

regionally, on the Community.[1] Only when a sophisticated background of harmonization is achieved will the right of establishment and the right to national treatment become relevant to the E.E.C. national.[2]

(*d*) *Secondary Community Legislation*

The first two Directives in this field were crucial in their application to the right of establishment: Directive 64/220, which concerned the suppression of restrictions on the movement and residence of E.E.C. nationals in respect of establishment and the provision of services;[3] and Directive 64/221, which requires co-ordination in local jurisdictions of the special regime applicable to foreigners in matters affecting 'ordre public', public security, and public health.[4]

Directive 64/220 is very similar in form to Directive 68/360 examined above. In this case the beneficiaries are those E.E.C. nationals who wish to provide services or participate in some non-salaried activity on the territory of another Member State, and the families of such persons.[5] Member States agree to permit the entry of E.E.C. nationals upon simple production of a passport or a national identity card,[6] and they recognize also the right of their nationals to leave their own State.[7] For a temporary stay of less than three months no residence permit is required, but in other cases permits will generally be issued for five years and they must be

[1] Mégret, op. cit., vol. III, pp. 102–6. Access to the liberal professions on the basis of national treatment may also be effected through bilateral treaties; see, for example, the Franco-Congolese Treaty of 15 August 1960: *Rev. crit. dr. int. pr.* (1965), 68 (note M. Simon-Depître). See also the convention signed between the Paris Bar and the Law Society, 12 April 1976; text in Law Society's *Gazette*, vol. 73 (5 May 1976), pp. 377–8.

[2] See Articles 59–66 of the Treaty for corresponding provisions in respect of the freedom to provide services within the E.E.C. For examples of the continuing efforts to secure wider recognition of qualifications, see Directive 75/362, which requires Member States to recognize medical qualifications obtained in other Member States and to facilitate the right to establishment; and also Directive 77/249, on facilitating the effective exercise by lawyers of freedom to provide services. See generally, Maestripieri, 'Freedom of Establishment and Freedom to supply Services', 10 C.M.L. Rev. (1973), 150; Bronkhorst, 'Freedom of Establishment and Freedom to Provide Services under the E.E.C. Treaty', 12 C.M.L. Rev. (1975), 245.

[3] J.O., 4 Mar. 1964, L 845/64; this is now amended and substituted by Directive 73/148: J.O., 28 June 1973, L 172/14.

[4] J.O., 4 Mar. 1964, L 850/64. This latter Directive is equally applicable to measures taken under Article 47 of the Treaty as to those taken under Article 52.

[5] Directive 73/148, Article 1.

[6] Directive 73/148, Article 3(1).

[7] Directive 73/148, Article 2(1). On the duty to issue passports or other travel documents, see above, pp. 40–1.

renewed automatically.[1] The only documents required to be produced are (*a*) the travel document under which the entrant gained admittance to the country;[2] and (*b*) proof that the entrant has the right to engage in the specified activity, that is, that it has been 'freed'.[3] Derogation is again permitted only for reasons of 'ordre public' etc.[4]

Both Article 48 and Article 56 anticipate the possibility of such limitations on the freedom of entry and residence as are justified by reasons of 'ordre public', public security, and public health. It has been argued that Directive 64/221 was issued in order to co-ordinate these concepts, which represent a retention of 'sovereign rights'.[5] In fact, and this point is argued more fully below,[6] 'ordre public' is itself a concept of Community law, which allows to Member States a certain margin of appreciation in matters considered to affect the national interest. The power of derogation is exceptional, and the validity of its exercise stands to be assessed in the light of the fundamental obligations undertaken by States Parties to the Treaty of Rome, and to the express limitations on the area of discretion which are required by Directive 64/221. This Directive applies to questions of entry, to the issue of residence permits or their renewal, and to expulsion. In no case, however, may restrictions be imposed to serve economic ends.[7]

Health matters are dealt with quite simply. Article 4(1) of the Directive, together with the annexed list of diseases and disabilities, declares the circumstances in which entry may be refused, or the first residence permit denied.[8] However, where such diseases or disabilities arise after a residence permit has already been issued,

[1] Directive 73/148, Article 4(1), (2). The same rights extend to family members: ibid.

[2] Cf. Lyon-Caen, *Droit social européen* (1969), para. 333: 'le droit d'entrée ne dépend que de la justification d'identité'.

[3] Directive 64/220, Article 5; Directive 73/148, Article 6. Under Article 55 of the Treaty a reservation is made in favour of the local State in respect of those occupations which involve the exercise of official, public authority. In *Reyners* v. *Belgian State* the European Court restricted the application of this provision to *activities*; it could not operate to deny access to occupations or professions as a whole: [1974] 2 C.M.L.R. 305, 324, paras. 49–53.

[4] Directive 73/148, Article 8. For the right of the self-employed to remain in the territory of a Member State after having exercised the right of establishment there, see Directives 75/34 and 75/36.

[5] Désmedt, 'La police des étrangers', *Cahiers de Droit Européen* (1966), 55–71.

[6] See below, pp. 300–6.

[7] Directive 64/221, Article 2(2).

[8] The list of diseases follows the International Sanitary Regulations No. 2 of the World Health Organization. Cf. France, décret du 5 janv. 1970, article 4 and Annex.

this provision does not justify either refusal to renew the permit or an order of expulsion.[1] The conditions for the imposition of restrictions on grounds of 'ordre public' or public security are less clearly defined, but certain guidelines are laid down. First, any action taken or proposed must be related solely to the personal conduct of the individual concerned.[2] Neither a criminal conviction by itself, nor the mere expiry of an identity card, may justify the refusal to renew a permit or the making of an order of expulsion.[3] While a criminal conviction will naturally be relevant to any consideration of the alien's personal behaviour, in a decision in 1968 a German court emphasized that other factors were also to be taken into account before the discretion to expel was exercised. A criminal conviction may be the lawful condition for the exercise of discretion, but alone it was not a sufficient ground for an adverse decision.[4] In a later decision, a different court affirmed that expulsion should be founded on the character of the individual alien, but it also noted that the authorities have a wide margin of appreciation in the matter and that, in effect, the interests of the State outweigh those of the alien.[5]

More recently the formative influence of Community law concepts has become more noticeable. The courts of the Federal Republic of Germany have been particularly critical of the actions of the authorities, and have been keen to set the limits of discretion with some precision. In one case, for example, the court declared that it would be a misuse of discretion for the authorities to limit the exercise of their judgment to establishing simply the existence of one of the conditions for expulsion. In all cases the exercise of power must be based on the principle of proportionality.[6] Elsewhere it has been

[1] Directive 64/221, Article 4(2); cf. United Kingdom Immigration Act 1971, section 30.

[2] Directive 64/221, Article 3(1); the meaning of 'personal conduct' was amplified by the European Court in *Van Duyn* v. *Home Office* [1975] 1 C.M.L.R. 1, 14, paras. 13, 17–18; and *Bonsignore* v. *Oberstadtdirektor*, *Köln* [1975] 1 C.M.L.R. 472.

[3] Directive 64/221, Article 3(2), (3).

[4] *VerwRspr*. Bd. 19, S. 964 (decision of the Bundesverwaltungsgericht, 1968). The case involved a conviction for manslaughter on the grounds of diminished responsibility; the court considered that there was a possibility of similar acts in the future and therefore a danger to 'ordre public' and public safety. See also *Re Deportation of a Belgian National* [1974] 1 C.M.L.R. 107, decision of the OVG, Münster, 1972.

[5] *VerwRspr*. Bd. 20, S. 844 (decision of the Oberverwaltungsgericht, Rheinland-Pfalz, 1969). The court considered Directive 64/221 and also the similar provisions of Article 2(2) of the Treaty of Establishment with Italy.

[6] *BVerwGE*. Bd. 35, S. 291, 292–3, 296 (1970). This decision involved interpretation of the 1927 Treaty of Establishment with Turkey, but the principles stated are of general

held that 'ordre public' as used in Article 48(3) of the Treaty, and in Regulations and Directives made thereunder, is a concept of Community law and not necessarily to be identified with any similar concept current in any of the national legal systems of the Member States.[1] This, essentially, is the view also of the European Court of Justice, as expressed in *Van Duyn* and *Bonsignore*. In the latter case, the Court mentioned that any departure from the rules concerning free movement by way of recourse to the exceptional powers is to be strictly construed.[2]

In addition to the substantive guarantees, Directive 64/221 anticipates a number of procedural guarantees. For example, Article 5 creates a presumption in favour of the E.E.C. national and, while insisting that decisions on individual applications must be taken with all due dispatch,[3] it provides for 'conditional entry' in the meantime.[4] The reasons for any refusal to renew or to issue a residence permit and for any order of expulsion must be given to the person affected, unless this would be contrary to the interests of national security.[5] Notice of the decision must also be given and at least fifteen days allowed for departure to those still awaiting the first residence permit, or one month to others.[6] Articles 8 and 9 require that there should be available some form of appeal or review against adverse decisions, and the individual concerned is to enjoy the same possibility of challenging administrative action as is enjoyed by nationals. Where no recourse to a court of law is available, or where such remedy can only be against the legality of the decision, or where it has no suspensory effect, then review must be permitted by some body independent of that which took the original decision.[7]

application. See also *Re Residence Permits* [1964] C.M.L.R. 5; *Re Expulsion of an Italian National* [1965] C.M.L.R. 285, which both affirm that the court may determine for itself whether the alleged reasons relating to 'ordre public' etc. exist.

[1] *City of Wiesbaden* v. *Barulli* [1968] C.M.L.R. 239, 242.

[2] [1975] 1 C.M.L.R. 472, 486, para. 2.

[3] Directive 64/221, Article 5(1). Decisions must be taken within six months at the latest.

[4] Detention pending decision is not, therefore, permitted. Cf. United Kingdom Immigration Act 1971, section 4(2); Sch. 2, para. 16; *State* v. *Royer* [1976] 2 C.M.L.R. 619, 640; *R.* v. *Boucheran*, *The Times*, 31 Oct. 1977 (European Court of Justice).

[5] Directive 64/221, Article 6. Article 5(2) authorizes the receiving State to seek details of a person's past record from the State of origin, but this is to be done on an informal, rather than regular or systematic basis.

[6] Ibid., Article 7. Less time may be allowed in cases of urgency.

[7] Ibid., Article 9 (1). Cf. France, décret du 5 janv. 1970, article 11, which establishes the special review procedure for E.E.C. nationals in France.

The E.E.C. Treaty and subordinate legislation have introduced a special regime for the benefit of the nationals of Member States. These advantages accrue primarily to those who desire to contribute economically to the Community, but in practice this cannot be considered a restricted category. While international law protects the minimum rights of the alien abroad, the E.E.C. national is also protected against future changes in the law which may adversely affect both citizens and foreigners.[1] At the same time he enjoys the protection of Community law and Community law concepts, which override the provisions of local jurisdictions. In this way significant restrictions are placed upon areas of State discretion which are commonly characterized in terms of 'sovereign rights'. The entry of the nationals of Member States to the territory of other Members is in practice dependent upon the simple proof of identity and status. Once within the frontiers, the migrant must comply with the established system of residence permits, but here he enjoys substantive rights as regards their issue, together with important procedural rights of appeal and review. Despite suggestions to the contrary,[2] the discretionary State powers retained in the 'ordre public' clause cannot be used to frustrate the fundamental principle of free movement. The competence which is affirmed stands to be interpreted in the light of the treaty obligations assumed and the provisions of the particular legal order which that treaty has created.[3] The reduction of free-movement and establishment provisions to so many details emphasizes the failings of many earlier, and some contemporary, bilateral treaties, which have been content to abide by generalities.[4] The unique feature of the E.E.C. regime is that movement between Member States is governed by the provisions of Community law, which alone determines the validity or invalidity of measures of implementation taken by State authorities; the provisions of local law remain of relevance, but they may only be imperfect reflections of Community law requirements.

However, the fact remains that bilateral treaties and agreements dealing with the right of establishment cannot be forgotten. Alien merchants and others have long conducted their affairs under the protection of such treaties; it remains to be seen whether the word

[1] Treaty of Rome, Articles 53 and 62.

[2] e.g. Wybo, *Discrimination et Marché Commun* (1966), p. 111.

[3] See further below, pp. 194–5.

[4] For example, the Anglo-Japanese Treaty of Establishment 1963: 478 U.N.T.S. 86; see further below, p. 195.

'establishment' as used in such a context is a term of art, and whether it can be seen to entail any well-defined rights and benefits.

(3) BILATERAL TREATIES OF ESTABLISHMENT

Historically, treaties of commerce and friendship have employed a variety of stock phrases purporting to express norms of international law applicable between the parties. Treaties have guaranteed that nationals of each party shall 'enjoy the full protection and security required by international law',[1] or that they shall benefit from the most-favoured-nation standard, that is, from treatment on a footing not inferior to the most favoured third State,[2] or that they shall be accorded 'national treatment'. At first glance there might appear to be a sufficient body of customary international law in this field to lend weight and content to the standard provisions of bilateral treaties.[3] However, in many respects these standards were not only uncertain, but were also inadequate to the main purpose, which was to secure non-discrimination with respect to treaty nationals or commercial enterprises. For example, the most-favoured-nation clause never in fact prohibited a State from discriminating or raising barriers against aliens as a class. The development of the 'national treatment' clause as the norm was intended to overcome these drawbacks, but it too was accompanied by substantial disadvantages. In many cases it could be argued that the standard of national treatment did not even meet the minimum requirements of international

[1] Wilson, *The International Law Standard in Treaties of the United States* (1953), pp. 87–105. See also Neufeld, *The International Protection of Private Creditors from the Treaties of Westphalia to the Congress of Vienna (1648–1815), passim.*

[2] Schwarzenberger, 'The Most-Favoured-Nation Standard in British State Practice', 22 *B.Y.I.L.* (1945), 96; id., *International Law and Order* (1971), ch. 8. The benefits of the Treaty of Rome are limited, for the most part, to the 'ressortissants' of States signatory thereto, especially in the case of Articles 52–9. It has been observed that, where individual States members have concluded treaties with third States, 'les ressortissants de l'État tiers qui ne participe pas à cette communauté et qui, dès lors, n'a pas souscrit aux obligations inhérentes à cette participation, ne peuvent pas se prévaloir, en vertu d'une clause de la nation la plus favorisée, des avantages resultant de cette communauté': *Droit des Communautés Européennes*, para. 1859. See also, *Le Statut de l'étranger et le Marché Commun*, 57ème Congrès des Notaires de France (1959), E.S. de la Marnière, *Introduction*, pp. 16–20. Note Article 234 of the Treaty of Rome, which obliges Member States to take all necessary steps to eliminate any incompatibilities resulting from agreements with third States, and which emphasizes that Treaty advantages are inseparably linked to the creation of common institutions.

[3] Cf. the parallel development in the nineteenth century of standards of protection for the admitted alien and in respect of compensation for expropriated property: Wilson, op. cit., pp. 87–105. See also Schwarzenberger, *International Law* (1957), vol. I, p. 207.

law, while in other cases disparity between national systems in regard to, for example, the establishment of enterprises, made it impossible to set up an equitable and reciprocal regime.[1] Together with these doubts and uncertainties, most treaties of commerce and establishment included a reservation to the effect that, while nationals of each contracting party enjoyed the right of entry, such 'right' was subject to compliance with local immigration and police laws. When problems arose over particular exclusions, States Governments were never quite sure of their footing.[2] Diplomatic protests did not usually follow upon individual exclusions, but there are a number of examples of remonstrance when exclusion took the form of discrimination against certain classes or groups of citizens. Occasionally, such discriminations were considered justifiable in the light of the terms of the treaty. For example, the Law Officers of the Crown in 1886 came to the conclusion that the treaty right of British subjects to 'free' admission to the United States, which was based on Article I of the Convention of Commerce between Great Britain and the United States of 1815, was confined to the inhabitants of the territories of Her Majesty in Europe and was subject always to the laws and statutes of the United States. It could not, therefore, be properly invoked by Her Majesty's Government in support of the claim of British subjects of Chinese origin to exemption from the Chinese Exclusion Act and to free admission to the United States.[3]

This Convention was again in point in the matter of the admission of British nationals, free persons of colour, which was impeded by the laws of South Carolina. The Foreign Office advanced the construction that a condition attached to the enjoyment of a right granted by treaty must be construed as only regulating the exercise of that right; it could not justly be construed as authorizing its entire extinction. With reference to the proviso in the Treaty that the liberty of free admission was to be subject always to the laws and statutes of the two countries respectively, the Foreign Office contended that these very words implied that the liberty was to exist

[1] Piot, 'Of Realism in Conventions of Establishment', *Clunet* (1961), 38–84; Walker, 'United States Commercial Treaties Today', in *De lege pactorum*, Essays in honour of R. R. Wilson (ed. D. D. Deener) (1970), p. 258.

[2] See, for example, the controversy over the interpretation of Articles I and XI of the Anglo-Russian Treaty of Commerce and Navigation 1859: 6 *B.D.I.L.* 29–32. See also, *Memorandum of Grievances of British Subjects of the Jewish Faith* (1912); 6 *B.D.I.L.* 32–42.

[3] 6 *B.D.I.L.* 20.

and to be enjoyed and exercised, and that it was therefore impossible to maintain that the proviso could sanction a law, the effect of which must be utterly to prevent that liberty from being exercised and enjoyed, or from existing at all. However, the Queen's Advocate then advised:

The condition attached to the enjoyment of a right granted by Treaty should certainly be construed as regulating, and not as authorising its entire extinction; but the condition in this case does not operate as an extinction of the right to the general body of Her Majesty's subjects, but to a particular class only, and if known to be in existence when the Treaty was signed, might have been intended as an exception to the general right.[1]

Another instance of discrimination arose in relation to the Anglo–Russian Treaty of Commerce and Navigation of 1859,[2] and Russian policy regarding the admission of Jews. The Treaty followed the usual form and it was provided that the stipulations as to freedom of commerce etc., 'in no way affect the laws, decrees and special regulations regarding commerce, industry and police, in vigour in each of the two countries, and generally applicable to all foreigners'.[3] The question for determination was whether British Jews were thereby subject to the considerable number of laws in Russia which discriminated against persons of that particular creed. Her Majesty's Government somewhat reluctantly concluded that it was unable to object to such discriminations, which had been tacitly accepted since 1859, and expressly in 1862 and 1881. It was admitted, however, that:

the claim of the Russian Government to be entitled to define for itself classes of undesirables is capable in practice of very wide extension, and might lead to results entirely inconsistent with the Treaty .... The Russian claim must be reduced within limits, but it is not easy to see where the limits are to be placed, while reserving the right to exclude persons who may properly be considered undesirables.[4]

[1] Ibid., p. 22. [2] *Hertslet's Commercial Treaties*, vol. X, p. 1057.

[3] Article I.

[4] 6 *B.D.I.L.* 37. In a Memorandum submitted by British Jews on the Government's interpretation and its view that British Jews in Russia were not suffering the same disadvantages as Russian Jews, it was alleged that the Russian Government was claiming to apply to British Jews certain special laws and regulations in the Passport Statute and the commercial code entirely different from the special administrative system which governed native Jews. The opinion was put forward that these restrictions were not justified by the Treaty because they did not apply to foreigners generally, but only to a single class defined by reference to a difference of religious opinion.

The Assistant Legal Adviser, Mr. Hurst, while accepting that the general right of entry must be read subject to the implied right of the contracting parties to exclude individuals whose presence will be harmful to the territory, nevertheless felt that the onus of showing that such individuals were harmful ought to rest on the excluding power. He added:

I do not think that logically it is possible for the excluding Power to claim a higher right than that; in fact it might well be argued that from the strict point of logic the implied exception only extends to cases where the parties are agreed as to the harmful effect of the individual . . . to be excluded, but on the whole I think that the sounder rule would be that a party is entitled to exclude where it can demonstrate to the satisfaction of a reasonable person that the individuals . . . would have a harmful effect . . . . In practice, however, it does seem to me that there has been a tendency on the part of foreign nations to accept exclusion laws without demur—at any rate so far as individuals are concerned—without calling upon the excluding State to justify its act . . . . My own conclusion is that unless Russia can demonstrate that the presence of a Jew in Russia is harmful in its effects she is not entitled under her Treaty with Great Britain to exclude them altogether when they are of British nationality.[1]

However, it was not this opinion which prevailed, and the Lord Chancellor concluded that the Treaty's objects and scope were prima facie restricted to what reciprocal privileges in commerce and navigation imply, and that police regulations and the power to make them do not fall within the range of those restrictions on sovereignty which the Treaty contemplated. Furthermore, it could not be asserted that the wording of the Treaty was such as to have effected a surrender of the inherent sovereign right of restricting the entry of individuals on grounds unconnected with their nationality.[2] In consequence, no protest was made to the Russian Government, a policy decision which was motivated also by the fear that any complaint to that Government would encourage it to terminate the Treaty by formal notice, to the detriment of all concerned.[3]

[1] Minute, 6 Sept. 1912: 6 *B.D.I.L.* 38–9.

[2] Lord Haldane to the Foreign Office, 1912: 6 *B.D.I.L.* 40–1.

[3] Cf. *Dudley Mann's Case* (1852): Whiteman, I *Damages in International Law*, 464. This case concerned the refusal by the Russian legation to visa Mr. Mann's passport, which was alleged to be in violation of Article I of the Treaty of Commerce and Navigation of 1832 between the United States and Russia. In reply to a request to the United States Government that a demand for damages of not less than $100,000 be submitted to the Russian Emperor, the Secretary of State, Everett, noted that while the power reserved to Russia to exclude those deemed dangerous probably had some limits, 'it

These cases may be contrasted with another instance of class discrimination against British subjects, apparently in violation of treaty rights. In 1896 the question arose whether a new law of the South African Republic constituted a violation of Article XIV of the London Convention of 1884.[1] This law provided that persons should not be at liberty to enter or reside in the Republic unless they could show affirmatively that they had the means or ability to support themselves, whereas the only condition imposed by the Convention was that they should conform themselves to the laws of the Republic. Her Majesty's Government considered that this new law was more than an ordinary police law, and that it was discriminatory in the sense that it imposed an additional burden which it might be difficult for many of the poorer, though perfectly respectable, immigrants to satisfy. A protest to the Government of the South African Republic was made along these lines.[2]

In many cases, certainly, the rule against exclusion in violation of treaty seems to have been honoured more in the breach than in the observance. In the *Chinese Exclusion Case* in 1889, the United States Supreme Court held that although the exclusionary Act of 1888 was in contravention of the treaties made with China in 1868 and 1880, it was not on that account to be restricted in its enforcement. In the opinion of the Court, treaties were of no greater legal force than an Act of Congress and were subject to such Acts as Congress might pass for their enforcement, modification, or repeal.[3] In 1893 in a

would not be safe to deny to . . . governments the right of judging for themselves . . . which course of policy in this respect is required by the great law of self-preservation. What we deny to other powers we must disclaim for ourselves; and this government could never give up the right of excluding foreigners whose presence they might deem a source of danger to the United States.'

[1] *Hertslet's Commercial Treaties*, vol. XVII, p. 12.

[2] 6 *B.D.I.L.* 26–9.

[3] *Chae Chan Ping* v. *United States* 130 U.S. 581 (1889). The Court also declared that the power to exclude foreigners is an incident of sovereignty and that the right to its exercise cannot be granted away or restrained on behalf of anyone. See Hackworth, *Digest*, vol. III, pp. 717 et seq. Whiteman. I *Damages in International Law* 418; *Shizuko Kumanomido* v. *Nagle* 40 F.2d 42, 44 (1930); *In Re Pezzi* 29 F.2d 999, 1002 (1928). In *McCandless* v. *United States, ex parte Diabo* 25 F.2d 71 (1928) the court held that Article III of the Jay Treaty, which gave to Indians dwelling on either side of the United States–Canada boundary the right 'freely to pass and repass . . . into the respective territories and countries of the two parties' was not abrogated by the War of 1812 and that the applicant could not therefore be deported for entering the United States under the provisions of the Treaty. Article IX of the Jay Treaty was considered in a decision of the Supreme Court in 1830, in which it was noted that the Article related to the rights of nationals of both countries to hold and dispose of land as if they were natives and not

Report to the President on a proposed Bill to suspend immigration for one year, the Secretary of State, Foster, declared:

I am not aware of any treaty which specifically purports to limit or restrict the right of this Government to control immigration into the United States .... Treaty provisions granting the right of entry, travel or residence in this country generally contain in some form the conditions of subjection to the laws of the land .... It is doubtful whether any of these treaty provisions guaranteeing rights of travel, residence, etc., were intended or can be construed to be restrictive of the right of the contracting governments to control immigration into their respective territories.[1]

During the late nineteenth and early twentieth centuries assertions continued to be made to the effect that immigration was a matter of purely domestic concern.[2] Nevertheless, developments were in hand which were to give important practical weight to the hitherto vague concept of a right of establishment, and to secure its more effective recognition both in municipal law and in the provisions of contemporary treaties.

aliens, and that it was therefore within those terms of the Treaty which were intended to be permanent, which operated in time of war as of peace, and which dealt with permanent territorial arrangements: *Society for the Propagation of the Gospel in Foreign Parts* v. *New Haven* 8 Wheat. 464. In 1928 the Supreme Court itself also dealt with Article III, but it distinguished the nature of that Article from that of Article IX. The latter might be implemented in war as in peace whereas Article III, which dealt with passage across the border, could not; in addition, Article IX could be said to have given a vested right intended to be perpetual, while Article III could not be so described. In effect the rights recognized in *ex parte Diabo* were limited to Indians who had been accepted and enfranchised as citizens of Canada: *Karnuth* v. *United States*, *ex parte Albro* 279 U.S. 231 (1928). See further *Francis* v. *R.* [1955] 4 D.L.R. 760, where a Canadian court followed the Supreme Court and held that Article III of the Treaty had expired with the War of 1812, even if Article IX had not. Cf. *United States Treaties in Force*, 1 Jan. 1962, which declares that only Articles IX and X of the Treaty continue in force.

[1] Moore, *Digest*, vol. IV, p. 154. See also Hackworth, *Digest*, vol. III, pp. 718, 768–9, and the account of the negotiations, treaties, and laws concerning immigration from China in Moore, op. cit., pp. 189 et seq.

[2] e.g. Sixth International Conference of American States 1928: 'The delegation of the United States desires . . . to state that the control of immigration is a matter of purely domestic concern, representing the exercise of a sovereign right and that, as far as the United States of America is concerned, the authority of its Congress in immigration matters is exclusive.' Cited in Wilson, *United States Commercial Treaties and International Law* (1960), pp. 28–9. This attitude is supported in municipal law by the courts' adoption of the 'political question doctrine'—the notion that questions which are in their nature political can only be answered by Congress or the President and are beyond the scope of judicial review: *Fong Yue Ting* v. *United States* 149 U.S. 698 (1892); *Nishimura Ekiu* v. *United States* 142 U.S. 651 (1892); *Baker* v. *Carr* 369 U.S. 186, 217 (1962); Konvitz, *Civil Rights in Immigration* (1953), pp. 3–6.

The United States Immigration Act of 1924 brought the classification of 'treaty-merchant' into the general category of non-immigrants.[1] It was considered desirable, in the words of one commentator,

that there be created a status which would be consistent with the spirit of existing commercial treaties, by permitting natural persons to enter the country on a basis somewhat less permanent than that accorded full immigrants, but more favourable than that enjoyed by temporary visitors having visas valid for a relatively short time.[2]

Such treaty-merchants were described by the statute, as amended in 1932, as 'aliens entitled to enter the United States solely to carry on trade between the United States and the foreign State of which [they are nationals] under and in pursuance of a treaty of commerce and navigation'.[3] The 1932 amendment emphasized that the trade must be reciprocal and not merely local, and it extended the statutory provision in respect of treaties subsequently concluded. The emphasis upon trade and the status of 'merchant' has been underlined in a number of court decisions. Thus, for example, a Chinese teacher was held not to be a person engaged in 'trade' within the meaning of the Treaty of 1880 between China and the United States.[4] In an earlier case, the Supreme Court made the following observations in regard to the status of a treaty-merchant:

The confounding of occupations—that of salesman or manager with that of merchant—cannot be accepted. A merchant is the owner of a business; a salesman or manager, a servant of it, and especially so under the immigration law. The policy of the law must be kept in mind. It is careful to distinguish between the status of merchant and those below that status.[5]

[1] 43 Stat. 153, section 3(6). See also complaints by the Japanese Government that this statute otherwise contravened the 'Gentleman's Agreement' of 1907 by providing, in section 13, that 'no alien ineligible to citizenship shall be admitted to the United States': Konvitz, op. cit., pp. 3-6.

[2] Wilson, *United States Commercial Treaties and Internatonal Law*, pp. 32 et seq.

[3] The right of entry extended also to the alien's wife and unmarried children under 21, if accompanying or following to join him.

[4] *Jeu Jan Wan* v. *Nagle* 9 F.2d 309 (1925).

[5] *Dharandas Tulsidas* v. *Insular Collector of Customs* 262 U.S. 258, 264 (1923). Cf. *Shizuko Kumanomido* v. *Nagle* 40 F.2d 42, 44 (1930), where it was held that a Japanese subject, the editor but not the proprietor, of a Japanese newspaper published in San Francisco, was engaged in trade within the meaning of Article 1 of the Treaty with Japan of 1911. The Treaty expressly provided that Japanese subjects shall have the right to 'employ agents of their choice . . . incident to or necessary for trade'.

The category of treaty trader has been maintained in the Immigration and Nationality Act 1952,[1] and non-immigrant status continues to be accorded to those who qualify under treaty.[2] However, the trade in question must now be 'substantial' and it must also be carried on 'principally' between the United States and the foreign State of which the treaty trader is a national. The 1952 Act introduces a further category of treaty alien, the 'treaty investor', who is characterized as one who comes solely to develop and to direct operations of an enterprise in which he has made or is about to make a substantial investment.[3] The treaty-investor innovation has figured frequently in commercial treaties concluded after 1952.[4] In most other cases, however, the treaty trader will either be self-employed or, if in the service of another, then his employer will be a person or organization of the same nationality as the non-immigrant. But if the latter is to benefit from the statute and the treaty, it is necessary that he be engaged in supervisory or executive duties, or that he have some special qualifications.[5] The Department of State recently expressed concern at the way in which these special categories were used by aliens coming for employment in organizations operated by aliens permanently resident in the United States. New regulations were therefore issued, redefining the conditions for classification as a non-immigrant treaty trader or treaty investor.[6]

[1] Section 101(a)(15)(E); 8 U.S.C. s. 1101(a)(15)(E).

[2] The nationality of the spouse and children is irrelevant, for their rights and their classification are dependent upon the status of the treaty alien: 22 C.F.R. 41.40(c); 41. 41(b).

[3] Cf. United Kingdom practice: 1973 H.C. No. 79, paras. 33–4; 1973 H.C. No. 81, paras. 29–30.

[4] In the Treaty of Friendship, Commerce and Navigation concluded with the Republic of Ireland in 1950 (206 U.N.T.S. 269) reference was made simply to entry for the purposes of 'carrying on trade between the territories of the two parties and for the purpose of engaging in related commercial activities': Article I(1). Compare Article I(1) of the similar treaty concluded with Japan in 1953 (206 U.N.T.S. 143), which added, '(b) . . . the purpose of developing and directing the operations of an enterprise in which they have invested or in which they are actively in the process of investing, a substantial amount of capital.'

[5] Gordon and Rosenfield, *Immigration Law and Procedure* (rev. ed., 1974), ch. 2, p. 55. Thus, a book-keeper does not have 'special qualifications', and knowledge of Japanese is not itself sufficient: *Nippon Express Inc.* v. *Esperdy* 261 F. Supp. 561 (1966); nor is an electronics technician with limited training, experience, and earnings, and with no supervisory or executive functions within the treaty: *Tokyo Sansei* v. *Esperdy* 298 F. Supp. 245 (1969).

[6] 22 C.F.R. 41.40(a)(2) and 41.41(a)(3). The revised regulations are printed in 69 A.J.I.L. (1975), 142–3.

The conditions which generally apply to non-immigrants apply also to treaty aliens, and the right of entry or the right to most-favoured-nation treatment[1] will be qualified by reference to the usual reservations permitting measures of exclusion or restriction necessary to maintain public order, and to protect public health, morals, or safety.[2] If nationals from either Contracting Party cannot bring themselves within the category of trader or investor, then, as a general rule, they do not enjoy any advantages over aliens from third States.[3] At most, the treaty will ensure that the alien benefits from certain minimum civil rights in the matter of liberty of the person,[4] that he will receive national treatment in respect of social security matters,[5] that he will enjoy national treatment and most-favoured-nation treatment as regards access to the courts[6] and in respect of compensation for the expropriation of property.[7]

However, both the national-treatment clause and the most-favoured-nation clause are of little practical application. In the Treaty of Establishment between France and the United States of 1959, the most-favoured-nation standard appears in only two areas, tax and exchange.[8] The emphasis is once again on the particular economic aims of the treaty, represented in the form of the treaty trader and investor.[9] Although reservation is made in respect of current laws and regulations on admission and residence, the two Contracting Parties, in the Protocol and Joint Declarations, state

[1] e.g. Treaty with Ireland 1950, loc. cit., Article I (1)(a).

[2] Ibid., Article I(1)(b); (3). See also Minutes of Interpretation for the clarification of Article 1(3). Cf. Treaty with Japan 1953, loc. cit., Article I(3).

[3] Treaty with Ireland 1950, Article I(1)(b); Article 20(5); Treaty with Japan 1953, Article I(1)(c); Article 21(4). Cf. *BVerwGE* Bd. 36, S. 45 (1970), a case which concerned the interpretation of the treaty of establishment between Germany and Turkey. The appellant, a Turk, objected to the fact that his residence permit was so restricted as to prevent him setting up his own business. The court held, *inter alia*, that he could not rely on the treaty which permitted entry and establishment only in accordance with the laws (at p. 49). See also *VerwRspr.* Bd. 21, S. 335, 347; *VerwRspr.* Bd. 27, S. 194 (Bayer. VGH. 1975).

[4] Treaty with Ireland 1950, Article 2(1); Treaty with Japan 1953, Article 2(1): 'the most constant protection and security, in no case less than that required by international law'.

[5] Treaty with Ireland 1950, Article 4; Treaty with Japan 1953, Article 3.

[6] Treaty with Japan 1953, Article 4.

[7] Ibid., Article 6(3), (y). Schwarzenberger, *Foreign Investments and International Law* (1969), pp. 162 ff.

[8] Piot, 'La Convention d'Établissement du 25 novembre entre la France et les États Unis d'Amérique', *Ann. Fr.* (1960), 953–72, at p. 955.

[9] Article II(1)(a), (b).

that such measures are not to be applied so as to curb, at base, engagement in the economic activities envisaged. The Joint Declaration is founded on reciprocity, and both Governments undertake to apply in the most liberal manner possible the powers conferred by their respective legislatures in matters of entry, residence, and establishment.[1] But this statement of policy applies only to Article II of the Treaty, and the Joint Declaration is much vaguer about liberalizing and facilitating the entry and establishment of those not involved in the favoured occupations of investment and bilateral trade.[2]

It is useful to contrast the treaties concluded by the United States with the Treaty of Commerce, Navigation and Establishment of 1963 between the United Kingdom and Japan.[3] This Treaty is remarkable principally for the way in which it maintains, purely and simply, the stock clauses of the most-favoured-nation, national treatment, and the international standard. The rights of entry, residence, engagement in business, and departure, are expressed in terms of the most-favoured-nation,[4] and other civil rights are founded upon one or other standard, or a combination of standards.[5] It is true that the Preamble calls for fair and equitable treatment and a liberal interpretation of the provisions, but the terms themselves are couched in generalities. Frequent references to most-favoured-nation and national treatment are no substitute for positive rights and remedies directly effective in municipal law. By contrast, the United States treaty with Japan, with its declaration of specific benefits for traders and investors, comes far closer to the realization of commercial ends.

(4) CONCLUSIONS

In the absence of any rule of customary international law prescribing the right to enter a foreign State, treaties and treaty standards

[1] Protocol, Section 2(b).

[2] Cf. Article 1, décret-loi du 17 juin 1938: industrial and commercial activities by aliens in France are geared in their extent to what is permitted to the Frenchman in the aliens' home States, and the extent to which reciprocity exists is a question of appreciation for the authorities: Piot, *Ann. Fr.* (1960), at p. 962.

[3] 478 U.N.T.S. 86; Almond, 'Anglo–Japanese Commercial Treaty of 1963', 13 I.C.L.Q. (1964), 925; Schwarzenberger, *Foreign Investments and International Law*, pp. 34–6.

[4] Article 3(1), (4).

[5] Articles 7, 14, 28.

continue to provide the basis for a reasonable programme of establishment on the bilateral plane. Early treaties did little more than guarantee recognition of the alien's legal personality. Nowadays, greater protection is secured through provisions which guarantee basic human rights and approximate the alien to the national, for example, in matters of social security. This tendency was marked first by a movement away from most-favoured-nation treatment towards national treatment. More recently progress has been made to the point of special guarantees, written into a treaty and reinforced by provisions of municipal law. The high point at the present time is the special regime operating within the E.E.C. The formal requirements for admission and residence amount to little more than a check on identity; in addition, social security rights have been assured on a Community-wide basis, the grounds for exclusion and expulsion have been limited, and certain procedural rights ensured.

Regional plans such as this, which entail the over-all co-ordination of national regimes, are clearly the most effective in creating substantive rights in favour of the alien. For the time being, however, considerable attention must continue to be paid to the less complete, but often quite effective, provisions of bilateral treaties. These have served not only to raise the level of the general standard of treatment, but also to implement the principle of non-discrimination, in the first instance, in regard to the reception of treaty aliens. Today it is possible to view the bilateral treaty as an important adjunct to the principles and standards of general international law, and as a major source of the detailed content of those standards.

A number of general conclusions can be drawn from the preceding survey of State practice in matters of entry and exclusion.

1. States continue to enjoy a wide discretion in regard to the entry of aliens. The choice of grounds for exclusion is largely a matter for each State to decide upon.

2. Rules of international law have nevertheless made a limited impact on the broad power. So, for example, it can be said that the State's freedom of decision is limited by the principle of non-discrimination on racial grounds, and by the rule forbidding the return of refugees to a place of persecution.

3. It is common also to find further restrictions deriving from a State's treaty obligations; some will be bilateral, intended to regulate

commerce and establishment between the parties; and others will have a broader base, for example, those designed to secure human rights on a regional basis. There is also some evidence in State practice of increased recognition of the 'right to family unity', in the sense that the individual admitted for settlement should be entitled to have his family join him.

4. However, in those areas in which specific rules do not apply it remains difficult, if not impossible, to define with precision (*a*) the circumstances in which the broad power may be said to have been abused; and (*b*) the consequences of such an abuse.

PART III

EXPULSION

INTRODUCTION

THE WORD 'expulsion' is commonly used to describe that exercise of State power which secures the removal, either 'voluntarily', under threat of forcible removal, or forcibly, of an alien from the territory of a State. Municipal laws show little consistency, but a distinction is sometimes drawn between expulsion and deportation, the latter being confined to proceedings initiated at the port of entry and designed to effect departure after refusal of admission. In the United States, 'deportation statutes' were first passed to facilitate the removal of illegal immigrants, but it will be seen that over the years deportation has developed its own peculiar regime.[1]

The first and most general condition which is held to limit the power to expel is that its exercise should be confined to aliens. This limitation flows from the nature of the legal relationship which exists between the expelling State and the State of which the alien is a national. Thus, the duty of a State to receive its nationals expelled from another State has been described as the corollary of the 'right' of expulsion,[2] but observations of this kind leave many questions unanswered. It is a matter for debate to what extent a State is free to expel persons long established on its territory, who may be considered to have acquired the effective nationality of that State.[3] Moreover, it is far from clear that a State is under a duty to receive those of its nationals who have been unlawfully expelled from

[1] Konvitz, *Civil Rights in Immigration* (1953), pp. 93–6. The status of the illegal entrant varies from State to State; sometimes he remains susceptible to summary removal, while in other cases he benefits to the full from due process provisions and the right of appeal. See *R.* v. *Governor of Pentonville Prison ex parte Azam* [1973] 2 All E.R. 765.

[2] For typical descriptions of this right-duty relationship, see Schwarzenberger, *International Law* (3rd ed., 1957), vol. I, p. 361; Oppenheim, *International Law* (8th ed., 1955), vol. I, pp. 645–6. See also the *Nottebohm Case*, I.C.J. Rep., 1955, p. 4, per Judge Read, dissenting, at pp. 34, 47–8; *R.* v. *Secretary of State, ex parte Thakrah* [1974] Q.B. 684; and the Solicitor-General in debate on the Commonwealth Immigrants Bill 1968: 'Where one nation-State expels the citizens of another and the citizen presents himself at the frontiers of his own State, that State is bound by obligation to the expelling State to accept him': 759 H.C. Deb., col. 1581.

[3] Brownlie, *Principles of Public International Law* (2nd ed., 1973), p. 506.

another State, at least in so far as the duty to admit is one which is owed between States alone.[1]

Although it might appear that international law limits a valid exercise of the power of expulsion to aliens, actual State practice is more equivocal. For example, in one case on appeal from Canada the Judicial Committee of the Privy Council ruled that whether or not the word 'deportation' was limited in its application to aliens was an open question, depending upon the construction of the particular statute in which it was found. Nationality *per se* was not a relevant consideration.[2] Now, international law clearly permits the revocation of nationality in certain circumstances, but the governing principle is, that a State may not manipulate its competence in order to avoid its international obligations. While, for example, fraud and misrepresentation commonly figure as grounds for the revocation of citizenship by naturalization[3] which are acceptable in international law, nevertheless, where denationalization takes place solely in order to give an air of legality to arbitrary expulsion, then it is merely one element of the wrongful conduct as a whole.[4] Fischer Williams proposed that, whereas positive international law does not forbid a State unilaterally to sever the relationship of nationality so far as the individual is concerned,

> still a State cannot sever the tie of nationality in such a way as to release itself from the international duty, owed to other States, of receiving back a person denationalized who has acquired no other nationality, should he be expelled as an alien by the State where he happens to be.[5]

In 1960, for example, it was said on behalf of Her Majesty's Government that no other State can be required to accept a stateless deportee, and that the power of deportation was not, therefore, available in a case in which a person's naturalization had been re-

[1] On the human rights aspect of the duty of admission; see above, pp. 136–7.

[2] *Co-operative Committee on Japanese Canadians* v. *Attorney-General for Canada* [1947] A.C. 87, at p. 105; see also *Ebrahim Vazir* v. *State of Bombay* [1954] A.I.R. (S.C.). 229 and cf. the exclusion provisions of the United Kingdom Prevention of Terrorism (Temporary Provisions) Act 1974, section 3, now substantially re-enacted by the 1976 Act of the same name.

[3] See British Nationality Act 1948, section 20.

[4] Brownlie, *Principles of Public International Law* (2nd ed.), pp. 383–4, 391. See also *Oppenheimer* v. *Cattermole* [1975] 2 W.L.R. 347, per Lord Cross of Chelsea at pp. 365–370; for comment on earlier stages in the proceedings, see Mann, 89 L.Q.R. (1973), 194 and Merrills, 23 I.C.L.Q. (1974), 143.

[5] 'Denationalisation', 8 *B.Y.I.L.* (1927), 45, at p. 61. See also Schwarzenberger, op. cit., vol. I, p. 377.

voked following conviction for espionage offences.[1] The municipal act of deprivation of citizenship does not *per se* justify the subsequent application to the individual of the international measure of expulsion.[2]

THE TRADITIONAL VIEW OF THE POWER OF EXPULSION

The competence to expel is usually accepted by States, by international tribunals, and by writers as the necessary concomitant of the State's powers in regard to the admission and exclusion of aliens.[3] It is frequently justified by reference to the public interests of the State and as an incident of sovereignty. In 1869, the United States Secretary of State, Mr. Fish, observed:

> The control of the people within its limits, and the right to expel from its territory persons who are dangerous to the peace of the State are too clearly within the essential attributes of sovereignty to be seriously contested.[4]

A successor to this office described the powers of exclusion and expulsion as 'incidents of sovereignty based on the fundamental right of self-preservation', and he inclined to the view that such rights could not be impliedly surrendered.[5]

Writers seem to be at one in agreeing that the power at least exists. Thus, Oda states the common view:

> The right of a State to expel, at will, aliens, whose presence is regarded as undesirable, is, like the right to refuse admission of aliens, considered as an attribute of sovereignty of the State. . . . The grounds for expulsion

[1] 606 H.C. Deb., col. 1176 (case of Klaus Fuchs), cited in *Contemporary Practice* VIII, 9 I.C.L.Q. (1960), 253, 305.

[2] A suggestion to the contrary by Ghai in 67 A.S.I.L. Proc. 122, 126 (1973) is quite without authority, as indeed are a number of other assertions made in the course of discussion of 'Expulsion and Expatriation in International Law: The Right to Leave, to Stay and to Return'. On occasional resort to the sanction of exile by States, see Donnedieu de Vabres, *Traité élémentaire de droit criminel*, no. 613; Batiffol and Lagarde, *Droit international privé* (1970), Titre II, ch. 1, pp. 194–7; *The French Communards' Case*, 6 *B.D.I.L.* 231–2; *Hochmann's Case*, 1899, ibid., p. 235. More recent examples of the expulsion of citizens may be found in 14 *Review of the International Commission of Jurists*, June 1975, pp. 3–8.

[3] See *Musgrove* v. *Chun Teeong Toy* [1891] A.C. 272; *Nishimura Ekiu* v. *United States* 142 U.S. 651 (1892); *Nottebohm Case*, I.C.J. Rep., 1955, p. 4, per Judge Read, dissenting, at p. 46; 6 *B.D.I.L.* 9–77; Hackworth, *Digest*, vol. III, 549–52, 690–707, 717 ff.

[4] Moore, *Digest*, vol. IV, p. 74; Whiteman, *Digest*, vol. 8, p. 620.

[5] Secretary of State Polk (1920), Hackworth, *Digest*, vol. III, p. 692.

of an alien may be determined by each State by its own criteria. Yet the right of expulsion must not be abused.[1]

The eighth edition of Oppenheim also accepts the general principle, but again suggests certain undefined limitations: 'Although a State may exercise its right of expulsion according to discretion, it must not abuse its right by proceeding in an arbitrary manner.'[2] The idea of discretion, of freedom of decision within limits, is the subject of pertinent discussion by Schwarzenberger.[3] He concludes somewhat cautiously:

It is arguable whether sovereign States have absolute discretion regarding the expulsion of foreigners or whether, in this respect, the minimum standard of civilization imposes limitations on the exercise of untrammelled domestic jurisdiction. However this may be, *within the limits in which international law permits the expulsion of foreigners*, this right involves the duty of the home State to receive its nationals.[4]

Thus, in the view of some writers at least, the power or competence to expel is to be seen not so much in terms of an absolute right, but rather as an exercise of controlled discretion. Expulsion requires justification, but although, as Oppenheim observes, an expelling State will hardly admit to not having just cause, 'the borderline between discretion and arbitrariness, although elastic, is a real one, and in a case of doubt it is for an impartial organ to determine whether it has been overstepped.'[5] The power of expulsion is a discretion, not absolute, but limited by the rules and standards of international law.

The power or competence was placed squarely in the context of a legal relationship between States by Judge Read in his dissenting opinion in the *Nottebohm Case* :

[1] Oda, 'The Individual in International Law', in Sørensen, ed., *Manual of Public International Law* (1968), p. 469, at p. 482.

[2] *International Law* (8th ed.), vol. I, p. 611.

[3] Note the analogous role of discretion in nationality matters, discussed by Schwarzenberger, *International Law* (3rd ed.), vol. I, p. 359.

[4] Ibid., p. 360, emphasis supplied. See also at p. 207 for a view of the international minimum standard transforming unlimited into limited territorial jurisdiction over aliens.

[5] *International Law* (8th ed.), vol. I, p. 693. See also *Zerman's Case*, Moore, *International Arbitrations*, vol. IV, p. 3348; *Boffolo Case*, U.N. Rep., vol. X, p. 528; O'Connell, *International Law* (2nd ed., 1970), p. 705; Brownlie, op. cit., pp. 505–6; Politis, 6 Hague *Recueil* (1925—I), 5.

by admitting the alien, the State, by its voluntary act, brings into being a series of legal relationships with the State of which he is a national . . . . The receiving State becomes subject to a series of legal duties vis-à-vis the protecting State, particularly the duty of reasonable and fair treatment. It acquires rights vis-à-vis the protecting State, particularly the rights incident to local allegiance and the right of deportation to the protecting State. At the same time the protecting State acquires correlative rights and obligations vis-à-vis the receiving State, particularly a diminution of rights as against the individual resulting from the local allegiance, the right to assert diplomatic protection and the obligation to receive the individual on deportation . . . . The scope and content of the rights are . . . largely defined by positive international law.[1]

In the case before him, Judge Read concluded that just such a relationship came into being between Guatemala and Liechtenstein on Nottebohm's admission to the former State after his naturalization in the latter. This relationship could not be brought to an end by the unilateral action of one of the parties: 'It was open to Guatemala to terminate the position by deportation [of Nottebohm to Liechtenstein], but not to extinguish the right of Liechtenstein to protect its own national without the consent of that country.'[2] This analysis still holds good. In the typical case the admission of an alien sets up a bilateral legal relationship, and the resulting rights and obligations bear directly on the exercise of the power of expulsion. Today, it is also necessary to accord due consideration to those obligations which are more broadly based, deriving their force from multilateral conventions and from general international law. So it will be necessary not only to analyse the function, justification, and manner of expulsion, but also to see what States do, what they claim for themselves, and object to in others.

[1] I.C.J. Rep., 1955, p. 4, at p. 47.

[2] Ibid., p. 48; cf. the Judgment of the Court, ibid., at p. 18.

XI
THE FUNCTION OF EXPULSION IN GENERAL INTERNATIONAL LAW

(1) INTRODUCTION

THE ESSENTIAL function of expulsion is the protection of the State and the preservation of that which in continental jurisprudence is described as 'ordre public', public morality, and public health. An exercise of the power to expel, therefore, must be related to these purposes, and an expulsion which is not executed in good faith may be a breach of the obligations of the acting State.[1] Of course, the principle of good faith in international law is advantageously presumptive, and it will never be very easy to establish *mala fides* on the part of the expelling State. As will be seen, State practice admits of a considerable margin of appreciation in such matters.

(a) *First Examples*

It is accepted that expulsion is justified for activities in breach of the local law,[2] and, further, that the content of that local law is a matter for the expelling State alone.[3] Expulsion following judicial sentence and expulsion which is ordered by the executive on general political grounds are readily distinguishable, but here too, in respect to the latter, it is accepted that the 'policy' of each nation must determine whether it will permit the continued residence of the alien.[4]

[1] Comparison may be made with the requirement of *bona fides* in municipal law. In *R.* v. *Governor of Brixton Prison, ex parte Soblen* [1963] 2 Q.B. 243, the court emphasized that a deportation order made on the ground that the alien's presence was not conducive to the public good would be struck down if it were shown that the Home Secretary did not *honestly* hold such an opinion. Such a ruling shows that the Home Secretary's power is one of controlled discretion, although in practice the evidentiary burden may be very difficult to satisfy. For similar judicial insistence on the relation of statutory discretion to the 'aim and purpose' of the statute in question, see *Padfield* v. *Minister of Agriculture* [1968] A.C. 997.

[2] *Dr. Hoby's* case 1843: 6 *B.D.I.L.* 113 (preaching contrary to local laws in favour of the established church).

[3] Cf. the general principles which govern questions of local competence on the one hand, and international opposability on the other hand; see *Anglo-Norwegian Fisheries Case*, I.C.J. Rep., 1951, p. 116.

[4] *Miss Dawkin's* case 1870: 6 *B.D.I.L.* 122–3.

In 1894 it was stated that,

in the opinion of Her Majesty's Government if the law ... permits the expulsion ... of persons whose presence is dangerous to public order, an expulsion on such ground lawfully carried out according to the municipal law could not be taken exception to, on any ground of international law, by a power whose subjects had been so expelled.[1]

Statements of this nature, which tend only to hint at control, reinforce the impression of an uncontrolled and uncontrollable power. On closer examination, however, significant qualifications are apparent, especially in the case of expulsions allegedly based on 'political' reasons. Thus, in 1883, the Law Officers advised:

where ... the expulsion does not result from a judicial sentence, but from the act of the Executive, Her Majesty's Government is entitled to scrutinise the facts; and if the action of the Executive has been arbitrary and unfriendly, or the mode of its enforcement unnecessarily harsh or oppressive, may properly make the matter the subject of protest or representation.[2]

Judicial inquiry, with its basis in formal investigation and the proof of facts, is a surer guard against abuse than the free exercise by governments of a power of expulsion based on vague and indefinite allegations.[3]

These issues were exemplified by the case of *Mr. Raphael*, who was expelled from Italy in 1907.[4] The Italian Government defended its action on two specific grounds: the provisions of the local law; and the inherent right of every State to expel undesirable aliens. On the second point the Law Officers advised:

This right exists in the abstract ... but its exercise is subject to at any rate two important qualifications: (1) that it is not restrained by the provisions of municipal law—as it probably is in the present case; and (2) that it is not exercised towards the subject of a friendly power without any apparent justification.[5]

Throughout their advice the Law Officers manifest a desire to keep the Italian Government to their original defence and not to permit

[1] *Haiti Case* 1894: ibid., p. 124. See also on expulsions from Zambia, 1966: 725 H.C. Deb., col. 1880; *British Practice*, 1966, p. 111.

[2] Cases of *Misses Charlesworth* and *Booth* 1883: 6 *B.D.I.L.* 167, 169.

[3] *Expulsions from the Capitulations Countries. Turkey 1860–1893*: 6 *B.D.I.L.* 199, 202–3.

[4] 6 *B.D.I.L.* 151.

[5] Ibid., p. 152. See also the arguments of the Italian Government in favour of an uncontrolled discretion: ibid., p. 153.

recourse to vague and general principles. At the same time they accepted that if the Italian Government did admit that the law had been erroneously applied, they would maintain that the mistake had been made in the *bona fide* exercise of his discretion by the official at fault, and that therefore no compensation was due as of right. But in the view of the Law Officers, this prospect alone was no reason not to ask both for compensation and for the revocation of the order of expulsion.[1]

(*b*) *First Propositions*

On the strength of these first few examples, certain preliminary points can be made:

1. States have the 'right', or 'power' or 'competence' to expel aliens.
2. This competence may be exercised in the discretion of the State, and on the grounds which it deems fit.
3. That discretion is confined by reference to its function and purpose.
4. Its exercise is subject to the requirement of justification, although a margin of appreciation is left to the expelling State.

The third and fourth points are usually summarized by writers and by governments in a description of the right of expulsion as a right which must not be abused by proceeding in an arbitrary manner.[2] In 1966, Her Majesty's Government set out the principles which govern the decision whether or not to make representations regarding the expulsion of United Kingdom citizens from Commonwealth countries:

> We . . . reserve the right to make representations to any Commonwealth Government in any individual case if the manner in which the power . . . is exercised causes hardship, or seems to be arbitrary or unjust . . . .This is different from representations, which we cannot make, concerning the operation of the laws of a country perfectly correctly according to their concept of their laws.[3]

[1] Compare *Mr. Luxenburg's* case 1908, in which it was accepted that compensation as of right could not be demanded for a false arrest which was based on a *bona fide* mistake: 6 *B.D.I.L.* 297.

[2] Oppenheim, *International Law* (8th ed., 1955), vol. I, p. 691; *Expulsions from Zambia* 1966: 730 H.C. Deb., col. 1582.

[3] 733 H.C. Deb., cols. 1223–5, quoted in *British Practice*, 1967, pp. 112–14.

(2) EXPULSION AND THE DOCTRINE OF ABUSE OF RIGHTS

References to function and purpose and to the good faith of the expelling State invite consideration of the doctrine of abuse of rights. This doctrine presents but another aspect of the general issue, whether the right of expulsion is uncontrolled or whether, if the intention behind it is to do harm, it ceases to be an exercise of discretion and becomes unlawful.[1] For example, the 'right' of expulsion may be exercised with the intention of effecting a *de facto* extradition, or in order to expropriate the alien's property, or even for the purposes of genocide, as by mass expulsions over desert frontiers. In such cases the exercise of the power cannot remain untainted by the ulterior and illegal purpose.

It is still a matter of controversy whether a doctrine of abuse of rights even exists in international law.[2] Where States' freedom of action is already limited by customary or conventional law, the doctrine can be of little significance; but, admittedly, customary and conventional rules are often lacking with respect to the entry and removal of aliens. At that point the doctrine may be called in aid. Abuse of rights can then be seen to occur whenever a State avails itself of its rights in such a way as to inflict an injury on another State which cannot be justified by a legitimate consideration of its own advantage; that is to say, when its actions, although strictly speaking 'legal', are coloured by bad faith.[3] While this characterization may be ambiguous, the doctrine can be seen to involve two elements in particular: the recognition of certain rights in favour of the State, and an exercise of those rights in some way contrary to fundamental rules.[4] After examining a number of expulsion cases,

[1] Consider also the principle established in the law of tort by the decision in *Wilkinson* v. *Downton* [1897] 2 Q.B. 57, to the effect that an act done which is calculated or intended to do harm, and which actually results in harm, is actionable, even though it is not strictly a trespass. See also *Hollywood Silver Fox Farm Ltd.* v. *Emmett* [1936] 2 K.B. 468, and cf. *Rattray* v. *Daniels* (1959) 17 D.L.R. (2d) 134; *Bradford Corporation* v. *Pickles* [1895] A.C. 587.

[2] Cf. Schwarzenberger, *International Law and Order* (1971), ch. 6.

[3] See I.C.J. Pleadings, *Nottebohm Case* (*Liechtenstein* v. *Guatemala*), vol. I, pp. 48, 364; Oppenheim, *International Law* (8th ed.), vol. I, p. 691: 'Although a State may exercise its right of expulsion according to discretion, it must not abuse its right in proceeding in an arbitrary manner'; Hyde, *International Law* (1947), vol. I, p. 230: 'Arbitrary action either in the choice of the individual expelled, or in the method of expulsion, would indicate an abuse of power.'

[4] Kiss, *Abus de droit en droit international* (Thèse, Paris, 1952), p. 11. See also Brownlie, *Principles of Public International Law* (2nd ed., 1973), p. 432: 'what is involved is the

Politis concluded that the requirement of 'abuse' was satisfied where the expulsion was arbitrary, was effected with insufficient motive, was in excess of power, or was otherwise affected by some fault on the part of the State authorities.[1] It was his view that the admission and expulsion of aliens generally was an area almost unregulated by international law, and that if the power of expulsion were the logical consequence of the sovereignty of the State, then the doctrine of abuse of rights was necessary in order to relate its exercise more precisely to considerations of humanity.[2]

Further elaboration of the doctrine has been undertaken by Kiss, who concludes that it is a general principle of international law: 'dans les domaines où une autre règle du droit international ne limite pas le pouvoir discrétionnaire des Gouvernements Étatiques, le principe interdisant l'abus de droit est appliqué.'[3] In Kiss's view, decisions and actions on matters affecting expulsion do not sufficiently show repeated conformity to a norm, accompanied by a conviction that the norm is a rule of law, to warrant the finding of any rules. Abuse of rights must therefore be called in aid to regulate those perhaps less significant matters upon which positive international law has nothing particular to say.[4]

(*a*) *The Doctrine before International Tribunals*

The doctrine of abuse of rights has received little recognition in international tribunals, and it has not been used explicitly to ground liability.[5] In the case concerning *German Interests in Polish Upper Silesia*, for example, the Permanent Court made only a passing reference to the theory, excluded it in the instant case, and noted

determination of the qualities of a particular category of permitted acts: is the power or privilege dependent on the presence of certain objectives?'

[1] Politis, 'La théorie de l'abus des droits', 6 Hague *Recueil* (1925—I), p. 5 at p. 107. And see to similar effect, Lauterpacht, *The Function of International Law in the International Community* (1933), p. 289.

[2] Politis, art. cit., pp. 101, 108.

[3] Kiss, op. cit., pp. 145, 194–6.

[4] Kiss, op. cit., pp. 139–41: 'la distinction entre l'existence du droit et les modalités dont ce droit est exercé—chose 'tout à fait indépendante de l'existence de droit'—est caractéristique: elle paraît une affirmation très nette de la conception de l'abus de droit.' These remarks were, however, confined to the legality of conditions such as a time limit for departure, imposed on the person expelled. Questions involving the treatment of that person were, in Kiss's view, already adequately covered by the rules and standards of international law.

[5] Brownlie, op. cit., pp. 430–2, cases cited at p. 431.

that abuse of rights or bad faith could not be presumed.[1] In the *Nottebohm Case* Liechtenstein relied to some extent upon the doctrine as indicating the illegality of Nottebohm's expulsion and Guatemala's refusal to readmit him:

While in principle a State is entitled to expel aliens from its territory, this right is subject to the qualifications common to the exercise of any right in international law and especially compelling in this instance, that it may not be exercised unjustifiably, arbitrarily, or in such a way as to constitute an abuse of rights. . . . If an alien acquires by long residence in a State a right to continue to reside there, a right which international law protects by prohibiting his arbitrary expulsion, it follows that that right continues to exist even if the alien temporarily departs. . . . In such cases the refusal to re-admit . . . amounts to an abuse of the right to regulate the admission of aliens.[2]

Liechtenstein sought damages for the unlawful arrest, detention, and expulsion of Nottebohm, and the refusal to readmit him, together with more general damages for unlawful interference with and deprivation of property. Had the Court been prepared to deal with the merits of the case, it would have had to consider whether Nottebohm's expulsion and the refusal to readmit had been effected in order to expropriate his property. The fact that more than one hundred different proceedings were subsequently initiated in order to deprive Nottebohm of his proprietary interests might thus have moved the Court to consider the expelling State's underlying intentions. It would then have had to weigh up the arguments on behalf of Guatemala, to the effect that the decision on readmission had been taken 'dans l'exercice de sa compétence essentiellement nationale dont il ne doit rendre compte à personne'. In further support of this point, Guatemala also alleged that, 'dans l'état actuel du droit l'admission ou le refus d'admission d'étrangers échappe à toute limitation ou réglementation internationale et par suite à tout contrôle extérieur.'[3] Moreover, the doctrine of abuse of rights could not be applied to security matters in particular, and to the exercise of an assumed absolute, discretionary competence in general.

[1] P.C.I.J. (1926), Ser. A, No. 7, pp. 30, 37–8.

[2] I.C.J. Pleadings, *Nottebohm Case*, Memorial of the Liechtenstein Government, at pp. 48, 53. See below, pp. 259–61 on the recognition by United States courts of a limited right of re-entry in favour of resident aliens.

[3] I.C.J. Pleadings, *Nottebohm Case*, Duplique of the Guatemalan Government, p. 505 at p. 542. It was also suggested that the conferment of nationality on Nottebohm by Liechtenstein itself constituted an abuse of rights *vis-à-vis* Guatemala.

In his Second Report on State Responsibility, Professor Ago characterizes international responsibility primarily in terms of the breach of an international obligation.[1] On the role of 'abuse of rights' he notes:

> the question is one of substance involving the existence or non-existence of a 'primary' rule of international law—the rule whose effect is apparently to limit exercise by the State of its rights, or, as others would maintain, its capacities, and to prohibit their abusive exercise. . . . If it was recognised that existing international law should accept such a limitation and prohibition, the abusive exercise of a right by a State would inevitably constitute a violation of the obligation not to exceed certain limits in exercising that right, and not to exercise it with the sole intention of harming others. . . . If the existence of an internationally wrongful act was recognised in such circumstances, the constituent element would still be represented by the violation of an obligation and not by the exercise of a right.[2]

This approach is far preferable to that of Politis, for example, who takes the sovereign power of the State as his first premiss and then seeks to confine it by imposing upon it the doctrine of abuse of rights. If the power of expulsion is seen in its proper context, that is, as but one right in the compex legal relationship between receiving State and protecting State, then the limitations which international law demands in its exercise become apparent. Although it cannot be affirmed that the doctrine exists as a general principle of positive law, nevertheless the concept of abuse of rights is still helpful in focusing attention on the intentions which motivate expulsion and on the manner of its execution.[3]

(*b*) *The Uganda Expulsions 1972*

Awareness of the general notion also invites an appreciation of the fact that, in certain circumstances, expulsion may well be but one aspect of something else, such as expropriation. In August 1972, President Amin of Uganda announced that he was asking Britian to take responsibility for all United Kingdom citizens of Asian origin resident in Uganda, 'because they are sabotaging the economy'.[4] A

[1] U.N. Doc. A/CN.4/233: Yearbook of the I.L.C., 1970—II, p. 177 at p. 191.

[2] Ibid., p. 193. See also Yearbook of the I.L.C., 1973—I, p. 19, para. 12.

[3] Note the related concept of 'incomplete privilege', Brownlie, op. cit., pp. 452–3, 506.

[4] *The Times* and the *Guardian*, 5 Aug. 1972. See also the *Guardian*, 6 July 1972, for deportation measures against other foreigners, particularly Senegalese, for alleged criminality.

time limit of three months was set for their departure and stringent controls were introduced to restrict the transfer of funds abroad. The expulsion order was implemented by two presidential decrees. These in effect made continued residence illegal, and actual departure was encouraged by the threat that Asians who remained behind would be herded into concentration camps. The Immigration (Cancellation of Entry Permits and Certificates of Residence) Decree 1972, made on 9 August 1972,[1] cancelled the specified documents which had previously been issued to any person of Asian origin, extraction, or descent who was a citizen of the United Kingdom, India, Pakistan, or Bangladesh. An absolute discretion was retained to reinstate any such permit holder. The Declaration of Assets (Non-Citizen Asians) Decree 1972, signed on 4 October but made retroactive to 9 August,[2] provided that no person leaving Uganda by reason of the earlier decree was to transfer 'any immovable property, bus company, farm, including livestock, or business to any other person'.[3] Further provisions were made for every 'departing Asian' to declare his assets and to effect transfer of his property or business to an agent.[4] In return, every such Asian was to be given a receipt and the Minister was directed to keep a register of properties so declared.[5] A penalty of 50,000 shillings or two years' imprisonment or both was imposed for non-compliance.[6]

Originally the expulsion order was destined to affect Asian citizens of Uganda as well, but after pressure from other African governments and the description of this facet of his policy as racialist,[7] President Amin changed his mind.[8] In fact large numbers of

[1] Printed in 11 Int. Leg. Mat., pp. 1388–9. See also Uganda Immigration Act 1969 (No. 19), section 9(1); Plender, 'The Exodus of Asians from East and Central Africa: Some Comparative and International Law Aspects', 19 Amer. J. Comp. Law. (1971), 287; Sharma and Wooldridge, 'The Expulsion of the Ugandan Asians', 23 I.C.L.Q. (1974), 397; 67 A.S.I.L. Proc. (1973), 122–40.

[2] 11 Int. Leg. Mat., pp. 1389–91.

[3] Section 1(a), (2). Subsections (b) and (c) prohibited mortgages of such properties and, in the case of companies, the issue of new shares, any change in the salaries of staff, or the appointment of new directors or any variation in their terms of service or remuneration.

[4] Section 2(1), (2). Such agent was responsible for looking after the property until transferred by sale to a Uganda citizen: section 2(3). Section 6 anticipated the possibility of an agent leaving Uganda for good or otherwise becoming incapable of acting, in which case the Minister was to appoint a trustee.

[5] Sections 2(5); 3.

[6] Section 5. Section 4 made provision for the sale of the properties declared, but none in respect of the purchase money.

[7] The *Guardian*, 22 Aug. 1972 (President Nyerere).

[8] The *Guardian*, 23 Aug. 1972.

Ugandan citizens were deprived of their status by reason of 'defects' said to have been found in their original registration. Many of those affected became stateless, and they were issued with emergency travel documents under the auspices of the United Nations High Commissioner for Refugees.[1] In the General Assembly the United Kingdom at first pressed for a debate on the expulsion as an important and urgent matter. While affirming the United Kingdom's duty to admit its nationals, the Foreign Secretary stressed the humanitarian aspects. The Uganda authorities argued that the matter was entirely within the reserved domain of domestic jurisdiction. They denied that there was any danger to the lives of United Kingdom citizens, or that assets were being confiscated. The British representative replied that the issues transcended domestic jurisdiction and that the hardships caused by the collective expulsions of members of an ethnic group raised humanitarian issues germane to the wide purposes of the Charter of the United Nations. Eventually, the United Kingdom agreed not to press for a debate in the General Assembly after an indication that Uganda was willing to discuss an extension of the deadline and an offer of mediation from President Mobutu of Zaïre.[2] At the same time, attempts to secure positive action from the United Nations Commission on Human Rights were also defeated.[3] In a strictly bilateral sense it may be doubted to what extent any duty was owed to Uganda. However, for the most part, the British Government accepted the responsibility which it had for its citizens, and which it owed also to other States faced with an influx of refugees. There was some controversy over

[1] The *Guardian*, 23 Oct. 1972. Co-operation was also arranged with the Intergovernmental Committee for European Migration and the Red Cross. Clearly, no State was absolutely bound to receive the stateless Asians, and India and African countries bordering on Uganda declared that they would not admit them. However, the Uganda authorities were able to rely on both the good offices of the United Nations High Commissioner and the adherence of most European States to international conventions on refugees and stateless persons. Cf. Schwarzenberger *International Law*, vol. I, p. 377.

[2] The *Times* and the *Guardian*, 30 Sept. 1972. In fact no extension was granted, although the Ugandan authorities gave certain assurances to the Secretary-General of the United Nations that there would be no maltreatment or oppression, that no property was being confiscated, and that departing Asians were being allowed to take with them their personal effects and up to £50 in cash: *Guardian*, 5 Oct. 1972. President Mobutu, on the other hand, informed the Secretary-General that Amin had agreed to a further three months: the *Guardian*, 6 Oct. 1972.

[3] See debate in the Sub-Commission on the Prevention of Discrimination and the Protection of Minorities: E/CN.4/Sub.2/SR. 636–50, 651, 656–63 (Aug. 1972). On the general issue and on the rights of immigrants as minorities, see E/CN.4/Sub.2/SR. 673–676, 686 (Sept. 1973).

stateless Asians separated from their families who still retained United Kingdom citizenship, but this was eventually resolved in favour of the refugees.

There can be little doubt that the Uganda expulsions contravened the rules and principles of international law. The expulsions were unprovoked; allegations of 'sabotaging the economy' and transferring funds abroad were never substantiated.[1] If such charges had been proved, they might have warranted repressive measures against the responsible individuals, but not against the whole of one racially distinct minority. Expulsion purportedly based on nationality, but in fact selective by reference to racial or ethnic criteria, clearly offends against the principle of non-discrimination. In addition, there was considerable evidence of harassment and a general failure on the part of the Uganda authorities, particularly the army, to respect the life and dignity of those affected.[2] Although a period of three months might be considered reasonable, it was a period of widespread confiscation of personal and other property, and little or no indication had been given of any intention or willingness to pay compensation.[3] This fact itself suggests that the

[1] The suggestion that the Asians of Uganda brought upon themselves their own expulsion by not marrying with or otherwise integrating into the African population (Ghai, *Problems of a displaced minority: the new position of East Africa's Asians*, Minority Rights Group, Report No. 16) amounts to nothing less than the condemnation of a minority for being a minority.

[2] See, for example, reports in the *Guardian*, 22 Dec. 1972; The *Times*, 26 Sept. 1972.

[3] The Properties and Business (Acqusition) Decree 1975 and the Assets of Departed Asians (Amendment) Decree 1975 both declare that the Government of Uganda 'shall pay compensation' to the Government of former owners or departed Asians. Provision is made for a Board of Valuers, who are to value property 'in accordance with the laws and practices prevailing in Uganda'. As regards actual payment, both decrees provide: 'The compensation shall be paid within such period as the Minister may determine having regard to the period within which the said property or business may generate sufficient income to offset the amount of the compensation payable.' The decrees purport to make provision for the possibility that claimant Governments may be dissatisfied with valuations made, and it is declared that any such Government may inform the Government of Uganda of its objections. If no friendly settlement is reached, the matter may be referred by either Party to an 'Arbitration Tribunal' whose awards, 'notwithstanding any other law to the contrary', are to be final and binding on both Governments. The Tribunal is to consist of seven members, each Government to appoint three members, and a seventh, the chairman, to be appointed by agreement of the six from the ranks of advocates of the High Court of Uganda of not less than five years' standing. In the event of a failure to agree, the appointment is to be made by the Chief Justice of Uganda. In July 1976 the United Kingdom Government broke off diplomatic relations with Uganda, and no progress had till then been made on the issue of compensation. For its part, it might be expected that the United Kingdom would have substantial objections both to the

expulsions were effected, in part at least, for the purposes of an unlawful expropriation. The value of the property left behind has been variously estimated at between £100m. and £500m., and the United Kingdom Government informed the Government of Uganda that it reserved all rights in respect of these matters.[1]

(*c*) '*Confiscatory expulsion*'

The United Kingdom adopted a similar stand in regard to the property of its citizens following the expulsions from Egypt in 1956[2] and, in retaliation, the Government imposed exchange control restrictions on Egyptian banks in London. The issues between the parties were finally settled by agreement and, in return for the lifting of exchange control, the United Arab Republic agreed to lift sequestration measures; to return British property, with certain exceptions; and to pay £27,500,000 in full and final settlement for the property retained and for injury or damage to property incurred prior to 1959.[3] It is clear that the intention to expropriate without compensation because it denies the essential function of expulsion, may also deny to that act the character of a *bona fide* exercise of discretion.[4]

A useful analogy is to be found in the principles applicable to

formulae for assessment and payment of compensation and to the attempt to subordinate the issue entirely to the jurisdiction of local tribunals, so excluding resort to applicable standards of international law.

[1] In January 1976 the Uganda Government paid a lump sum of $1,627,115 to the Indian Government for the claims of its citizens. In August 1977 the United Nations High Commissioner for Refugees received $662,181 as the first payment for 1,705 claims by Asians of undetermined nationality submitted through U.N.H.C.R. The balance of the total $4,868,416 is to be paid over ten years, without interest. For the United Kingdom's position, see 868 H.C. Deb., Written Answers, col. 2751; 878 H.C. Deb., cols. 439–50; 883 H.C. Deb., cols. 1557–8.

[2] 200 H.L. Deb., col. 633. In a letter to the Secretary-General of the United Nations the Foreign Secretary condemned the expulsions for their 'brutal haste' and 'indiscriminate nature': 561 H.C. Deb., col. 589.

[3] United Kingdom–United Arab Republic Agreement concerning Financial and Commercial Relations and British Property in Egypt 1959 (Cmnd. 639): 9 I.C.L.Q. (1960), 288 ff. For later developments see *British Practice*, 1964—I, pp. 65–6, 1964—I, p. 206; Exchange of Notes regarding the Use of British non-resident blocked Bank Accounts in Egypt, Mar. 1973, U.K.T.S. No. 49 (1973): Cmnd. 5290.

[4] Note the analogous approach adopted by municipal courts in relation to the exercise of statutory powers. In *Brownsea Haven Properties Ltd.* v. *Poole Corporation* [1957] 3 W.L.R. 669 [1958] 2 W.L.R. 137 (C.A.), the court condemned the corporation's introduction of a one-way street system through the use of a general police power to control traffic temporarily in times of processions and the like. The corporation had earlier failed in its application for such a system under the proper legislation. Cf. *Backhouse* v. *Lambeth L.B.C.*, *The Times*, 14 Oct. 1972.

confiscatory taxation.[1] The limitations on the 'sovereign power' of taxation have been succinctly stated by Albrecht and they may be extended, *mutatis mutandis*, to the case of 'confiscatory expulsion':

According to the doctrine of the sovereign right of taxation, and in the absence of special treaty provisions, there would seem to be no basis in international law for objections to the exercise by a State of its right to tax where there is no discrimination against aliens. . . . Nevertheless, an exception must be made in the case of confiscatory taxation, for it is a rule of international law that confiscation, or expropriation without compensation, is illegal. There is little difference in the practical effects of confiscation and confiscatory taxation. Surely, then, confiscation in the guise of taxation cannot be permitted when confiscation itself is prohibited. A State may tax aliens without unfair discrimination under international law only so long as the taxation is not confiscatory. When taxation becomes confiscatory, it becomes illegal.[2]

In like manner, it is reasonable to conclude that where expulsion becomes confiscatory, it also becomes illegal.

(*d*) *Expulsion for Other Ulterior Motives*

The power of expulsion may be similarly employed as an instrument of genocide or mass murder, and in such cases it is then but one aspect of the greater wrong. Two recent incidents contained elements which suggested that the action taken was intended or calculated to do harm. In retaliation for Iran's policy over navigation on the Shatt-al-Arab river, Iraq expelled large numbers of Iranians from that country in April and May 1969. The expulsions were carried out at a moment's notice and in circumstances of great brutality, with bus-loads of refugees being deposited in the border towns. The Iranian Government complained to the Security Council on 12 May, protesting against the 'arrests, expulsions and tortures' inflicted by the Iraqi authorities on the deported Iranians.[3] Later the same year, the Ghanaian Goverment tightened controls over the resident alien population both for economic reasons and because, it was said, some 90 per cent of those known to have criminal records or be in prison were aliens. The result of the Government's directive was that a mass exodus took place in conditions of

[1] *British Practice*, 1964—II, pp. 202–6; 1965—I, pp. 45–6.

[2] Albrecht, Taxation of Aliens in International Law', 29 *B.Y.I.L.* (1952), 145 at p. 172; cited in *British Practice*, 1964—II, pp. 202–3; on respect for acquired rights, see below, pp. 255–61.

[3] Keesing's *Contemporary Archives*, 1969–70, 23544a.

great panic, and by the end of January 1970 it was estimated that some 200,000 African aliens had quit the country. The Government of Togo closed its border after receiving 40,000 refugees, and some 100,000 Nigerian nationals were accommodated in camps in their own country. Following representations from neighbouring States, Ghana took steps to allay the panic and set up its own camps in an effort to deal with all those who wished to regularize their status. The Government denied that it was at any time contemplating a mass expulsion of aliens, but by then the frantic flight along the roads leading to the frontiers had already begun.[1] In practice, there may be little difference between forcible expulsion in brutal circumstances, and 'voluntary removal' promoted by laws which declare continued residence illegal and encouraged by threats as to the consequences of continued residence.[2] The introduction of a new regime of permits can quite effectively secure the *de facto* expulsion of aliens. In order to establish or negative good faith, consideration must therefore be given to all the circumstances, including the reasons underlying the measures taken and their actual consequences.

(3) EXPULSION TO A PARTICULAR STATE AS THE BREACH OF AN INTERNATIONAL OBLIGATION

The question remains, whether expulsion to a particular State can ever amount to a breach of an international obligation. In one field the States Parties to the 1951 Convention relating to the Status of Refugees have indeed undertaken obligations limiting their competence in the matter.[3] However, even as amended by the 1967 Protocol, this Convention does not guarantee a right of entry or residence as such.[4] Nevertheless, it has already been noted how Articles 32 and

[1] Keesing's *Contemporary Archives*, 1969–70, 23824; the *Guardian*, 11, 12 Dec. 1969, 22 Jan. 1970. For similar actions by the Zanzibari regime, see the *Guardian*, 14 Oct. 1971; the *Observer*, 17 Oct. 1971; for reciprocal action between Kenya and Tanzania, see the *Guardian*, 20 Dec. 1974; and for the expulsion of Kurds from Iraq to Turkey and Iran, see *The Times*, 18 Jan. 1974. Note Brownlie's suggestion that expulsion which causes specific loss to the national State receiving groups without adequate notice would ground a claim for indemnity as for incomplete privilege: op. cit., p. 506.

[2] On General Amin's threat to set up 'concentration camps' for those who remained in Uganda after the deadline, see *The Times*, 14, 15 Sept. 1972; the *Guardian*, 14 Sept. 1972.

[3] 189 U.N.T.S. 150.

[4] Article 31(1) does require States Parties generally to refrain from penalizing refugees for illegal entry. See further above, pp. 137-42.

33 of the Convention severely limit the competence of States to expel the refugee.[1] Moreover, it may be reaffirmed that the prohibition on the return of refugees to places of persecution has established itself as a general principle of international law, binding on States automatically and independently of any specific assent.[2]

Depending on the particular circumstances, breach of the rule will therefore involve international responsibility towards other contracting parties, and perhaps also towards the international community as a whole, or towards some regional institution.[3] International obligations which have a regional basis will continue to be of importance in the protection of individual rights, particularly while States remain reluctant to embody the subjective right of asylum in any multilateral treaty.[4] Bilateral recognition of the principle of non-extradition of political offenders, although important as one aspect of asylum, tends to understate the broader, humanitarian issues. Some attempts were made to establish the principle of non-extradition on a regional basis during the negotiations which led to the 1957 European Convention on Extradition, but these were largely frustrated by certain fundamental differences of opinion. Two attitudes were never finally reconciled: the first reflected the view that extradition should be generally facilitated, the chief aim being the suppression of crime; and the second, the 'restrictive' view, which demanded the introduction of humanitarian considerations.[5]

The differences are readily apparent in those provisions which deal with the political-offence exception. Article 3(1) of the Convention forbids the extradition of those accused of political offences, or of offences connected with political offences, and provides that the requested party shall determine the character of the particular offence. The form adopted did not receive unanimous agreement among the Committee of Experts, especially by reason of its mandatory character. The Committee therefore decided that reservations should be permitted under Article 26.

Subsection (2) attempts to take account of the humanitarian aspect and provides that extradition shall not be granted,

[1] See above, pp. 139–40. [2] See above, pp. 141–2.

[3] See *Second Report on State Responsibility*, Roberto Ago, Special Rapporteur: U.N. Doc. A/CN.4/233; Yearbook of the I.L.C., 1970—II, p. 177.

[4] See the views of the Sixth Committee: U.N. Doc. A/6912, paras. 64, 65; cf. I.L.C. *Survey of International Law*: U.N. Doc. A/CN.4/245, pp. 191 et seq. G.A. Res. 2780 (XXVI), 3 Dec. 1971.

[5] See generally, *Explanatory Report on the European Convention on Extradition*, Council of Europe, 1969.

if the requested Party has substantial grounds for believing that a request for extradition has been made for the purpose of prosecuting or punishing a person on account of his race, religion, nationality or political opinion, or that the person's position may be prejudiced for any of these reasons.[1]

The practice common in European bilateral treaties of excluding the assassination of a Head of State from the class of political offences is recognized by subsection (3).[2] Once again this was not accepted by all the delegations and it was anticipated that there would be further reservations on this point. This express acceptance by the framers of the Convention that States Parties should be able to make reservations to various provisions is one element which will affect the weight to be accorded to those provisions as evidence even of a regional custom.[3] Certain general conclusions, however, are possible:

1. There is no general or customary rule of international law which forbids the extradition of 'political offenders'. This view is supported both by the variety of State practice and by the fact that decision on the character of a given offence is left, inevitably, to the authorities of the requested party;[4] it is a unilateral action only occasionally limited by express treaty obligations.[5]

2. The general principle must now be interpreted in the light of the rule which requires the refusal of surrender on humanitarian grounds, that is, where the individual is likely to be prejudiced by reason of irrelevant distinctions or where there is a possibility of the violation of fundamental human rights.[6]

[1] Cf. United Kingdom Fugitive Offenders Act 1967, section 4; *Fernandez* v. *Government of Singapore* [1971] 1 W.L.R. 987.

[2] Such a provision is commonly called an 'attentat' clause, and seems to have originated in the Belgian law of 1856: 6 *B.D.I.L.* 668–9. Although it will depend on the precise role of the Head of State within a given system, in many cases assassination will be the most political of all political crimes. See also section 4(5), Fugitive Offenders Act 1967; article 3, 1922 United States–Venezuela Extradition Treaty: 49 L.N.T.S. 435.

[3] *North Sea Continental Shelf Cases*, I.C.J. Rep., 1969, p. 3 at pp. 38–9; *Asylum Case*, I.C.J. Rep., 1950, p. 266 at pp. 276–7; but cf. Baxter, 129 Hague *Recueil* (1970—I), 48–51.

[4] Note the reservation made to Article 3(3) by Denmark, Norway, Sweden, Switzerland, and Finland.

[5] e.g. under the Genocide Convention 1949 or Articles 1, 2, European Convention on the Suppression of Terrorism 1977.

[6] Ibid., Article 5; see further above, pp. 143–4.

3. There is no general or customary rule of international law which excludes assassination of a Head of State or member of government from the category of political offence.[1]

Although proposed with specific reference to a European context, these conclusions are capable of wider application. Refugees and political offenders are particularly susceptible of violation of basic human rights, and it is these considerations which dominate questions concerning their entry, expulsion, or extradition. A treaty regime such as that established by the 1951 Refugees Convention, with its emphasis on human rights, raises the possibility of exceptions to the general rule that a State is not free to take up the claims of those who are not its nationals.[2] Once such exceptions are recognized, then a third State or other subject of international law would acquire the standing necessary to take up the case of an alien likely to be expelled to any State in which he may face persecution or punishment, whether that State be his own or not.[3] For it may be that certain obligations are owed by States *erga omnes*, some deriving from customary international law, others from particular treaties. The present state of international law favours the latter and, especially, the circumstances of membership in some regional organisation endowed with competence to take action. The concept of generalized obligations owed to the international community as such may not, for the moment, offer a very profitable line of inquiry.

(*a*) '*Locus standi*' *under the European Convention on Human Rights*

The involvement of third parties, whether they be States or organizations, in the protection of the individual against arbitrary expulsion can be seen under the European Convention on Human Rights. The European Commission has recognized that, in certain circumstances, expulsion may amount to inhuman or degrading

[1] Cf. Articles 7, 8, Convention on the Prevention and Punishment of Crimes against Internationally Protected Persons 1973.

[2] Further exceptions were expressly mentioned by the International Court of Justice in the *Reparations for Injuries Case*, I.C.J. Rep., 1949, p. 174 at p. 181.

[3] There is no doubt that a State may protest where its own national is expelled to a third State in which he is then prosecuted. See the case of *Greville Wynne*, a British subject deported from Hungary to the U.S.S.R., to face prosecution for political offences, specifically, espionage. The extradition procedure was not used, and the United Kingdom protested about the circumstances in which his removal had taken place: *Contemporary Practice*, 1962—II, pp. 210–14; 1963—I, p. 27. Cf. the *Soblen Case*, below, pp. 226–8.

alleged breaches of the Convention by another High Party to the Commission. It does not have to show the breach of any obligation owed to itself. The State which brings a complaint under Article 24, 'is not to be regarded as exercising a right of action for the purpose of enforcing its own rights, but rather as bringing before the Commission an alleged violation of the public order of Europe.'[3] Thus, every State Party to the Convention has an independent and sufficient interest in the fulfilment of its obligations. It is therefore open to any such State to allege that the expulsion of an individual, whatever his nationality and wherever he might be sent, constitutes a violation of the European Convention. An expulsion which violated the rights and freedoms guaranteed would incur the international responsibility of the State, in so far as its action amounted to the breach of an international obligation owed to the regional community. In practice, such violation might be based either on a failure by the State to permit to the individual the usual guarantees of extradition procedure,[4] or on the nature of the regime to which it was proposed to remove him.[5] It thus becomes possible to challenge the arbitrary and undesirable consequences which may follow from a 'straitforward application of the immigration laws'.[6]

[1] Application 984/61. And note Application 1082/63: 6 *Yearbook* 480.

[2] Application 434/58: 2 *Yearbook* 354, 373.

[3] Application 788/60 (*The Pfunders Case*): 4 *Yearbook* 139, 142, See also Resolution of the Standing Committee of the Consultative Assembly, June 1967 (Doc. B (67) 37), especially paragraph 10; Fawcett, *The Application of the European Convention on Human Rights* (1969), pp. 272–7.

[4] For example, the rule against the surrender of political offenders, the rule of specialty, and the general requirement that the requesting State make out a prima facie case. Cf. Article 6, European Convention on Human Rights.

[5] For example, by reference to Article 3, the prohibition on torture, inhuman or degrading treatment or punishment.

[6] In 1972, two Moroccan Air Force officers who had been involved in the attempted assassination of the King of Morocco were summarily returned to that country from Gibraltar under the provisions of the local immigration laws. They were subsequently executed: the *Guardian*, 18, 19 Aug. 1972; *The Times*, 19, 22 Aug. 1972; the *Observer*,

(*b*) *The Practice of 'Disguised Extradition'*

In the practice known as 'disguised extradition', the usua cedure is for the individual to be refused admission at the requ a foreign State, and for him to be deported to that or any State which wishes to prosecute or punish him. The effect override those usual provisions of municipal law which comı permit the legality of extradition proceedings to be contesteu anu allow for the submission of evidence to show that the individual is being pursued for political reasons.

While the legality of the resort to immigration laws for such purposes has long been controversial,[1] it may also be argued that the immigration laws have a supporting role to play in the international control of criminals, and that therefore *de facto* extraditions made under those laws are justified.[2] It may indeed be a little spurious to demand the use of extradition proceedings in a State which has already decided, as a matter of immigration policy, that the alien will not be allowed to remain. Be that as it may, the established and primary purpose of deportation is to rid the State of an undesirable alien, and that purpose is achieved with the alien's departure. His destination, in theory, should be of little concern to the expelling State, although in difficult cases it may put in issue the duty of another State to receive its national who has nowhere else to go. Unlike extradition, which is based on treaty, expulsion gives no rights to any other State and, again in theory, such State can have no control over the alien's destination. In exclusion proceedings, States generally assume a greater latitude in regard to the destination to which the individual is to be removed, and it is not uncommon

20 Aug. 1972, 14 Jan. 1973. In December 1973, the European Commission on Human Rights declared as admissible the petition of the widow of one of the officers, alleging that the detention and return to Morocco of her husband after he had sought asylum in Gibraltar were contrary to Articles 3, 5(4), and 8 of the European Convention: Council of Europe Communiqué C(73) 28. In August 1974 a friendly settlement was announced, under which the British Government made a payment of £37,500 *ex gratia*, and the application was withdrawn: *The Times*, 14 Aug. 1974 (*Amekrane* v. *United Kingdom*).

[1] See the Circular Letter of 19 Mar. 1907 to Officers and Employees of the Immigration Service, in which the United States Government condemned the practice: Hackworth, *Digest*, vol. III, pp. 717 f.; see also ibid., vol. IV, p. 30. In *Strongford's* case in 1906, the Home Office showed its awareness that an alien's own State might have cause for complaint if he were to be deported to some other State which wanted to put him on trial: 6 *B.D.I.L.* 238. See also *Glen's* case 1910: ibid., pp. 239–40; *Christmann's* case 1912: ibid., p. 241.

[2] Shearer, *Extradition in International Law* (1971), ch. 3, pp. 68, 78 ff.

to secure his removal to the port of embarkation.[1] The wide choice available to State authorities and accepted in practice must be reviewed against the fact that the excluded alien will only rarely be entitled to appeal against the proposed destination or to arrange for his own departure.[2] Once he has passed the frontier, however, State practice frequently allows him to benefit from certain procedural guarantees. Thus, he may be able to appeal, not only against the expulsion itself, but also against the proposed destination, and he may be given the opportunity of securing entry to another country of his choice.[3] Of course, in the final analysis, if no other State is willing to receive him, then the only State to which the alien can lawfully be removed is his State of nationality or citizenship. If he is unable to secure admission elsewhere, his appeal against removal will commonly fail.[4]

(*c*) *Municipal Law Controls*

The case for simplified extradition procedures will continue to be strongly argued, particularly between allied or friendly States.[5]

[1] e.g. Immigration Act 1971, Sch. 2, para. 8(1)(c); compare Sch. 3, para. 1(1). For examples of exclusions on request, see Evans, 'Acquisition of Custody over the International Fugitive Offender—Alternatives to Extradition: A Survey of United States Practice', 40 *B.Y.I.L.* (1964), 77, at pp. 83–4 and *passim*.

[2] *Ma* v. *Barber* 357 U.S. 185 (1958); cf. Immigration Act 1971, section 17(1), (5).

[3] e.g. 66 Stat. 212 (1952), 8 U.S.C. s. 1253(a). Cf. Immigration Act 1971, sections 15, 17, 5(6); Sch. 3, para. 4; *R.* v. *Governor of Brixton Prison, ex parte Sliwa* [1952] 1 All E.R. 187.

[4] *Secretary of State* v. *Croning* [1972] Imm. A.R. 51; *Secretary of State* v. *Fardy* [1972] Imm. A.R. 192; *Ali* v. *Secretary of State* [1973] Imm. A.R. 19, 33 (C.A.); this decision of the Court of Appeal is somewhat surprising given the clearly mandatory character of the relevant immigration rule: 'A deportation order will not be made against a person if the only country to which he can be removed is one to which he is unwilling to go owing to well-founded fear of [persecution].' (See for example, H.C. No. 81, para. 57.) The principle of ultra vires would lead one to suppose the illegality of any purported deportation order which would have the effect of securing the return of the appellant to a State of persecution. It is not clear that this point was raised before the Court, whose decision may therefore be considered as arrived at *per incuriam*. See also Article 25, Aliens Law of Venezuela 1925, cited by de Boeck, 18 Hague *Recueil* (1927—III), 447 at p. 452. Note also the provisions of French law which excuse an alien who fails to depart if he shows that it is impossible for him to leave French territory: ordonnance de 2 nov. 1945, article 27; Dalloz, 1967, Somm. 79 (*Moravek*).

[5] See, for example the arrangement between the United Kingdom and the Republic of Ireland contained in the Backing of Warrants (Ireland) Act 1965; see also the inter-NATO provisions for the surrender of military deserters: 199 U.N.T.S., 67; *R.* v. *Thames Justices, ex parte Brindle* (C.A.) [1975] 3 All E.R. 71.

For developments in Anglo-Irish relations and for a useful summary of past practice, see McCall-Smith and Magee, 'The Anglo-Irish Law Enforcement Report in Historical and Political Context', [1975] Crim. L. Rev. 200.

Delay and expense are reduced, and expulsion under the immigration laws circumvents the inconveniences of a weak case, the absence of the offence charged from the extradition treaty, and even the lack of a treaty itself.[1] Yet it is apparent that modern expulsion laws have been developed with some regard being paid to the requirements of due process and to the desirability of a right of appeal. To this extent, these laws reflect the growth of human rights principles and they may be taken as some evidence of contemporary State attitudes to the rights of individuals.

In the past it has often been difficult for one threatened with expulsion ever to challenge an order, or to question its merits. In *R.* v. *Secretary of State, ex parte Château-Thierry*[2] the Court of Appeal held that under the Aliens Restriction Act 1914 it was wholly within the discretion of the Secretary of State whether or not to allow the alien the privilege of arranging his own departure. The fact that the alien was a political refugee was again a matter for the Minister to consider in his discretion, and it was not for the court to determine whether the power of deportation might lawfully be used to secure the mutual surrender of military deserters.[3] In effect the Minister might, by designating a particular vessel, secure the alien's departure to any desired country.[4]

Although in this case the tone of the judgment is in favour of an arbitrary and uncontrolled power, other decisions have emphasized the limits, admittedly wide, within which the Home Secretary's discretion is confined. In *Sarno's* case in 1916,[5] the court stated that if it appeared that a misuse of the power conferred upon the Executive was imminent, then the court was free to deal with the matter. In *Sacksteder's* case, two years later, the court again ruled that it might go behind an apparently valid order for the arrest and detention of an alien against whom a deportation order has been made if it is a 'mere sham not made *bona fide*'.[6] By contrast, in *Muller* v. *Superintendent, Presidency Jail, Calcutta*,[7] the Supreme Court of

[1] See *Re D'Emilia* 24 I.L.R. 499.

[2] [1917] 1 K.B. 922.

[3] See also *Abdou* v. *Attorney-General of Kenya* [1951] I.L.R., Case no. 80, p. 282; *R.* v. *Chiswick Police Station Superintendent, ex parte Sacksteder* [1918] 1 K.B. 578; O'Higgins, 'Disguised Extradition: The *Soblen* Case', 27 M.L.R. 521. Cf. *R.* v. *Zausmer* (1911) 7 Cr. App. Rep. 41.

[4] Cf. *R.* v. *Governor of Brixton Prison, ex parte Sliwa* [1952] 1 All E.R. 187.

[5] *R.* v. *Governor of Brixton Prison, ex parte Sarno* [1916] 2 K.B. 742.

[6] [1918] 1 K.B. 578.

[7] [1955] I.L.R., p. 497.

India expressly held that the fact that a request for extradition had been made did not fetter the decision of the Government to choose the less cumbrous procedure of expulsion. The Government had a discretion to expel an alien in conformity with its territorial supremacy and no question of good faith could arise merely because the Government had exercised the right of choice which the law conferred.

(*d*) *The* Soblen Case

In the United Kingdom the *locus classicus* is without doubt the decision of the Court of Appeal in the *Soblen* affair.[1] Dr. Soblen, although admitted in fact to the United Kingdom for urgent medical treatment, was refused leave to land and detained under the Aliens Order 1953.[2] A deportation order was then made against him under Article 20(2)(b) of that Order on the ground that the Secretary of State deemed his departure to be conducive to the public good. Dr. Soblen challenged the validity of the deportation order, *inter alia*, on the ground that an alien refused leave to land under Article 1 of the Order could not thereafter be deported under Article 20 and that, even if valid on its face, the order was being used for the unlawful purpose of extraditing a political fugitive for a non-extraditable offence. This challenge was rejected by the Court of Appeal, which held that the provisions for the removal of those refused leave to land and the provisions enabling the deportation of those already admitted were not mutually exclusive, but were 'cumulative and complementary'.[3] It was further held that the Home Secretary might deport an alien to the State of his nationality even though he had fled after conviction for a non-extraditable offence, and even though a request had been received for his return.[4] It was lightly

[1] *R.* v. *Governor of Brixton Prison, ex parte Soblen* [1963] 2 Q.B. 243. See also Goodhart, 'Extradition and Deportation', 79 L.Q.R. 41; O'Higgins, art. cit. Thornberry, 'Dr. Soblen and the Alien Law of the United Kingdom', 12 I.C.L.Q. (1963), 414–74.

[2] Articles 1, 8(4). The legality of his detention was unsuccessfully challenged in *R.* v. *Secretary of State, ex parte Soblen* [1963] 1 Q.B. 829.

[3] This finding clouds the distinction between exclusion and deportation proceedings which even today may have significant consequences for the individual. For the alien who has been admitted benefits fully from the right of appeal against removal and against destination. If, however, it emerges that he was never given leave to land, he may be removed summarily and without any trial on the merits: Immigration Act 1971, Sch. 2, para. 8. The alien is then once again left to his common-law remedy of habeas corpus: *R.* v. *Governor of Pentonville Prison, ex parte Azam* [1973] 2 W.L.R. 949, per Lord Denning at p. 960.

[4] Soblen had been convicted and sentenced to life imprisonment in the United States for espionage offences.

suggested that if the Home Secretary had acted simply at the request of a foreign State, that might be unlawful, but Lord Justice Donovan made the following pertinent comment:

If country A is an ally of country B, each of them may well think it conducive to the public good of their own citizens that they should co-operate to see that a national of one of them who gives defence information to a common potential enemy, should not escape the consequences inflicted upon him by due process of law.[1]

His Lordship also remarked that if the deportation order was to be regarded as invalid, it must be for some other reason than the consequence to which it would lead.[2] Lord Denning, however, was somewhat more explicit in his description of the grounds upon which the court exercises control. He said:

it depends on the purpose with which the act is done. If it was done for an authorised purpose, it was lawful. If it was done professedly for an authorised purpose, but in fact for a different purpose with an ulterior object, it was unlawful. . . . Was there a misuse of the power or not? The courts can always go behind a deportation order in order to see whether the powers entrusted by Parliament have been exercised lawfully or no.[3]

If it could be shown that the deportation order was a sham in that the Home Secretary did not genuinely consider it to be in the public interest to expel the alien, then a challenge on these grounds would succeed. But there was no such evidence in this case for attributing to the Home Secretary anything in the nature of a sham or want of *bona fides* or any unlawful or improper purpose.[4]

The evidentiary burden is thus considerable, and it may well be increased by the Executive's refusal to reveal the evidence relating to its decision. But if that burden can be satisfied, the court has the power to strike down the deportation order. This illustrates an approach to the power of expulsion that is common in municipal systems and also the meaning of the presumption that expulsion must follow only from a decision reached 'in accordance with the law'. Due process excludes arbitrariness and the requirement flows from international law itself. The international standard is reflected in the practice of States and in their municipal laws. This is some evidence

[1] [1963] 2 Q.B. 243 at p. 310. See also 664 H.C. Deb., col. 805.
[2] [1963] 2 Q.B. 243 at p. 307. *Sed quaere*; see above p. 224, note 4.
[3] Ibid., at p. 302. Cf. Donovan L.J., at p. 308.
[4] Ibid., at p. 305. Cf. Article 18, European Convention on Human Rights.

of a sufficient *opinio juris* and strong support for the proposition that the discretionary power of expulsion is confined by the rules of international law. As in municipal law, so also in determining whether there has been a breach of an international obligation the fact of delivery up to persecution may bear directly on the question of *bona fides*. The power of expulsion is a discretionary power limited by reference to its function and, while the margin of appreciation left to States is wide, it is not beyond control. Actual decisions may be a matter of policy, and local courts may consider them non-justiciable,[1] but it does not follow from this that the power may be exercised in bad faith, dishonestly, or for some ulterior and unlawful purpose.

(4) CONCLUSIONS RELATING TO THE FUNCTION OF EXPULSION

The preliminary propositions set out above[2] can now be expanded in the light of the first part of this study:

1. States have the 'right', or 'power', or 'competence' to expel aliens.

2. The function of this competence is to protect the essential interests of the State; it is a measure of self-defence.

3. The competence to expel may be exercised in the discretion of the State, and on the gounds which it deems fit.

4. That discretion is, however, limited as to its extent by reference to its function and purpose. The power must be exercised in good faith and not for some ulterior motive, such as genocide, confiscation of property, or the surrender of an individual to persecution.

[1] *R.* v. *Governor of Pentonville Prison, ex parte Azam* [1973] 2 W.L.R. 949, per Lord Denning M.R., at pp. 962–3.

[2] At p. 208.

XII

THE JUSTIFICATION FOR EXPULSION

THE INQUIRY into the function and purpose of expulsion has provided the first indication of the limits which confine this discretionary competence of States. The further requirement of justification follows both from the aim and purpose of expulsion, which is the protection of the State, and from that obligation owed by the 'receiving State' to the 'protecting State', which is to accord a certain standard of treatment to the nationals of the latter admitted to its territory.

(1) THE CONCEPT OF 'ORDRE PUBLIC'

Continental jurisprudence frequently prescribes as the basis of expulsion reasons of 'ordre public', public safety, and public morality. A summary of the meaning to be given to these terms and the conditions of their application may be found in the European Convention on Establishment 1955.[1] Section I of the Protocol declares that each Contracting Party shall have the right to judge by national criteria the reasons of 'ordre public', national security, public health, or morality, the circumstances which constitute a threat to national security or an offence against 'ordre public' or morality, and whether the reasons for expulsion are of a 'particularly serious nature'.[2] This is a treaty provision apparently confined to the regime

[1] European Treaty Series, No. 19.

[2] See also Section III, which provides that the concept of 'ordre public' is to be understood in the wide sense generally accepted in continental countries and that this embraces, for example, exclusion for political reasons. However, Contracting States undertake, in the exercise of their rights, to give particular consideration to family ties and periods of residence. There is little authority for approximating 'ordre public' to the concept of 'public policy', at least as that is understood in the law of the United Kingdom; see the *caveat* entered by the Editor in the report of the decision of the European Court of Justice in *Van Duyn* v. *Home Office* [1975] 1 C.M.L.R. 1, 6, 12; compare the views of the Metropolitan Magistrate in *R.* v. *Secchi* [1975] 1 C.M.L.R. 383, 394 with those advanced by Advocate General Mayras in *Bonsignore* v. *Oberstadtdirektor, Köln* [1975] 1 C.M.L.R. 472, at pp. 476, 580, 485.

in question, but there are good reasons for taking it as expressing the general standard of international law. As regards both the grounds for expulsion and the separate question of whether an individual qualifies within those grounds, the expelling State is in the best position, and is, indeed, the only authority competent to pronounce upon such matters. Practice accepts that it is for each State to determine whether the continued residence of aliens is desirable. In *Ben Tillett's* case in 1898, the arbitrator observed that there was no difference between the parties on this point:

the right of a State to exclude from its territory foreigners when their dealings or presence appears to compromise its security cannot be contested. . . . Moreover, the State in the plenitude of its sovereignty judges the scope of the acts which lead to the prohibition.[1]

And yet the liberty is not complete. Rules of international law stand at the perimeter and occasionally pass through to impose specific obligations. A considerable margin of appreciation is left to States, but it is a margin that has its own limits. The expelling State is required to balance its own interests against those of the individual. It is, therefore, obliged to take account of the alien's acquired rights or legitimate expectations,[2] and to arrive at a decision which bears a reasonable relationship to the facts.

It has been doubted whether the State is obliged to prove the legitimacy of its reasons for expulsion,[3] and in one case the tribunal held that when expulsion is based on grounds of public policy it will not, as a rule, review the decision of the competent State authorities.[4] But this appears to be a little extreme, and the better view is that the expelling State must show 'reasonable cause', for 'ordre public' is not a term without meaning, and it is not the shorthand description of a sovereign and absolute power. In the *Guardianship of Infants Case*, Judge Lauterpacht described it as a 'general legal conception', a 'general principle of law', whose content stood to be determined by reference to the practice and experience of municipal law.[5] Admit-

[1] 6 *B.D.I.L.* 124 at p. 147. See also *Expulsion of Missionaries from the Sudan 1964*: 692 H.C. Deb., col. 9; *Expulsions from Austria 1963*: 682 H.C. Deb. (Written Answers), col. 164; both cited in *British Practice*, 1964—I, p. 63, 1963—II, p. 127.

[2] See below, pp. 255–61.

[3] O'Connell, *International Law* (2nd ed., 1970), p. 707; Brownlie, *Principles of Public International Law* (2nd ed., 1973), p. 506.

[4] *Re Hochbaum*, Ann. Dig., 1933–4, Case No. 134; Decisions of the Upper Silesian Arbitral Tribunal, vol. 5, p. 140, at p. 162.

[5] I.C.J. Rep., 1958, p. 55 at p. 92. See further below, pp. 295–7.

tedly, his words were directed to the limitation of 'ordre public' as an implied reservation to treaty obligations, but the evidence of State practice suggests that a similar view is valid for expulsion matters, even in the absence of specific conventional obligations.

(*a*) *The Requirement of 'reasonable cause'*

Expulsion is a drastic measure which, by its very nature, presupposes substantial justification. In *Zerman's* case[1] the character of the individual expelled was notorious and he suffered no pecuniary loss by reason of his expulsion. Nevertheless, the arbitrator, Sir Edward Thornton, awarded substantial damages. Whereas expulsion on mere suspicion might be warranted in time of war or other disturbances, no such circumstances existed in this case and 'reasons of safety' could not be advanced as a sufficient ground. If the Mexican Government had had good reasons for the expulsion, then it was at least under an obligation of proving its charges before the Commission. Mere suspicion was disallowed again in the case of *Lorenzo Oliva* in 1903.[2] The decision in this dispute was given by the Mixed Claims Commission established to resolve certain matters between Italy and Venezuela.[3] It should be noted, however, that the Commission's awards were largely based on the admission of liability by the Venezuelan Government where the claim was for injury to the person and 'wrongful' seizure of property.[4] The same Commission gave the decision in the *Boffolo Case*[5] and the propositions which it there formulated have since been frequently cited: (1) every State possesses the general right of expulsion; but (2) expulsion should only be resorted to in extreme instances and must be accomplished in the manner least injurious to the person affected; (3) the State exercising the power must, when occasion demands, state the reason for such expulsion before an international tribunal, and, an insufficient reason or none being advanced, accept the consequences. The only reasons advanced in the present case were contrary to the Venezuelan Constitution and could not be accepted. Umpire Ralston maintained the distinction between the right to exercise a power and the rightful exercise of that power, and assumed that there was

[1] U.S.A.–Mexico Convention of 1863, case cited in Moore, *Internatonal Arbitrations*, vol. IV, p. 3348. See also Whiteman, I *Damages in International Law*, at p. 507.

[2] Whiteman, op. cit., pp. 429–30, 508.

[3] Italy–Venezuela, Protocol of 1903, U.N. Rep., vol. X, p. 479.

[4] Article IV.

[5] U.N. Rep., vol. X, p. 528.

jurisdiction to inquire into the reasons and circumstances of the expulsion.[1]

The Belgium–Venezuela Commission gave a decision to similar effect in the *Paquet Case*, and suggested also that the very refusal to give reasons to the government of the foreigner affected, characterized the expulsion as arbitrary.[2] However, it is doubtful to what extent the requirement of explicit reasons applies in cases other than those submitted to arbitration. In 1964, after an incident involving the expulsion of United Kingdom citizens from Tanzania, the view was expressed in Parliament that there was in fact no obligation to give reasons for deportation, although here they seem to have been apparent from the circumstances of the case.[3]

It is important that a requirement to give precise reasons should not be confused with an over-all requirement that expulsion should be based on 'reasonable cause'. This may appear to be only a matter of detail, but it gives substance to both the obligation not to proceed in an arbitrary manner and the right to judge reasons of 'ordre public' in the light of national criteria. States have not hesitated to protest where the alleged reasons constituted insufficient evidence that a just cause existed. Thus, in *Loubriel's* case in 1923, the United States expressed the opinion that justification allegedly based on 'motives of internal order' and 'reasons of gravity and facts well known to the Government of Venezuela' was too vague, and that it had a right to be informed in greater detail.[4]

Similarly, in the case of *Mr. Sawkins*, who was expelled from Cuba in 1847 for 'reserved political motives which cannot be revealed', the Queen's Advocate advised that a demand should be made for compensation and to secure his return.[5] Again, in *Davidson's* case in 1855, the Queen's Advocate expressed the opinion that the arbi-

[1] Ibid., p. 532. The Umpire also placed reliance on statements of principle in Calvo, *Dictionnaire du droit international*, and on the decisions in *Ben Tillett's* case and the case of *Orazio de Atellis*.

[2] U.N. Rep., vol. IX, p. 323 (1903). See also *Jaurett's* case (1904): Hackworth, *Digest*, vol. III, p. 690; Whiteman, I *Damages in International Law*, pp. 432–5, 506 (settled through diplomatic channels).

[3] 702 H.C. Deb. (Written Answers), col. 145; *British Practice*, 1964—II, pp. 209–10. Cf. case of *British Subjects at Bogotá 1831*: 6 *B.D.I.L.* 112.

[4] Hackworth, *Digest*, vol. III, pp. 699–700. Cf. Case of *Eugene Wiener*, Moore, *Digest*, vol. IV, pp. 82–5; Whiteman, I *Damages in Internatonal Law*, p. 425 (although the United States refrained from complaint in this case, it maintained the view that only the proof of facts justifying expulsion was sufficient, and not the simple assertion as to their existence).

[5] 6 *B.D.I.L.* 113.

trary expulsion of a British subject who had not been convicted of crime, without any previous legal proceedings, required substantial justification.[1] In *Fürst's* case in 1860 it was noted that the charges raised were of a 'vague and indefinite character, inconsistent with the admitted facts and unsupported by any proof or corroboration whatsoever'.[2] More recently the Secretary of State for Commonwealth Affairs expressed doubt as to the substance of reasons advanced by the Kenyan Government justifying expulsion in terms of the need to root out 'bad weeds' and those who defy the 'call for racial harmony'.[3] Faced with a simple assertion of 'ordre public', States governments have tended to go beyond and look to the facts. In 1883 the Law Officers of the Crown considered that whatever may have been the public excitement produced by Salvation Army meetings in Switzerland, there was hardly any ground for contending that the mere presence of two of its officers was a source of danger to the State.[4] By comparison, in *Mr. Gallenga's* case in 1860, the Queen's Advocate observed that there was some evidence to justify the revocation of a residence permit for 'political reasons' in troubled times, and no complaint was made.[5]

The insistence upon justification or reasonable cause which is so clearly common to these different cases emphasizes again the manner in which the competence to expel may be substantially confined; in this instance, by operation of the principle of good faith. More precise limitations will be seen to follow as a consequence of other factors, notably the impression of the concept of 'ordre public' and the influence of international standards of treatment.

(*b*) *The South African Expulsions 1900*

The incidence of civil disturbance is itself instructive in respect of those limits which bind the general class of exceptional State measures. It is accepted in the practice of States that such circumstances may justify the arrest and detention of suspects; but in one

[1] Ibid., p. 114.

[2] Ibid., pp. 119–21. In the opinion of the Queen's Advocate, Her Majesty's Government was entitled to require both an apology and adequate pecuniary compensation. See also *Mr. Raphael's* case, above, p. 207.

[3] 750 H.C. Deb., cols. 97–100, cited in *British Practice*, 1967, pp. 112–14.

[4] Case of *Miss Charlesworth* and *Miss Booth 1883*: 6 *B.D.I.L.* 167–70. See also regarding the deportation of Jesuit missionaries from Haiti for alleged collaboration in a plot: 4 *Canadian Yearbook of International Law* (1966), 244–5.

[5] 6 *B.D.I.L.* 119. Mr. Gallenga was expelled from Rome whither he had gone for the purpose of regularly sending contributions to *The Times*. The hostility of that paper towards the then Government of Rome was notorious.

case it was advised that a claim might be made for the unreasonable expulsion which followed, unless satisfactory evidence of involvement in the alleged plot was forthcoming.[1] This approach was maintained in regard to expulsions from Hawaii in the years 1895–1898.[2] Martial law might justify exceptional measures, but nothing justified unreasonable detention, maltreatment, and enforced departure.[3] The British Government, for example, not only insisted upon these standards in its relations with other States, but also applied them to itself in regard to expulsions from South Africa in 1900. In April of the following year the Government set up a Commission to examine the various claims for compensation. In the view of Her Majesty's Government, the validity of the expulsions derived from the authority of a military commander in a theatre of war, rather than from the sovereign capacity of a State. Nevertheless, the Government agreed, in response to the representations of a number of States, to pay compensation in respect of those who had been expelled without justification although, in the view of the Legal Adviser, this decision was founded in policy rather than strict law.[4] However, the principles generally relied upon are, without doubt, also applicable to expulsions in time of peace.

In preliminary discussions, the Legal Adviser observed that the right of expulsion was one to be exercised in an equitable manner and without undue prejudice or favour to the nationals of one foreign State as compared with the nationals of others.[5] The Foreign Office inclined to the view that the simple fact of expulsion, 'with its more or less inevitable attendant hardships or losses', should not itself be regarded as a sufficient ground for compensation.[6] However, the President-Designate of the Commission was eventually instructed:

[1] *Gowrie's* case 1896: 6 *B.D.I.L.* 178; see also the incident involving the Treaty with the Two Sicilies 1863: ibid., p. 336.

[2] 6 *B.D.I.L.* 178–3. On the annexation of Hawaii to the United States the claims were submitted to the United Kingdom–U.S.A. Claims Tribunal, but they were dismissed in 1925 on the ground that no liability had passed to the United States.

[3] The claims proposed were in some cases reduced by reason of the complainants, 'loose talk': 6 *B.D.I.L.* 190 (*Thomas* and *McDowall*).

[4] 6 *B.D.I.L.*, pp. 209 ff. Claims on behalf of their nationals were presented by the governments of Austria, Belgium, Denmark, France, Germany, Greece, Holland, Italy, Sweden and Norway, Russia, Spain, Switzerland, and the United States. A total of £1,294,216 was claimed, and a total of £107,140 was paid out, for the most part in lump-sum settlements to the governments of the claimants. See Whiteman, I *Damages in International Law*, pp. 497–511, especially on the outcome of the United States claim and the distribution of compensation.

[5] 6 *B.D.I.L.* 209 at p. 213.

[6] Ibid., at p. 214.

to investigate whether the power of expulsion is shown in any case to have been exercised unreasonably or capriciously, or whether it was attended in its exercise with the infliction of any unnecessary hardship . . . The principle . . . in these assessments should be that of fair and reasonable compensation for direct damage, excluding consequential damages except for natural and proximate consequences of the act complained of.[1]

In determining liability, and on the general question of the formulation of defences, the Commission made the following significant points:

Mere opinions—such as that a certain person has no claim to compensation—are of no value, unless supported by reasons and proof. . . . General statements—such as that a certain person was concerned in a plot, or was an 'undesirable'—are likewise useless, without authenticated reasons and proofs.[2]

Despite these encouraging beginnings, the general findings and conclusions of the Commission are open to criticism. In a confidential report, Sir John Ardagh, counsel for the British Government, recorded the difficulties with which he was faced.[3] He noted the lack of precise information and the frequent total absence of materials for justification and defence. On the arrests following the so-called 'Race Course plot', he wrote:

No accusation was made against them and no reason or explanation given for their summary arrest . . . [The] prisoners were neither tried, nor examined, nor told what they were accused of . . . [It] is very greatly to be regretted that in a measure which affected such a large number of foreign subjects, no step, with the exception of communicating with the Consuls, should have been taken to ascertain whether any culpability attached to them individually, or whether there were reasonable grounds for a proceeding of an apparently arbitrary nature in the event of an appeal to their Governments having to be answered.[4]

Referring to the Commission's awards of £5 and £10, Sir John Ardagh concluded that these were wholly illusory, 'as even a solatium or act of grace'.

The Commission's Report[5] proceeded on the dual assumption that a Military Commander has an 'absolute right' of expulsion and

[1] Ibid., at p. 216.

[2] 6 *B.D.I.L.*, at p. 218. Note also the general grounds which the claimant was required to establish in order to justify a claim, and the grounds for the disallowance of any such claim: ibid., at pp. 218–19. On the issue of damages, see below, pp. 278–80.

[3] 6 *B.D.I.L.*, at pp. 219–21.

[4] Ibid., at pp. 220–1.

[5] Ibid., at pp.223 ff.

that every State has an 'indisputable right to expel aliens whose presence is considered dangerous'. The claims fell into two main classes: on the one hand, those by employees of the Netherlands South African Railway Company; and on the other hand, the claims of those allegedly implicated in the various plots. Little regard was paid to the first class, and the Commission described the Company as 'a body actively hostile to Great Britain'. In the main, its attention focused on the manner in which the expulsions were carried out and the treatment accorded to those expelled. The allegations in these matters were rejected as wholly unfounded by the Commission, which also concluded that there were reasonable grounds for the deportation of all those suspected of complicity in the plots, and that the wide discretion was 'exercised with wisdom and moderation'.[1] In fact these findings bear little relation to the agreed awards. During the Commission's deliberations, Sir John Ardagh himself negotiated amicable settlements by way of lump-sum agreements, and these were in turn approved by the Commission.[2] It is apparent that the British Government accepted the criticisms made by Sir John Ardagh in his confidential report, and recognized the justice contained in his suggested settlements.

(2) GROUNDS FOR EXPULSION IN MUNICIPAL LAW

Attention may now be turned to the particular practice of States, in so far as that is reflected in the provisions of municipal law. The aim is to see what States do, what they claim for themselves, and what they object to in other States. By way of introduction, the results of the survey so far may be summarized as follows:

1. Expulsion is a measure designed for the protection of the State and for the preservation of 'ordre public'.

2. 'Ordre public' is a 'general legal conception' and its content is determined by law.

3. Whether or not reasons of 'ordre public' exist is open to impartial adjudication in the light of the prescribed function of

[1] Ibid., at pp. 229–30, 'and that the civilised world owes . . . a debt of gratitude for . . . [the adoption of] a policy of wholesale deportation in preference to one of suppression by force'. For examples of conventional arrangements expressly governing expulsion in time of war or other rupture of relations, see Lapradelle and Politis, *Recueil des arbitrages internationaux*, vol. I, pp. 550, 557.

[2] 6 *B.D.I.L.* 230. The Commission noted that the amounts agreed were larger than it would have awarded.

expulsion and of the international obligations owed by one State to another.

4. However, in practice, a considerable margin of appreciation is left to States to determine whether their national interests are affected by the continued presence of the alien.

Possible limitations upon the power of expulsion can be seen in the provisions of certain municipal systems. In the following survey attention is concentrated on four systems which have, on the whole, a reasonably well developed regime governing the entry and exit of aliens. However, the intention is not, without more, to propose as rules of customary international law those which commonly figure as rules of municipal law.[1] Indeed, it may be that the large measure of discretion which municipal systems concede to their respective executive authorities makes it less than usually possible to presume *opinio juris* on the basis of actual practice. Nevertheless, there can be no doubt of the important influence which the standards of international law have had on the manner of exercise of the power and on the development of the principle that decisions in such matters be 'in accordance with law'.[2]

(*a*) *United States Practice*

In the United States in 1798 an Act was passed which gave the President authority to order the departure of any alien whom he deemed to be dangerous.[3] In fact, the power was never used and the Act was allowed to expire after two years. Thereafter, and particularly towards the end of the nineteenth century, a number of statutes were enacted which introduced deportation as a sanction against those entering in violation of the law.[4] It was not until 1910 that a statute authorized the removal of lawfully admitted aliens on the ground of subsequent misconduct. Since that date the classes of deportable aliens have been increased, and deportation now operates both as an adjunct to the law on entry and exclusion and, on its own, to secure the removal of those later found, or considered, to be undesirable.[5]

[1] See the cautious approach adopted by Weis in respect to general principles of the law of nationality: *Nationality and Statelessness in International Law* (1956), p. 98; quoted, with comment, by Brownlie, 'The Relations of Nationality in Public International Law', 39 *B.Y.I.L.* (1963), 284, 312–13.

[2] See further below, pp. 263–5.

[3] 1 Stat. 570.

[4] e.g. 24 Stat. 504 (1888); 26 Stat. 1084 (1891).

[5] Gordon and Rosenfield, *Immigration Law and Procedure* (rev. ed., 1974), ch. 4.

The Constitution of the United States makes no mention of any power regarding the entry and removal of aliens, but the Supreme Court has held such power to be 'an inherent and inalienable right of every sovereign and independent nation, essential to its safety, its independence and its welfare'.[1] Because such power is inextricably bound up with international relations, the argument continues, its exercise is therefore in the hands of the executive branch and largely beyond the control of the courts, or 'with such opportunity for judicial review . . . as Congress may see fit to authorise or permit'.[2]

In practice, however, the constitutional requirements of 'due process' have been recognized as essential limitations upon the exercise of discretion, and these now guarantee certain procedural rights at least,[3] if they do not actually impose any substantive limitation upon the power of Congress to create new classes of deportable aliens.[4] In an early decision, the Supreme Court held that the Government was not competent under statute to take into custody an alleged illegal entrant and to deport him without first giving him an opportunity to be heard. Such hearing did not need to be in accordance with judicial proceedings, but should be that which was appropriate to the circumstances.[5] The full benefits of due process have been denied as a result of the nature which the courts have attributed to deportation proceedings. While admitting the severity of the measure, the tendency has been to describe them as civil and

[1] *Fong Yue Ting* v. *U.S.* 149 U.S. 698, 711 (1893); see also *Nishimura Ekiu* v. *U.S.* 142 U.S. 651 (1892); *Kleindienst* v. *Mitchell* 408 U.S. 753 (1972); *Perdroza-Sandoval* v. *INS* 498 F.2d 1254 (1974).

[2] *Carlsdon* v. *Landon* 342 U.S. 524 (1952), and note the dissent of Black J; *Circella* v. *Sahli* 216 F.2d 33 (1954). See also per Brewer J. dissenting in *Fong Yue Ting* v. *U.S.* 149 U.S. 698 (1893): 'The doctrine of powers inherent in sovereignty is one both indefinite and dangerous. . . The governments of other nations have elastic powers—ours is fixed and bounded by a written constitution. The expulsion of a race may be within the inherent powers of despotism' (at p. 737).

[3] Immigration and Nationality Act 1952, 8 U.S.C. s. 1252(b); *Nguyen Da Yen* v. *Kissinger* 528 F.2d 1194 (1975); *Casteneda-Delgado* v. *INS* 525 F.2d 1295 (1975).

[4] In *Hitai* v. *INS* 343 F.2d 466 (1965) the Court of Appeals, Second Circuit, held that the appellant could not rely on the guarantee of human rights without distinction contained in Article 55 of the United Nations Charter. This provision was not self-executing and the question of immigration was a policy decision of the legislative branch binding on the judiciary.

[5] *Yick Wo* v. *Hopkins* 118 U.S. 356 (1886); *Kaoru Yamataya* v. *Fisher* 189 U.S. 86 (1903) (The Japanese Immigrant Case); *Ludeck* v. *Watkins* 335 U.S. 160 (1948)—removal of enemy alien not subject to judicial review. Cf. *Netz* v. *Ede* [1946] Ch. 224; *R.* v. *Bottrill, ex parte Küchenmeister* [1947] 1 K.B. 41.

not criminal proceedings.[1] Deportation is not, therefore, punishment, and removal on account of conviction for crime cannot come within the prohibition on cruel and unusual punishment in the Eighth Amendment.[2] Yet at the same time there has been judicial recognition of deportation as a drastic penalty, such that the relevant statutes are to be strictly construed.[3]

But it seems that deportation statutes cannot be unconstitutional by reason of *ex post facto* provisions. In the leading case of *Harisiades* v. *Shaughnessy* the Supreme Court held that the United States had the power to expel an alien notwithstanding his long residence, that the exercise of this power violated neither due process nor freedom of speech, and that deportation because of membership of a 'subversive organization' prior to the effective date of the statute did not constitute an *ex post facto* law within the constitutional prohibition.[4] In addition, the alien who is subject to the 'civil' procedure of deportation cannot rely upon the otherwise far-reaching implications of the Supreme Court decision in the *Miranda Case*.[5] In criminal prosecutions this decision precludes the use of statements made by a person in custody unless he is first told of his right to remain silent and of his right to have a lawyer present at his interrogation.[6]

Despite these disadvantages, the expulsion process must involve what is sometimes characterized as 'procedural', as opposed to 'substantive', due process. In effect, this preserves the dichotomy generally assumed to exist between the reserved domain of 'sovereign' powers and the requirements of international law standards. In one case the Supreme Court expressly noted that without a hearing there would be no constitutional authority for deportation, and

[1] *Bugajewitz* v. *Adams* 228 U.S. 589 (1913), per Holmes J. at p. 591; *Zapp* v. *District Director of Immigration* 120 F.2d 762, 764 (1941).

[2] *Circella* v. *Sahli* 216 F.2d 33 (1954). The alien in question had been born in 1898, had entered the United States in 1902, and was ordered to be deported in 1954. See also *Santelises* v. *INS* 491 F.2d 1254 (1974); *Brea-Garcia* v. *INS* 531 F.2d 693 (1976). Cf. *Furman* v. *Georgia* 93 S.Ct. 2726, esp. per Brennan J. at pp. 2742–8.

[3] *Bronsztejn* v. *INS* 526 F.2d 1990 (1975).

[4] 342 U.S. 580 (1952). Cf. *Mandel* v. *Mitchell* 325 F. Supp. 620 (1971); reversed, *sub nom. Kleindienst* v. *Mitchell* 408 U.S. 753 (1972).

[5] *Miranda* v. *Arizona* 384 U.S. 436 (1966).

[6] *Pang* v. *INS* 368 F.2d 637 (1966); *Lavoie* v. *INS* 418 F.2d 732 (1969), cert. den. 400 U.S. 854 (1970); *Valeros* v. *INS* 387 F.2d 921 (1967); *Kung* v. *District Director* 356 F. Supp. 571 (1973); Haney, 'Deportation and the Right to Counsel', 11 Harv. Int. L.J. 177 (1970). Cf. United Kingdom Immigration Act 1971, Sch. 2, para. 4—the duty to answer questions is imposed on all who seek entry. In *U.S.* v. *Sacco* 428 F.2d 264 (1971) it was held that the alien registration acts do not violate the rule against self-incrimination because they are 'essentially non-criminal and regulatory provisions'.

that this constitutional requirement derives from the self-same source as the power of Congress to legislate.[1] In practice, while the remedies available to the alien tend to go only to the *legality* of the order of detention or deportation, and not to the merits,[2] it will be seen that the courts have developed the concept of legality beyond the merely formal meeting of statutory requirements.

It has been estimated that, in the law of the United States, the eighteen general classes of deportable aliens entail some 700 different grounds for removal.[3] An over-all view of the situation will suffice for present purposes.

The power of expulsion is applicable to all aliens, that is, to 'any person not a citizen or national of the United States'.[4] Any claim to citizenship is to be determined judicially, rather than by an administrative decision, in the deportation proceedings themselves, for the authorities only have jurisdiction if alienage is established.[5] Moreover, if the person concerned establishes a prima facie case of

[1] *Wong Yang Sung* v. *McGrath* 339 U.S. 33, 49–50 (1950); the Court also held that the provisions of the Administrative Procedure Act 1946 applied to deportation proceedings. This ruling was promptly negatived by the Immigration and Nationality Act 1952, s. 242(b), 8 U.S.C. s. 1252(b), prescribing an *exclusive* procedure for deportation: *Marcello* v. *Bonds* 349 U.S. 302 (1955). However, it has since been held that the 1946 Act *does* apply to determinations by the Secretary of Labor on whether to issue alien employment certification. Such certification is a necessary pre-condition to the taking-up of employment by an alien and it will only be granted if there is not enough local labour 'able, willing, qualified and available' to perform the work sought by the particular alien, and provided that employment of the alien will not adversely affect the working conditions and wages of U.S. workers. See *Secretary of Labor of the U.S.* v. *Farino* 490 F.2d 885 (1973); *First Girl, Inc.* v. *Regional Manpower Administrator* 499 F.2d 122 (1974); *Ratnayake* v. *Mack* 499 F.2d 1207 (1974).

[2] In *Vajtauer* v. *Commissioner of Immigration, New York* 273 U.S. 103 (1927) the Court held that want of due process is not established in habeas corpus proceedings merely by showing that the decision is erroneous, and that if there was some evidence supporting the order, that was sufficient. See now the requirement of 'substantial evidence', below, p. 267. Where the alien applies for 'discretionary relief', for example, suspension of deportation, the Attorney General is not required to give a hearing: 8 U.S.C. s. 1254(a)(1), (2). In *Jay* v. *Boyd* 351 U.S. 345 (1956) the Supreme Court held that the use of confidential information in security or public interest matters on such applications was reasonable; note dissenting judgments of Warren C.J. (at p. 361), Black J. (at p. 368), Frankfurter and Douglass JJ. (at p. 370).

[3] Gordon and Rosenfield, *Immigration Law and Procedure*, ch. 4, p. 5. The statute declares that all the enumerated grounds for deportation apply retrospectively, and the alien does not benefit from any period of limitation: 8 U.S.C. s. 1215(d).

[4] 8 U.S.C. s. 1101(a)(3).

[5] *Pignatello* v. *Attorney General* 350 F.2d 719 (1965); 8 U.S.C. s. 1105(a)(5). An application to file petition for naturalization does not give the alien any status, right, or immunity from the initiation of deportation proceedings until the question of naturalization is settled: *Millan-Garcia* v. *INS* 343 F.2d 825 (1965).

citizenship, this can be rebutted only by clear, unequivocal, and convincing evidence of fraud or error.[1]

Assuming that the question of alienage is not in issue, the grounds for removal fall into two main categories: those which derive from an entry in breach of the immigration laws, or continuing residence in breach of entry conditions; those which derive from conduct after entry. The statute provides that any alien shall be deported who at any time was within one or more of the classes of aliens excludable under the law at the time of entry.[2] This means, in effect, that the question of 'exclusion' is always open, and the fact that the alien has received permission to enter does not mean that the matter cannot be reviewed.[3]

Additional and extensive grounds for removal apply in respect of the alien's conduct after he has been admitted to the country. The statute provides for the deportation of any alien who, within five years of entry, is convicted of a crime involving 'moral turpitude', and is confined or is sentenced to confinement for a year or more.[4] Other specific crimes and offences may also lead to deportation. These include the offences of carrying or possessing an automatic weapon or 'sawn-off' shotgun,[5] offences involving prostitution[6] or the smuggling of aliens,[7] and also touch one who has become a public charge, in the opinion of the Attorney General, from causes not affirmatively shown to have arisen after entry.[8]

Wide provisions have also been enacted in order to deal with subversives of various kinds, and deportation is required of aliens both on account of their personal beliefs and advocacy and on account of their membership in or affiliation to certain designated organizations.[9] This covers, for example, anarchists and those who advocate opposition to all organized government, and those who are members of or affiliated to the Communist Party or any other totalitarian party

[1] *Lim* v. *Mitchell* 431 F.2d 197 (1970).

[2] 8 U.S.C. s. 1251(a)(1).

[3] See 8 U.S.C. s. 1251(a)(2), (3); (c); *Leon* v. *Murff* 250 F.2d 436 (1957). For provisions governing the removal of those who re-enter after deportation without the permission of the Attorney General, see 8 U.S.C. s. 1252(f); cf. United Kingdom Immigration Act 1971, sections 15(5), 16(1), 24(1); *R.* v. *Kelly* [1966] 1 W.L.R. 1556.

[4] 8 U.S.C. s. 1251(a)(4); *Circella* v. *Sahli* 216 F.2d 33(1954); *Hirsch* v. *INS* 308 F.2d 562 (1962); *Guerrero de Nodahl* v. *INS* 407 F.2d 1405, 1406–7; Gordon and Rosenfield, *Immigration Law and Procedure*, ch. 4, pp. 98–115.

[5] 8 U.S.C. s. 1251(a)(14).

[6] Ibid., s. 1251(a)(12), (18).

[7] Ibid., s. 1251(a)(13).

[8] Ibid., s. 1251(a)(8).

[9] 8 U.S.C. s. 1251(a)(6), (7).

of the United States or any other State, or who advocate the doctrines of world communism, etc. As a general rule, the alien must know what he is doing when he joins a designated organization, and it has been held that it is for the Government to produce evidence of 'meaningful association' with the organization.[1]

The immigration laws of the United States are among the most complex and detailed in the world, although the classes of deportable aliens which those laws lay down are those common to most systems. Deportation is accepted as the most appropriate sanction for (1) those who enter or remain in violation of law; (2) those convicted of serious crime; (3) those who otherwise offend against 'ordre public' or public morality; and (4) those who are politically undesirable. The details of the law represent a partial attempt to substitute rules for discretion—if an alien comes within class X, Y, or Z then, upon the order of the Attorney General, he shall be deported.[2] This approach is quite different from that of the law of the United Kingdom, France, or Germany, each of which, in its own way, employs the satisfaction of a general condition as the necessary prerequisite to the exercise of discretion and leaves a wide margin of appreciation to the executive to order deportation in 'security' cases.[3]

Expulsion under the United States law depends greatly upon the individual satisfying certain objective criteria. Whether these criteria exist is clearly a matter of fact which is capable of impartial determination, far more so than the question whether an alien's removal is 'conducive to the public good', or whether he 'constitue une menace pour l'ordre public', or whether 'seine Anwesenheit erhebliche Belange [des Staates] beeinträchtigt'. But this first impression of control given by United States law is a little deceptive. Although the fact of deportability must be established by clear, unequivocal, and convincing evidence, it will be seen that the powers of the Executive are less closely confined where the alien applies for 'discretionary relief', such as suspension of deportation, adjustment of status to that of permanent resident, or voluntary departure.

[1] *Gastelum-Quinones* v. *Kennedy* 374 U.S. 469 (1963); *Rowoldt* v. *Perfetto* 355 U.S. 115, 120 (1957). Cf. *Bridges* v. *Wixon* 326 U.S. 135, 143 (1945); Konvitz, *Civil Rights in Immigration* (1953), pp. 114–22.

[2] 8 U.S.C. s. 1251(a).

[3] See the criticism of the non-justiciability of 'security' matters in the United Kingdom by Street, 'The Prevention of Terrorism (Temporary Provisions) Act 1974', [1975] Crim. L. Rev. 192, 195–6.

(*b*) *United Kingdom Practice*

Although it is now generally assumed that the power to expel aliens is inherent in every sovereign and independent nation, it was never at any time very clear whether the exercise of this power lay within the prerogative of the Crown. There are a number of early dicta to the effect that the Crown may expel even alien friends.[1] There are also a number of historical examples[2] but little use seems to have been made of any such prerogative in the years after the revolution of 1688. What power there was resided in statute, the purpose of which seems to have been to enact the power, rather than to declare its continuing existence.[3] In *Attorney-General for Canada* v. *Cain*,[4] however, the Privy Council did not doubt that the Crown possessed the power to expel even a friendly alien from Canada, and to remove him to the country whence he came. The Board expressed the further view that, in the grant of the privilege of entry, the Crown might attach whatever conditions it deemed fit. Since 1905, the power of expulsion in the United Kingdom has been regulated by statute, but there are many more recent decisions which tend to reflect this return to primitive notions of 'sovereign' rights.[5]

The Aliens Act 1905 introduced a limited statutory power of expulsion. It provided (1) that if an alien was convicted of an offence for which he was liable to imprisonment without the option of a fine, the court might recommend his expulsion, either in addition to or in lieu of sentence;[6] (2) that if an alien were found within twelve months of his last arrival to be in receipt of poor relief, or to be living in insanitary conditions owing to overcrowding, or to have been convicted in a foreign country for an extradition crime, then

[1] e.g. Blackstone, I *Comm.* 366; Chitty, *Law of the Prerogatives of the Crown* (1820), p. 49.

[2] e.g. the expulsion of the Jews in 1290. See also Craies, 'The Right of Aliens to enter British Territory', 6 L.Q.R. (1890), 27; Sibley and Elias, *The Aliens Act and the Right of Asylum* (1906), pp. 70–1 and *passim*; Thornberry, 'Dr. Soblen and the Alien Law of the United Kingdom', 12 I.C.L.Q. (1963), 414; Haycraft, 'Alien Legislation and the Prerogative of the Crown', 13 L.Q.R. (1897), 165; 6 *B.D.I.L.* 83 ff.

[3] e.g. 33 Geo. III c. 4; 45 Geo. III c. 155; see 5 *B.D.I.L.* 98–101.

[4] [1906] A.C. 542, 546. Lord Atkinson based himself specifically on Vattel, *Law of Nations*, I, s. 231, II, s. 125.

[5] See the cases involving alien enemies: *Netz* v. *Chuter Ede* [1946] Ch. 224; *R.* v. *Bottrill, ex parte Küchenmeister* [1947] 1 K.B. 41, per Scott L.J., at p. 51; see also remarks of Lord Denning M.R., in *Schmidt* v. *Home Secretary* [1969] 2 Ch. 149, 168–9, 171, and *R.* v. *Governor of Pentonville Prison, ex parte Azam* [1973] 2 W.L.R. 949, 960, 963. Cf. Opinion of the Assistant Under-Secretary of State, 1901, 6 *B.D.I.L.* 211.

[6] Section 3(1)(a).

a court might, on proceedings taken, certify the facts to the Secretary of State.[1] There was no time limit for the expulsion of criminal aliens, but it is to be noted that the Secretary of State might only order expulsion after due recommendation or certification by the courts.[2] In the years to 1914 some 2,866 expulsion orders were made on the recommendation of a court, and there is some evidence of a corresponding reduction in the alien prison population. Most of the recommendations were carried out, although in some few cases no order was made in the light of various considerations, such as the youth of the offender, lack of friends in or connection with any other country, and long residence in the United Kingdom.[3]

With the outbreak of the First World War control of aliens was established on a new basis, and within one day there was passed an Act requiring all aliens to register with the police and giving the Home Secretary power to exclude or deport any alien without appeal.[4] As amended in 1919,[5] this statute and the Aliens Orders made thereunder remained the basis of control until 1973. In each case, leave to land was required and this might be given subject to conditions, for example, as to registration with the police or prohibiting employment.[6] It appears to have been completely within the discretion of the Secretary of State whether to revoke, vary, or cancel such conditions.[7] Similarly, extensive powers were granted to order the deportation of an alien, either on the recommendation of the court which had convicted him of an offence punishable with imprisonment, or in circumstances in which the Home Secretary deemed such deportation to be conducive to the public good.[8] In

[1] Section 3(1)(b).

[2] On the deficiencies of the recommendation procedure in practice, see Gainer, *The Alien Invasion* (1972), pp. 203–6; also Home Office Report, *Expulsion of Aliens*, 1914, and the Reports for the preceding years. On the exclusion provisions of this legislation see above, pp. 97–8.

[3] e.g. Home Office *Reports*, 1908, 1911, 1914.

[4] Aliens Restriction Act 1914; Parl. Deb., 5th Ser., 1914, vol. 65, cols. 1986–90. Cf. the provision for appeal to the Privy Council in the Aliens Act 1848: 6 *B.D.I.L.* 100.

[5] Aliens Restriction (Amendment) Act 1919.

[6] Aliens Order 1953, Article 5.

[7] Ibid., Article 5(3); but note Lord Denning's remarks on the premature withdrawal of permission to remain in *Schmidt* v. *Home Secretary* [1969] 2 Ch. 149, at pp. 170–1. For application of the Aliens Order 1920 and the Special Restriction (Coloured Alien Seamen) Order 1925, and their effect on all coloured seamen regardless of nationality, see, Little, *Negroes in Britain* (1957), pp. 63–7.

[8] Aliens Order 1953, Article 20(1). Under Article 21 the Home Secretary might give directions for the alien's removal with any dependants, on a ship or aircraft, and might specify the country to which he was to be returned. The alien was liable to be detained

most cases, the court's recommendation could be challenged on appeal against sentence, and occasionally account would be taken of mitigating factors such as the possibility of persecution,[1] and length of residence in the United Kingdom.[2] But after 1914 the Home Secretary's power was no longer tied to the recommendation of a court. He was free to order deportation on the grounds of public good, and this he might do regardless of recommendation, regardless even of conviction.[3] Although the courts declared their jurisdiction to go behind a deportation order in the case of a 'misuse' or 'unlawful' exercise of the power, in practice the evidentiary burden was difficult to satisfy and no allegation of improper purpose was ever upheld.[4] The courts refused to sit on appeal from the Home Secretary and declined even to demand that deportation proceedings provide opportunity for a hearing within the minimum requirements of the rules of natural justice.[5] In those days a very wide margin of appreciation was conceded to the executive.

Under the Commonwealth Immigrants Act 1962 the Secretary of

whenever a deportation order had been made and whenever consideration was being given to the recommendation of a court.

[1] *R.* v. *Zausmer* (1911) 7 Cr. App. Rep. 41.

[2] *R.* v. *Kleis* (1910) 4 Cr. App. Rep. 101; *R.* v. *Friedmann* (1914) 10 Cr. App. Rep. 72; and cf. *R.* v. *Grunspan* (1913) 8 Cr. App. Rep. 269. These cases were all decided under the Aliens Act 1905, when the recommendation of a court was an essential precondition to expulsion. For more recent expression of judicial attitudes to the recommendation for deportation, see *R.* v. *Caird* (1970) 54 Cr. App. Rep. 499, 510; *R.* v. *Baidoo* (1971) 55 Cr. App. Rep. 253, 255; *R.* v. *Anderson* [1972] 1 Q.B. 304.

[3] Expulsion for breach of landing conditions might be ordered either on public-good grounds or on the recommendation of a court after conviction for such breach under Aliens Order 1953, Articles 25 and 26. After 1956, and in pursuance of its obligations under the European Convention on Establishment, the Government permitted aliens resident for two years or more the privilege of making representations before the Chief Metropolitan Magistrate against any decision to deport. The Magistrate in turn might make his recommendation to the Home Secretary which, although not binding, was followed in practice: *Report of the Wilson Committee on Immigration Appeals*, Cmnd. 3387, para. 53, Appx. VII, Table 7.

[4] *R.* v. *Governor of Brixton Prison, ex parte Sarno* [1916] 2 K.B. 742; *R.* v. *Secretary of State, ex parte Château-Thierry* [1917] 1 K.B. 922; *R.* v. *Chiswick Police Station Superintendent, ex parte Sacksteder* [1918] 1 K.B. 578; *R.* v. *Governor of Brixton Prison, ex parte Bloom* (1920) 124 L.T. 375.

[5] *R.* v. *Inspectors of Leman Street Police Station, ex parte Venicoff* [1920] 3 K.B. 72; *Musson* v. *Rodriguez* [1953] A.C. 530; *Schmidt* v. *Home Secretary* [1969] 2 Ch. 149. Cf. *Ridge* v. *Baldwin* [1964] A.C. 40. The main categories of aliens deported on public-good grounds were the mentally disordered, criminals in respect of whom no recommendation for deportation had been made by the court, 'destitute malingerers', 'persistently unsatisfactory workers', aliens who refused to leave after their permission had expired, students who refused to study, and security cases: 649 H.C. Deb., cols. 423–4.

State was empowered for the first time to order the deportation of a Commonwealth citizen, but this power was limited to the occasion of a recommendation by the court which had convicted him of an offence punishable with imprisonment.[1] The power of the court was also limited, and no recommendation was to be made against such citizen who satisfied the court that he was 'ordinarily resident' in the United Kingdom at the date of conviction and that he had been continuously so resident for at least five years prior to that date.[2] This Act also provided for the prosecution of Commonwealth citizens who entered or remained in breach of the immigration laws, and they might be convicted and, on the recommendation of the court, deported.[3] The prosecution, conviction, and recommendation were essential pre-conditions to an exercise of the power of expulsion, and it was not until the Immigration Act 1971 that a general power to deport for the public good was introduced in respect of Commonwealth citizens. It was recommended in 1965[4] that the Home Secretary should have the power to repatriate those who evaded immigration controls or who remained beyond their permitted time, and this was eventually enacted in the Immigration Appeals Act 1969.[5]

The Act of 1962, in fact, made it no offence for Commonwealth citizens to enter the United Kingdom without being examined by an immigration officer. If they did so, and remained unexamined for the statutory period of twenty-four hours, then they could not be prosecuted or required to submit to examination. They could only then be deported if subsequently convicted for a criminal offence and recommended for deportation.[6] In 1969, the Immigration Appeals Act introduced rights of appeal against, *inter alia*, a decision to vary

[1] Commonwealth Immigrants Act 1962, section 6. The power was limited to those who had attained the age of 17: ibid., section 7 (1). British protected persons and Irish citizens were also liable to be deported, but provision was made for appeal against the recommendation as against a sentence of the court: ibid., section 8 (4).

[2] Ibid., section 7(2). In calculating the period, no regard was to be paid to continuous periods of detention exceeding six months. The limited statutory recognition of a 'vested right of residence' is carried over into the new law; see below, p. 249.

[3] Ibid., section 4(1).

[4] *Immigration from the Commonwealth*, Cmnd. 2739, para. 25.

[5] See now Immigration Act 1971, section 3 (5).

[6] *N.B. D.P.P.* v. *Bhagwan* [1970] 3 W.L.R. 501, in which the House of Lords adopted a restricted interpretation of the 1962 Act in view of the 'common law rights of British subjects' to enter the United Kingdom. See also *R.* v. *Governor of Pentonville Prison, ex parte Azam* [1973] 2 W.L.R. 949; Immigration Act 1971, sections 4(2), 16(1), (2); Sch. 2, para. 9.

conditions of entry for both aliens and Commonwealth citizens, and any decision to deport for breach of conditions or otherwise without a recommendation of the court. For the first time an alien might challenge a decision that his removal was conducive to the public good, and both adjudicators and the Immigration Appeals Tribunal were empowered to review any discretionary decision, where they were of the opinion that the discretion should have been exercised differently.[1] This statutory innovation gave belated recognition to the substantive requirements of due process. It accepted the principle that the executive's power is one of controlled discretion and reflected the impact of international standards, particularly the pressure exerted by developments in the light of the European Convention on Human Rights.

Despite the recommendations of the Wilson Committee on Immigration Appeals,[2] the Government of the day attempted to grant an appeal against decisions or actions of the Home Secretary which were based on political reasons, and also those based on reasons of national security. A special procedure was introduced, with appeal directly to a specially constituted Tribunal.[3] But this was no appeal in the ordinary sense of the word: evidence could be presented by the Government in the absence of the appellant and his advisers,[4] and the Tribunal's decision was not binding on the Secretary of State.[5] This was well illustrated by the *Dutschke* affair in 1970,[6] where the Tribunal upheld the decision to refuse permission to remain on the ground that the appellant was 'likely to be a security risk in the future'. The new law has abandoned any formal procedure in security and political cases, and the Government's view was

[1] Immigration Appeals Act 1969, section 8(1); see now Immigration Act 1971, section 19.

[2] Cmnd. 3387, paras. 143–4.

[3] Immigration Appeals Act 1969, section 9. For aliens the special procedure was applicable not only in national security cases, but also where the decision or action was taken wholly or mainly in the interests of the relations between the United Kingdom and any other country or otherwise on grounds of a political nature: Aliens (Appeals) Order 1970 (S.I. 1970 No. 151), article 8.

[4] Immigration Appeals Act 1969, section 9 (3); Aliens (Appeals) Order 1970, article 8(3). The Wilson Committee objected to just this sort of procedure: Cmnd. 3387, para. 144. Cf. 754 H.C. Deb., col. 457.

[5] Immigration Appeals Act 1969, section 9 (2).

[6] For a critical analysis of the procedure and of the decision of the Tribunal, see Hepple, 'Aliens and Administrative Justice: The Dutschke Case', 34 M.L.R. 591 (1971). See also the *Guardian* 19, 23 Dec. 1970, 9, 19, 20 Jan. 1971; *The Times*, 30 Nov. 1970, 9 Jan. 1971; the *Sunday Times*, 1, 8 Nov., 18 Dec. 1970.

expressed in 1971 by Lord Windlesham in the House of Lords: 'These cases, by their very nature, require political judgments to be made as to what does or does not constitute a threat to the security of the state or what amounts to undesirable political activity.'[1] Although he enjoys no legal right of appeal, the non-patrial alien or Commonwealth citizen remains free to challenge the legality of his detention by way of the writ of habeas corpus. This is not, however, entirely satisfactory and the procedure involved tends to remove the 'margin of appreciation' farther from control.

The Immigration Act 1971 applies controls to all non-patrials,[2] and provides that they shall be liable to deportation (1) for failure to comply with a condition attached to their leave to enter or for failure to depart at the expiry of such leave;[3] (2) if the Secretary of State deems deportation to be conducive to the public good;[4] (3) if another person to whose family he or she belongs is or has been ordered to be deported;[5] (4) if, after attaining the age of 17, and having been convicted for an offence punishable with imprisonment, the court recommends deportation.[6] In addition, specific powers are laid down for the summary removal of 'illegal entrants',[7] and for the compulsory repatriation of mental patients.[8]

[1] 320 H.L. Deb., col. 998; 819 H.C. Deb., cols. 375–7. Provision has now been made for informal representations to be put before an advisory committee: ibid. The procedure was invoked against an Italian, *Franco Caprino*, in 1975, but the decision to deport was revoked before the committee sat: the *Guardian*, 4, 11, 14, 25 Jan. 1975; *The Times* 23 Jan. 1975. It was first actively employed against two United States citizens, *Agee* and *Hosenball* in 1977. Whatever may have been the advice tendered by the committee, the Home Secretary, Mr. Merlyn Rees, maintained his decision to deport on the grounds of national security in both cases: 919 H.C. Deb., cols. 1567–72; 926 H.C. Deb., cols. 495–507; 519–21; 719–24; 379 H.L. Deb., cols. 1563–7. In a debate on the Prevention of Terrorism Bill in 1974 the Home Secretary said that 'exclusion orders are concerned with national security, rather than with judicial issues': 881 H.C. Deb., col. 637.

[2] The power to deport does not apply to any diplomatic agent or other person entitled to like immunity: Immigration Act 1971, section 8(3); Immigration (Exemption from Control) Order 1972 (S.I. 1972 No. 1613), articles 3, 4.

[3] Immigration Act 1971, section 3(5)(a).

[4] Ibid., section 3(5)(b); this is the first time that 'public good' grounds have been applied to Commonwealth citizens.

[5] Immigration Act 1971, section 3(5)(c).

[6] Ibid., section 3(6). A person is deemed to have attained the age of 17 at the time of conviction if he appears to the court to have done so, on consideration of any available evidence: ibid., section 6(3)(a).

[7] See *R.* v. *Governor of Pentonville Prison, ex parte Azam* [1973] 2 W.L.R. 949 (C.A.); [1973] 2 All E.R. 765 (H.L.).; *R.* v. *Bangoo* [1974] Crim. L.R. 765.

[8] Immigration Act 1971, section 30, amending Mental Health Act 1959, section 90. This power applied previously only to aliens; it may be exercised where the Home

The Immigration Act does recognize the notion of a 'vested right of residence', at least as regards Commonwealth and Irish citizens who were ordinarily resident in the United Kingdom at the entry into force of the Act.[1] They may not be deported on grounds conducive to the public good if they are ordinarily resident at such date, if they are so resident at all times thereafter and at the date of the Secretary of State's decision.[2] Once they have been ordinarily resident for five years, they are also immune from deportation on any ground at all.[3] It is for the individual concerned to show that he comes within the benefit of these exceptions,[4] but it is provided that if he has at any time become ordinarily resident in the United Kingdom, he is not to be treated as having ceased to be so merely because he remained in breach of the immigration laws.[5]

A right of appeal is granted to any non-patrial who is adversely affected by a decision to restrict or vary the conditions of his admission.[6] But, as has been noted, the right of appeal is denied if the Secretary of State certifies that the individual's departure would be conducive to the public good, as being in the interests of national

Secretary is satisfied that it is in the interests of the patient to remove him. Cf. earlier agreements for the mutual retention of lunatics: 6 *B.D.I.L.* 104–6. Provision is also made for 'assisted repatriation': section 29. Payment of expenses is not to be made unless it is shown that it is in the individual's interest to leave the United Kingdom to reside permanently elsewhere, and that he wishes to do so; see 320 H.L. Deb., col. 1000. On earlier practices which secured the 'voluntary' departure of a person from the Realm, see O'Higgins, 'Voluntary Deportation', [1963] Crim. L.Rev. 680; 6 *B.D.I.L.* 98; Habeas Corpus Act 1679, sections 11, 12, and 13; *R.* v. *Ayu* [1959] 1 W.L.R. 1264; *R.* v. *McCartan* [1958] 1 W.L.R. 933; *Yager* v. *Musa* [1962] Crim. L. Rev. 240; *R.* v. *East Grinstead JJ., ex parte Doeve* [1968] 3 W.L.R. 920.

[1] Immigration Act 1971, section 7(1); cf. Commonwealth Immigrants Act 1962, section 7(2), now repealed. Resident aliens are to be considered as having received indefinite leave to land and to remain: Immigration Act 1971, section 1(2), but they still continue to be liable to deportation.

[2] Immigration Act 1971, section 7(1)(a).

[3] Ibid., section 7(1)(b), (c). In calculating the five-year period, similar principles on imprisonment apply as under the earlier legislation: ibid., section 7(3), (4). Cf. the use of a twenty-year residence requirement as a condition of immunity from exclusion from Great Britain in respect of a citizen of the United Kingdom who may be suspected of involvement in terrorism: Prevention of Terrorism (Temporary Provisions) Act 1974, section 3(4).

[4] Immigration Act 1971, section 7(5).

[5] Ibid., section 7(2). See the interpretation of this provision adopted by Lord Denning M.R., in *R.* v. *Governor of Pentonville Prison, ex parte Azam* [1973] 2 W.L.R. 949, 958–9, followed in *Secretary of State* v. *Aluko* [1974] Imm. A.R. 90.

[6] Immigration Act 1971, sections 3(3)(a); 14. But note *Suthendran* v. *Immigration Appeal Tribunal* [1976] 3 W.L.R. 725 (H.L.).

security or of the relations between the United Kingdom and any other country, or for reasons of a political nature.[1]

Where a deportation order is made on the recommendation of a court, there is no appeal within the statutory system. Any court which has the power to sentence the individual for the offence may recommend deportation, unless the court commits him to be sentenced or further dealt with by another court.[2] No deportation order may be made while it is still open to the person concerned to appeal against the relevant conviction, sentence, or recommendation, or while such appeal is pending.[3] The Immigration Rules set out the factors to be considered in deciding whether or not to implement the recommendation of the court and it is emphasized that in each case the public interest is to be balanced against any compassionate circumstances.[4]

Finally, deportation may be ordered for breach of the conditions of admission, or generally on grounds relating to the public good.[5] In the former case, the Immigration Rules declare that deportation will normally be the proper course, although the merits will always be considered.[6] An appeal may be made to the adjudicator in the first instance, and thence with leave to the Immigration Appeal

[1] Ibid., section 14(4); *Statement of Immigration Rules for Control after Entry: Commonwealth Citizens*, 1973 H.C. No. 80, paras. 4–5, 27; ibid., *E.E.C. and other Non-Commonwealth Nationals*, 1973 H.C. No. 82, paras. 4–5, 25. On the continuing availability of habeas corpus, see *R.* v. *Governor of Brixton Prison, ex parte Soblen* [1963] 2 Q.B. 243; above, pp. 226–8; *R.* v. *Governor of Pentonville Prison, ex parte Azam* [1973] 2 W.L.R. 949. Note, however, the emphasis which is given to *subjective* powers of appreciation in the Prevention of Terrorism (Temporary Provisions) Act 1974, esp. sections 1(2), 3(1), (2); cf. *Liversidge* v. *Anderson* [1942] A.C. 206.

[2] e.g. committal to the Crown Court under the Magistrates Courts Act 1952, section 29, as amended by the Courts Act 1971, section 56, Sch. 8, para. 3. See also Crompton, 'The Power to Recommend Deportation', 126 Justice of the Peace 660 (1962); Rogerson, 'Deportation', Public Law (1963), 305; Zellick, 'The Power of the Courts to Recommend Deportation', [1973] Crim. L.R. 612.

[3] Immigration Act 1971, section 6(2), (4), (5); 1973 H.C. No. 80, para. 35; 1973 H.C. No. 82, para. 42. A person convicted on indictment may appeal against the recommendation to the Court of Appeal (Criminal Division), with leave of that Court (Criminal Appeal Act 1968, sections 9, 11(1)), and a person convicted by a magistrates' court may appeal against the recommendation to the Crown Court (Magistrates Courts Act 1952, section 83(1), (3), as amended by the Courts Act 1971, section 56, Sch. 9).

[4] 1973 H.C. No. 80, paras. 38–41; 1973 H.C. No. 82, paras. 45–8; *Derrick* v. *Secretary of State* [1972] Imm. A.R. 109; *Jordan* v. *Secretary of State* [1972] Imm. A.R. 201.

[5] Immigration Act 1971, sections 3(5)(a), (b). No appeal lies in national security or political cases: ibid., section 15(1).

[6] 1973 H.C. No. 80, para. 42; 1973 H.C. No. 82, para. 49; *Secretary of State* v. *Aluko* [1974] Imm. A.R. 90.

Tribunal.[1] Deportations on the ground of public good will generally occur in two types of case. In the first, deportation in effect will be on the ground of criminality, for example, where the individual has been convicted, but the court has made no recommendation, or where criminal activities are only suspected and not proven. Other grounds, such as vagabondage or living off social security, may also be relevant. Where deportation is ordered, there is a right of appeal direct to the Tribunal,[2] save in those cases directly involving national security or political reasons.[3] Here the individual must rely, if at all, on the common-law remedies, such as habeas corpus.[4]

The grounds for removal of aliens in United Kingdom law bear obvious similarities to those current in the municipal law of the United States of America. They may be summarized as follows:

1. Entry in breach of law.
2. Breach of the conditions attached to permission to land.
3. Involvement in criminal activities.
4. Offences against 'ordre public', including political matters and matters affecting national security.

In respect to the fourth general category, United Kingdom law is remarkable for the wide measure of discretion which it leaves to the executive; it is only with difficulty that such areas may be subjected to the control of detailed rules.

(c) *Other Regimes*

Regimes for the control of aliens within national frontiers vary considerably between States, and in the countries of continental Europe the system of residence permits is a common feature. For example, in France, three categories of permits are employed, involving distinctions between temporary, ordinary, and privileged residents.[5] The permit for privileged residents constitutes recognition

[1] Immigration Act 1971, section 15(1); Sch. 3, paras. 2, 3. No order of deportation may be implemented pending the outcome of any appeal, but detention or control of the appellant may be required. See also The Immigration Appeals (Procedure) Rules 1972 (S.I. 1972 No. 1684).

[2] Immigration Act 1971, section 15(7)(a); *Derrick* v. *Secretary of State* [1972] Imm. A.R. 109.

[3] Immigration Act 1971, section 15(3). On appeals against destination, see below, p. 273.

[4] See below, pp. 272–3.

[5] Ordonnance du 2 nov. 1945. E.E.C. nationals are subject to their own regime; see, for example, ordonnance du 28 août 1969 (D. 1969. 335); décret du 5 janv. 1970 (D.

of the special status acquired by aliens long established in France. It may be issued to aliens with uninterrupted residence of at least three years, who were aged 35 or more at the time of admission.[1] It is valid for ten years and is renewable as of right (en plein droit). Its validity extends to the whole of metropolitan France and it cannot be restricted by individual measures, although residence in certain *départements* may be curtailed. The holders of these permits are dispensed from the *cautio judicatum solvi*,[2] and they may only be deprived of their status by decision of the Minister of the Interior. In addition, they are not subject to 'refoulement' as a consequence of the withdrawal of or failure to renew their permit, and they may be dealt with only in expulsion proceedings.[3]

In the Federal Republic of Germany, the residence of aliens is also made subject to possession of a residence permit (Aufenthaltserlaubnis).[4] There is no express provision for a hearing on applications for such permits, but this is required indirectly by Article 103 of the Constitution (Bonner Grundgesetz, 1949), which leads in turn to the possibility of an appeal against a prejudicial decision.[5] Residence permits may be applied for either before or after admission, although there is no appeal in the former case.[6] Work permits (Arbeitserlaubinisse) are also required, as in France, and recent legislation provides that these may be either restricted to a particular job with a

1970. 54); décret du 25 mai 1971 (D. 1971. 227); ordonnance no. 72–1242 du 29 déc. 1972 (D. 1973. 58); loi no. 73–628 du 10 juill. 1973 (J.O. 11 juill. 1973). Under the Franco–Algerian Agreement of 27 Dec. 1969 Algerians also reside in France under 'un régime spécifique privilégié'. They are issued with a special 'certificat de résidence' allowing them to travel, reside, and work freely. It has been held that this certificate differs not only in name but also in nature from the ordinary 'carte de séjour': Ch. Crim., Aix-en-Provence (*Kheili Lakhaar ben Brahim*), 1 Mar. 1973, Rec. Dalloz Sirey, 1973 (2).

[1] Ordonnance du 2 nov. 1945, article 16.

[2] Ordonnance du 2 nov. 1945, article 17. There are also additional advantages in matters of employment.

[3] Ibid., article 18. The bearer automatically loses his status if absent from France for six months or more without previous authorization: ibid., modified by décret du 14 août 1968. On 'acquired rights' see further below, pp. 255–61.

[4] Ausländergesetz 1965, Article 2(1), 1965 BGBl. I, 353. Special provision is also made for E.E.C. nationals; see Article 2(3) and *Aufent/EWG*, 1969 BGBl. I, 1, implementing E.E.C. Directive 64/221, Article 3(1). Entry without a permit, where that is required, and residence without such a permit are punishable with a fine and up to one year's imprisonment: *AuslG*., Article 47(1), (2). Arbeitserlaubnisse may be limited in time, restricted to particular areas, or made subject to other conditions: ibid., Article 7.

[5] Grundgesetz, Article 19(4); Schiedermair, *Handbuch des Ausländerrechts der Bundesrepublik Deutschland* (1968), pp. 214–27; *AuslG*. Article 6(1).

[6] *AuslG*. Article 5; Schiedermair, op. cit., p. 226.

specified employer or unlimited.[1] Unrestricted work permits may be issued where the applicant has been regularly employed for the last five years, where he has married a German national who is ordinarily resident in the Federal Republic, where he is ordinarily resident himself and has been granted privileged status (Aufenthaltsberechtigter), or where he has been recognized as a refugee by the German authorities.[2] The special permit is valid for five years and, after ten year's residence, is subject to no further time limit.[3] Unless the alien is in an exempted category, the issue of work permits generally is conditional on possession of the requisite residence permit, but a work permit may also be issued to one whose deportation has been temporarily suspended.[4]

The special class, 'Aufenthaltsberechtigter', is the source of substantial benefits for the long-term resident, who has established roots and economic ties in the Federal Republic. The Ausländergesetz 1965 permits this title of 'privileged resident' to be granted to aliens resident for at least five years who have adapted themselves economically and socially to local life. Those who qualify and who benefit from this status are not subject to area restrictions, to time limits or other conditions, and the grounds upon which they may be expelled are substantially reduced.[5] The alien has no right to the grant of these privileges, but once his status has been recognized he cannot then be reduced to the residence permit class, although he continues to be liable to expulsion on the limited grounds.[6]

Both the French and German systems employ the 'refus de séjour' as an intermediate stage between lawful residence and expulsion. The alien whose residence permit is refused or withdrawn comes under a duty to leave with due dispatch, although he is not at that

[1] Verordnung über die Arbeitserlaubnis für nichtdeutsche Arbeitnehmer, 1971 BGBl. I, 152, Articles 1, 3.

[2] Ibid., Article 2.

[3] Ibid., Article 4. The law declares the circumstances in which a work permit may be refused or withdrawn (ibid., Articles 6, 7), but any such decision must be supported by reasons (ibid., Article 14), which may thereafter be challenged.

[4] Ibid., Article 5.

[5] *AuslG.* Articles 8, 10(1), 11(1). Cf. *Expulsion of a Foreign National (Germany) Case* 32 I.L.R. 255.

[6] The *AuslG.* simply declares that the alien 'kann' be granted privileged status: Article 8(1). In certain circumstances the residence permit and the status of privileged resident terminate automatically, as where the alien ceases to hold a valid passport or where he loses or changes his nationality: ibid., Article 9; Schiedermair, op. cit., pp. 143–8.

time generally subject to police measures.[1] Expulsion itself is predicated upon more substantial grounds. French law is not very specific in the matter, but simply authorizes the expulsion of an alien whose presence 'constitue une menace pour l'ordre public ou le crédit public'.[2] German law on the other hand describes in some detail eleven grounds which may justify expulsion in such a way as to impose distinct and significant restrictions on the discretion of the authorities.[3] In France and in Germany the alien who is ordered to be expelled comes at once under a duty to leave. In practice, a reasonable time is allowed for departure and expulsion will be delayed pending the outcome of any appeal.[4] The departure itself is encouraged by the imposition of penalties for failure to leave[5] and, in the Federal Republic of Germany, by provisions which authorize the physical removal (Abschiebung) of the alien.[6] In France, the emphasis is on repeated prosecution for illegal residence, rather than forcible removal.[7] German law makes no specific provision in re-

[1] *AuslG.* Articles 2(1)(1), 47(1); Schiedermair, op. cit., pp. 168–70; cf. *VerwRspr.* Bd. 23 S. 84 (Bayer. Obersten Landesgericht 1971). Cf. the similar effect created by criminal provisions of the Immigration Act 1971, section 24 of which provides for the offence of knowingly remaining in the United Kingdom without leave. In fact the actual number of 'physical' deportations is low; see ordonnance du 2 nov. 1945, article 19. French law and practice frequently refer to withdrawal and refusal of residence permits as measures of 'refoulement' : Batiffol and Lagarde, *Droit international privé* (1970), pp. 190 ff. The holders of ordinary and privileged permits must be dealt with in expulsion proceedings: décret du 30 juin 1946, articles 8, 9.

[2] Ordonnance du 2 nov. 1945, article 23. For the limits of judicial and administrative review, see below, pp. 263–5 and ordonnance du 2 nov. 1945, articles 24–8. Expulsion may also be ordered by the *Préfets* of frontier and coastal *départements.*

[3] *AuslG.* Article 10(1). A general provision is retained to order the expulsion of an alien when 'seine Anwesenheit erhebliche Belange der BRD aus anderen Gründen beeinträchtigt': ibid. Article 10(1), Nr. 11. Schiedermair has noted that expulsion under this essentially political provision cannot be effectively challenged on appeal, 'weil es sich insoweit um eine Regierungsakt und nicht um eine Verwaltungsakt handelt'; op. cit., p. 163. See below, pp. 298–9 for examples of the further limits imposed by the courts on the discretion of the authorities. Cf. *VerwRspr.* Bd. 18 S. 737 (OVG, Hamburg, 1967); *VerwRspr.* Bd. 21 S. 353 (BVerwGe, 1970); *VerwRspr.* Bd. 21 S. 981 (OVG Münster, 1969); *VerwRspr.* Bd. 21, S. 982 (VG, Baden-Württemberg, 1970); *BVerfGE.* Bd. 34, S. 211 (1973); *BVerfGE.* Bd. 35, S. 382 (1973).

[4] Ordonnance du 2 nov. 1945, articles 24, 25. It has been held that the provisions for appeal against expulsion in article 25 apply only to those aliens who show that they have entered France lawfully and who hold residence permits: Cons. d'État, 2 fév. 1962, Annuaire français de droit international (1963), 997. Cf. *VerwRspr.* Bd. 19 S. 481, 483; *AuslG.* Article 12(1); Schiedermair, op. cit., p. 169.

[5] Ordonnance du 2 nov. 1945, article 27; Cass. Crim., 20 janv. 1932, Sirey 1935, I, 33. *AuslG.* Articles 9(1)(4), 47(1), (2).

[6] *AuslG.* Article 13; note the limitations imposed by Article 14. *VerwRspr.* Bd. 23, S. 84.

[7] Cf. Batiffol and Lagarde, op. cit., p. 157.

spect of destination, and the first choice is given to the alien.[1] It is generally accepted that the State of nationality is obliged to receive the alien,[2] although both France and Germany have concluded a number of bilateral treaties expressly to govern the return of those expelled.[3]

(*d*) *Grounds for Expulsion Summarized*

The municipal law systems examined display a perhaps unremarkable consistency in their choice of grounds for expulsion. Generally, an alien will render himself liable to deportation if he qualifies under one or more of the following heads:

1. Entry in breach of immigration law.
2. Breach of the conditions of entry; for example, working without a work permit.
3. Becoming a 'public charge', to include illness and 'living off social security'.
4. Involvement in criminal activities.
5. Involvement in 'undesirable' political activities or otherwise offending against 'ordre public'.

It is only rarely that local laws will make expulsion mandatory for the alien who comes within the above categories.[4] Executive authorities generally retain wide discretionary powers in regard to the final decision in such matters, and also in regard to the exercise of the residuary power to deport for political or security reasons.

(3) EXPULSION AND RESPECT FOR 'ACQUIRED RIGHTS'

In the provisions of municipal law it is commonly accepted that, in exercising their discretion, State authorities must also take the interests of the individual into account, and weigh them in the

[1] It has been suggested that for the State to select a destination would be to involve the authorities in an interference within the reserved domain of other States: Schiedermair, op. cit., p. 171. On the effect of expulsion, see *VerwRspr*. Bd. 19, S. 481 (OVG, Münster, 1967).

[2] Schiedermair, op cit., p. 178.

[3] In France, known as 'conventions de prise en charge de personnes à la frontière': Batiffol and Lagarde, op. cit., p. 198; in the Federal Republic, as 'Übernahme-' or 'Schubabkommen'; *AuslG*. Article 22; Schiedermair, op. cit., pp. 178, 227 ff.

[4] The absolute exclusion of alien stowaways in United States law (8 U.S.C. s. 1182 (a)(18)) is exceptional.

balance with the competing demands of 'ordre public'.[1] Thus, it will be relevant to consider, for example, length of residence in the State, the conduct and character of the individual, family and other connections, and compassionate circumstances.[2] In addition, the discretion must be exercised with due regard for acquired or vested rights. In its Judgment in *German Interests in Polish Upper Silesia* the Permanent Court of International Justice referred to provisions of the Geneva Convention 1922 which *confirmed* the obligation of the States involved 'to recognise and respect *rights of every kind* acquired before the transfer of sovereignty by private individuals, companies and juristic persons.'[3] Later the Court emphasized that the principle of respect for acquired or vested rights was 'a principle, which as the Court has already had occasion to observe, forms part of generally accepted international law.'[4] Although in principle the property and contractual rights of individuals depend in every State upon municipal law,[5] this does not exclude conformity of the latter with the standards of international law, at least in so far as the rights of foreigners are concerned.[6]

(*a*) *The Meaning of 'Acquired Rights'*

In the form in which it is usually proposed, the doctrine of respect for acquired rights is commonly limited to rights 'properly vested under municipal law . . . of an assessable value'.[7] Whether such a limitation is fully justified in view of the Permanent Court's reference to 'rights of every kind' is open to debate. However, if the restrictive interpretation is adopted, then its terms do not include the interests or 'legitimate expectations' of those who have established themselves within a State's territory solely by virtue of a period of substantial residence, whether or not accompanied by

[1] The jurisprudence of the Federal Republic of German refers expressly to '*die gebotene Abwägung* zwischen dem öffentlichen Interesse und dem privaten Interesse des Ausländers an weiteren Aufenthalt in Inland' (*BVerfGE*. Bd. 35, S. 382 (1973)).

[2] Cf. United Kingdom *Immigration Rules for Control after Entry* (*Commonwealth Citizens*): 1973 H.C. No. 80, paras. 38–41; (*E.E.C. and other non-Commonwealth Nationals*): 1973 H.C. No. 82, paras. 45–8. See also 731 H.C. Deb. (Written Answers), col. 45.

[3] P.C.I.J. (1926), Ser. A, No. 7, p. 21, emphasis supplied.

[4] Ibid., p. 42. See also *German Settlers in Poland*, P.C.I.J. (1923), Ser. B, No. 6 at pp. 35, 36.

[5] See *Panevezys-Saldutiskis Railways Case* (1939), Ser. A/B, No. 76, p. 18.

[6] Schwarzenberger, *International Law* (3rd ed., 1957), vol. I, p. 204.

[7] O'Connell, *International Law*, p. 763. This description would, of course, cover most cases of 'confiscatory expulsion'.

engagement in some profession. Thus, in *Joblonsky* v. *German Reich*[1] the Upper Silesian Arbitral Tribunal noted:

as a rule the freedom to use one's working capacity and to exercise a profitable activity which rests on the general principle of industrial liberty does not constitute a subjective vested right. For such a right to exist there must be some title of acquisition and the recognition by the law of some concrete power.

Hence it may be argued that the 'right of residence' or the right to earn a living is not protected as such, and that international responsibility is not engaged until some injury to the person or property occurs. The view has even been advanced that States in East Africa do not accept the principle of a vested right of residence or rights to carry on a business or profession,[2] and the fact that many Asians and others have been expelled from East Africa, even though long resident or born there, is called in aid in support of this proposal. But such arguments do no more than beg the question. Of perhaps greater significance for the purposes of international law is the more general practice in East Africa of *gradually* implementing policies of 'Africanization', which is in keeping with the principle of respect for acquired rights. On the general issue, there is now a growing body of law which seeks to protect the individual in the enjoyment of rights which defy assessment in pecuniary terms. Thus it may be that the State in which the alien finds himself owes certain obligations to the international community as a whole, while other, more specific, obligations are owed to the protecting State. The latter obligations derive from the legal relationship between the two States which is constituted by the presence of the alien on the former's territory.

Expulsion is a measure primarily directed to the protection of the interests of the State. It is not essentially a measure for the punishment of aliens, although obviously its effects may be devastating.[3]

[1] Ann. Dig. 1935–7, Case No. 42. Cf. Commonwealth Immigrants Act 1962, section 7(2), and now the Immigration Act 1971, section 1(2), (5) and especially section 7. See also *Niederstrasser* v. *Polish State*, Ann. Dig. 1931–2, Case No. 33 (licence to exercise a profession not as such protected by the Germano–Polish Convention 1922); *Hausen* v. *Polish State*, Ann. Dig. 1933–4, Case No. 40 (the obligation to respect rights of every kind did not extend to the alleged acquired right to continue employment as a teacher); case of *Lazar Rokach*, American–Turkish Claims Settlement, *Opinions and Report* prepared by F. K. Nielsen (1937), pp. 503, 508; Amerasinghe, *State Responsibility for Injuries to Aliens* (1967), pp. 148 ff.

[2] 67 A.S.I.L. Proc. 122 (1973), at pp. 125–6 (Yash P. Ghai).

[3] In the view of the present writer, it is both undesirable and unnecessary to adopt the habit of certain municipal courts, which is to characterize deportation as 'not punishment',

The alien who is admitted for any substantial period of time, and especially one who is admitted for permanent residence, has many interests which require protection. He may establish himself in business, he may marry and have children. His interests will not all come within the limited doctrine of acquired rights, but overall he has what may be loosely called 'legitimate expectations'.[1] No significant distinction is to be drawn between the refusal to renew permission to remain and the premature withdrawal of such permission.[2] In many cases of established residence the alien who is refused permission to remain will be as badly off as one whose permission is suddenly withdrawn, and in both cases there exists the possibility of an infraction of personal and property rights. A straightforward classification of the alien's continued residence as involving nothing greater than a 'privilege' solves nothing. It certainly does not meet the argument that discretion in the granting of privileges is, and requires to be, confined by rules of law.[3]

and from that characterization to deduce certain consequences, such as the absence of a right of appeal. See, for example, *Muller* v. *Superintendent*, *Presidency Jail*, *Calcutta*, [1955] I.L.R. 497 (Supreme Court of India); *Bugajewitz* v. *Adams* 228 U.S. 589 (1913), per Holmes J., at p. 591: 'nor is the deportation a punishment; it is simply a refusal by the government to harbour persons whom it does not want'. In *Lavoie* v. *INS* 418 F.2d 732 (1969) the court held that deportation proceedings were civil and not criminal; the VIth Amendment guarantees declared and affirmed in *Miranda* v. *Arizona* 384 U.S. 436 (1966) did not, therefore, apply; but cf. *Woodby* v. *INS* 385 U.S. 276 (1966), at p. 285; *Gastelum-Quinones* v. *Kennedy* 374 U.S. 469 (1963), at p. 479. More recently, in *Santelises* v. *INS* 491 F.2d 1254 (1974), the civil nature of the proceedings was held to mean that deportation could not amount to 'cruel and unusual punishment' contrary to the VIIIth and XIVth Amendments; compare the view of the Supreme Court on capital punishment (*Furman* v. *Georgia* 92 S.Ct. 2726 (1972), esp. per Brennan J. at pp. 2742–2748), and on expatriation (*Trop* v. *Dulles* 356 U.S. 86 (1958), at p. 102). With reference to the law of the Federal Republic of Germany, Schiedermair has observed: 'die Ausweisung ist im übrigen eine Verwaltungsmassnahme und keine Strafe' and therefore the principle *ne bis in idem* does not apply where expulsion is ordered after conviction and punishment. A similar conclusion was reached in *U.S.* v. *Ramirez-Aguilar* 455 F.2d 486 (1972).

[1] See *Schmidt* v. *Secretary of State* [1969] 2 Ch. 149, particularly the judgment of Lord Denning M.R., at pp. 170–1, and his discussion of *Re H.K.* (*an infant*) [1967] 2 Q.B. 617 and *R.* v. *Secretary of State*, *ex parte Avtar Singh* (Divisional Court, 25 July 1967, unreported). In *Birdi* v. *Secretary of State* (1975) 119 S. J. 322 Lord Denning suggested that the notion of 'legitimate expectations' would apply in favour of any illegal entrant who arrived in the United Kingdom before 1 January 1973 and who thus came within the terms of the amnesty announced by the Home Secretary on 11 April 1974.

[2] Cf. Immigration Act 1971, section 14; *Wilson Committee on Immigration Appeals*, Cmnd. 3387, paras. 128–30; Leacock, 'Prohibited Immigrants and Illegal Entrants under Barbados and United Kingdom Immigration Laws', 23 I.C.L.Q. (1974), 160.

[3] See Davis, *Discretionary Justice*, pp. 130, 172–6, on the analogous problems in the United States procedure on parole—'only a privilege'.

The wider doctrine of 'legitimate expectations' received a certain amount of recognition in the diplomatic exchanges of the past,[1] but of greater relevance today is the approach adopted in municipal law. In the United States, most attempts to broaden the protection of due process have failed on account of the non-criminal character of deportation. Increased awareness that the consequences of deportation may be far more devastating than imprisonment has not significantly affected actual decisions; however, it is clearly a factor to be considered in the course of the exercise of discretion.

(*b*) *A Vested Right of Residence?*

Before the courts of the United States it has been argued that the resident alien, of all people, will frequently have established strong family ties and acquired property interests, and that these and other relevant considerations together amount to a 'vested right of residence' worthy of greater protection than is provided by mere procedural guarantees.[2] In *Harisiades's* case, however, the Supreme Court observed that by withholding his allegiance from the United States the alien leaves outstanding a foreign call on his loyalties:

> So long as the alien elects to continue the ambiguity of his allegiance his domicile here is held by a precarious tenure. That aliens remain vulnerable to expulsion after long residence is a practice bristling with severities. But it is a weapon of defence and reprisal confirmed by international law as a power inherent in every State.[3]

The language may be a little archaic, but the sentiments persist and the concept of a vested right of residence remains unaccepted by

[1] *Haiti (1890); Withdrawal of Trading Licences:* 6 *B.D.I.L.* 346–7. See also ibid., pp. 154–5 in respect of a similar incident in 1911–12; *Dr. Gamble's* case 1852, ibid., p. 347, in which the Queen's Advocate advised that a claim for compensation might be pressed for the sudden and unmotivated order by the Mexican authorities that the complainant suspend his medical practice. More recently, note remarks by the Secretary of State on the refusal of re-entry by the Cyprus Government to an alien resident for over 40 years: 706 H.C. Deb., cols. 184–5, cited in *British Practice*, 1965—I, pp. 45–7. See above, p. 249, for recognition of the rights of those settled or ordinarily resident in the United Kingdom by the Immigration Act 1971.

[2] *Mignozzi* v. *Day* 51 F.2d 1019 (1931), per Learned Hand J. at p. 1021: 'To root up all those associations which we call home, to banish him to be an outcast in a country of whose traditions and habits he knows nothing and where his alienage is a daily living fact, not a legal imputation—these are consequences whose warrant we may properly scrutinize with some jealousy and insist that logic shall not take the place of understanding.' Cf. *R.* v. *Friedmann* (1914) 10 Cr. App. Rep. 72.

[3] 342 U.S. 580. And note *Shaughnessy* v. *Mezei* 345 U.S. 206 (1953). Cf. *Nottebohm Case*, I.C.J. Rep. 1955, p. 4, per Judge Read, dissenting, at p. 47.

the courts of the United States; whatever right the alien may have, it is not generally such as may be opposed to the paramount power of Congress to determine whether he shall be permitted to remain.

In several other cases, however, it has been held that a *resident* alien who departs from and then returns to the United States is not thereby liable to be *excluded*, and that he is entitled to be dealt with only in deportation proceedings.[1] In *Stacher* v. *Rosenberg* in 1963,[2] the District Court of California held that a resident alien could not be removed in exclusion proceedings where he had planned his whole trip and his return while domiciled and personally present in the United States. In addition, the court observed that there was in fact no other country to which the alien, a resident for over fifty years, could be deported.[3] Noting that the alien's 'undesirability' arose from conduct since admission, the court stated that his was the typical case for which the expulsion procedure was designed and intended.[4] This approach was affirmed by the Supreme Court in *Rosenberg* v. *Fleuti* in the same year.[5] In the Court's view, the statutory provision that an alien having a lawful permanent residence in the United States should not be regarded as making an 'entry' into the United States if his departure to foreign parts was not intended or reasonably to be expected by him,[6] should be so intepreted as to protect resident aliens only briefly absent. An alien does not make an entry, and does not thereby become liable to be excluded, unless he intended to depart in a manner which can be regarded as 'meaningfully interruptive' of his permanent residence.[7] So far, these decisions mark the limit to the substantive protection which the courts are prepared to allow. There has been but little advance since *Harisiades*, and although the alien resident will not now be arbi-

[1] *Chew* v. *Colding* 344 U.S. 590 (1953).

[2] 216 F. Supp. 511 (1963).

[3] Ibid., pp. 513, 514.

[4] 216 F. Supp. 511, 513, 514.

[5] 374 U.S. 449 (1963).

[6] Immigration and Nationality Act 1952, section 101(a)(13); 8 U.S.C. s. 1101(a)(13). In *Palatian* v. *INS* 502 F.2d 1091 (1974) a majority of the court held that there was a 'meaningful interruption of permanent residence' where the alien went to Mexico and returned after two and a half days with 55 pounds of untaxed marijuana. He could, therefore, be dealt with in exclusion proceedings.

[7] *Di Pasquale* v. *Karnuth* 158 F.2d 878, 879 (1949), per Learned Hand J: (alien had taken overnight sleeper from Buffalo to Detroit on route passing through Canada) 'it is well that we should be free to rid ourselves of those who abuse our hospitality; but it is more important that the continued enjoyment of that hospitality, once granted, should not be subject to meaningless and irrational hazards.' The judge referred also to the alien's 'vested right of residence'.

trarily excluded, he gains no special privilege of exemption from the deportation law.[1]

Both French law and German law also recognize that the long-resident alien occupies a position different from that of one who has just arrived or who is still on the point of initial entry.[2] His special status warrants special protection, and there is an increasing readiness on the part of States to restrict expulsion to grounds of the most serious nature. Any alien who is deported suffers a punishment distinctive by reason of his alienage, and the longer he has been resident in the host country, the greater will be the hardship. At the present time it cannot be said that there is a rule of general international law which forbids the expulsion of resident aliens, but there is a generality of practice sufficient to indicate the special position of this class. This is balanced by recognition of the fact that the receiving State is entitled to expect more from the resident alien than from the transient alien. Thus, it is the former who may on occasion be called upon to perform military service,[3] and who is required to submit to the jurisdiction and to seek his remedies in the local courts.[4] In return, State practice as evidenced by the content of the municipal systems examined suggests a restriction on the permissible grounds for expulsion, together with a requirement for a more thoroughgoing examination of the individual's interests and expectations.

[1] *Rodriguez-Romero* v. *INS* 434 F.2d 1002 (1970). This protection may nevertheless be fairly substantial, for the grounds of exclusion are far wider than those for deportation.

[2] See the category of 'résidents privilégiés', above, pp. 251–2 in French law; and also the category of 'Aufenthaltsberechtigter' in the law of the Federal Republic of Germany, above, pp. 252–3.

[3] See Opinion of the King's Advocate 1824, on the question of the liability of British subjects to military service in the Netherlands: 6 *B.D.I.L.* 248–9. In the United States aliens admitted for permanent residence must register for selective service within 6 months after admission and they are liable to be drafted after one year's residence: section 5(a)(3), Military Selective Service Act, as amended, 50 U.S.C. App. 455(a)(3); 32 C.F.R. 1611.5. In the past non-immigrants were also liable to be drafted if they remained in the U.S. beyond one year. Relief could be obtained, particularly under the provisions of bilateral treaties, but this resulted in disqualification from naturalization and other immigration benefits. Under present law as amended in 1971 (85 Stat. 348; 50 U.S.C. App. 451(a)), an alien admitted as a non-immigrant is not required to register for military service and is not subject to induction while he maintains his lawful non-immigrant status.

[4] See *Mr. Crutchett's* case 1864: 6 *B.D.I.L.* 252–3. Note also the influence here of the so-called 'link factor': *Aerial Incident 1955* (Israel *v.* Bulgaria), I.C.J. *Pleadings*, 1959, pp. 530–1. It may also be necessary to consider the case where the long-resident alien may have acquired the 'effective nationality' of the host State; see Brownlie, *Principles of Public International Law* (2nd ed.), p. 506; *Nottebohm Case*, I.C.J. Rep., 1955, p. 4, at p. 23.

(4) CONCLUSIONS RELATING TO THE JUSTIFICATION FOR EXPULSION

1. Justification for expulsion is demanded by reason of the function and purpose of the power, and the requirement of good faith.

2. State practice accepts that expulsion is justified:
   (*a*) for entry in breach of law;
   (*b*) for breach of the conditions of admission;
   (*c*) for involvement in criminal activities;
   (*d*) in the light of political and security considerations.

3. In determining whether its interests are adversely affected by the continuing presence of the alien, or whether there is a threat to 'ordre public', the expelling State enjoys under international law a fairly wide margin of appreciation.

4. 'Ordre public' remains a 'general legal conception', the content of which is determined by law. Whether or not reasons of 'ordre public' exist is open to impartial adjudication in the light of the prescribed function of expulsion and of the international obligations which each State owes.

5. The principle of good faith and the requirement of justification, or 'reasonable cause', demand that due consideration be given to the interests of the individual, including his basic human rights, his family, property, and other connections with the State of residence, and his legitimate expectations. These must be weighed against the competing claims of 'ordre public'.

XIII

THE MANNER AND FORM OF EXPULSION

AN EXPULSION which is founded on just cause may nevertheless be tainted by the manner in which it is carried out. Oppenheim notes that as deportation is not, theoretically, a punishment, it must be effected with as much forbearance as the circumstances and conditions allow.[1] The expulsion must, in the first instance, be permitted by the local law, and, further, be effected only in pursuance of a decision reached in accordance with law.[2] The latter requirement precludes arbitrariness and is derived directly from the standards of general international law.

(1) THE RIGHT TO A HEARING

Less settled is the question whether a hearing must be permitted to the alien. This point was taken by the Arbitrator in the *Chevreau* affair, which arose out of the expulsion and alleged ill-treatment of a Frenchman by the British military authorities in Persia.[3] The Arbitrator concluded that Chevreau's arrest might have been justified, but he noted that the British authorities were thereafter under a duty to proceed to a full inquiry without delay. M. Chevreau ought to have been informed of the suspicions against him and to have been given an opportunity to state his own case.[4] The French Government in fact claimed no express indemnity for the deportation itself, apart from the general claim in respect of arrest, detention,

[1] *International Law* (8th ed., 1955), vol. I, p. 694.

[2] See the cases of *Jaurett* and *Scandella*, both involving summary expulsion from Venezuela in breach of the local law. In the first case, that law permitted only the expulsion of those foreigners who had not established their domicile, and in the latter case the alien was denied the hearing to which he was entitled. Both claims were settled by agreement: Whiteman, I *Damages in International Law*, pp. 432–6; Hackworth, *Digest*, vol. III, p. 696.

[3] France–Great Britain, *compromis* of 4 Mar. 1930, U.N. Rep., vol. II, p. 1113.

[4] U.N. Rep., vol. II, p. 1113, at p. 1125.

ill-treatment, and loss of property.[1] By their *compromis*, the parties had requested the arbitrator to decide whether the arrest, detention, and deportation had taken place in circumstances which gave rise to a claim in international law.[2] Both parties also accepted that the rules to be applied were those previously laid down by the various international commissions, and that, whereas the facts alleged might give rise to an international claim, such claim was ill founded if the measures had been taken in good faith and on reasonable suspicion, particularly in a zone of military operations.

The right to a hearing was given a limited recognition in the code adopted by the Institute of International Law in 1892.[3] Article 21 of the code declared that every individual expelled had the right to have recourse to a court or administrative tribunal passing judgment completely independent of the government. Such a hearing was to be granted in all cases where the individual claimed to be a national or maintained that his expulsion was contrary to law or treaty. Where political issues were involved, however, it was conceded that the expulsion might take place before any appeal was heard. Many States do, in practice, permit some form of review of, if not appeal against, expulsion orders, but it has not been found easy to apply the concept of denial of justice in this area. Arbitrators and others have never satisfactorily resolved the dichotomy between due process and what they have characterized as 'sovereign powers'. In *Ben Tillett's* case, for example, the arbitrator concluded that Belgium was not liable for the summary expulsion of a political agitator without accusation or criminal charge.[4] The Government, in evaluating the facts and ordering the expulsion, had acted 'in the plenitude of its sovereignty', and the case then turned solely on the question of whether there had been any ill-treatment.

A more recent attempt to introduce the requirement of a hearing is to be found in Article 13 of the Covenant on Civil and Political Rights. This declares that, except where compelling reasons of national security otherwise require, the alien shall be allowed to submit reasons against his expulsion and to have his case reviewed by the competent authority. Although many States do make provision

[1] Ibid., p. 1129. A total sum of £2,100 was allowed, representing £2,000 for the arrest and detention and £100 for the loss of a violin. The evidence of ill-treatment was held insufficient to found a claim in international law.

[2] Article II of the *compromis*, U.N. Rep., vol. II, p. 1115.

[3] XII Annuaire de l'Institut de droit international (1892–4) 218, 222.

[4] 6 *B.D.I.L.* 124–50.

for some sort of a hearing, it is doubtful whether Article 13 can be regarded as expressing a rule of *lex lata*. Thus, the requirement is commonly subject to wide exceptions and there are few restrictions on the quality or character of the 'competent authority'.[1]

(*a*) *Judicial Review*

A useful distinction may be maintained, however, between the notion of a hearing and appeal on the one hand, and the availability of judicial review on the other. Not infrequently States will reserve to the executive branch the power of appreciating the facts and reasons behind an expulsion, while they will permit the judicial branch to review the legality of their actions. For example, under French law, expulsion may be ordered where the presence of the alien represents 'une menace pour l'ordre public ou le crédit public'.[2] Certain guarantees are declared in favour of lawful residents and provision is made for a right to be heard, except in cases of absolute emergency so certified by the Minister.[3] The judicial tribunals are not entitled to question the occasion for an expulsion order or the reasons which lie behind it.[4] Moreover, the administrative tribunals are not permitted to review the appreciation of fact upon which is based either the conclusion that the alien is a danger to 'ordre public' or that the occasion is one of urgency.[5] But they may decide on the *legality* of the order of expulsion,[6] and this involves consideration of the question whether there has been an 'excès ou détournement de pouvoir'.[7]

[1] Note the rejection by the Committee of Experts of the proposals to include similar, but more detailed, rights for aliens in the Fourth Protocol of the European Convention on Human Rights, below, pp. 286–90.

[2] Ordonnance du 2 nov. 1945, article 23.

[3] Ibid., articles 24, 25, and 26.

[4] Cour de Cassation (Ch. crim.), arrêt du 17 déc. 1937 (*Keledjian*), *Clunet* 1938, p. 485; arrêt du 20 déc. 1966 (*Yahia Ali*), *Rev. cr. dr. int. privé*, 1967, p. 517, note Aymond; Dalloz. 1967. 19.

[5] Cons. d'État, arrêt du 24 oct. 1952 (*Eckert*), *Clunet* 1953, p. 67; *Yahia Ali*, loc. cit. This approach resembles that adopted by United States courts in certain cases, and which is known as the 'political question doctrine'; see Konvitz, *Civil Rights in Immigration* (1953), p. 44; *Baker* v. *Carr* 369 U.S. 186 (1962), at p. 217. Cf. the view taken by courts in Scotland of certain provisions of the Act of Union 1707 and to the effect that any obligations which that Act may impose upon the Westminster Parliament are not justiciable: *MacCormick* v. *Lord Advocate* 1953 S.C. 396; *Gibson* v. *Lord Advocate* (1975) S.L.T. 134.

[6] Cons. d'État, arrêt du 4 fév. 1955 (*Molinelli-Wells*), *Rev. prat. dr. admin.* (1955), p. 85.

[7] Cf. Batiffol and Lagarde, *Droit international privé* (1970), pp. 194 ff.

(2) RIGHTS OF APPEAL IN MUNICIPAL LAW

It is not uncommon to find that the review of legality is supplemented by local provision for a full hearing on the merits.

(*a*) *United States Practice*

In the United States, for example, the decision to commence deportation proceedings is within the discretion of the Attorney General, but this is not uncontrolled, and a decision may be subject to judicial review if it is motivated by some unconstitutional reason, such as race, religion, colour, or other arbitrary classification.[1] In practice, deportation proceedings will be commenced with the issue and service of an order to show cause why the alien should not be deported, and the alien will only normally be arrested where this is in the public interest or if he is likely to abscond.[2] The order to show cause must state the grounds upon which the prima facie case of deportability is based, in such a way as to enable the alien to meet the allegations against him. Although attempts to introduce the full requirements of judicial process have generally failed, the statute itself does provide for the minimum rights essential to a fair hearing.[3] This hearing takes place before an immigration judge,[4] who is empowered to determine deportability, to make orders of deportation, to permit voluntary departure, to determine the country to which the alien is to be removed, to pass on applications to withhold deportation on the ground of anticipated persecution,[5] to determine the validity of visas, etc., and to take any other appropriate and consistent action.[6] The immigration judge is authorized to conduct the whole hearing, and to this end may administer oaths, present and receive evidence, interrogate, examine, and cross-examine witnesses.[7]

[1] *U.S.* v. *Sacco* 428 F.2d 264, 271 (1970); note also the difference between exclusion and deportation proceedings, and the inapplicability of the *Miranda* rules; see above, p. 239.

[2] 8 U.S.C. s. 1252(a).

[3] Ibid., s. 1252(b).

[4] Formerly known as a 'special inquiry officer'; the new designation was introduced in 1973: 8 C.F.R. 1.1(1), as amended by 38 F.R. 8590.

[5] See references cited below, p. 268, n. 4.

[6] 8 C.F.R. 242.8(a). Certain matters are reserved to the District Director, such as waiver of inadmissibility and the question of refugee status.

[7] No immigration judge may conduct a hearing in any case in which he has previously acted in an investigating or prosecuting capcity: 8 U.S.C. s. 1252(b).

The statute expressly provides that the alien shall be given reasonable notice of the case and of the time and place of the hearing; that he may be represented by counsel at his own expense; that he shall have a reasonable opportunity to examine the evidence against him, to present his own evidence, and to cross-examine Government witnesses.[1] It is further expressly provided that no decision of deportability shall be valid unless 'based upon reasonable, substantial and probative evidence'.[2] Furthermore, the burden of proof is on the government in most cases, although it is incumbent on the alien to show the time, manner, and place of his entry into the United States.[3]

If the alien admits that he is liable to deportation, then in certain circumstances he may be allowed the privilege of voluntary departure.[4] In all other cases the immigration judge is required to prepare a full and reasoned decision which is based on the evidence received. This decision may then be made the subject of an administrative appeal to the Board of Immigration Appeals,[5] at the

[1] This rules out the possibility of the government relying upon confidential evidence. It is otherwise in exclusion cases and in applications for discretionary relief: *Jay* v. *Boyd* 351 U.S. 345 (1956); 8 C.F.R. 242.17(a).

[2] 8 U.S.C. s. 1252(b). This significant guarantee was developed by the courts from a requirement of 'sufficient' evidence (*Goncalves-Rosa* v. *Shaughnessy* 151 F. Supp. 900 (1957)), to one of 'substantial' evidence (*Liacakos* v. *Kennedy* 195 F. Supp. 630 (1961)), and finally to a Supreme Court ruling that no order for the deportation of a resident alien may be made unless it is found by clear, unequivocal, and convincing evidence that the facts alleged as grounds for deportation are true (*Woodby* v. *INS* 385 U.S. 276 (1966)). In this case the Court observed (at p. 285): 'To be sure, a deportation proceeding is not a criminal prosecution. . . . But it does not syllogistically follow that a person may be banished from this country upon no higher degree of proof than applies in a negligence case.' Cf. *Lim* v. *Mitchell* 431 F.2d 197 (1971); and see 8 U.S.C. s. 1105a(a)(4); 8 C.F.R. 242.14(a). See also *Tuan* v. *INS* 531 F.2d 1337 (1976), where the immigration judge's decision was upheld, and *Ribeiro* v. *INS* 531 F.2d 179 (1976), where the deportation order was struck down, the Government having failed to establish deportability by clear, unequivocal, and convincing evidence.

[3] 8 U.S.C. s. 1361, which also provides that the alien may rely upon, and request the production of, visas etc. Where the government's case is based upon the alien having become a public charge under s. 1251(a)(3) or (8), it is for the alien to show otherwise.

[4] 8 U.S.C. s. 1251(b); s. 1254(e). The discretion to permit voluntary departure applies in all cases other than those where there is reason to believe that the alien is deportable under s. 1251(a)(4), (5), (6), (7), (11), (12), (14), (15), (16), (17), (18), i.e. generally, as a subversive, criminal, prostitute, drugs offender, or one involved in violation of the aliens registration requirements. The Attorney General may authorize the payment of removal expenses if this is in the best interests of the country. In the case of *Brea-Garcia* v. *INS* 531 F.2d 693 (1976) voluntary departure was denied by reason of the applicant's adultery, which fact indicated that he was 'not of good moral character'.

[5] 8 C.F.R. 242.21. The immigration judge may re-open the hearing at any time before the Board of Immigration Appeals secures jurisdiction over the appeal.

instance of either the alien or the Commissioner of the Immigration Service. The Board is entitled to exercise any of the Attorney General's powers in the course of its review of the decision of the immigration judge. It is expected to use its own judgment and is not subject in the exercise of discretion to any limitations or standards set by the Attorney General.[1] After review by the Board, a decision remains open to challenge in the courts on the ground that it is illegal or arbitrary or that it involved a denial of due process.[2]

Destination. Where it is decided that the alien shall be deported, it is then necessary for the immigration judge to specify the State to which he may be removed. The alien is given first choice, and removal may be ordered to the State designated by him if that State is willing to admit him and unless the Attorney General considers that this would be prejudicial to the interests of the United States. If the first choice fails, it is for the immigration judge to order deportation to any State or country of which the alien is a national or citizen. If that country in turn is unwilling to receive him, then there is a discretionary power to seek removal to any one of seven different destinations, including the State from which the alien entered the U.S.A., the State in which he was born, and, finally, any country which is willing to receive him.[3] It remains within the discretion of the Attorney General whether or not to suspend deportation and to adjust the status of the alien to that of a permanent resident.[4] This power may be exercised in favour of those resident

[1] *Jarecha* v. *INS* 417 F.2d 220 (1969).

[2] The only remedy available is that of habeas corpus, and all prior administrative remedies must be first exhausted: 8 U.S.C. s. 1105(a)(9), (c). Cf. *Vajtauer* v. *Commissioner of Immigration* 273 U.S. 103 (1927); *R.* v. *Peterkin, ex parte Soni* [1972] Imm. A.R. 253 (Divisional Court).

[3] 8 U.S.C. s. 1253(a). See *Staniszewski* v. *Watkins* 80 F. Supp. 132 (1948); *Hudak* v. *Uhl* 20 F. Supp. 928 (1937); also *Chan* v. *McFarlane* 34 D.L.R. (2d) 179 (1962).

[4] 8 U.S.C. s. 1254(a); 8 C.F.R. 242.17(a). On 'anticipated persecution' as a ground for appeal against deportation, see 8 U.S.C. s. 1254(h), as amended in 1965 (79 Stat. 911, s. 11(f)). For the provision in action, see *Fu* v. *INS* 386 F.2d 750 (1967); *Mercer* v. *Esperdy* 234 F. Supp. 611 (1964); *Blazina* v. *Bouchard* 286 F.2d 510 (1961); *Glavic* v. *Beechie* 225 F. Supp. 24 (1963); *Kovac* v. *INS* 407 F.2d 102 (1969); cf. *Berdo* v. *INS* 432 F.2d 824 (1970); *Chim Ming* v. *Marks* 505 F.2d 1170 (1974); *McCaud* v. *INS* 500 F.2d 355 (1974); *Leung* v. *INS* 531 F.2d 166 (1976); *Daniel* v. *INS* 528 F.2d 1278 (1976). In the case of *Cisternas-Estay* v. *INS* 531 F.2d 155 (1976) it was held that the Board of Immigration Appeals had not abused its discretion by denying asylum to the Chilean applicants where it was not shown that there was a 'clear probability' the petitioners would be subject to persecution. It was also held that the Immigration and Nationality Service had not abused its discretion by relying in part on a letter from the Office of Refugee and Migrant Affairs of the Department of State, commenting on the requests and noting that the government fled from was now removed from power. The court

in the United States for at least seven years,[1] who are of good moral character, and whose deportation would result in extreme harship to the spouse, parent, or child of a United States citizen or alien resident. In each case it is for the applicant to show that he is eligible for discretionary relief and, moreover, that the discretion should be exercised in his favour.[2]

(*b*) *United Kingdom Practice*

In the United Kingdom appellate bodies were established by the Immigration Appeals Act 1969 after recommendations by the Wilson Committee.[3] They are continued by the Immigration Act 1971 and are empowered to review the decisions of the Secretary of State or any immigration officer. In most cases appeal lies in the first instance to an adjudicator, and section 19 of the Act provides that he shall allow the appeal if he considers (1) that the decision or action in question was not in accordance with the law or with any immigration rules applicable to the case; or (2) where the decision or action involved the exercise of a discretion by the Secretary of State or any officer, that the discretion should have been exercised differently.[4] In the exercise of his functions, the adjudicator may review any determination of a question of fact upon which the decision was based, but it is expressly provided that, where the decision or action is otherwise in accordance with the Immigration Rules, a refusal to depart from those rules shall not be construed as an exercise of discretion.[5] In one case it was held that the latter restriction prohibited the adjudicator from allowing an appeal on considerations of natural justice:

To urge that for reasons of natural justice these rules should not be applied . . . can really only mean that the Secretary of State is being requested . . . to depart from the rules. This he has refused to do and since

observed that there was no evidence of any personal hostility displayed by the government towards the petitioners. See also Evans, 'The Political Refugee in United States Immigration Law', 3 *International Lawyer* (1969), 204.

[1] Ten years' residence and 'extremely unusual hardship' are required if discretionary relief is to be granted to these liable to deportation as subversives, criminals, prostitutes, drug offenders, or for having been involved in violation of the aliens registration laws.

[2] 8 C.F.R. 242.17(d).

[3] Report of the Wilson Committee on Immigration Appeal, Cmnd. 3387.

[4] Immigration Act 1971, section 19(1)(a); in any other case he is to dismiss the appeal section 19(1)(b).

[5] Section 19(2).

his decision is in accordance with the Immigration Rules, such decision cannot be treated as having involved the exercise of a discretion.[1]

In certain cases, such as those involving the 'public good',[2] appeal lies directly to the Immigration Appeals Tribunal. This is also the procedure where a deportation order is made against the wife or children under 18 of any person who is himself ordered to be deported.[3] Before any such 'family order' is made, the Secretary of State will consider, for example, how long the family has been resident, what ties they have in the United Kingdom other than with the deportee, and whether the wife can maintain herself and her children in the foreseeable future without relying on public funds. These provisions are directed solely at the wife, and it appears that the Immigration Rules, unlike the statute itself, do not envisage the woman either as breadwinner and head of the family, or as principally liable to be deported.[4] In the past, other discriminatory provisions operated against women. Thus, if a woman who was settled in the United Kingdom happened to marry a non-patrial, she had no right to have her husband settle with her. This rule applied even in the case of a woman who was a citizen of the United Kingdom and who herself had the right of abode. Both this practice and the rule by which wives were denied the separate use of family passports were justified by the Government on the ground that they conformed with international usage,[5] and that the prohibition on husbands and fiancés operated as an acceptable and useful barrier against people 'marrying their way through the controls'.[6] The rules were amended in 1974, and a woman settled in the United Kingdom is now entitled

[1] *Secretary of State* v. *Glean* [1972] Imm. A.R. 84, 88.

[2] See above, pp. 250–1.

[3] Immigration Act 1971, section 15(7)(b), (c). Any member of such family may depart voluntarily if he does not wish to appeal or if his appeal is dismissed: *Statement of Immigration Rules for Control after Entry* (*Commonwealth Citizens*), 1973 H.C. No. 80, paras. 44–8; *Statement of Immigration Rules for Control after Entry* (*E.E.C. and other Non-Commonwealth Nationals*), 1973 H.C. No. 82, paras. 51–5.

[4] Cf. Immigration Act 1971, section 5(4).

[5] On international passport practice, see 814 H.C. Deb., cols. 227–8; 817 H.C. Deb., col. 871 (1971); 829 H.C. Deb., cols. 967–8; 838 H.C. Deb., cols. 978–80 (1972); for the change in United Kingdom practice, see statement by Lord Balniel, 860 H.C. Deb., col. 1595 (1973). On the alleged international practice that the family should follow the head of the household (male), see 846 H.C. Deb., cols. 36, 40–1 (1972); 849 H.C. Deb., col. 663 (1973). See also *Secretary of State* v. *Dumont* [1972] Imm. A.R. 119; cf. Spouses (Equal Treatment) Bill 1974, presented to the House of Lords by Lord Avebury.

[6] 851 H.C. Deb., col. 640 (1973).

to have her husband or fiancé join her.[1] Certain other concessions are also made to the independent status of women. Thus, it is provided that a wife is not to be regarded as part of the family if she is living apart from her husband, and her deportation will not normally be considered if she has herself qualified for settlement in the United Kingdom. Children approaching the age of 18, if they have spent some years in the United Kingdom, or if they have left the family and established themselves, are also not normally to be deported.[2]

This attitude to the family may be briefly compared with that current in the courts of the Federal Republic of Germany. There it has been held, for example, that, by virtue of Article 6(1) of the Grundgesetz, a German spouse has such an interest in the proposed deportation of husband or wife, that he or she is entitled to be a party to the proceedings.[3] Other cases have consistently affirmed that marriage and the family are institutions demanding the most positive protection of the courts,[4] and the presumption thus raised operates as a most significant limitation upon the discretion of the authorities.

In the United Kingdom, on the other hand, a number of rules operate effectively to bar the review of discretionary powers. Under the old law, for example, it was provided that an extension of stay 'may be granted' to a Commonwealth trainee if the Department of Employment submitted a favourable report to the Home Office.[5] It

[1] 1973 H.C. No. 79, new paras. 47, 48, 49 substituted by Cmnd. 5715 (1974); 1973 H.C. No. 81, new paras. 42, 43, 44 substituted by Cmnd. 5717 (1974); these new rules came into force on 27 June 1974. The husband or fiancé does not have an *absolute* right to settle: *Vasiljevic* v. *Secretary of State* [1975] Imm. A.R. 100; [1976] Imm. A.R. 44.

[2] 1973 H.C. No. 81, paras. 44–8; 1973 H.C. No. 82, paras. 51–5.

[3] *VerwRspr.* Bd. 25, S. 337 (BVerwG. 1973).

[4] See *VerwRspr.* Bd. 25, S. 81 (Hesse, VGH, 1972); ibid., S. 333 (BVerwG. 1973); ibid., S. 337 (BVerwG. 1973); *BVerfGE.* Bd. 37, S. 217, 247 (1974); *BVerwGE.* Bd. 42, S. 148 (1973); ibid., S. 299 (1975). Compare practice in other jurisdictions; in the United Kingdom it has been held additionally that an alien may not generally object to expulsion on the ground that he or she is married to a national: *C.* v. *E.* (1946) T.L.R. 326; *R.* v. *Hannah Fine* (1912) 29 T.L.R. 61 (C.C.A.); Aliens Order 1953, article 20(5); see now Immigration Act 1971, section 5(2). See also Cons. d'État, 8 mars 1939, *Nouv. Rev. de dr. int. privé* (1939), p. 456. In Canada it has been held that an alien woman may not resist expulsion on the ground that she is the mother of a child who is a citizen by birth: *Louie Yuet Sun* v. *The Queen* 32 I.L.R. 252; and a similar conclusion was reached in the United States: *Aalund* v. *Marshall* 461 F.2d 710 (1972).

[5] Cmnd. 4295 (Commonwealth Citizens: Control after Entry), para. 18. See the similar provision in 1973 H.C. No. 80, paras. 15–16, and compare 1973 H.C. No. 82, para. 14 (student employees who are foreign nationals). There is no appeal against the decisions

was held that the discretion only comes into play where a favourable report is received, and that without such report the immigration officer does not enjoy any choice between alternative courses of action. In another case, the Tribunal has ruled that the applicant who seeks an extension of stay must bring himself within one or other of the categories set out in the rules. For example, he must qualify as a person of independent means or as a person setting up in business on his own account. It is not permissible to pick certain factors from one category and to add them to certain factors from another category, as as to arrive at some composite type of immigrant. The categories are bound by the rules and exceptions must be a matter for special decision by the Secretary of State. They are not, therefore, subject to review as an exercise of discretion.[1]

The issue of discretion will be of particular importance where deportation is ordered on the grounds of public good, otherwise than in security and political cases. The Tribunal will then be required to weigh the interests of 'ordre public' against those of the individual,[2] and an indication of the correct approach was given by the Divisional Court in *R.* v. *Peterkin* (*Adjudicator*), *ex parte Soni*.[3] On an appeal against the refusal of an entry certificate, the adjudicator had taken the view that he should not interfere with the decision unless it could be shown that the entry certificate officer, in the exercise of his discretion, had taken into account some matter which he ought to have excluded or had failed to take into account some matter which he ought to have included. This restricted view of his role was rejected by the Court. In its judgment, it reaffirmed that the actions of inferior tribunals remain subject to the controlling jurisdiction of the superior courts and the prerogative remedies of certiorari and mandamus. In the opinion of the court, the adjudicator was required[4] to apply his mind afresh to the problem presented by the facts and to determine what in his judgment was the correct exercise of discretion.[5] He had erred in law in following a

of the Department of Employment: *Latiff* v. *Secretary of State* [1972] Imm. A.R. 76. Compare United States law, above, p. 240, note 1.

[1] *Secretary of State* v. *Martin* [1972] Imm. A.R. 146; *R.* v. *Immigration Appeals Tribunal, ex parte Martin* [1972] Imm. A.R. 257 (Q.B.D.).

[2] Cf. *Jordan* v. *Secretary of State* [1972] Imm. A.R. 201.

[3] [1972] Imm. A.R. 253.

[4] Under the Immigration Appeals Act 1969, section 8(1)(a)(ii), re-enacted in Immigration Act 1971, section 19(1)(a)(ii).

[5] Here he ought to have considered anew the degree of hardship which would be caused to a girl if she had to leave England in order to live with her husband in his own country.

rule previously applied with some strictness by the Court of Appeal to the exercise of discretion by a High Court Judge. In the circumstances of the case, however, the Divisional Court declined to interfere while it was still open to the appellate tribunal to deal with the error. But, as the Lord Chief Justice observed, 'our supervisory powers are still available if in the end, when the appellate system has worked outside it, injustice or breach of the law remains.'[1]

It is important once again to note the interaction between the statutory system of appeals and the common-law remedies. The former provides the appellant with the means of challenging the merits of a policy decision. It also allows the exercise of discretion to be confined and permits due recognition to be given to competing considerations. The common-law remedies, such as certiorari, mandamus, and habeas corpus, do not generally intrude upon the 'policy' side of decision-making,[2] but influence and structure the exercise of power by requiring it to conform with certain minimum conditions of fairness, and by controlling abuse. They define, as it were, the outer fringes of the power, and represent the substance of that requirement of international law, that decisions be in accordance with and controlled by the law.

It is to these remedies in particular that one must look when the statutory rights are excluded, for clearly control may be hampered by the Secretary of State's certificate that national security or political reasons are involved. The common-law remedies operate to prevent manifest abuse, but there is still much to be said in favour of the independent development of something akin to the continental and E.E.C. concept of 'ordre public'.[3]

Destination. Finally, in respect of the United Kingdom, it may be noted that, although rights of appeal against deportation are frequently restricted, in all cases the individual concerned has a right of appeal against directions for his removal on the ground that he ought to be removed, if at all, to a country or territory specified by him and other than the one named in the directions.[4] In most cases, a person to be deported will be removed to the State of which he is a national or which has most recently issued him with a travel

[1] [1972] Imm. A.R. 253, at p. 257.

[2] See *R.* v. *Governor of Pentonville Prison, ex parte Azam* [1973] 2 W.L.R. 949, per Lord Denning M.R., at pp. 962–3.

[3] Note in particular *Reyners* v. *Belgian State* [1974] 2 C.M.L.R. 305 and *Van Duyn* v. *Home Office* [1975] 1 C.M.L.R. 1, and see further below, pp. 302–4.

[4] Immigration Act 1971, section 17.

document.[1] It has been held that an appeal against proposed destination will only succeed, *inter alia*, if the appellant can show another State which is willing to receive him.[2] In each case consideration is to be given to the public interest generally, and to any additional expense which may fall on public funds.[3]

(c) *A Hearing as an International Obligation*

An appeal on the merits is clearly a procedural and substantive advantage, but it is the 'review of legality' which is principally inherent in the requirement that a decision on expulsion be 'in accordance with law'.[4] It is remarkable that municipal law generally is not content simply to review the form of an order of expulsion, but that it is prepared also to examine the possibility of an absence of *bona fides*. This factor points up the character of the power as a controlled discretion and is further evidence of the limits which States admit to their powers. International law demands that an alien be permitted to obtain redress for wrongs done to him by the State in which he is present. The content of that law may, to a wide degree, be a matter of purely domestic concern. Indeed, the expelling State is in the best position, perhaps is the only authority competent, to pronounce upon such matters. Nevertheless, as Commissioner Nielsen observed in the *Neer Case*, there is clear recognition of the limits to sovereign competence in respect of matters which are the subject of domestic regulation: 'the domestic law and the measures employed to execute it must conform to the requirements of . . . international law, and . . . any failure to meet these requirements is a failure to perform a legal duty.'[5]

[1] 1973 H.C. No. 80, para. 54; 1973 H.C. No. 82, para. 61. State practice suggests that the principle of 'returnability' which attaches to the issue of a passport is now a rule of customary international law. See above, pp. 44–6.

[2] *Secretary of State* v. *Croning* [1972] Imm. A.R. 51; *Secretary of State* v. *Fardy*, ibid.. p. 192; *Ali* v. *Immigration Appeals Tribunal*, [1973] Imm. A.R. 19, 33.

[3] Appeal may also be made against the refusal to revoke a deportation order: Immigration Act 1971, section 15(1)(b); *Dervish* v. *Secretary of State* [1972] Imm. A.R. 48 (humanitarian aspects considered at pp. 49–50); *Secretary of State* v. *Udoh* [1972] Imm. A.R. 89; see also 1973 H.C. No. 80, para. 56; 1973 H.C. No. 82, para. 63.

[4] Note the availability of habeas corpus declared by the court in *R.* v. *Governor of Brixton Prison, ex parte Soblen* [1963] 2 Q.B. 243 and *R.* v. *Governor of Pentonville Prison, ex parte Azam* [1973] 2 W.L.R. 949. Consider also *R.* v. *Liverpool Corporation, ex parte Liverpool Taxi Fleet Operators' Association* [1972] 2 Q.B. 299—the court would not interfere with a 'policy' decision, but it could and should intervene to ensure that the Council acted fairly and after due regard to conflicting interests; cf. *Liversidge* v. *Anderson* [1942] A.C. 206.

[5] U.N. Rep., vol. IV, p. 60 (1926); see also *British Practice*, 1964—I, p. 63, 1966, pp.

This notion of an 'objective duty' is inherent in Ago's description of international responsibility in terms of an 'internationally wrongful act', which itself springs from the failure to carry out an 'international obligation'.[1] That expulsion should be in accordance with the local law expresses also the rule which is prescribed by international law, and it is essential that the further consequences of that rule should not be ignored. Thus, the local law is required to conform with the standards of international law:[2] it must not therefore offend against the norm of non-discrimination, and may not permit the use of expulsion as an instrument of genocide, persecution, or confiscation. The prescriptive requirement of decisions in accordance with the law necessarily implies that the discretion is confined and that decisions are controlled by the law. A full appeal on the merits, or even some special administrative tribunal which hears representations, may not be demanded, especially in political and security matters where the executive enjoys the widest margin of appreciation. But the rule of international law requires that there be available some procedure whereby the underlying legality of executive action can be questioned, such as the writ of habeas corpus in common-law jurisdictions.[3] The additional requirement of a hearing on the merits or of an opportunity to make representations, although commonly found in municipal systems, cannot be said to have gained recognition as a rule of international law. The principle, however, may be offered *de lege ferenda*. But there can be no doubt that the first rule, which denies the arbitrary and capricious nature of expulsion, is to be accepted *de lege lata*.

(3) PERSONAL TREATMENT OF THE ALIEN: DECISIONS OF TRIBUNALS

Expulsion may not only be unlawful in the circumstances considered above, but it may also be tainted by reason of the personal treatment

111–12, 1967, pp. 112–13. Cf. Article 4, Draft Articles on State Responsibility, Yearbook of the I.L.C., 1973—I, pp. 5 ff.

[1] *Second Report on State Responsibility*, U.N. Doc. A/CN.4/233: Yearbook of the I.L.C., 1970—II, p. 177, at pp. 187, 190 ff.

[2] *N.B. Anglo–Norwegian Fisheries Case*, I.C.J. Rep. 1951, p. 116.

[3] This principle follows also from the standards of equality and national treatment and non-discrimination in the matter of legal remedies; see Articles 14, 16, and 26, International Covenant on Civil and Political Rights 1966, which 'embody and crystallize' pre-existing rules of customary international law. Cf. *North Sea Continental Shelf Cases*, I.C.J. Rep. 1969, p. 3, at pp. 37–41. See above, pp. 66–74.

afforded to the individual by the expelling State. In *Dillon's* case, heard in 1928 before the Mexico–U.S.A. General Claims Commission,[1] Commissioner Nielsen noted that the sovereign right of expulsion was not denied by the United States Government, but that complaint was centred on the manner of the expulsion. Mexico and the United States had agreed, by the General Claims Convention of 1923, that all claims outstanding between the parties were to be decided 'in accordance with the principles of international law, justice and equity'.[2] Nielsen noted that although there may be no rule as to the precise and proper methods of expelling an alien, 'when resort is had to a use of unnecessary force or other improper treatment there may be ground for a charge . . . account being taken of the manner in which expulsion might have been effected.'[3]

In an earlier case, an American citizen expelled from Mexico with unnecessary cruelty was awarded $2,000, even though it appears that the expulsion was based on proper grounds.[4] The Umpire, Sir Edward Thornton, noted: 'There is no excuse for the cruelty with which the claimant appears to have been treated . . . and the unnecessary and painful march to which he was subjected together with his subsequent imprisonment.' The *Maal* case in 1903 involved the expulsion of a Dutch citizen from Venezuela.[5] The measure had been accompanied by a variety of indignities, including the stripping of the complainant in public, and this was held to be

[1] U.N. Rep., vol. IV, p. 368. On standards of treatment generally, see *Falcon's* case (1926), U.N. Rep., vol. IV, p. 104; *Garcia's* case (1926), ibid., p. 119; *Hopkins's* case (1926), ibid., p. 41.

[2] Article I, Mexico–U.S.A. General Claims Convention, 8 Sept. 1923, U.N. Rep., vol. IV, p. 11. Compare the Special Claims Convention of the same year for claims arising from 'revolutionary acts': ibid., p. 779. Article II of this Convention declared that settlement was to be in accordance simply with justice and equity, and not according to the generally accepted rules and principles of international law, for the Mexican Government felt 'morally bound to make full indemnification'.

[3] U.N. Rep., vol. IV, p. 368 at pp. 369–70. Cf. the case of *Hannah Jenkins*, American-Turkish Claims Settlement, cited in Nielsen, *Opinions and Report* (Washington, D.C., 1937), p. 463: 'It is probably a correct view that the departure of an alien from a nation's territory may be compelled by virtue of a sovereign right, the precise methods of whose exercise are not prescribed by international law. The legal right to this harsh measure undoubtedly exists.' (At page 465.) In the circumstances of this case, there was no evidence of arbitrary action upon which an international claim could be based.

[4] *Gourrier's* case (1868): Whiteman, I *Damages in Internatonal Law*, pp. 483–4, 507; see also *Snelling's* case, ibid.

[5] U.N. Rep., vol. X, p. 730: Whiteman, I *Damages in International Law*, pp. 488 ff., 507. See also *Boffolo* case, U.N. Rep., vol. X, p. 528; *Affaire Chevreau*, ibid., vol. II, p. 1113; *Orazio de Atellis*, Moore, *International Arbitrations*, p. 3333 (injury to health and reputation; obliged to leave through fever-ridden port).

unnecessary and oppressive, going beyond what would have been justifiable in the admittedly troubled times. The Netherlands and Venezuela agreed that the claims between them were to be decided according to justice, 'upon a basis of absolute equity without regard to objections of a technical nature or the provisions of local legislation'.[1] Five hundred dollars in gold were awarded in this case solely for the indignities, the Commission noting that expulsion is justified only where the foreigner's presence is detrimental to the welfare of the State, and when accomplished 'with due regard to the convenience and personal and property interests of the person expelled'.

In so far as such statements express general principles they continue to be valid; in each case it will be necessary to consider the circumstances of any arrest or detention which may precede expulsion. If the arrest is wrongful or the detention unreasonable, these facts will aggravate the damages which may be due for unlawful expulsion. The obligations which a State owes in these matters are clearly established and any breach will involve the guilty State in international responsibility.[2] It should be noted that detention may not only be too long, but may also be unreasonably short, leaving the alien no time in which to arrange his affairs. These matters also must be taken into account in assessing the damage done.[3]

In recent years the British Government has continued to protest about the conditions in which expulsions are carried out. In 1966, for example, the United Kingdom High Commissioner in Nigeria expressed concern at both the absence of any reason given for the expulsion of a resident journalist and the shortness of notice. Although the decision itself was not reconsidered, a temporary postponement in its execution was obtained.[4] In 1967, strong representations were made on the expulsion of twelve United Kingdom citizens from Kenya on twenty-four hours' notice. Although there was express recognition of the Kenyan Government's right of expulsion, complaint was made about the shortness of notice and the general lack of consideration.[5]

[1] Mixed Claims Commission, Netherlands–Venezuela 1903, Protocol Article I, U.N. Rep., vol. X, p. 709.

[2] See *Dillon's* case, U.N. Rep., vol. IV, p. 368; *Neer* case, ibid., p. 60; *Janes's* case, ibid., p. 82.

[3] See, for example, *Jaurett's* case (1904), Whiteman, I *Damages in International Law*, p. 433; *Orazio de Atellis*, Moore, *International Arbitrations*, p. 3333.

[4] 731 H.C. Deb. (Written Answers), col. 45: *British Practice*, 1966, pp. 111–15.

[5] 750 H.C. Deb., cols. 97–100: *British Practice*, 1967, pp. 112–14. See also on

(4) COMPENSATION FOR EXPULSION

There is a distinct lack of cases involving claims for expulsion alone, and protecting States frequently confine themselves to diplomatic representations and protest. This fact or tendency is good evidence of the reluctance of States to seem to deny to others powers which they may themselves need at some future date. However, in other cases, expulsion is often to be found as one of the heads in a wider claim for damages. Clearly, personal injury and property loss are among the most important of such heads, and serve to raise the issue of international responsibility.

In the assessment of damages for wrongful expulsion, Whiteman notes that consideration is generally given to the following matters:[1] (*a*) the expenses of removal and return; (*b*) actual property losses; (*c*) interruption to established business ventures;[2] (*d*) the number of dependants; (*e*) the character of the claimant;[3] (*f*) the indignity involved in the expulsion; and (*g*) the affront to the claimant's State.[4] The Commission set up by the British Government after the South African expulsions of 1900 drew a clear distinction between actual pecuniary loss, for which damages were recoverable, and so-called 'moral' damages, which were not recoverable. In *Charilaos's* case,[5] the Commission was faced with a total claim of £616 for loss of property, together with a claim for the loss of £2 to £3 per day from the claimant's tea-room. The Commission first disallowed £281, as no cogent evidence had been produced as to the existence of various items, including cash, securities, and jewellery. Next, it was noted

detention without trial and the duty to permit access by consuls: ibid., pp. 116–17; 6 *B.D.I.L.* 178 ff. Note *Ben Tillett's* case, 1898, in which the British Government, admitting the right to expel, nevertheless argued that arrest was unnecessary and was accompanied by hardship. The arbitrator deduced the permissibility of means necessary to ensure expulsion from the general right to expel (6 *B.D.I.L.* 124ff., 147). On the facts, the allegations of ill-treatment were found to be unproven.

[1] Whiteman, I *Damages in International Law*, p. 513.

[2] *Gowen and Copeland's* case, ibid., p. 491; $20,000 allowed for loss of guano deposits and exploitation rights.

[3] Compare *Boffolo's* case, a man of 'low character' who was permitted to return within a month—$380, with *Oliva's* case, a man of standing and character and recognized by the Venezuelan Government as a worthy concessionary—$7,720, plus an indemnity for business losses.

[4] It may be that the State can also claim for the loss incurred by receiving groups of nationals without adequate notice; see Brownlie, *Principles of Public International Law* (2nd ed., 1973), p. 506.

[5] 6 *B.D.I.L.* 227 ff.

that furniture values depreciated in time of war by about 75 per cent, and the claim was again correspondingly reduced. The full value of clothes and a bicycle was allowed but, 'on the reasonable assumption that the values [had] been inflated', the provisional total was then reduced by one-half to £59. A further reduction of £14 was then made because the Consul who acted for Greece would not vouch the respectability of the claimant, and there was no evidence as to other means of livelihood or whether the furniture and effects had been left in good order. On the other hand, the full value of stock-in-trade (£45) was allowed, and the final total arrived at was £90.

The general findings of the Commission have been criticized above, and it is impossible to say that their approach in this one case would be typical of other arbitral tribunals. Each case will depend on its own particular facts, but it is clear that the major difficulties will arise in respect of the evidence concerning property and other interests. In arranging for the distribution of the lump sum which it received on behalf of American claimants, the United States Government distinguished between three classes: those wrongfully deported who suffered no loss of property and no hardship—these were entitled only to nominal damages; those wrongfully deported and who did suffer in consequence—these were to be treated generously; and those who were rightly deported, but who were treated with unnecessary severity—these were entitled to some consideration.[1] In making its awards, the United States Government paid particular attention to business and property losses which were capable of more precise measurement.[2] In the *Phelps* claim, for example, the loss was corroborated and an award was made to the full extent. In many cases, however, little corroborative evidence was available, and consideration was then given to the circumstances of arrest, detention and deportation as the basis for other awards. These were substantial where no reasons for the arrest and deportation were forthcoming, and where the claimant had not been allowed to communicate with friends.[3] In one case the claim was rejected because the claimant had suffered 'no damage by his deportation from South Africa to his home in America'.[4]

[1] Whiteman, I *Damages in International Law*, p. 498.

[2] See the breakdown of awards in Whiteman, op. cit., pp. 501–6.

[3] e.g. cases of *Anderson* and *Crus*, Whiteman, op. cit., pp. 504–5.

[4] *Maloney's* case, ibid., p. 505. The claimant had been a bartender, had been continually under the eyes of the police, and was well known as a 'longstall for pickpockets'. Actual pecuniary loss and indignity are not essential prerequisites to an award of

While there is ample support for the principle that compensation is due for injuries caused by an unlawful expulsion, the question of re-admission remains open. It will often be demanded in the course of diplomatic protest and negotiation,[1] but the position may be that the expelling State is entitled to consider the payment of a sufficient sum of money as adequate compensation. If this is, indeed, the case, then the discretionary power of States is considerably widened and the consequences of a breach of international obligations significantly reduced.[2]

(5) CONCLUSIONS RELATING TO THE MANNER AND FORM OF EXPULSION

1. General international law imposes as a precondition to the validity of an order of expulsion the requirement that it be made in accordance with law.

2. An order of expulsion will only be in accordance with law if

(*a*) it is permitted under the local law;

and either

(*b*) the alien is allowed a hearing and appeal on the merits;

or

(*c*) there exists an effective remedy (judicial review), whereby the legality of the exercise of power can be challenged.

3. Expulsion proceedings generally must be carried out in accordance with the general standards which international law has established for the treatment of aliens. There must be no ill-treatment or torture and due regard must be paid to the dignity of the individual and to his basic rights as a human being.

4. International responsibility attaches to the expelling State which acts in breach of its international obligations, and com-

damages, and these may be allowed where the other wrongs done to the alien are aggravated': Whiteman, op. cit., p. 514; *Zerman's* case, Moore, *Internatonal Arbitrations*, vol. IV. p. 3348.

[1] See remarks by the Secretary of State on the refusal of re-entry by the Cyprus Government to an alien resident for over forty years: 706 H.C. Deb., cols. 184–5, cited in *British Practice*, 1965—I, pp. 46–7.

[2] See Brownlie on 'incomplete privilege': *Principles of Public International Law* (2nd ed.), pp. 452–3.

pensation may be demanded by the State of which the alien is a national. Although re-admission of the alien may be demanded, State practice does not support the existence of an obligation in the matter; the payment of damages and the making of an apology are generally considered sufficient.

XIV
THE IMPRESSION OF TREATY OBLIGATIONS UPON THE GENERAL POWER OF EXPULSION

(1) INTRODUCTION

EXPULSION MAY not only be accomplished in such a way as to depart from the standards of general international law, but it may also violate obligations expressly assumed in treaties. Bilateral treaties of commerce and establishment play a major role in putting nationals of States parties in a privileged position in matters of entry and expulsion, but due regard must be paid also to the compelling effect of multilateral treaties and other international instruments, whose primary concern is with human rights. The importance of such instruments in the setting of standards was considered above,[1] although some caution was advised in the evaluation of recent conventional provisions, particularly in view of the low level of ratifications. While the details of such provisions still fail to qualify as rules of customary international law, and while the entry into force of the principal covenants did not occur until early 1976, nevertheless the agreements in question may yet indicate the content of present human rights standards. Thus, there is throughout an insistence on certain minimum rights, on the procedural guarantees of due process and the right of appeal, and on the recognition of the rule of law as the very minimum protection against arbitrary treatment.

Rights of greater substance will usually result from bilateral treaties, and in general such rights are of most importance once the treaty alien has secured admission and has established himself in business.[2] In the past, diplomatic protest frequently followed the

[1] See above, pp. 66–74.

[2] But treaties do operate to secure admission. In the case *Re Nakane and Okazake* 13 Brit. Col. Rep. 370 (1908) the provisions of a provincial immigration act discriminating against 'orientals' were held inoperative in so far as subjects of the Japanese Empire were concerned. The 1907 Treaty between Canada and Japan, which had been enacted by federal statute of the same year, expressly provided for full liberty to enter, travel or reside in favour of the nationals of both parties. See also the categories 'treaty trader'

application of discriminatory policies to treaty aliens in matters of admission,[1] and the situation was much the same in regard to expulsion or conditions of residence. In 1874, the United States Secretary of State, Mr. Fish, suggested that a law or ordinance affecting those of a specific faith might be the sort of law which the commercial treaty with Russa of 1832 expressly anticipated would also apply to treaty nationals.[2] Nevertheless, in the case of one *Rosenstrauss* he concluded that the withholding of a trading licence solely on account of religious faith appeared to be in direct violation of the said treaty.[3]

In the case of *Orazio de Atellis*,[4] the United States Government claimed that the expulsion violated not only the rights secured to inhabitants by the Constitution, but also infringed the United States–Mexico treaty of 1832 which guaranteed to the citizens of each country, while within the jurisdiction of the other, 'special protection' to their 'persons and property', leaving 'open and free the tribunals of justice'.[5] Essentially, the treaty anticipated the protection of interests and the availability of a right of appeal, but it was never suggested that a treaty of commerce might abolish altogether the right of expulsion. In the *Gardner* case, the Board of Commissioners said:

> It is not to be presumed that either nation, by any article or stipulation of the treaty . . . intended to deprive itself of taking a reasonable measure of precaution against an injury likely to result immediately from the residence of one national in the territory of another.[6]

This view has been reaffirmed in other contexts, and there seems to be a presumption that, in the absence of express provisions to the contrary, treaties of friendship, commerce, and navigation 'should

and 'treaty investor' provided for in the United States Immigration and Nationality Act 1952, s. 101(a)(15)(E); 8 U.S.C. s. 1101(a)(15)(E), and in such treaties as that concluded with Japan in 1953, Article I: 206 U.N.T.S. 143. 69 A.J.I.L. 142–3 (1975).

[1] 6 *B.D.I.L.* 37 ff.

[2] Moore, *Digest*, vol. IV, p. 111. See similarly, *Mr. Lewisohn's* case 1881–1882, 6 *B.D.I.L.* 158 ff.; German discriminations against American Jews, Hackworth, *Digest* vol. III, 643 ff.

[3] Moore, *Digest*, vol. IV, pp. 112–13. See also the case of *Pinkos*, ibid., pp. 114–16; case of the *Mormon missionaries* in Switzerland, 1924, Hackworth, *Digest*, vol. III, p. 697.

[4] Moore, *International Arbitrations*, vol. IV, p. 3333.

[5] Cf. case of *Alexander A. Atocha*, Whiteman, I *Damages in International Law*, p. 469.

[6] Whiteman, op. cit., p. 476 and note to p. 497. In fact, Gardner was a confidence trickster who had never owned the silver mine which he claimed to have lost, nor had he been expelled.

not be considered as renouncing such an important attribute of sovereignty as the right of expulsion'.[1] Where such treaties exist, it will be assumed that the immigration laws continue to apply and that expulsion remains available. But, at the same time, it must follow that the general power is limited in view of those obligations which the parties have agreed to bear. Only occasionally will the parties agree to limit expulsion to serious infractions of 'ordre public',[2] but it is more common to find express and reciprocal guarantees in the matter of access to the courts and in the provision of rights of appeal. It is this type of provision which, by submitting discretionary powers to control by the law, ensures a certain protection against arbitrary treatment.

(2) EXPULSION AND THE EUROPEAN CONVENTION ON HUMAN RIGHTS AND FUNDAMENTAL FREEDOMS

The European Convention does not, by its express terms, guarantee the right of residence in any particular State.[3] Nevertheless, it is apparent that both a refusal of admission and an order of expulsion may be prohibited indirectly, in the sense that their execution would amount to the violation of some other protected right, such as those covered by Articles 3, 5, 8, and 14 of the Convention. In one case, the Commission observed: 'L'expulsion d'un étranger peut, dans certaines conditions exceptionelles, constituer un traitement inhumain ou dégradant au sens de l'article 3 . . .'[4] Regard must also be had, in matters of both entry and expulsion, to the special position occupied by the family.[5] Forcible removal or the refusal of entry

[1] United States Department of State to the Consul General at Hamburg 1912, on the question whether Articles VI and VIII of the Convention of Friendship, Commerce and Navigation of 1827 between the United States and the Hanseatic Republics stood in the way of expulsion. Opinion cited in the case of *Lazar Rokach*, American–Turkish Claims Settlement, *Opinions and Report*, F.K. Nielsen (1937), p. 503 at p. 509. See also Moore, *Digest*, vol. IV, p. 80; Hackworth, *Digest*, vol. III, p. 692.

[2] e.g. Article 2(2), Italy–Germany Treaty of Friendship, considered in decision of the Oberverwaltungsgericht, Hamburg (1966): *VerwRspr*. Bd. 18, S. 737. See also decision of the Bundesverwaltungsgericht (1971): *BVerwGE*. Bd. 37, S. 227 (Germany–Greece, Treaty of Establishment).

[3] Application 238/56: 1 *Yearbook* 205; Application 434/53: 2 *Yearbook* 354; Application 3325/67: 10 *Yearbook* 528; see also *Residence of an Alien Trader (Germany) Case* [1954] I.L.R. 209.

[4] Application 984/61: *Recueil* 6. The Commission had in mind the expulsion of an individual to a State in which he faced persecution or the death penalty.

[5] See *Patel et al.* v. *United Kingdom*, Decision of the Commission on Admissibility of Applications 4478/70, 4486/70, 4501/70 (Oct. 1970).

might well effect the separation of husband and wife, and to that extent could constitute a breach of Article 8 of the Convention. In Application 2535/65 *v.* Federal Republic of Germany,[1] the applicant alleged just such a breach in regard to the proposed deportation of her husband on account of his many criminal convictions. In the circumstances, the Commission declared the claim inadmissible as being manifestly ill-founded. It noted that the applicant had the opportunity of leaving Germany with her husband and of living with him in Austria, his own State. The applicant had married after the expulsion order had been made, and consequently knew the situation and the risks involved.[2]

In fact this case illustrates just one aspect of the position which currently prevails in German municipal law. Under the Federal Constitution, general international law and the specific provisions of bi- and multilateral treaties are incorporated into the local law.[3] Where treaties such as the European Convention on Human Rights, the European Convention on Establishment, or the Treaty of Rome are concerned, the individual can plead his treaty rights before the national courts.[4] For example, in a decision in 1956, the Federal Administrative Court (Bundesverwaltungsgericht) held that, by virtue of Article 6 of the Constitution and Article 8 of the European Convention, the family is under the 'special protection' of the State.[5] The alien threatened with expulsion in this case had subsequently married a German woman who was mother to a number of illegitimate children. In the view of the court, due regard must be paid to the likely effect of the order of expulsion on the family. If the unity and the integrity of the family are likely to be compromised, then it is essential that the interests of family protection be taken into account and set against the competing demands of 'ordre public'.[6] These conditions had not been fulfilled and the expulsion was accordingly annulled. The discretionary power which the authorities enjoyed was thus to be confined within the limits of its

[1] *Recueil* 17, p. 28.

[2] See also Application 3898/68 *v.* United Kingdom, cited in *Case Law Topics* No. 2, pp. 10–11.

[3] *Grundgesetz*, 1949, Article 25.

[4] Schiedermair, *Handbuch des Ausländerrechts der Bundesrepublik Deutschland* (1968). p. 22.

[5] Cited in 2 *Yearbook* 584.

[6] Note the 'public interests' set out in Article 8(2). The court in this case accepted the family as a unit, even though the husband had no parental connection with the children born prior to the marriage.

essential function, namely, the protection of the State. The demands of public interest are not absolute and they can, and must, yield where the interests of the family are dominant. By contrast, the expulsion of a divorced husband and father was upheld in a more recent decision. The divorce, said the court, had removed the appellant from the family unit, but again it noted that even the divorced parent without custody has a right of access, and this too must be weighed in the balance against the public interest.[1] A similar view has been taken of the relationship between child and parents, although it is admitted that the weight to be accorded to this factor will vary, depending on the closeness in fact of the relationship.[2]

(*a*) *The Fourth Protocol*

Although the alien may be able, indirectly, to invoke one or more of the rights guaranteed by the Convention, there are obvious deficiencies in this sort of protection. The Council of Europe has attempted in the past to encourage States to accept more specific obligations in favour of aliens, and in 1968 the Fourth Protocol to the Convention entered into force.[3] However, many of the provisions which were originally intended to benefit aliens were substantially altered by the Committee of Experts.[4]

Article 2 of the Protocol prescribes freedom of movement and residence for everyone lawfully within the territory of a State Party and for the freedom of everyone to leave any country, including his own.[5] These rights are subject to the usual restrictions 'in accordance with law and necessary in a democratic society', but here again it is to the substance of the rights and of the permitted restrictions that one must look, in order to ascertain the limits within which the State's discretion is confined.[6] The final wording of this Article represents

[1] *VerwRspr.* Bd. 19, S. 960, decision of the Oververwaltungsgericht, Münster (1968); see also, *VerwRspr.* Bd. 18, S. 14 (Bundesverfassunsgericht, 1966); *VerwRspr.* Bd. 20, S. 332 (OVG, Münster, 1968); *VerwRspr.* Bd. 22, S. 359 (BVerwGe, 1970); *BVerwGE.* Bd. 35, S. 291, 296–7 (1970).

[2] *BVerwGE.* Bd. 42, S. 299 (1975).

[3] Jacobs, *The European Convention on Human Rights* (1975), pp. 182–8.

[4] The Protocol entered into force on 2 May 1968 between Denmark, Iceland, Luxembourg, Norway, and Sweden. By 31 December 1970 it had also been ratified by Austria, Belgium, the Federal Republic of Germany, and Ireland: *Explanatory Reports on the Second to Fifth Protocols to the European Convention on Human Rights* (Council of Europe, 1971) (Doc. H (71) 11).

[5] Fourth Protocol, Article 2(1)(2). Cf. Article 12(1)(2), International Covenant on Civil and Political Rights.

[6] Article 2(3), and note the somewhat wider provision of paragraph (4). Cf. Article 12(3), Covenant on Civil and Political Rights, which appears to be narrower in scope.

a compromise between the recommendations of the Consultative Assembly and the Committee of Experts. For example, the word 'lawfully' was substituted for 'legally' in order to take account of the wide discretionary powers commonly granted to administrative authorities in matters of entry and exclusion. It was also agreed by the Committee that an alien who is admitted under certain conditions of entry which he transgresses can no more be regarded as 'lawfully' in the country.[1] In addition, it should be noted that Article 2 does not grant or guarantee the right to work to aliens lawfully present, nor does it ensure freedom of choice in the matter of place of work. To regulate the issue of work permits in the light of social and economic needs is therefore quite permissible.

Article 3 of the Protocol declares that no one shall be expelled[2] by means of either an individual or a collective measure from the State of which he is a national, and that no one shall be deprived of the right to enter the territory of the State of which he is a national.[3] This provision may raise particular problems in regard to nationality. The Committee of Experts proposed the inclusion of a clause to the effect that 'a State would be forbidden to deprive a national of his nationality for the purpose of expelling him',[4] but this was dropped because of doubts about the wisdom of touching on the controversial character of denaturalization measures. In subsection (2), the phrase 'No one shall be deprived of the right to enter' was substituted for the original wording, 'Everyone shall be free to enter' in order specifically to permit to States the power to investigate claims to nationality at the port of entry, and also to permit the imposition of any necessary quarantine measures.[5]

It is the content of Article 3 which remains the basis of the continuing failure of the United Kingdom to ratify the Fourth Protocol.

[1] Council of Europe, *Explanatory Reports*, pp. 40–1.

[2] The Committee preferred 'expelled' to 'exiled', even though it applies normally only to aliens. Expulsion was to be understood in its usual sense, to drive away from a place, but it was agreed that extradition was not included: Council of Europe, *Explanatory Reports*, p. 47.

[3] Note *Patel et al.* v. *United Kingdom*. Cf. Article 12(4), International Covenant on Civil and Political Rights: 'no one shall be arbitrarily deprived of the right to enter his own country'. The Committee rejected this formulation of 'his own country' as being vague and imprecise.

[4] Council of Europe, *Explanatory Reports*, pp. 47–8.

[5] Council of Europe, *Explanatory Reports*, p. 48. However, it was accepted that the right declared was not absolute, in the sense of a right to remain in that territory. Thus, the extradited criminal sentenced in another State would not enjoy an unconditional right to seek refuge in his own State: ibid., p. 49.

Under the Commonwealth Immigrants Act 1968, and now under the Immigration Act 1971, the United Kingdom authorities have the power to deport or otherwise remove non-patrial United Kingdom citizens. As a rule, such citizens will be removed to that Commonwealth territory to which they can be said to 'belong'. Alternatively, when permission to land has been refused, the prospective entrants may be subjected to the 'shuttlecocking' procedure which involves removal to the point of embarkation for the United Kingdom.[1] Immigration control as currently practised by the United Kingdom demands the mandatory exclusion of any non-patrial United Kingdom citizen who arrives without a special voucher or other entry clearance.[2] Acceptance of the obligations in Article 3 of the Protocol would entail a complete review of existing controls, and continued distinctions between different classes of United Kingdom citizens would constitute violations of Article 3 alone and in conjunction with Article 14.[3]

Some sort of solution would appear to be provided by Article 5(4) of the Protocol. This provides that the territory to which the Protocol applies, and each territory to which it is applied by declaration of a Contracting Party, shall be treated as separate territories for the purposes of the references in Articles 2 and 3 to the 'territory of a State'. Article 5(1) makes provision for the extension of the Protocol to any territories for the international relations of which the Contracting State is responsible. If the United Kingdom were to take advantage of this provision, it would be entitled to continue to exclude and expel those United Kingdom citizens who derive their status from connection with a dependent territory. Immigration controls could be maintained, for example, in respect of United Kingdom citizens from Hong Kong. However, the United Kingdom would not be entitled to maintain such restrictions against United Kingdom citizens resident in independent countries, such as Uganda or Kenya, which are not within the purview of Article 5(1). The

[1] In *Patel et al.* v. *United Kingdom* the Government argued that if a person were sent repeatedly back and forth between different countries, that might ultimately raise a question under Article 3 of the Convention, which prohibits inhuman treatment. Otherwise Article 3 was directed solely at the prevention of physical or mental maltreatment and suffering and could not be extended to a refusal of entry under immigration laws: *Decision of the Commission as to Admissibility*, 10 Oct. 1970, pp. 23–4. But the Commission felt that such measures raised issues of law and fact properly dealt with on an examination of the merits: ibid. 35–7.

[2] 1973 H.C. No. 79, para. 38.

[3] Note the observations of the Commission in *Patel's* case, loc. cit., p. 36.

necessary changes in the immigration laws do not, at the present time, appear to be acceptable to the Government of the United Kingdom.

Finally, Article 4 of the Protocol prohibits the collective expulsion of aliens. This was inserted solely on the initiative of the Committee of Experts, and it bears little or no relation to what was actually proposed by the Consultative Assembly. The latter body wished to include wide-ranging provisions regulating the individual expulsion of aliens, but these were rejected by the Committee of Experts.[1] The Assembly had proposed:[2] (1) a lawfully resident alien[3] should be expelled only if he endangers national security or offends against 'ordre public' or morality; (2) except where imperative reasons of national security otherwise require, an alien who has been lawfully resident for more than two years in the territory of a Contracting Party should not be expelled without first being allowed to avail himself of an effective remedy before a national authority within the meaning of Article 13 of the Convention; (3) an alien who has been lawfully residing for more than ten years should be liable to expulsion only for reasons of national security or if the reasons mentioned in (1) are of particularly serious nature.[4]

For a number of reasons, the Committee of Experts was unwilling to touch on the question of individual expulsions. It argued that these were adequately covered already by Article 3 of the European Convention on Establishment, and that further provisions would result in the risk of conflict between the two sets of rules.[5] More to the point was the refusal of the Committee to accept any express limitations on the reasons which may justify expulsion. A majority maintained that the State concerned should alone be competent to appreciate the reasons which, according to its own law, might lead to expulsion,[6] and that such matters were not the proper subject of

[1] Cf. the limitations on the expulsion of individual aliens in Article 13, International Covenant on Civil and Political Rights, 1966.

[2] Council of Europe, *Explanatory Reports*, pp. 49–50.

[3] Note the intended restriction by way of the word "lawfully", above, p. 287.

[4] Note the decisions of German courts, which have largely adopted these criteria in respect of treaty aliens and as a general basis for controlling the discretion of the authorities: below, pp. 289–9. Note also the notions of "Aufenthaltsberechtigter", "résident privilégié", and "settled" Commonwealth citizen, in German, French, and United Kingdom law respectively.

[5] On Article 3, see further below, p. 294.

[6] Recognition was given to the overriding principle that "the decision of expulsion must be taken in accordance with law", i.e. within the reasons and procedure provided by internal law: Council of Europe, *Explanatory Reports*, p. 51. A provision permitting review of the *legality* of expulsion proceedings was considered acceptable, but not a substantive appeal going to the merits.

control by the organs of the Convention.[1] These conclusions are, perhaps, the more surprising in the light of the obligations which States have assumed under Article 15 of the Convention.

(*b*) *The Example of Emergency Measures taken under Article 15*

Paragraph (1) of this Article permits States Parties, in time of war or other public emergency threatening the life of the nation, to take measures derogating from their obligations under the Convention. This exceptional competence is qualified by the condition that the measures taken be those strictly required by the exigencies of the situation, and providing that they are not inconsistent with the States' other obligations under international law.[2] The words 'public emergency threatening the life of the nation' suggest the application of an objective test to the facts in any given situation, and this has been the interpretation adopted by the Court and the Commission. In the first *Cyprus* case (Greece *v.* United Kingdom),[3] the Commission ruled that it was competent to declare on the existence of a public danger and on whether the measures taken were required, although 'the Government should be able to exercise *a certain measure of discretion* in assessing the extent strictly required by the exigencies of the situation'.

In the *Lawless Case*,[4] the approach of the Court reflects a similar view, although its concern was primarily with the facts of the situation and the notion of a 'margin of discretion' was not called directly in aid. The provisions of Article 15, and of the second paragraph of each of Articles 8 to 11,[5] are open to both an objective and a subjective interpretation. The latter has been rejected in practice, and neither the Commission nor the Court will accept a Government's simple assertion in the matter as conclusive. It has been argued,[6] and this is in line with what has been said earlier on expulsion in general international law, that the 'margin of appreciation' occupies a middle position in these interpretations. The State enjoys a certain freedom of decision largely because it is in the best position to know the relevant facts, and because it is best placed to

[1] Council of Europe, *Explanatory Reports*, p. 51.

[2] Additional restrictions are imposed by paragraphs (2) and (3).

[3] Application 176/56: 2 *Yearbook* 177.

[4] 4 *Yearbook* 438.

[5] These paragraphs permit restrictions on the rights and freedoms guaranteed which are reasonably necessary in a democratic society.

[6] Fawcett, *The Application of the European Convention on Human Rights* (1969), p. 248.

assess the measures which those facts may reasonably require. Whereas the existence of the facts can be determined objectively, the State's actions on the facts are controlled by the requirements of reasonableness and good faith. Thus, the measures taken must not be employed for purposes other than the intended purposes. Article 18 of the Convention declares: 'The restrictions permitted under this Convention to the said rights and freedoms shall not be applied for any purpose other than those for which they have been prescribed.' This important provision expresses the essence of the notion of abuse of rights in international law, and the municipal law prohibitions on bad faith and 'détournement de pouvoir'.[1]

(*c*) *Procedural Guarantees for Aliens*

In further debate on the Fourth Protocol, the Committee of Experts studied the possibility of including certain procedural guarantees in favour of aliens about to be expelled. These would have provided for a hearing and the opportunity to make representations before the competent authority, except in cases where the State considered that compelling reasons of national security required otherwise. The Committee rejected this proposal on the ground that to limit guarantees to those of a procedural nature was insufficient—it was better to have no provision at all. First, the guarantees would not apply where the State 'considers' compelling reasons otherwise required.[2] Secondly, the 'competent authority' might well be the same body which had taken the original decision, and there could, therefore, be no guarantee of impartiality.

(*d*) *Conclusions regarding the European Convention*

The Committee's response reflects the continuing desire of governments to retain the broadest margin of appreciation in their dealings with foreign nationals, and for the time being discretion in this area must remain only indirectly confined by the Convention. Development of the concept of a 'European public order', however, could prove to be the means by which all States Parties came to recognize their own interest in and concern with the treatment of

[1] See Application 493/59: 4 *Yearbook* 322, in which the applicant alleged that his detention in Ireland was ordered by the Government not for the purposes of preserving 'ordre public' but in order to remove a political opponent.

[2] Cf. *Lawless Case*, above. But note Applications 7729/76 and 7917/77 (*Agee* v. *United Kingdom*); *R.* v. *Secretary of State, ex parte Hosenball* [1977] 1 W. L. R. 766.

aliens throughout the Continent. The guarantees which the Convention does provide reflect closely those standards of general international law examined above. There can be no doubt that an expulsion would also be in breach of the Convention if it resulted in personal injury or damage to the property of an alien, if it was executed in breach of the local law, or without due consideration being given to the alien's family, or if it led to the alien's removal to a State in which he faced political or other persecution. Although States alone may be competent to decide upon the adequacy of the reasons for expulsion, the Convention clearly requires that the alien be permitted to challenge the legality of his arrest and detention.[1] The fundamental assumption throughout the Convention is that discretionary powers are subject to control, and that State actions which are arbitrary, in that they are inspired by bad faith or otherwise reveal a 'détournement de pouvoir', may be challenged.

(3) EXPULSION AND TREATIES OF ESTABLISHMENT

As their name implies, treaties of commerce and establishment operate to make easier the entry, residence, and business activities of nationals in the territories of the States parties. The word 'establishment' is not confined to entry alone, but is a term of art applicable to all the provisions of a commercial treaty which affect the activities of aliens. The treaty itself will commonly attempt to lay down standards of treatment whose general object is non-discrimination with regard to treaty nationals and companies, and these standards may be expressed in terms of most-favoured-nation treatment, national treatment, or treatment in accordance with the international law standard.[2] As a general rule, treaty provisions of this nature are not to be so construed as to affect existing laws on entry

[1] Article 5(1)(f), (4).

[2] Wilson, *United States Commercial Treaties and International Law* (1960). On 'national treatment' see Piot, 'Of Realism in Conventions of Establishment', *Clunet* (1961), 38–84; Walker, 'United States Commercial Treaties Today', in *De lege pactorum*, Essays in honour of R. R. Wilson (ed. Deener) (1970), p. 258. On the most-favoured-nation clause, see Schwarzenberger, 'The Most-Favoured-Nation Standard in British State Practice', 22 *B.Y.I.L.* (1945), 96; *International Law and Order* (1971), ch. 8; *Third Report* by Endre Ustov, Special Rapporteur, U.N. Doc. A/CN. 4/257. On the international law standard, see Wilson, *The International Law Standard in Treaties of the United States* (1953), pp. 87–105. See also Neufeld, *The International Protection of Private Creditors from the Treaties of Westphalia to the Congress of Vienna (1648–1815)* (1971), *passim*.

and residence, or the power to enact future regulations.[1] In addition the rights prescribed are limited by reference to the aims of such treaties, namely, the encouragement of bilateral trade and investment.[2] There is, therefore, an underlying assumption that the power of expulsion is retained, although the aims and purposes of the treaty in question indicate the confines of State discretion. The power of expulsion cannot be used in such a way as to frustrate those aims and purposes, and it is in this light that one should view the reservation common to treaties of establishment, which permits either party to apply measures necessary to maintain public order.[3]

The fact that the treaty alien remains liable to expulsion is frequently balanced by provisions which guarantee to him national and most-favoured-nation treatment regarding access to the courts,[4] and protection and freedom from unlawful molestation in no case less than that required by international law.[5] Today, the rights of access to the courts and to the equal application of justice are firmly established in general international law, whereas, in an earlier period, they resulted most frequently from the provisions of bilateral treaties.[6] These general principles are strengthened by the rule that a State may not adduce deficiencies in its own law with a view to avoiding its obligations, either generally, under customary international law, or specifically, under treaty.[7]

(*a*) *Reserved Powers in Treaties of Establishment*

The total effect of treaty stipulations may not seem to be very great. There will be the usual affirmation of civil rights and freedoms,

[1] See, for example, *VerwRspr.* Bd. 23, S. 220 (BVerwG. 1971), on interpretation of the German–Iranian Treaty of Establishment 1929.

[2] Treaty of Friendship, Commerce and Navigation between the United States and Ireland 1950, Article I (206 U.N.T.S. 269); see also the Protocol, para. 1 and the Minutes of Interpretation. Treaty of Friendship etc. between the United States and Japan 1953, Article I (206 U.N.T.S. 143). Treaty of Friendship etc. between the United Kingdom and Japan 1963, Article 3 (478 U.N.T.S. 86); Almond, 'Anglo–Japanese Commercial Treaty of 1963', 13 I.C.L.Q. (1964), 925. See also Treaty of Commerce, Establishment and Navigation between the United Kingdom and Iran 1959 (Cmnd. 698): *Contemporary Practice* VIII, 9 I.C.L.Q. (1960), 391 ff. (this treaty is not in force).

[3] e.g. U.S.A.–Japan Treaty 1953, Article 1(3); U.S.A.–Ireland Treaty 1950, Article 1(3).

[4] e.g. U.S.A.–Japan Treaty 1953, Article 4; cf. United Kingdom–Japan Treaty 1963, Article 7.

[5] e.g. U.S.A.–Ireland Treaty 1950, Article 2; U.S.A.–Japan Treaty 1953, Article 2.

[6] Neufeld, op. cit., pp. 100 ff.; see also Roth, *The Minimum Standard of International Law applied to Aliens* (1949), pp. 181, 185.

[7] *Treatment of Polish Nationals Case*, P.C.I.J. (1932), Ser. A/B, No. 44, p. 24.

and to that extent the treaty national may be protected against arbitrary executive action. Some guarantees may also be given in respect of legally acquired rights or interests and, for example, expropriation is often limited to public purposes and to the prompt payment of just compensation.[1] The laws and regulations which govern admission, residence, and expulsion are expressly retained, but the treaty will call for their liberal application. It follows also that entry and residence must be equitably accorded, for they are the necessary pre-conditions to the exercise of those economic rights which it is the aim and purpose of the treaty to secure.[2] However, in practice little or no clear restriction is offered in respect of the reasons of 'ordre public' which may be called upon to justify expulsion. Thus, the European Convention on Establishment 1955 expressly provides that each Contracting Party shall have the right to judge reasons of 'ordre public' by national criteria.[3] A limited right of appeal is called for in the case of treaty aliens lawfully resident in the territory of Contracting Parties for two years or more, and they are to be allowed to make representations against their removal before the competent authority.[4] Most States Parties permit representations on the merits to be made before some sort of advisory committee, while at the same time the normal judicial proceedings are left open, by which the alien may challenge the legal basis of executive action.[5] The reasons of 'ordre public' which justify expulsion fall within that margin of appreciatiation which States enjoy. Action within the prescribed limits is only occasionally opened to

[1] e.g. U.S.A.–Japan Treaty 1953, Articles 5(1), 6(3)(4); United Kingdom–Japan Treaty 1963, Article 14.

[2] There will not necessarily be any liberalization in favour of those entering for purposes other than trade and investment: Piot, 'La Convention d'Établissement de 25 novembre 1959 entre la France et les États-Unis d'Amérique', *Ann. Fr.* (1960), 953, 957–8, 960, and *passim*.

[3] Article 3(1); Protocol, Section 1(a)(1), (3). The standard of national treatment is demanded in respect of access to the courts and administrative tribunals, in the protection of rights and interests: Article 7. Section 3 of the Protocol declares that 'ordre public' is to be understood in the wide sense generally accepted in continental countries, but as such it is clearly a concept of, and limited by, the law. Cf. *Guardianship of Infants Case*, below, pp. 295–7.

[4] Article 3(2).

[5] See the summary of available procedures in *First Periodical Report by the Standing Committee on the European Convention on Establishment* (*Individuals*), Council of Europe (1971), pp. 21–30. For details of the United Kingdom procedure prior to the introduction of the immigration appeals system, see *Report of the Wilson Committee*, Cmnd. 3387, paras. 53–4; *British Practice* 1964—II, 207–8, 1966, 115–16.

direct judicial challenge, as is the case, for example, in the Federal Republic of Germany.

(*b*) *'Ordre public' Reconsidered*

The fact remains that the extensive claims of State authorities and the apparent meaning of treaty stipulations regarding 'ordre public' can be deceptive. There is already a considerable body of authority for the view that 'ordre public' is not to be allowed to nullify obligations assumed under treaty, and it will be seen that this authority stands firmly opposed to one view of the concept which is often advanced. This view is perhaps best expressed by the following, not untypical, description:

['Ordre public'] ... est employé pour mettre en échec le norme ... invoqué de façon purement négative, sous forme d'exception; et il est donc de son essence d'être imprévisible dans son intervention et illimité dans son domaine. Il justifie d'avance la substitution d'un Droit d'exception au Droit en vigueur.[1]

Characterized in this way, the exception of 'ordre public' does indeed represent an unlimited reserve of sovereign power, awaiting application by public, executive, administrative, and judicial authorities.

(*c*) *'Ordre public' and the* Guardianship of Infants Case

In the *Guardianship of Infants Case*, the Swedish Government argued that not even a treaty can modify rules of 'ordre public', which guarantee the integrity of those legal principles whose respect is necessary and vital for the State.[2] To this claim for the exclusive application of certain internal laws, the Netherlands objected that, if it were allowed, the operation of 'ordre public' would enable any contracting State to destroy the very object of the Convention in dispute.[3] In this case, a Dutch child residing in Sweden had been placed and maintained under the Swedish regime of 'protective custody' and it was alleged that this constituted an impediment to the guardian's right to custody which was to be determined by the national law of the child.

[1] Lyon-Caen, 'La réserve d'ordre public en matière de liberté d'établissement et de libre circulation' (1966), 2 *Rev. trim. de dr. eur.* 693, 694.

[2] 1958 I.C.J. *Pleadings, Guardianship of Infants Case* (Netherlands *v.* Sweden), pp. 42, 44, 122.

[3] Ibid., pp. 99–100. See also *Belgian Linguistics Case*, above, pp. 55–7.

Sweden maintained its view that the 1902 Hague Convention must be interpreted as containing a reservation authorizing, on the ground of 'ordre public', the overruling of a foreign law which would normally be recognized as the proper law. In its judgment, the Court did not feel obliged to pronounce upon the Swedish contention,[1] but a number of views were expressed in separate opinions on the purview and scope of 'ordre public'.

Judge Lauterpacht stated the general princple that a State is not entitled to whittle down its treaty obligations concerning one institution by enacting in the sphere of another institution provisions whose effect is to frustrate the operation of a crucial aspect of the treaty.[2] In his opinion, 'ordre public' did cover the institution of exceptional measures for the protection of minors, even to the exclusion of guardianship.[3] In addition, this was a principle which must be recognized as a general principle of law in the field of private international law:

> the notion of 'ordre public' ... being a general legal conception, its content must be determined in the same way as that of any other general principle of law in the sense of Article 38 [of the Statute of the International Court of Justice] ... namely, by reference to the practice and experience of the municipal law of civilised nations in that field.[4]

On the general applicability of 'ordre public' in treaty relations, he noted:

> When [the] State is bound by a treaty in relation to a particular subject-matter it can invoke public order *only if, in case its action is challenged, it is prepared to submit the legality of its action to impartial decision.* It is that jurisdiction which removes the notion of and recourse to 'ordre public' from the orbit of uncertainty, pure discretion and arbitrariness and which endows the treaty with the character of an effective legal obligation.[5]

Judge Spender was even less willing to compromise.[6] He characterized 'ordre public' as a concept of municipal law and noted that

[1] I.C.J. Reports, 1958, p. 55, at p. 70. The Court dismissed the Netherlands claim by a majority of 12–4. In its view, the 1902 Hague Convention concerning the Guardianship of Infants did not cover protection of children and young persons as this was understood by the Swedish law. In addition, the law in question did not and could not have any extra-territorial effect.

[2] Ibid., Separate Opinion, p. 79 at p. 83.

[3] Ibid., pp. 89–90.

[4] Ibid., p. 92.

[5] Ibid., p. 100, emphasis supplied.

[6] I.C.J. Rep. 1958, Separate Opinion, pp. 120 et seq.

treaty and conventional obligations were to be faithfully observed; the two did not mix and the provisions of municipal law could not prevail over those of treaty or convention.[1] If any such reservation were implied, it would be of such an indefinable character, so variable and unpredictable, so dependent upon the will of the parties, that there would be very little left in the legal sense of any obligations.

These views, and particularly those expressed by Judge Lauterpacht, can be usefully applied to the reservations of 'ordre public' which have been met in treaties of commerce and establishment, and also in provisions of municipal law. Unbridled resort to the let-out clause of 'ordre public' could easily defeat the whole object of such treaties, although some caution is perhaps necessary in considering the extent to which States parties would be willing to make these provisions justiciable. In a related municipal decision, however, the United States Court of Appeals was called upon to apply the public policy exception in the United Nations Convention on the Recognition and Enforcement of Foreign Arbitral Awards.[2] It was the court's view that public policy was to be narrowly construed:

> To read the public policy defence as a parochial device protective of national political interests would seriously undermine the Convention's utility. This provision was not meant to enshrine the vagaries of international politics under the rubric of 'public policy'. Rather, a circumscribed public policy doctrine was contemplated by the Convention's framers and every indication is that the United States, in acceding to the Convention, meant to subscribe to this supranational emphasis.[3]

The case against 'ordre public' or public policy as a wide-ranging let-out clause is even stronger where a multilateral treaty provides the basis for a regional arrangement and for the judicial settlement of disputes. It is very strong indeed where economic, social, and legal relationships are brought under one regime, as in the E.E.C.[4]

[1] Ibid , p. 128. Judge Spender concluded that there could therefore be no 'reservation, exception or exclusion' of 'ordre public'; in the course of his judgment he referred expressly to the *Greco-Bulgarian Communities Case* P.C.I.J. (1930), Ser. B, No. 17, p. 32. See also I.C.J. Rep. at p. 130 and per Judge Cordova, dissenting, pp. 140–2; *Treatment of Polish Nationals Case*, P.C.I.J. (1932), Ser. A/B, No. 44 at p. 24.

[2] 330 U.N.T.S. 38 (1958); Article V(2)(b).

[3] *Parsons and Whitemore Overseas Co. Inc.* v. *Société Générale de l'Industrie du Papier* (1974), reported in 14 *Int. Leg. Mat.* (1975), 405, at pp. 507 f.

[4] See further below, pp. 299–306; also Lyon-Caen, art. cit., pp. 703–5.

(*d*) *'Ordre public' in the Jurisprudence of the Federal Republic of Germany*

An interpretation of 'ordre public' that allows for control has already been adopted by the courts of the Federal Republic of Germany, which have gone some considerable way towards giving it substantive meaning. These developments are not solely due to a familiarity with the clause in the local law, but represent also a response to its inclusion in many treaties to which the Federal Republic is a party. In two cases it was held that working without the requisite permit was contrary to 'ordre public',[1] and this conclusion was based upon the requirements of economic order and upon the presumption that entry under treaty must be in accordance with the immigration laws.[2] In each of these two cases the court was called upon to interpret the 1960 Treaty of Establishment between Germany and Greece, but to this end it applied the definition and interpretation of 'ordre public' to be found in the 1955 European Convention. In another case in 1970 a Turkish national had entered Germany under a similar treaty, but his residence permit was so restricted as to prevent him from setting up his own business.[3] The court noted that the issue of residence permits and the imposition of conditions was a matter for the discretion of the authorities, and the appellant was unable to rely in this case on any specific provisions of the treaty, which required that entry and establishment be in accordance with the laws. However, the court affirmed that the discretion of the authorities was subject to control by the courts, and that an exercise of that power which was *ultra vires* or otherwise improper could be struck down.[4] In the circumstances of this case, the fact that the appellant was married to a German woman was not itself sufficient reason to permit unconditional residence. Such a decision did not impose separation on the couple, although, in actual cases of expulsion, family and marriage considerations must be weighed against the public interests.[5] Other, more recent, cases have tended to give greater weight to the need to protect and pre-

[1] *VerwRspr.* Bd. 21, S. 335 and S. 347, decisions of the Bundesverwaltungsgericht, 1969.

[2] *VerwRspr.* Bd. 21, S. 347.

[3] *BVerwGE*, Bd. 36, S. 45.

[4] See Article 114, Verwaltungsgerichtsordnung (VwGO), 1960, BGBl. I, 17. Compare the powers of adjudicators under the Immigration Act 1971, section 19.

[5] e.g. *VerwRspr.* Bd. 25, S. 81 (VGH, Hesse, 1972); ibid., S. 333 (BVerwG. 1973); *BVerfGE.* Bd. 37, S. 217, 247 (1974); *BVerwGE.* Bd. 42, S. 148 (1973); ibid., S. 299 (1975).

serve the institutions of family and marriage. It has also frequently been emphasized that public safety and order, not revenge and punishment, are the proper issues which should underlie the decision on expulsion. Conviction for crime is not itself sufficient, although it may be a lawful pre-condition to the exercise of the discretion.[1] There will be a misuse of discretion if the authority limits the exercise of its judgment to establishing simply the existence of one of the conditions of expulsion, such as a conviction. Moreover, the authority must base the exercise of discretion upon the principle of proportionality. There must be facts which support the necessity of the measure, otherwise it does not justify its purpose:

Die Ausweisung [hat] nicht den Zweck ... ein bestimmtes menschliches Verhalten zu ahnden, sondern einer künftigen Störung der öffentlichen Sicherheit und Ordnung oder einer Beeinträchtigung sonstiger erheblicher Belange der BRD vorzubeugen.[2]

(4) EXPULSION AND THE EUROPEAN ECONOMIC COMMUNITY

One of the most basic principles of the E.E.C. is that of freedom of movement. One fundamental rule underpins the new regime, that in the application of the Treaty there is to be an end to discrimination based on nationality.[3] However, the self-same article which prescribes this 'règle de base' provides also that non-discrimination

[1] *VerwRspr.* Bd. 19, S. 964 (BVerwG. 1969); here expulsion following conviction for manslaughter was upheld—the case involved diminished responsibility, there was a possibility of repetition and consequently a danger to public order. See, by contrast, *VerwRspr.* Bd. 25, S. 81 (VGH, Hesse), where the expulsion order was annulled. Here, a wife had killed her brother-in-law who had indecently assaulted her; the court weighed up the competing interests, noted that the prerogative of mercy had been exercised in behalf of the wife, and came down in favour of keeping the family together. Compare *VerwRspr.* Bd. 20, S. 847 (BVerwG. 1969); and see *BVerfGE.* Bd. 38, S. 52 (1974).

[2] 'Deportation does not have as its purpose the punishment of some specific human behaviour, but rather the prevention of some future disturbance of public safety and 'ordre public' or some injury to other important interests of the Federal Republic of Germany.' *BVerwGE.* Bd. 35, S. 291, 293 (1970). Of particular importance is the recent decision of the Bundesverfassungsgericht (*BVerfGE.* Bd. 35, S. 382 (1973)) in which appeals by Arab students expelled after the Munich massacre were allowed. The court affirmed that the protection of the law guaranteed by Article 19 (4) of the Constitution applied in full to aliens. It also applied the principle of 'Interessenabwägung' and, in favour of the appellants, noted how serious expulsion would be for a medical student very nearly at the end of his studies. See also *BVerfGE.* Bd. 38, S. 52 (1974).

[3] Article 7. See Sundberg-Weitman, 'The Addressees of the Ban on Discrimination enshrined in Article 7 of the E.E.C. Treaty', 10 C.M.L. Rev. 71 (1973).

cannot be invoked where there are specific or particular rules which demand a different approach. In so far as the Treaty of Rome, in Articles 48 to 57, advances the cause of freedom of movement and the right of establishment, it also reserves to States Members the power to curtail those freedoms in the interest of 'ordre public', public safety, and public health.[1] Directive 64/221 attempts to confine and structure these concepts, to which Member States may resort on occasion in order to justify the refusal of admission, the refusal of a residence permit, and the expulsion of the E.E.C. national.

(a) *The Scope of Reserved Powers under the Treaty of Rome*

It has been argued that the inclusion of these 'let-out' provisions represents a significant retention of sovereign powers and pure discretion.[2] In view of what has been said above, however, it can be seen that they are not unlimited. They are confined indirectly, by the aims and purposes of the European Communities, and directly, by the express effect of Community law. Thus, Directive 64/221 provides, for example, that these exceptional powers may be exercised only on grounds which relate to the individual.[3] It is important to remember that the Community worker has a legal right to a residence permit and that therefore the provisions of 'ordre public' must operate by way of exception.[4] In a German case in 1962, it was held that the concept of 'ordre public' was to be understood in the wide sense current in continental countries, and reference was made to the Protocol of the European Convention on Establishment. Nevertheless, the court went on to declare that it had the power to examine the reasons advanced in order to establish whether they met the requirements of 'ordre public' as a matter of law.[5]

There have been further developments since that date. For example, the European Court of Justice has held that the term 'Community worker' is a term of Community law: 'If this could arise

[1] Articles 48(3), 56(1).

[2] Desmedt, 'La police des étrangers', 1966 *Cahiers de Droit Européen*, pp. 55, 56.

[3] Article 2(2); general economic grounds are absolutely ruled out. The exceptional character of any departure from the rules concerning freedom of movement was emphasized by the European Court of Justice in *Bonsignore* v. *Oberstadtdirektor*, *Köln* [1975] 1 C.M.L.R. 472.

[4] *Re Residence Permits* [1966] C.M.L.R. 5, decision of the Berlin Verwaltungsgericht (1962).

[5] *Re Residence Permits* [1966] C.M.L.R. 5. Cf. *Re Expulsion of an Italian National* [1965] C.M.L.R. 285.

from internal law, each State would then have the power to modify the concept of "migrant worker" and to eliminate certain categories at will from the protection of the Treaty.'[1] The same reasoning is equally applicable to the treaty concept of 'ordre public'.[2] In *City of Wiesbaden* v. *Barulli*, the court noted that since Directive 64/221 the legal bases of many earlier decisions had been altered, although even here a somewhat reserved approach was adopted.[3] The court felt that the definitions of that directive were fairly narrow:

> they do not create a particular concept of 'ordre public' of paramount significance. Consequently one must proceed from the concept customary in the countries concerned and so consider the definitions as modifications.... Here we are dealing with inter-state and supra-national law.[4]

The caution in this approach has been largely overtaken by events. For some time it had been argued that not only Regulations but also Directives might be so binding within the Community as to give rise to enforceable rights in favour of individuals.[5] The European Court of Justice took up this suggestion in a number of cases and in its judgments it has favoured individual rights deriving both from directly applicable treaty provisions and from directives, even, in the latter instance, in the absence of national legislation.[6]

[1] *Unger* v. *Bestuur der Bedrijfsvereniging voor Detailhandel en Ambachten* [1964] C.M.L.R. 319, 331.

[2] But note *Re Expulsion of an Italian Worker* [1965] C.M.L.R. 53, in which the OVG Münster concluded that the question whether an alien has violated 'ordre public' falls to be decided by German law, whether the power of expulsion is exercised under Articles 48(3) and 56(1) of the Rome Treaty or under Article 2(2)(ii) of the Treaty of Friendship between Germany and Italy. The latter provision declared that after a period of 'ordinary residence' of more than five years Italian nationals were only to be expelled from the Federal Republic on grounds of state security, or when the threat to public safety, order or morality is particularly grave. See also, *VerwRspr*. Bd. 20, S. 844, decision of the OVG Rheinland-Pfalz (1969) to similar effect. The court took note of Article 3(2) of the Directive 64/221, which declares that conviction alone is not a sufficient ground for expulsion, but held that the authorities had not, in the circumstances, abused their discretion.

[3] [1968] C.M.L.R. 239, decision of the Landgericht, Wiesbaden.

[4] [1968] C.M.L.R. 239, at p. 245. The court also referred to the freedom of people to move about, inquiring into or seeking work, as a privilege rather than a right: ibid., p. 246, *sed quaere*.

[5] See in particular, Bebr, 'Directly Applicable Provisions of Community Law: The Development of a Community Concept', 19 I.C.L.Q. (1970), 257, esp. at pp. 278, 289 ff.; Lipstein, *The Law of the European Economic Community* (1974), pp. 11, 27 ff.; *Corvelyn* v. *État Belge*, 5 *Cahiers de Droit Europeén* 343 (1969); *Re Deportation of a Belgian National* [1974] 1 C.M.L.R. 107 (OVG, Münster, 1972).

[6] See also *Re French Merchant Seamen* [1974] 2 C.M.L.R. 216; *Lütticke* v. *Hauptzollamt Sarrelouis* [1971] C.M.L.R. 674.

(*b*) *The Decision in* Reyners *v.* Belgian State

In *Reyners* v. *Belgian State*[1] the question for decision by the Court was whether a Dutch national was entitled, under the E.E.C. Treaty regime of establishment, to practise as 'avocat' in Belgium. In its Judgment, the European Court of Justice declared:

[26] In laying down that freedom of establishment shall be attained at the end of the transitional period, Article 52 thus imposes an obligation to attain a precise result, the fulfilment of which had to be made easier by, but not made dependent on, the implementation of a programme of progressive measures.
[27] The fact that this progression had not been adhered to leaves the obligation itself intact beyond the end of the period provided for its fulfilment.[2]

The consequence was that after the expiry of the transitional period the rule prohibiting discrimination on the ground of nationality was henceforth sanctioned by the Treaty itself, with *direct effect.*

(*c*) *The Decision in* Van Duyn *v.* Home Office

The Court went one step farther in the case of *Van Duyn* v. *Home Office*,[3] a decision given on a reference from the Chancery Division. The case arose out of the refusal to admit to the United Kingdom a Dutch national whose intention was to take employment with a branch of the Church of Scientology. This organization, although not illegal, was considered by the British Government to engage in activities contrary to public policy. In view of this, it was government practice to refuse admission to any alien seeking entry to the United Kingdom for the purpose of participation in the organization. Before the Court, the Government argued that it had done no more than exercise the right reserved to it in Article 48(3). It further argued that no directive could have direct effect by reason of the limitations said to exist in Article 189 of the Treaty. It was the view of the Court, however, that Article 48 of the Treaty and Article 3(1) of E.E.C. Directive 64/221 were both self-executing. In respect to Article 48, the Court noted:

[6] These provisions impose on Member States a precise obligation which does not require the adoption of any further measure on the part either of

[1] [1974] 2 C.M.L.R. 305.
[2] [1974] 2 C.M.L.R. 305, 327.
[3] [1975] 1 C.M.L.R. 1; [1975] 3 All E.R. 190; Simmonds, '*Van Duyn* v. *The Home Office*: The Direct Effectiveness of Directives', 24 I.C.L.Q. (1975), 419.

the Community institutions or of the Member States and which leaves them, in relation to its implementation, no discretionary power.[1]

It affirmed yet again that the exceptional right of derogation reserved to States in Article 48(3) continued subject to judicial control, and that national courts must protect the individual rights conferred by the generality of that Article.[2] In respect to the question of the direct effect of a provision contained in a directive, it was said:

[12] . . . It would be incompatible with the binding effect attributed to a directive by Article 189 to exclude, in principle, the possibility that the obligation which it imposes may be invoked by those concerned. In particular, where the Community authorities have, by directive, imposed on member States the obligation to pursue a particular course of conduct, the useful effect of such an act would be weakened if individuals were prevented from relying on it before their national courts and if the latter were prevented from taking it into consideration as an element of Community law.[3]

Finally, the Court set out in its Judgment matters relevant to the personal conduct of the individual, which might justifiably be taken into account in determining whether or not the exceptional right of derogation should be exercised.[4] Moreover, the Court appears expressly to have ignored the invitation extended to it in his submissions by Advocate General Mayras, which was, to restrict the concept of 'community public policy' ('ordre public') to an *economic* public policy.[5]

In addition to the foregoing, it is also settled that repressive measures against individual E.E.C. nationals are not justified by reason only of their criminal conviction,[6] or by the simple expiry of the individual's identity document.[7] Health reasons are specifically listed, and it is expressly provided that diseases or disabilities occurring after the initial residence permit has been issued do not justify either a refusal to renew such permit or an order of expulsion.[8]

[1] Judgment of the Court [1975] 1 C.M.L.R. 1, 14, at pp. 15–16.

[2] Ibid., para. 7. [3] Ibid., p. 16. [4] Ibid., paras. 17 et seq.

[5] Ibid., p. 11; compare the change of view adopted by Advocate General Mayras in his submissions to the Court in *Bonsignore* v. *Oberstadtdirektor*, *Köln* [1975] 1 C.M.L.R. 472, 475, 478–85, and *Rutili* v. *Minister of the Interior* [1976] 1 C.M.L.R. 140, 143, 145, 148–9.

[6] Directive 64/221, Article 3(2).

[7] Ibid., Article 3(3), (4).

[8] Ibid., Article 4 and Annex. Cf. United Kingdom Immigration Act 1971, section 30; Mental Health Act 1959, section 90. For some early examples of agreements for the mutual retention of lunatics, see 6 *B.D.I.L.* 103–6.

Furthermore, it has recently been held by the European Court that to expel an E.E.C. national 'pour encourager les autres', for general preventive reasons, is contrary to Community law.[1]

The manner of exercise of that discretionary power which remains to States Members is regulated by requirements as to procedural guarantees. There must be available some form of appeal against, or review of, decisions to refuse admission, to refuse the issue or renewal of a residence permit, or to order expulsion.[2] The Directive declares that the Community national shall have the same possibilities of review as are available to the local citizen in respect of acts of the administration,[3] but in regard to deportation proceedings, the reference to national treatment is clearly inapplicable. National authorities have, in many cases, opted for the informal procedure of permitting representations before an advisory committee. It is open to debate whether such procedures fulfil States' obligations under the Treaty, particularly as the appointment and membership of the committees remains in the hands of State authorities.

(*d*) *Conclusions regarding the E.E.C. regime*

The E.E.C. Treaty has created its own legal order, which is directly applicable both to Member States and to their nationals as a result of the partial transfer of sovereignty from those States to the Community.[4] Part of this Community law is comprised in the concept of 'ordre public'. To define this notion as a reserved element of 'sovereign rights' is to assume for Member States a way out of their obligations. The aims and purposes of the E.E.C. touch social, economic, and legal relationships in a manner beyond the countenance of most bilateral treaties of commerce and friendship, and beyond even the provisions of the European Convention on Establishment.

International standards as hitherto applied are still relevant, but they have been overtaken by a substantive law which is supra-national. Within the sphere of application of the Treaties, the legality of

[1] *Bonsignore* v. *Oberstadtdirektor, Köln* [1975] 1 C.M.L.R. 472; this decision was anticipated in *VerwRspr.* Bd. 25, S. 81 (VGH, Hesse, 1972).

[2] Directive 64/221, Articles 8, 9. Cf. France, décret no. 70–29 du 5 janv. 1970, D. 1970. 54, Article 11. Note the decision of the Cons. d'État, 11 déc. 1970, in which an expulsion order was struck down because the alien had not been granted the procedural guarantees provided for by the Franco–German Treaty of Establishment 1956: *Clunet*, 1971, 296, note Goldman; *Rev. cr. int. privé*, 1972, 81, note Aymond.

[3] Directive 64/221, Article 8. Note also the decision of the European Court of Justice in *Rutili* v. *Minister of the Interior* [1976] 1 C.M.L.R. 140.

[4] *Costa* v. *E.N.E.L.* [1964] C.M.L.R. 425.

action taken in the name of 'ordre public' stands to be determined by impartial decision. Otherwise, and this was made clear in the *Guardianship of Infants Case*, the notion of 'ordre public' would remain within the 'orbit of uncertainty, pure discretion and arbitrariness'.[1]

Article 7 of the Treaty of Rome proposes the general rule of no discrimination on the basis of nationality. Logically, therefore, the nationals of Member States should be subject to a general regime of 'ordre public' and not to those particular regimes which individual States may oppose to aliens *qua* aliens. The power to exclude or to expel is exceptional, the basis of the principle of free movement itself is the control of discretion. From these premisses it follows that the individual faced with the prospect of repressive measures is entitled to an effective judicial guarantee. Such guarantee in turn must be capable of recognizing those substantive rights with which the Community national is endowed. It is open to serious debate whether 'expulsion' itself is an acceptable sanction in a community which is based on national treatment and supra-national co-operation. It has been said that the principle of non-discrimination on the basis of nationality reaches beyond the establishment of the Community, and that it must not be ignored in its establishment.[2] Taking that as a starting-point, one may go on to the specific question, whether there is a presumption in favour of 'sovereign' powers, or a presumption in favour of Community law, in which every derogation is exceptional and must be justified. Within the E.E.C. it must be the latter presumption which is dominant. The regime benefits from the existence of machinery for the resolution of disputes; when the question of measures purportedly taken for reasons of 'ordre public' comes before the European Court of Justice, that Court finds itself dealing with but another concept of Community law. In order to ascertain the substance of that concept, the Court will look to the aims and purposes of the Treaty of Rome and, in particular, the content of Directive 64/221. It must apply the appropriate objective standards, bearing in mind the principle that 'ordre public' does not represent an area of pure discretion, permitting the avoidance of treaty obligations. Member States still retain a margin of appreciation, but their freedom of

[1] I.C.J. Rep. 1958, per Judge Lauterpacht at pp. 55, 100.

[2] Submission of Advocate General Lagrange in *Re Electric Refrigerators* [1963] C.M.L.R., at p. 294.

decision is now more closely confined.[1] In determining the weight to be given to their own interests, they must now pay due regard not only to the interests and rights of the individual, but also to the interests of the Community as a whole. 'Ordre public' is no longer to be judged solely in accordance with national criteria.

[1] *Rutili* v. *Minister of the Interior* [1976] 1 C.M.L.R. 140; Goodwin-Gill, '*Ordre public* and the limits to discretionary power', 92 L.Q.R. (1976), 353–7.

XV

A SUMMARY OF THE LIMITS ON THE POWER OF EXPULSION IN GENERAL INTERNATIONAL LAW

AN ANALYSIS of expulsion in the practice of States reveals that general international law is by no means silent as to the limits within which this power may be exercised. It is a power which is essentially discretionary, and international law operates to prescribe the extent of the power, and to regulate its manner of exercise. It is possible to go further now in the description of those limits than the somewhat generalized conclusions most usually found, for example, to the effect that the power of expulsion must not be exercised 'arbitrarily', 'unjustly', or 'without consideration'. It remains essential that any description of the power of expulsion in practice should take account of the legal context in which it finds its meaning. Expulsion serves as a measure to terminate the relationship of reciprocal rights and duties which is established between receiving and protecting States, by reason of the admission or presence of foreign nationals on the territory of the former. But if, in terminating that relationship, any of the obligations which it owes are violated by the expelling State, then international responsibility is invoked and a new set of legal relationships is established. It may also be necessary and advisable to take account of that putative theory of responsibility, which would embrace obligations owed *erga omnes*, or owed to some other subject of international law. The obligations concerning basic human rights and the principle of non-discrimination have been canvassed as falling within this class.

With this fundamental legal relationship between States as the point of departure, the role and limits of the discretionary power of expulsion may then be summarized:

1. The function of expulsion is to protect the essential interests of the State and to preserve 'ordre public'.

2. From its function, it follows that the power of expulsion

must not be 'abused'. If its aim and purpose are to be fulfilled, the power must be exercised in good faith and not for some ulterior motive, such as genocide, confiscation of property, the surrender of an individual to persecution, or as an unlawful reprisal.[1]

3. The function of expulsion, together with the requirement of good faith, involves the subsidiary point that expulsion requires 'justification'. The expelling State must show 'reasonable cause', although in determining whether its interests are adversely affected, or whether there is a threat to 'ordre public', international law allows that State a fairly wide margin of appreciation. However, 'ordre public' is a general legal conception, the content of which is determined by law.

4. The principle of good faith and the requirement of justification demand that due consideration be given to the interests of the individual, including his basic human rights, his personal interests, including family and other connections with the State of residence, his property interests, and other legitimate expectations. These require to be weighed against the competing demands of 'ordre public'.

5. General international law imposes as a precondition to the validity of an order of expulsion the requirement that it be made in accordance with law. This rule entails the further requirement that there should be available an effective remedy whereby an unlawful exercise of discretion may be challenged.

6. The expulsion itself must be carried out in accordance with the general standards which international law has established for the treatment of aliens. Due regard must, therefore, be paid to the dignity of the individual and to his basic rights as a human being.

Each of the above propositions indicates significant limitations upon the discretionary power to expel aliens. Considered in summary form, these limitations and the standards which they propose may appear too general; the manner of their more precise application has, however, been sufficiently indicated above. The emphasis

[1] There are difficulties in determining when a reprisal is lawful. Brownlie observes that, in principle, it should be a reaction to a prior breach of legal duty and be proportionate: *Principles of Public International Law* (2nd ed., 1973), p. 524.

on control of discretion and on the permissible limits of its exercise is commonly found in municipal law and, to that extent, may support the finding of a general principle. Municipal law accepts that, whether it be a civil or a criminal proceeding, deportation is a severe penalty which must be founded on serious reasons, In the systems examined, limited in number though they have been, there is recognition also of the requirement of a hearing as a necessary precondition to the making or execution of an order of expulsion. Some States will permit an appeal on the merits, while others simply allow the alien to put forward representations. But in every case it is open to the alien to challenge the legality of the measure, and to require that the law control not only formal illegality, but also the arbitrary or abusive exercise of power. Once again, the emphasis is on the inherently discretionary nature of the 'right' of expulsion. However, it may be noted that, while the standards of international law favour a system of appeals, it is recognized that exceptions may be made in 'security' cases. State practice indicates a possibly equivocal attitude to the exercise of power by others on such occasions, and this is some evidence of a claim to an absolute discretion in political or security matters. Nevertheless, there does not appear to be any objection in principle to the introduction of guiding rules even in this area; the requirement of good faith certainly stands already at the perimeter of the field of competence.

The rules and standards proposed receive additional support from the provisions of treaties. These do not only reflect the controls on discretion which are imposed by general international law, but seek also to define these controls with greater precision in the light of the express aims and purposes of the particular treaty. It may be that the most effective confinement of the discretionary power of expulsion can be achieved by way of the regional treaty-based organization such as the E.E.C. Here, in matters of entry and expulsion, the concern is with the development of Community law, as similarly, under the European Convention on Human Rights, the concern is with the concept of a European 'ordre public'. It has been suggested also that the measure of expulsion may well be incompatible with the development of a political, economic, and legal community. Expulsion is essentially a measure of self-defence, to be applied in the interests of the community as a whole. In many cases the local law will be adequate to cover criminal infractions, and it is debatable to what extent the discriminatory provision of expulsion is additionally justifiable. The power of expulsion is a sovereign right, in that it pertains to every State for that State's protection, but it is a power which is controlled and limited, particularly by treaty obligations, and generally, by the obligations imposed by customary international law.

SELECT BIBLIOGRAPHY

THE FOLLOWING list represents a selection of those articles and monographs which have been found to be most pertinent to the subject-matter of this book. General treatises on public international law have not been included, but separate mention may be made of the digests of past and present State practice, particularly,

HACKWORTH, Green Haywood. *Digest of International Law*, 8 vols., Washington, 1940–44.

KISS, Alexandre Charles. *Répertoire de la pratique française en matière de droit international public*, 7 vols., Paris, 1962–72.

MOORE, John Bassett. *Digest of International Law*, 8 vols., Washington, 1906.

PARRY, Clive. *British Digest of International Law*, Vols. 2b–7, Stevens, London, 1965, 1967.

WHITEMAN, Marjorie M. *Digest of International Law*, Vol. 1, Washington, 1963.

ALBRECHT, A. R. 29 *B.Y.I.L.* (1952), 145: 'The Taxation of Aliens under International Law.'

ALMOND, H. H. 13 I.C.L.Q. (1964), 925: 'The Anglo-Japanese Commercial Treaty of 1963.'

AMERASINGHE, C. F. *State Responsibility for Injuries to Aliens*, Clarendon Press, Oxford, 1967.

AUERBACH, Frank L. *Immigration Law of the United States*, Bobbs Merrill, New York, 3rd ed., Elizabeth J. Harper, ed., 1976.

BASDEVANT, S. *Les Fonctionnaires internationaux*, Paris, 1931.

BASTID, S. Rev. Cr. (1953), 467: 'L'Organisation européenne et le traitement réciproque des nationaux.'

BEBR, G. 19 I.C.L.Q. (1970), 257: 'Directly Applicable Provisions of Community Law: The Development of a Community Concept.'

BOEK, Charles de. 18 Hague *Recueil* (1927—III), 447–647: 'L'expulsion et les difficultés internationales qu'en soulève la pratique.'

BÖHNING, W. R. *The Migration of Workers in the United Kingdom and the European Community*, I.R.R./O.U.P., 1972.

—— 10 C.M.L. Rev. (1973), 81: 'The Scope of the EEC System of Free Movement of Workers.'

—— and STEPHEN, D. *The EEC and the Migration of Workers*, Runnymede Trust, 1971; Supplement, 1972.

BONTEMPS, Jean. *Liberté d'établissement et libre prestation des services dans le Marché Commun*, Brussels, 1968.

BORCHARD, Edwin M. *The Diplomatic Protection of Citizens Abroad*, New York, 1915.
—— A.S.I.L. *Proceedings* (1939), 51: 'The "Minimum Standard" of the Treatment of Aliens.'
BORELLA, François. 64 R.G.D.I.P. (1960), 301–34: 'Le Passeport.'
BOTTOMLEY, Arthur and SINCLAIR, Sir George. *Control of Commonwealth Immigration*, Runnymede Trust, 1970.
BOULBÈS, Raymond. *Droit français de la nationalité*, Paris, 1956.
BOWETT, Derek W. *The Law of International Institutions*, Stevens, London, 3rd ed., 1975.
BRANDON, M. 27 *B.Y.I.L.* (1950), 448: 'The United Nations Laissez-passer.'
BROSSARD, Jacques. *L'Immigration: les droits et pouvoirs du Canada et du Québec*, Les Presses de l'Université de Montréal, Montreal, 1967.
BROWNLIE, Ian. 39 *B.Y.I.L.* (1963), 284: 'The Relations of Nationality in Public International Law.'
CABLE, Vincent. *Whither Kenyan Asians?* Young Fabian Pamphlet, 1969.
CAMPBELL, Alan. *Common Market Law*, 2 vols. and supps., Longmans, London, 1969–.
CAVAGLIERI, Arrigo. 26 Hague Recueil (1929—I), 315–583: 'Règles générales du droit de la paix.'
CLUTE, Robert E. 'Nationality and Citizenship,' in R. R. Wilson, ed., *The International Law Standard and Commonwealth Developments*, Duke U.P., Durham, N.C., 1966, at pp. 100–36.
—— 'Extradition,' ibid., at pp. 207–28.
COLYER, W. T. *The Worker's Passport*, Labour Research Department, 1928.
CRAIES, W. F. 6 L.Q.R. (1890), 27: 'The Right of Aliens to enter British Territory.'
CROMPTON, I. W. 126 *Justice of the Peace* (1962), 660: 'The Power to recommend Deportation.'
DAVIS, Kenneth Culp. *Discretionary Justice—A Preliminary Inquiry*, University of Illinois Press, 1971.
DEAKIN, Nicholas, ed. *Immigrants in Europe*, Fabian Research Pamphlet, 1972.
DESMEDT, H. 1966 *Cahiers du Droit Européen*, 55–71: 'La police des étrangers'.
DE SMITH, S. A. *The New Commonwealth and its Constitutions*, Stevens, London, 1964.
—— 31 Cam. L.J. (1972), 1: 'Immigration Act 1971: Allons, Enfants de la Patrie.'
DIPLOCK, T. 32 *Grotius Society* (1946), 42: 'Passports and Protection in International Law.'

DOMAN, Nicholas R. 43 *Amer. Bar. Assoc. J.* (1957), 307: 'Do Citizens have the Right to Travel?'

EHRLICH, Thomas. 19 *Stanford L.R.* (1966–7), 129: 'Passports.'

EISSEN, Marc-André. 'L'Autonomie de l'Article 14 de la Convention Européenne de Droits de l'Homme dans la Jurisprudence de la Commission', in *Mélanges offerts à Polys Modinos*, Paris, 1968, at pp. 122–45.

ERDMANN, Ulrich. *Europäisches Fremdenrecht*, Albert Metzner Verlag, Frankfurt-am-Main, 1969.

EVANS, Alona E. 40 *B.Y.I.L.* (1964), 77: 'Acquisition of Custody over the International Fugitive Offender—Alternatives to Extradition: A Survey of United States Practice.'

—— 3 *The International Lawyer* (1969), 204: 'The Political Refugee in United States Immigration Law.'

EVANS, J. M. *Immigration Law*, Sweet and Maxwell, London, 1976.

FAWCETT, James E. S. *The Application of the European Convention on Human Rights*, Clarendon Press, Oxford, 1969.

FOOT, Paul, *Immigration and Race in British Politics*, Penguin, London, 1965.

FRANÇOIS, J. P. A. 53 Hague *Recueil* (1935—III), 358–69: 'Le problème des apatrides.'

FRASER, C. F. *Control of Aliens in the British Commonwealth of Nations*, Hogarth, London, 1940.

GAINER, Bernard. *The Alien Invasion*, Heinemann, London, 1972.

GARRARD, John A. *The English and Immigration*, I.R.R., Oxford, 1971.

GHAI, Y. *Problems of a displaced minority: the new position of East Africa's Asians*, Minority Rights Group, Report No. 16,

—— and GHAI, D. *The Asian Minorities of East and Central Africa*, Minority Rights Group, Report No. 4, 1971.

GOODHART, A. L. 79 L.Q.R. (1963), 41: 'Extradition and Deportation.'

GORDON, Charles and ROSENFIELD, Harry. *Immigration Law and Procedure*, 2 vols., Mathew Bender, New York, rev. ed., 1974.

GRAHL-MADSEN, Atle. *The Status of Refugees in International Law*, 2 vols., Sijthoff, Leiden, 1966, 1972.

HAWKINS, Freda. *Canada and Immigration: Public Policy and Public Concern*, McGill Queen's, 1972.

HAYCRAFT, T. W. 13 L.Q.R. (1897), 165: 'Aliens Legislation and the Prerogative of the Crown.'

HEPPLE, Bob. *Race, Jobs and the Law in Britain*, Penguin, London, 2nd ed., 1970.

—— 34 M.L.R. (1971), 501: 'Aliens and Administrative Justice: The *Dutschke* Case.'

HIGGINS, Rosalyn. *The Development of International Law through the Political Organs of the United Nations*, R.I.I.A., Oxford, 1963.

HIGGINS, Rosalyn. 49 *International Affairs* (1973), 341–57: 'The Right in International Law of an Individual to enter, stay in and leave a Country.'

INGLES, Jose. *Study of Discrimination in respect of the Right of Everyone to leave any Country, including his own, and to return to his Country*, U.N. Doc. E/CN.4/Sub.2/229/Rev.I (1964).

JACOBS, F. G. *The European Convention on Human Rights*, Clarendon Press, Oxford, 1975.

JENKS, C. Wilfred. *The Headquarters of International Institutions*, R.I.I.A., 1945.

JENNINGS, Robert Y. 20 *B.Y.I.L.* (1939), 98: 'International Law and the Refugee Question.'

JONES, Mervyn. 22 *B.Y.I.L.* (1945), 121: 'Who are British Protected Persons?'

—— *British Nationality Law and Practice*, Clarendon Press, Oxford, 1947.

—— *British Nationality Law*, rev. ed., Clarendon Press, Oxford, 1956.

JOSEPH, Cuthbert. *Nationality and Diplomatic Protection: The Commonwealth of Nations*, Sijthoff, Leiden, 1970.

JUSTICE. *Going Abroad—A Report on Passports*, Barry Rose, 1974.

KAUFMANN, Erich. 54 Hague Recueil (1935—IV), 313–615: 'Règles générales du droit de la paix.'

KIMMINICH, Otto. *Der internationale Rechtsstatus des Flüchtlings*, Carl Heymans Verlag, Köln, 1962.

—— *Asylrecht*, Luchterhand, Berlin, 1968.

KISS, A. C. *Abus de Droit en Droit International*, Paris, 1952.

—— *Ann. Fr.* (1957), 478–89: 'La Convention Européenne et la Clause de la Nation la plus favorisée.'

KONVITZ, Milton R. *The Alien and the Asiatic in American Law*, Cornell U.P., New York, 1946.

—— *Civil Rights in Immigration*, Cornell U.P., New York, 1953.

KOZIEBRODSKI, L. B. *Le Droit d'asile*, Sijthoff, Leiden, 1962.

KRENZ, F. E. 15 I.C.L.Q. (1966), 90: 'The Refugee as a Subject of International Law.'

LAUTERPACHT, Sir Hersch, *The Function of International Law in the World Community*, Clarendon Press, Oxford, 1933.

—— 21 *B.Y.I.L.* (1944), 58: 'The Law of Nations and the Punishment of War Crimes.'

—— 9 Cam. L.J. (1947), 330–48: 'Allegiance, Diplomatic Protection and Criminal Jurisdiction over Aliens.'

—— 70 Hague *Recueil* (1947—I), 5–108: 'The International Protection of Human Rights.'

—— *International Law and Human Rights*, Stevens, London, 1950.

—— *The Development of International Law by the International Court*, Stevens, London, 1958.

LESTER, Anthony and BINDMAN, Geoffrey. *Race and Law*, Penguin, London, 1972.
LEWIN, K. 2 C.M.L. Rev. (1964–65), 300–24: 'The Free Movement of Workers in the Countries of the EEC.
LILLICH, R. 69 A.J.I.L. (1975), 359: 'The Diplomatic Protection of Nationals Abroad: An Elementary Principle of International Law under Attack.'
LOWENSTEIN, E. *The Alien and the Immigration Law*, Oceana, New York, 1958.
LUCAS, J. R. *The Principles of Politics*, Clarendon Press, Oxford, 1966.
LYON-CAEN, Gérard. *Droit social européen*, Dalloz, Paris, 2nd ed., 1972.
—— 2 *Rev. trim. de dr. eur.* (1966), 693: 'La réserve d'ordre public en matière de liberté d'établissement et de libre circulation.'
MACDONALD, Ian A. *Race Relations and Immigration Law*, Butterworths, London, 1969.
—— *The New Immigration Law*, Butterworths, London, 1972.
MCKEAN, W. A. 44 *B.Y.I.L.* (1970), 177: 'The Meaning of Discrimination in International and Municipal Law.'
MACKENZIE, N., ed. *The Legal Status of Aliens in Pacific Countries*, Oxford U.P., 1937.
MCNAIR, Lord (Arnold Duncan McNair). 28 *B.Y.I.L.* (1951), 172: 'Extradition and Exterritorial Asylum.'
MAESTRIPIERI, G. 10 *C.M.L. Rev.* (1973), 150: 'Freedom of Establishment and Freedom to Supply Services.'
MANSON, E. 4 *Jour. Soc. Comp. Leg.* (1902), 114: 'The Admission of Aliens.'
MEGRET, Jacques, ed. *Le Droit de la Communauté Economique Européenne*, 4 vols., Brussels, 1970– .
MORGENSTERN, Félice. 26 *B.Y.I.L.* (1949), 327: 'The Right of Asylum.'
NAMBIAR, K. R. 7 *Indian Journal of International Law* (1967), 526: 'The Right to a Passport.'
NASCIMENTO E SILVA, G. E. Do. 13 I.C.L.Q. (1964), 124: 'The Vienna Conference on Consular Relations.'
NEUFELD, H. *The International Protection of Private Creditors from the Treaties of Westphalia to the Congress of Vienna (1648–1815)*, Sijthoff, Leiden, 1971.
O'CONNELL, D. P. *State Succession in Municipal and International Law*, 2 vols., Cambridge U.P., 1967.
O'HIGGINS, Paul. [1963] *Crim. L. R.*, 680: 'Voluntary Deportation.'
—— 27 M.L.R. (1964), 521: 'Disguised Extradition: The *Soblen* Case.'
PANHUYS, H. F. van. *The Role of Nationality in International Law*, Sijthoff, Leiden, 1959.
PARKER, R. 40 *Virginia L. R.* (1954), 853: 'The Right to go Abroad: to have and to hold a Passport.'

PARRY, Clive. *Nationality and Citizenship Laws of the Commonwealth and the Republic of Ireland*, 2 vols., Stevens, London, 1957, 1961.

PIOT, Alice. *Ann. Fr.* (1960), 953–72: 'La Convention d'Établissement du 25 novembre 1959 entre la France et les États Unis d'Amérique.'

—— *Clunet* (1961), 38–84: 'Of Realism in Conventions of Establishment.'

PLENDER, R. 19 *Amer. J. Comp. Law* (1971), 287: 'The Exodus of Asians from East and Central Africa: Some Comparative and International Law Aspects.'

—— *International Migration Law*, Sijthoff, Leiden, 1972.

—— 23 I.C.L.Q. (1974), 709: 'The New French Nationality Law.'

POLITIS, Nicolas. 6 Hague *Recueil* (1925—I), 1–121: 'Le problème des limitations de la souverainété et la théorie de l'abus des droits dans les rapports internationaux.'

RAWLS, John. *A Theory of Justice*, Clarendon Press, Oxford, 1972.

REALE, E. 50 Hague *Recueil* (1934—IV), 89–187: 'Le problème des passeports.'

ROCHE, T. W. E. *The Key in the Lock*, Murray, London.

ROTH, A. H. *The Minimum Standard of International Law Applied to Aliens*, Sijthoff, Leiden, 1949.

SALMOND, Sir John W. 17 L.Q.R. (1901), 270, Part I; 18 L.Q.R. (1902), 49, Part II: 'Citizenship and Allegiance.'

SCHIEDERMAIR, Rudolf. *Handbuch des Ausländerrechts der Bundesrepublik Deutschland*, Alfred Metzner Verlag, Frankfurt-am-Main, 1968.

SCHWARZENBERGER, G. 22 *B.Y.I.L.* (1945), 96: 'The Most-Favoured-Nation Standard in British State Practice.'

—— *International Law and Order*, Stevens, London, 1971.

SHARPE, R. J. *The Law of Habeas Corpus*, Clarendon Press, Oxford, 1976.

SHEARER, I. A. *Extradition in International Law*, Manchester U.P., 1971.

SIBLEY, N. W. and ELIAS, Alfred. *The Aliens Act 1905 and the Right of Asylum*, Clowes & Sons, London, 1906.

SIMMONDS, K. R. 21 I.C.L.Q. (1972), 307: 'Immigration Control and Free Movement of Labour: A Problem of Harmonization.'

—— 24 I.C.L.Q. (1975), 419: '*Van Duyn* v. *The Home Office*: The Direct Effectiveness of Directives.'

SINHA, S. P. *Asylum and International Law*, Nijhoff, The Hague, 1971.

STREET, Harry. [1975] *Crim. L.R.* 2: 'The Prevention of Terrorism (Temporary Provisions) Act 1974.'

THORNBERRY, Cedric. 25 M.L.R. (1962), 654: 'Law, Opinion and the Immigrant.'

—— 12 I.C.L.Q. (1963), 414–74: 'Dr. Soblen and the Alien Law of the United Kingdom.'

—— *The Stranger at the Gate*, Fabian Research Pamphlet, 1964.

TURACK, Daniel C. *The Passport in International Law*, Lexington Books, Mass., 1972.

VAN DER MEERSCH, W. J. Ganshof, ed. *Droit des Communautés EuroPéennes*, Brussels, 1969.

VECCHIO, Georgio del. 4 *Sydney L. R.* (1962–64), 205: 'The Evolution of Hospitality.'

VERDROSS, A. 37 Hague *Recueil* (1931—III), 327–409: 'Règles internationales concernant le traitment des étrangers.'

VIERDAG, E. W. *The Concept of Discrimination in International Law*, Nijhoff, The Hague, 1973.

WALKER, H. 'United States Commercial Treaties Today,' in *De lege pactorum*, Essays in honor of Robert R. Wilson, David R. Deener, ed., Duke U.P., Durham, N.C., 1970, at pp. 258–69.

WASSERMAN, Jack. 3 *The International Lawyer* (1969), 254: 'The Undemocratic, Illogical and Arbitrary Immigration Laws of the United States.'

WEIS, Paul. *Nationality and Statelessness in International Law,* Stevens, London, 1956.

WEISSMANN, Gunter. *Ausländergesetz*, Walter de Gruyter, Berlin, 1966.

WHITE, Gillian. *The Nationalization of Foreign Property*, Stevens, London, 1961.

WHITEMAN, Marjorie M. *Damages in International Law*, 3 vols., Washington, 1937–43.

WILLIAMS, D. W. 23 I.C.L.Q. (1974), 642: 'British Passports and the Right to Travel.'

WILLIAMS, Glanville. 10 Cam. L.J. (1948), 54: 'The Correlation of Allegiance and Protection.'

WILLIAMS, Sir J. Fischer. 8 *B.Y.I.L.* (1927), 45: 'Denationalisation.'

WILSON, Robert R. *The International Law Standard in Treaties of the United States*, Harvard U.P., Cambridge, Mass., 1953.

—— *United States Commercial Treaties and International Law*, Hauser Press, New Orleans, 1960.

ZELLICK, G. [1973] Crim. L.R. 612: 'The Power of the Courts to recommend Deportation.'

INDEX

UNIV DUNELM

3 0104 00025447 8

This book should be returned on or before the last date shown below, unless it is previously recalled by the Library when it must be returned immediately.

Fines are incurred on overdue books (see Library Regulations).

CLASS No. 341·515

AUTHOR GOODWIN-GILL

ACCESSION No. AGJ 612